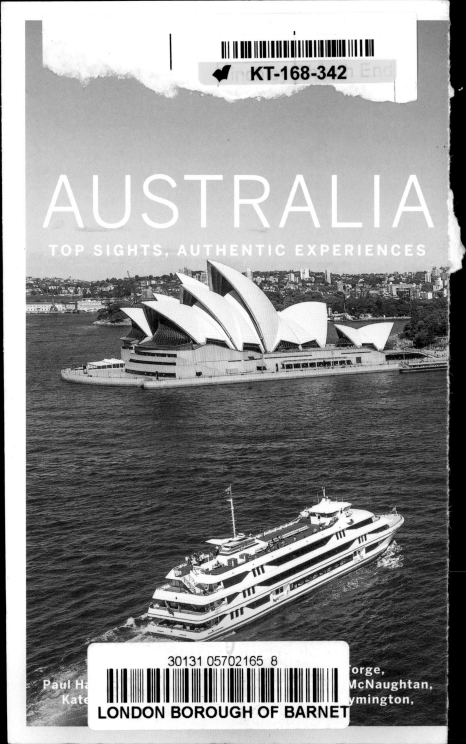

KT-168-342

AUSTRALIA

TOP SIGHTS, AUTHENTIC EXPERIENCES

Paul Ha...   ...orge,
...McNaughtan,
Kate...   ...ymington,

Contents

AL PARK

PAPUA NEW GUINEA

Torres Strait

Thursday Island — Cape York

Weipa

Coral Sea

Cape York Peninsula

Gulf of Carpentaria

SOUTH PACIFIC OCEAN

Daintree National Park

Port Douglas

Cairns

Great Barrier Reef

Townsville

Mt Isa

Airlie Beach

Mackay

Winton

QUEENSLAND

Rockhampton

Simpson Desert

ngs

Birdsville

Charleville

Bundaberg

Fraser Island

Lake Eyre North

Lake Eyre South

TH ALIA

Noosa

BRISBANE

Bourke

Eyre insula

Port Augusta

Broken Hill

NEW SOUTH WALES

Tamworth

Coffs Harbour

Port Macquarie

GREAT DIVIDING RANGE

E & RALIA'S NS p207

Adelaide

Mildura

Hay

Newcastle

Lord Howe Island (NSW)

Albury

ACT

VICTORIA

Mt Kosciuszko

Ballarat

Geelong

Tasman Sea

King Island

Bass Strait

Flinders Island

Launceston

TASMANIA

INDONESIA

Savu Sea

Timor Sea

Melville Island

Bathurst Island

Darwin ◉

Jabiru ●

Arnhem

**KAKAD
NATIO
p249**

Joseph Bonaparte Gulf

Katherine ●

Kununurra ●

Daly Waters

Cape Leveque

The Kimberley

Tennant Creek ●

**NORTHER
TERRITOR**

Broome ◉

INDIAN OCEAN

Port Hedland ◉

The Pilbara

Karratha ◉

North West Cape

Gibson Desert

**ULURU &
THE OUTBACK
p233**

Ali
Sp

Exmouth ●

Little Sandy Desert

Coober Pedy ●

Shark Bay

**WESTERN
AUSTRALIA**

Yulara ●

Uluru-
Kata Tjuta
National Park

SO
AUST

● Mt Magnet

Great Victoria Desert

Geraldton ●

**Kalgoorlie-
Boulder** ●

Nullarbor Plain

Eucla ●

**PERTH &
MARGARET RIVER
p267**

◉ **Perth**
Fremantle

Great Australian Bight

**ADELA
SOUTH AU
WINE REG**

Bunbury ●

Esperance ●

Margaret River ●

Albany ●

SOUTHERN OCEAN

Ⓝ 0 _____ 500 km
0 _____ 250 miles

Welcome to Australia

Australia is the unexpected: a place where the world's oldest cultures share vast ochre plains, stylish laneways and unimaginably blue waters with successive waves of new arrivals from across the globe.

Most Australians live along the coast, and most of these folks live in cities. It follows that urban life here is a lot of fun! Sydney is the glamorous poster child with world-class beaches and a glorious harbour, but Australia's other cities bring much to the table.

Australia's landscapes are just as diverse, from lush tropical and temperate rainforests to the remote rocky outcrops of Uluru, Kakadu and the Kimberley. To understand many of these places means walking in the footsteps of the First Peoples on earth. Whether you're tracing outlines of rock art more than 20,000 years old in Kakadu National Park, floating in the azure waters of Rottnest Island or admiring the iconic sights of Sydney Harbour, where the Eora Nation traded for centuries: you are on Indigenous land.

Beset with islands and deserted shores, Australia's coastline is wild and wonderful. Animating these splendid places is wildlife like nowhere else on the planet: kangaroos, crocodiles, wombats, wallabies, platypus, crocodiles, dingoes and 700-plus bird species.

When it comes to food, Australia plates up a multicultural fusion of European techniques and fresh Pacific-rim ingredients – aka 'Mod Oz' (Modern Australian). Seafood plays a starring role, though you'll always find beef, lamb and chicken at Aussie barbecues. To wash all it down, Australian beers, wines and whiskies are world-beaters.

> *Beset with islands and deserted shores, Australia's coastline is wild and wonderful.*

Sydney Harbour

Aboriginal and Torres Strait Islander people should be aware that this book may contain images of or references to deceased people.

Australian Parliament House (p86)
ARCHITECT: ROMALDO GIURGOLA;
IMAGE: PHILLIP MINNIS/SHUTTERSTOCK ©

Plan Your Trip
Australia's Top 12

CARL CHAPMAN/ALAMY ©

Great Barrier Reef & the Daintree

Kaleidoscopic coral and ancient rainforest

The Unesco World Heritage–listed Great Barrier Reef is a complex, 2000km-long ecosystem populated with dazzling coral and tropical fish. Underwater nirvana! Back on dry land, the Daintree is another Unesco darling, enveloping visitors in prehistoric ferns and twisted mangroves spilling onto brilliant white-sand beaches.

1

TOURISM NT/DAVID KIRKLAND

SARAWUT KONGANANTDECH/SHUTTERSTOCK ©

Uluru & the Outback

Big boulders and endless desert skies

No matter how many times you've seen it on postcards, nothing prepares you for the burnished grandeur of Uluru as it first appears on the outback horizon. With its remote desert location, deep cultural significance and dazzling natural beauty, Uluru is an essential Australian pilgrimage. Equally captivating is Kata Tjuta, with mystical walks, sublime sunsets and ancient desert cultures.

Top: Uluru (p236); above: Kata Tjuta (p240)

Kakadu National Park

Wilds and wildlife in the tropical Top End

Kakadu is like another world. This staggering array of Aboriginal art (and living Aboriginal culture), lush wetlands, ancient gorges and abundant wildlife is spread across nearly 20,000 sq km of Australia's Top End. Visitors – whether they choose to simply dip in with a day's guided tour or take the plunge on a longer camping trek – find it hard to shake this land that time forgot. Brolga, Kakadu National Park (p249)

PARKS AUSTRALIA ©

4

Sydney

An iconic city that's beachy and beautiful

Sydney's big-ticket sights – the Sydney Opera House, the Rocks and Sydney Harbour Bridge – top most people's lists. But to really catch Sydney's vibe, spend a day at the beach. Stake out some sand at Bondi Beach and plunge into the surf; or hop on a harbour ferry to Manly for a swim, a surf or a walk along the sea-sprayed promenade to Shelly Beach. Ahhh, this is the life! Sydney Opera House (p38)

5

Great Ocean Road

A classic Australian road trip

The Twelve Apostles – craggy rock formations jutting out of wild waters – are one of Victoria's most vivid sights, but it's the 'getting there' journey along the Great Ocean Road that doubles their impact. Drive slowly along roads that curl beside spectacular Bass Strait beaches and holiday villages, then whip inland through temperate rainforest studded with small towns and big trees.

F PHOTOGRAPHY R/SHUTTERSTOCK ©

Byron Bay

Counter-cultural mecca by the sea

Australia's most easterly point, big-hearted Byron Bay (just Byron to its mates) is an enduring icon of Australian culture. Families on holiday, hippies, surfers and sun-seekers from across the globe gather by the foreshore at sunset, drawn to this spot by fabulous restaurants, a chilled pace of life and an astonishing range of activities on offer. But mostly they're here because this is one of Australia's most beautiful stretches of coast. Tallow Beach (p102)

6

The Whitsundays

Set sail through a tropical archipelago

You can hop around a whole stack of tropical islands in this sea-faring life and never find anywhere with the sheer beauty of Queensland's Whitsundays. Travellers of all monetary persuasions launch yachts from party-town Airlie Beach or from sprawling Hamilton Island and drift between these lush green isles in a slow search for paradise (you'll probably find it in more than one place).

Beach resort at Hamilton Island (p140)

Melbourne

Soul, style and substance down south

Why the queue? Oh, that's just the line to get into the latest hot 'no bookings' restaurant in Melbourne. The next best restaurant, chef, cafe, barista, bar or food truck may be the talk of the town, but there are things here the locals would never change: the leafy parks and gardens, the crowded trams and the passionate sporting allegiances. On alleyway walls, the city's world-renowned street-art scene expresses Melbourne's fears, frustrations and joys.

9

Margaret River

Wild coast and world-class wines

South of Perth, the Margaret River region showcases two quintessential Aussie love affairs. For a start, this is one of Australia's most respected wine regions, with all manner of other culinary highlights on show. And then there's a rather dramatic coastline where big breaks attract surfers and landscape photographers alike. It's a fine combination and one of Western Australia's best-loved escapes. Far left: Vasse Felix (p285), left: coast at Margaret River

WILLIAM ROBINSON/ALAMY ©

ALEXANDER KONDAKOV/ALAMY ©

Adelaide & South Australia's Wine Regions

MEGAPIXELES.ES/SHUTTERSTOCK ©

Fine wines and refined urban vibes

Flying enticingly under the tourist radar, 'SA' is home to Adelaide – a charming city with burgeoning arts, food and laneway bar scenes – and a cavalcade of world-class wine regions. Sip shiraz in the Barossa Valley or McLaren Vale, or pinot noir in the cool Adelaide Hills. Happy days!

ARCHITECT: NONDA KATSALIDIS
IMAGE: CHAMELEONSEYE/SHUTTERSTOCK ©

Hobart

History and hip culture hand in hand

Hobart is Australia's second-oldest city, and perhaps its prettiest. The city's idiosyncratic island culture has been boosted of late by flourishing food and arts scenes, with MONA at the helm – an innovative, world-class museum described by its owner as a 'subversive adult Disneyland'. But Hobart's antique vibes endure: Salamanca Place and Battery Point evoke colonial days that somehow don't seem so far gone. Mona (p190)

SUE MARTIN/SHUTTERSTOCK ©

Canberra

Australia's cultural and political heart

The major drawcard in Australia's purpose-built capital city is a portfolio of lavishly endowed museums and galleries. Institutions such as the National Gallery of Australia, National Museum of Australia, National Portrait Gallery and Australian War Memorial offer visitors a fascinating insight into the country's history and culture, both ancient and modern. Australian War Memorial (p85)

Plan Your Trip
Need to Know

When to Go

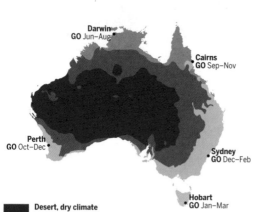

Darwin
GO Jun–Aug

Cairns
GO Sep–Nov

Perth
GO Oct–Dec

Sydney
GO Dec–Feb

Hobart
GO Jan–Mar

- Desert, dry climate
- Dry climate
- Tropical climate, wet/dry seasons
- Warm to hot summers, mild winters

High Season (Dec–Feb)
- Summer: wet season up north, bush fires in the south.
- Accommodation price rises, busy beaches.
- Festivals season: arts, food, film, music.

Shoulder (Mar–May & Sep–Nov)
- Warm sun, clear skies, cool nights.
- Coastal areas busy at Easter with families.
- Autumn colours are atmospheric in Victoria, Tasmania and South Australia.

Low Season (Jun–Aug)
- Cool wintry days down south; mild and sunny up north.
- Lower tourist numbers; some attractions keep slightly shorter hours.
- Head for the desert, the tropical north, or whale-watching spots.

Currency
Australian dollar ($)

Language
English, plus Djam-barrpuyngu, Pitjant-jatjara, Warlpiri, Tiwi, Murrinh-Patha, Kunwin-jku of 120 Indigenous languages

Visas
All visitors to Australia need a visa, except New Zealanders. There are several different visas available from short-stay visitor visas to working-holiday visas.

Money
Australian dollars is the only currency accepted. You won't have much trouble finding an ATM (cashpoint) but be aware, transaction fees are high.

Mobile Phones
Either set up global roaming, or pick up a local SIM card with a prepaid rechargeable account on arrival in Australia.

Time
Australia has three main time zones: Australian Eastern, Central and Western Standard Time. Sydney is on AEST, which is GMT/UCT plus 10 hours.

Daily Costs

Budget: Less than $200

o Hostel dorm bed: $40

o Double room in a basic motel: $100–150

o Simple main meal: $15–20

o Short bus or tram ride: $5

Midrange: $200–350

o Double room in a B&B or hotel: $150–250

o Brunch in a good cafe: $25–40

o Small gig or show: $30

o Short taxi ride: $25

Top End: More than $350

o Double room in a top-end hotel: from $250

o Upmarket three-course meal: $125 per person

o Theatre or festival tickets: from $100 per person

o Domestic flight between two main cities: from $100

Opening Hours

Most attractions close Christmas Day; many also close on New Year's Day and Good Friday.

Banks & post offices 9.30am–4pm Monday to Thursday; until 5pm Friday

Cafes 7am–5pm; some close later

Petrol stations & roadhouses 8am–8pm; some open 24 hours in cities

Restaurants Lunch noon–2.30pm and dinner from 6pm

Shops 9am–5pm Monday to Saturday (sometimes Sunday)

Supermarkets 7am–9pm; some open 24 hours

Useful Websites

Lonely Planet (www.lonelyplanet.com/australia) Destination information, hotel bookings, traveller forum and more..

Tourism Australia (www.australia.com) Main government tourism site with loads of visitor info.

Bureau of Meteorology (www.bom.gov.au) Nationwide weather forecasts and weather warnings.

Parks Australia (www.environment.gov.au/topics/national-parks) Get excited about Australia's cornucopia of national parks and reserves.

Arriving in Australia

Sydney Airport AirportLink trains run to the city centre every 10 minutes from 4.20am to 1am (30-45 minutes). Prebooked shuttle buses service city hotels. A taxi into the city costs approximately $55 (30 minutes).

Melbourne Airport SkyBus services run to the city (20 minutes), leaving every 10 to 30 minutes 24 hourly. A taxi into the city costs around $50 (25 minutes).

Getting Around

Australia is the sixth-largest country in the world: how you get from A to B requires some thought.

Van or car Travel at your own pace, explore remote areas and visit regions with no public transport.

Plane Fast track your holiday with affordable, frequent, fast flights between major centres.

Bus Reliable, frequent long-haul services around the country. Not always cheaper than flying but you'll get a better sense of scale.

Train Slow and not inexpensive, but the scenery is great! Australia has some bucket-list rail journeys, so plan ahead.

For more on **getting around**, see p323 ➡

Plan Your Trip
Hotspots for...

Beaches

With this much coastline to play with, it's no surprise that daily life for many Australians involves a trip to the beach. Enjoy!

DARREN TIERNEY/SHUTTERSTOCK ©

Sydney (p35)
Sydney's fab beaches range from surf-strewn bays to sheltered harbour swim-spots: irresistible!

Bondi Beach
Sydney's biggest, best and most 'braggadocious' (p44).

Byron Bay (p97)
Everyone comes to Byron for the beaches, from wild ocean shores to sheltered sandy nooks.

Watego's Beach
Chill on the sand at hidden Watego's Beach (p102).

Great Ocean Road (p173)
Along Victoria's photogenic Great Ocean Road are a string of amazing surf beaches (bring your wetsuit).

Bells Beach
Enjoy riding Bells' epic point break (p178).

Islands

Australia has thousands of islands...8222 of them, in fact! From tropical to windswept, there's one waiting for every kind of traveller.

ISABEL WEBSTER/SHUTTERSTOCK ©

The Whitsundays (p131)
Check yourself into a resort or go sailing around this pristine Queensland archipelago.

Hayman Island
Reigns supreme in the luxe resort scene here (p141).

Southern Reef Islands (p120)
The northern Great Barrier Reef gets all the press, but its southern isles are low-key and lovely.

Lady Musgrave Island
Offers brilliant snorkelling and castaway vibes (p120).

Fremantle (p274)
You could argue that 'Freo' is an island of culture...but offshore lies a true island gem.

Rottnest Island
Has cute quokkas and a troubling history (p275).

Indigenous Culture

With artefacts dating back more than 50,000 years, Australia's Indigenous culture is ancient, rich and varied.

TOURISM NT/JEWELS LYNCH ©

Uluru-Kata Tjuta National Park (p236)
Much more than big boulders: learn about local Aboriginal mythology, laws, customs and religion.

Kata Tjuta Cultural Centre
Book an Indigenous guide for the Rock (p236).

Kakadu National Park (p249)
Discover ancient Aboriginal rock-art galleries and experience 'bush tucker' on an Indigenous-led tour.

Kakadu Animal Tracks
Visit Kakadu's famous rock-art galleries (p252).

Alice Springs (p243)
Alice is the epicentre for authentic Aboriginal arts from right across central Australia.

Araluen Arts Centre
Excellent galleries and a performance theatre (p244).

Wildlife

From marine mammals to marsupials, birds and reptiles, Australia overflows with native wildlife. Meeting these locals is worth planning your trip around.

FLO129/SHUTTERSTOCK ©

Great Barrier Reef (p109)
Turtles, dugongs, sharks, manta rays, crabs, eels and unbelievable numbers of tropical fish.

Sealife Spotting
Head to the reef from Cairns or Port Douglas (p126).

The Daintree Rainforest (p118)
Queensland's tropical Daintree buzzes with birds, frogs, insects, even wandering cassowaries.

Crocodile Spotting
Crocodile Express (p128) runs Daintree River tours.

Sydney (p35)
Experience Australia's eccentric wildlife at Sydney's excellent, accessible zoos and aquariums.

Taronga Zoo
This zoo (p55) is worth a visit for the ferry ride alone.

Plan Your Trip
Essential Australia

SHUANG LIU/SHUTTERSTOCK ©

Activities

Australia's richly varied terrain is ripe for exploration, and there are very few limits on where you can go or what you can do. On land, there is hiking, skiing, cycling and mountain-biking trails to pursue, while the diving, snorkelling and other aquatic sports are world class.

Shopping

Australia's big cities can satisfy most consumer appetites with international brands, local brands, and markets for the more unusual gifts and souvenirs. Smaller towns tend towards speciality retail: home-grown produce, local art and homemade crafts as well as the usual high-street stores in larger towns. It's possible to get a refund (p319) on goods tax paid if you plan ahead.

Eating

Australia's culinary scene has transformed over the last few decades. Just about everywhere, the country's culinary offerings are filled with flavour and innovation, informed by a commitment to fresh ingredients and bequeathed endless variety by the extraordinary diversity of peoples who have come here from around the world (bringing their recipes with them) and now call Australia home.

Drinking & Nightlife

Australians enjoy a few drinks, although an increased health consciousness is dampening the hedonistic spirit. Pubs have always been the reliable workhorses of the drinking and social scene, but dance clubs, rock venues, cocktail bars and wine bars also feature in cities and some towns. Venues with great views, open-air beer gardens, and roof terraces for smokers, provide the perfectly Aussie backdrop to while away an afternoon with the locals.

Entertainment

Australia's dynamic and richly varied cultural life is reflected in its entertainment options, ranging from epic sporting events and thriving live-music scenes in venues both big and intimate, to theatre and arts festivals like Adelaide Festival (p217). Australians enjoy European performance expressions like classical music, opera and ballet. An interest in Aboriginal cultural entertainment has developed in recent years, most notably in dance (check out Bangarra Dance Theatre; www.bangarra.com.au) and music.

★ Best Restaurants

Quay (p60)

Brae (p179)

Attica (p165)

Sounds of Silence (p239)

Icebergs Dining Room (p63)

From left: Bourke St Mall, Melbourne; Quay (p60), Sydney

Plan Your Trip
Month by Month

JAVENG/SHUTTERSTOCK ©

January

January yawns into action as Australia recovers from its collective New Year hangover. Festival season kicks off with outdoor music festivals; Melbourne hosts the Australian Open. It's wet season up north.

✿ Australia Day

The date when the First Fleet landed in 1788, 26 January, is for some Australia's 'birthday' (www.australiaday.org.au) celebrated with BBQs, fireworks and nationalistic flag-waving. Aboriginal Australians refer to it as Invasion Day or Survival Day and a growing chorus is calling for Australia to 'change the date'.

☆ Australian Open

Held in Melbourne in late January, the Australian Open (p308) draws tennis fanatics from around the planet. The city centre buzzes with international visitors there to take in the action the courtside.

February

February is usually Australia's hottest month: humid and sticky up north as the wet season continues; often baking hot in South Australia and Victoria. Locals return to school and work while the sun shines on.

☆ Adelaide Fringe

All the acts that don't make the cut (or don't want to) for the more highbrow Adelaide Festival end up in the month-long Fringe (p217), second only to Edinburgh's version. Hyperactive comedy, music and circus acts spill from the Garden of Unearthly Delights in the parklands.

✿ Sydney's Gay & Lesbian Mardi Gras

Mardi Gras (www.mardigras.org.au) is a decades-old festival that runs into March and culminates in a flamboyant parade along Sydney's Oxford St that attracts 300,000 spectators. After-party tickets are like gold.

SAMANTHAINALAOHLSEN/SHUTTERSTOCK ©

March

March is harvest time in Australia's vineyards; and in recent years it has been hot, despite its autumnal status.

☆ WOMADelaide

This annual festival (p217) of world music, arts, food and dance is held over four days in Adelaide's luscious Botanic Park, attracting crowds from around Australia. Eight stages host hundreds of acts, with plenty for children to enjoy too.

☆ Adelaide Festival

Culture vultures absorb international and Australian dance, drama, opera and theatre performances at this ultra-classy annual event. Australia's biggest multi-arts festival (p217).

April

Melbourne and the Adelaide Hills are atmospheric as European trees turn golden then maroon. Up north the rain is abating and the desert temperatures are becoming

★ Top Events

Australian Open, January

Adelaide Fringe, February

WOMADelaide, March

Gourmet Escape, November

manageable. Easter means pricey accommodation everywhere.

☆ Tjungu Festival

The month of April in the Red Centre sees the dynamic Tjungu Festival (www.ayersrockresort.com.au/tjungu take over Yulara, with a focus on local Aboriginal culture.

May

The dry season begins in the Northern Territory, northern Western Australia and Far North Queensland, offering relief from humidity. A great time of year to visit Uluru.

From left: Rod Laver Arena, host to the Australian Open (p308); Sydney's Gay & Lesbian Mardi Gras (p318);

June

Winter begins: snow falls across the southern Alps ski resorts and football crowds fill grandstands across the country. Peak season in the tropical north: waterfalls and outback tracks are accessible (accommodation prices less so).

July

Pubs with open fires, cosy coffee shops and empty beaches down south; packed markets, tours and accommodation up north. Bring warm clothes for anywhere south of Alice Springs.

✳ Melbourne International Film Festival

Right up there with Toronto and Cannes, MIFF (www.miff.com.au) has been running since 1952 and has grown into a wildly popular event; tickets sell like piping-hot chestnuts in the inner city. Myriad short films, feature-length spectaculars and documentaries flicker across city screens from late July into early August.

August

August is when southerners, sick of winter's grey-sky drear, head to Queensland for some sun. Approaching the last chance to head to the tropical Top End and outback before things get too hot and wet.

✳ Alice Desert Festival

Central Australian visual arts, music, dancing, exhibitions and street performers (www.alicedesertfestival.com.au). Starts in August and runs right through to October.

September

Spring heralds a rampant bloom of wildflowers across outback WA and SA, with flower festivals happening in places such as Canberra and Toowoomba. Football finishes and the Spring Racing Carnival begins.

☆ AFL Grand Final

The pinnacle of the Australian Football League (AFL) season is this high-flying spectacle (p151) in Melbourne, watched (on TV) by millions of impassioned Aussies.

Tickets to the game are scarce, but at half-time everyone's neighbourhood BBQ moves into the local park for a little amateur kick-to-kick.

October

The weather avoids extremes everywhere: a good time to go camping or to hang out at some vineyards (it's a dirty job, but someone's gotta do it...). The build-up to the rains begins in the Top End – *very* humid.

✳ Melbourne Festival

This annual arts festival (www.melbournefestival.com.au) offers some of the best of opera, theatre, dance and visual arts from Australia and the world. It starts in early October and runs through to early November.

November

Northern beaches may close due to 'stingers' – jellyfish in the shallow waters off north Queensland, the NT and WA. Outdoor events ramp up; the surf life-saving season flexes its muscles on beaches everywhere.

☆ Melbourne Cup

On the first Tuesday in November, Australia's premier horse race (p308) chews up the turf in Melbourne during the Spring Racing Carnival. The city takes the day off and many host picnics or bet on the race, though increasing awareness of the injuries to horses is tempering some celebrations.

✗ Gourmet Escape

The culinary world's heavy hitters descend on regions from Margaret River to Swan Valley for four days of culinary inspiration (www.gourmetescape.com.au); celebrity chefs like Nigella Lawson and Rick Stein are often on the program, as are accessible, family-friendly events.

December

Ring the bell: school's out! Holidays usually begin a week or two before Christmas. Cities are packed with shoppers and the weather is desirably hot. Up north, monsoon season is under way: afternoon thunderstorms bring pelting rain.

Plan Your Trip
Get Inspired

Read

Our Magic Hour (Jennifer Down; 2016) A young woman's meditation on life and loss via suburban Melbourne and Sydney.

Welcome to Country (Marcia Langton; 2018) Your comprehensive guide to Indigenous Australia, and stunningly illustrated to boot.

True History of the Kelly Gang (Peter Carey; 2000) Fictionalised recreation of Australia's most controversial bushranger.

Benang (Kim Scott; 1999) A powerful, magical story of discovery and belonging.

Wake in Fright (Kenneth Cook; 1961) Disturbing picture of outback Australia.

Watch

Radiance (1998) Three Aboriginal sisters return to their childhood home, and wounds of the past are reopened.

Sweet Country (2017) A brutal colonial history is retold in this ode to the country western.

The Adventures of Priscilla, Queen of the Desert (1994) A bus, drag queens and the great Australian outback.

Muriel's Wedding (1994) A devastating story of love and friendship told with classic Aussie humour.

Mad Max (1979) Mel Gibson gets angry in this ground-breaking stunt phenomenon.

Listen

1000 Forms of Fear (Sia; 2014) Electro-pop anthems for the 21st century.

My Island Home (Warumpi Band; 1988) A love song to Australia's north.

Back in Black (AC/DC; 1980) Australian rock comes of age.

From Little Things Big Things Grow (Paul Kelly & Kev Carmody; 1992) The land rights movement gets a soundtrack.

Marryuna (Baker Boy; 2017) 50 Cent meets Arnhem Land royalty.

Above: Bondi Coogee Walk (p46)

Plan Your Trip
Five-Day Itineraries

Way Out West

Plenty of Australians have never been to Western Australia – it's so far from the east coast it could be another country! Spend five days checking out Perth and Fremantle, with a day-trip ferry ride to Rottnest Island to cycle and swim.

①

③

Perth (p274) Bright and perky, Perth is an upbeat city a long way from anywhere, but is perfectly self-contained. 🚗 30 mins to Fremantle

①

Rottnest Island (p275) A ferry jaunt from Fremantle, 'Rotto' is a beautiful car-free isle with a chequered history. Discover hidden beaches on a bike.

③

② **Fremantle** (p279) 'Freo' is a raffish port town full of musicians, students and artists, which equals good times! ⚓ 30 mins to Rottnest Island

Southern Scenic

Culture and coffee, sport and street art – Melbourne is Australia's hippest city. Further south, scenic Great Ocean Road tracks west – a classic Aussie road trip. Keep driving and you'll hit impressive Adelaide, with world-beating wine regions on tap.

Adelaide (p207) Spend a day in underrated Adelaide, a sassy city with brilliant bars and even better restaurants.
🚗 1 hr to McLaren Vale Wine Region

McLaren Vale Wine Region (p212) Daytrip south of Adelaide to our fave SA wine region: McLaren Vale's Mediterranean-like vineyards produce Australia's best shiraz.

Melbourne (p143) Ride Melbourne's trams between the MCG, jazzy laneway bars, Chinatown and top-flight restaurants.
🚗 1½ hrs to Great Ocean Road

Great Ocean Road (p173) This photogenic surf-coast route passes tall forests, beach towns and amazing rock formations – allow two days.
🚗 6½ hrs to Adelaide

Plan Your Trip
10-Day Itinerary

Cities Big & Small

Over 10 days you can experience the best of Sydney, Australia's brightest big city, and the gorgeous Blue Mountains. Short flights away are two of Australia's most beguiling small cities – Canberra and Hobart – with the arts and history to the fore.

Sydney (p35) Australia's big-smoke demands four days. Scale Sydney Harbour Bridge, explore the Rocks and take a harbour cruise.
🚗 2 hrs to Blue Mountains

Blue Mountains (p75) Two scenic Blue Mountains days: bushwalking, caving, abseiling or just ogling a vast sandstone canyon. 🚗 2 hrs to Sydney, then ✈ 1 hr to Canberra

Canberra (p81) Spend two days in Australia's custom-built capital, with museums, galleries and (of course) Parliament House. ✈ 1½ hrs to Hobart

Hobart (p187) Little Hobart is big on charm. Check out historic Salamanca Place, eat in North Hobart and spend a day at mesmerising MONA.

Plan Your Trip
Two-Week Itinerary

Best of Australia

Two weeks to explore one of the largest countries on the planet will never be enough, but if you plan carefully and don't mind flying, you can get a taste of Australia's greatest hits: the reef, the rock, the wildlife and the big-city lights.

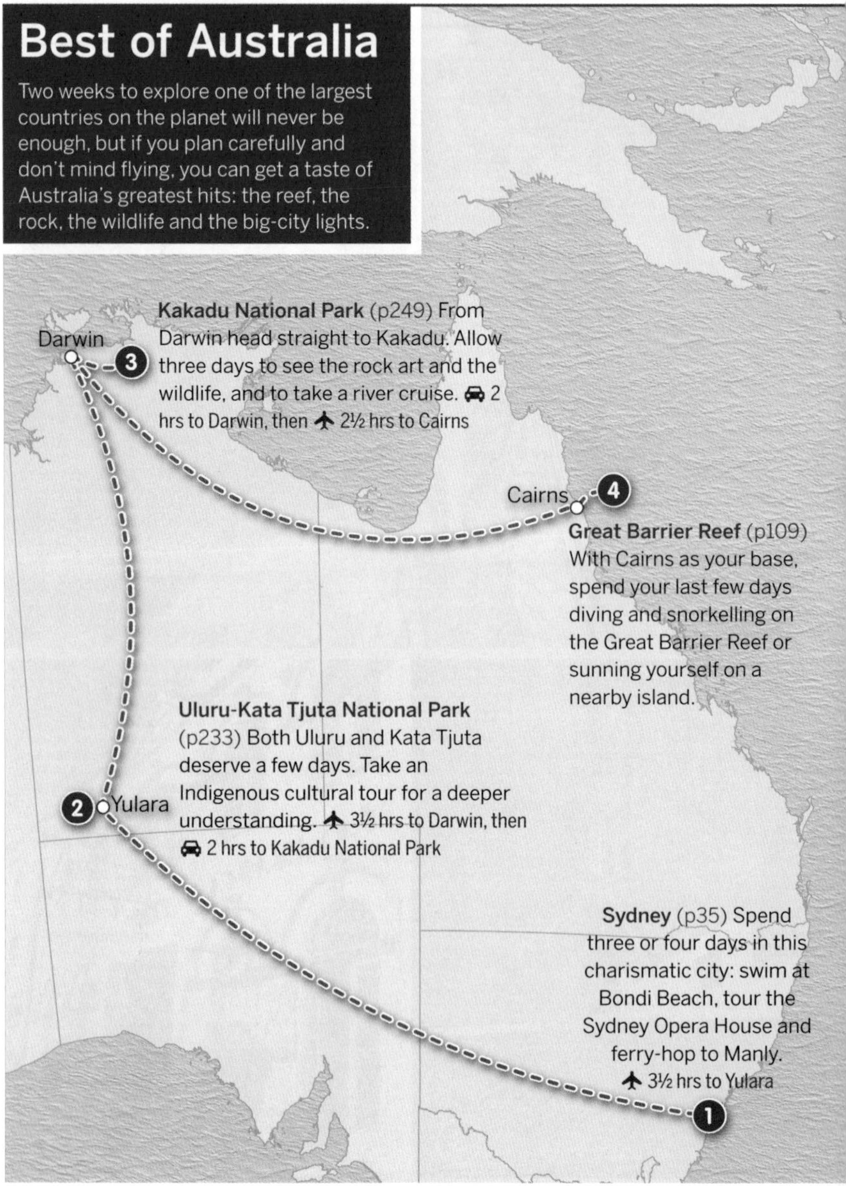

Kakadu National Park (p249) From Darwin head straight to Kakadu. Allow three days to see the rock art and the wildlife, and to take a river cruise. 🚗 2 hrs to Darwin, then ✈ 2½ hrs to Cairns

Darwin

Great Barrier Reef (p109) With Cairns as your base, spend your last few days diving and snorkelling on the Great Barrier Reef or sunning yourself on a nearby island.

Cairns

Uluru-Kata Tjuta National Park (p233) Both Uluru and Kata Tjuta deserve a few days. Take an Indigenous cultural tour for a deeper understanding. ✈ 3½ hrs to Darwin, then 🚗 2 hrs to Kakadu National Park

Yulara

Sydney (p35) Spend three or four days in this charismatic city: swim at Bondi Beach, tour the Sydney Opera House and ferry-hop to Manly. ✈ 3½ hrs to Yulara

Plan Your Trip
Family Travel

Australia for Kids

Don't underestimate the vast distances in Australia: the open road may be just the tonic for stressed-out parents, but it's probably not numero uno on the kids' hit list. Australia's cities, however, abound with attractions designed for bright young minds and bodies of boundless energy: museums, zoos, aquariums, interactive technology centres, amusement parks...

Lonely Planet's *Travel with Children* contains a wealth of useful information, hints and tips.

Sleeping & Eating

Top-end hotels and many (but not all) midrange hotels cater for children. B&Bs, however, often market themselves as sanctuaries from all things child-related.

Dining with children in Australia is relatively easy. At all but the flashiest places children are commonly seen. Kids are usually more than welcome at cafes,

while bistros and clubs often see families dining early. Many fine-dining restaurants discourage small children (assuming that they're all ill-behaved).

Most places that do welcome children don't have kids' menus, and those that do usually offer everything straight from the deep fryer – crumbed chicken and chips etc. You might be best finding something on the normal menu (say a pasta or salad) and asking the kitchen to adapt it to your child's needs.

Medical & Safety

Australia has high-standard medical services and facilities: items such as baby formula and disposable nappies (diapers) are widely available.

Major hire-car companies will supply and fit child safety seats, charging a one-off fee of around $25 or a per-day rate. Call taxi companies in advance to organise child safety seats. The rules for travelling in taxis

MARINA J/SHUTTERSTOCK ©

with kids vary from state to state: in most places safety seats aren't legally required, but must be used if available.

Change Facilities & Babysitters

Most shopping centres and all cities and major towns have public baby-change facilities; ask the local tourist office or city council for details. It is your legal right to publicly breastfeed anywhere in Australia.

If you want to leave Junior behind for a few hours, many of Australia's licensed childcare agencies offer casual care. Search for 'Baby Sitters' and 'Child Care Centres' in the online *Yellow Pages,* or contact the local council for listings.

Kids' Discounts

Child and family concessions often apply to accommodation, tours, admission fees and transport, with discounts as high as 50%

★ **Best for Kids**

Sydney Sea Life Aquarium (p52)

AFL footy at the Melbourne Cricket Ground (p151)

Territory Wildlife Park (p259)

Snorkelling the Great Barrier Reef (p112)

Taronga Zoo (p55)

off the adult rate. However, the definition of 'child' varies from under 12 years to under 18 years. Accommodation concessions generally apply to children under 12 years sharing the same room as adults. On the major airlines, infants travel free provided they don't occupy a seat – child fares usually apply between the ages of two and 11 years.

Above: Sydney Sea Life Aquarium (p52)

Sydney Tower Eye (p51)

SYDNEY

Royal Botanic Garden (p48)

The Rocks (p48)

Sydney Opera House (p38)

Sydney Harbour Bridge (p40)

Circular Quay & the Rocks
Seamlessly combines the historic with the exuberantly modern. Major sights and great eating and drinking.

SYDNEY HARBOUR BRIDGE

SYDNEY OPERA HOUSE

Manly
The surf's good, the bars and eateries appeal, and it's the gateway to the beautiful Northern Beaches.

City Centre & Haymarket
Upmarket shopping, eating and sightseeing, with raffish Chinatown providing the yin to the CBD's yang.

Kings Cross & Potts Point
The Cross is still gloriously down at heel, the antidote to which is refined, leafy Potts Point.

Darling Harbour & Pyrmont
Unashamedly touristy, Darling Harbour dazzles with waterside bars, restaurants and museums. Pyrmont maintains historic vibes.

BONDI BEACH

Bondi, Coogee & the Eastern Beaches
Sydney sheds its suit and tie and chills on the eastern beaches. Bondi is the biggest and best.

Newtown & the Inner West
Students, bookshops, cafes and pubs: Newtown and the inner-west 'burbs are Sydney's bohemian zone.

Surry Hills & Darlinghurst
Sydney's hippest and gayest neighbourhoods are also home to its most interesting dining and bar scene.

Paddington
A byword for eastern-suburbs elegance, this is Sydney's fashion and art heartland.

Central Sydney Map (p50)
Kings Cross, Darlinghurst & Woolloomooloo Map (p54)

Sydney at a Glance...

Sun-kissed, sophisticated and self-confident: Sydney is the capital to which all the other Australian cities aspire. Encircling one of the world's most beautiful natural harbours, the city is flush with Aussie icons: the Sydney Harbour Bridge, Sydney Opera House and Bondi Beach.

But wait – there's more! Spectacular Sydney also hosts magnificent museums and restaurants, a vivacious performing-arts scene and yet more sublime beaches. As the sun sets, hip bars and clubs light up as locals wage war against sleep... So wake up! Sydney is as good as it gets.

Sydney in Two Days

Start by exploring the Rocks and Circular Quay, then follow the harbourside walkway to the **Royal Botanic Garden** (p48) and the **Art Gallery of NSW** (p49). Catch an evening show at the **Sydney Opera House** (p39).

Next day, climb the **Harbour Bridge** (p41), then soak up the scene at **Bondi** (p45) and take the clifftop walk to Coogee. Hoof it back to Bondi for dinner; **Icebergs Dining Room** (p63) has bodacious views.

Sydney in Four Days

Jump on a ferry on day three and chug across the harbour to **Manly** (p55) for a surf lesson, with a debriefing beer at **Manly Wharf Hotel** (p68). That night, head to stylin' Surry Hills for dinner.

On day four, dig into Sydney's convict heritage at the **Hyde Park Barracks Museum** (p49), head to Chinatown for dinner, then hit the small bars nearby.

KETBKTI/SHUTTERSTOCK ©

Giraffes at Taronga Zoo (p55)

Arriving in Sydney

Airport shuttles (from $22), taxis (from $45) and trains (from $16) head into the city from **Sydney Airport** (p71), 10km south of the city centre. Interstate trains arrive at **Central Station** (p71) in the CBD, and long-haul buses at the adjacent **Sydney Coach Terminal** (p71).

Sleeping

Your choice of neighbourhood will inform the tone of your Sydney experience. Circular Quay, the Rocks and the city centre have famous sights and myriad eating and drinking options. Surry Hills and Darlinghurst are much hipper, with fab bars and gay clubs. Glebe and Newtown are grungier and bookish, while Bondi and the beach 'burbs are backpacker-surfer central.

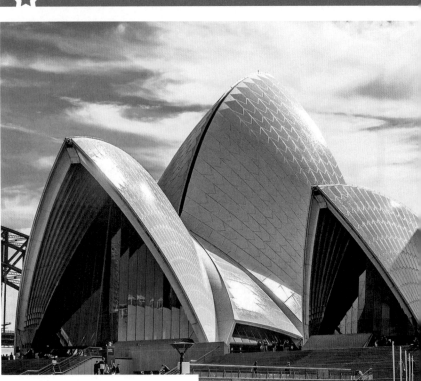

Sydney Opera House

Come face to face with Sydney's number-one symbol. On a sunny day the Opera House is postcard-perfect, its curves a pinnacle of architectural expression.

Great For...

☑ Don't Miss

Catch a show: take a glass of bubbles outside during interval and admire the harbour.

Design & Construction

Danish architect Jørn Utzon's competition-winning 1956 design is Australia's most recognisable visual image. It's said to have been inspired by billowing sails, orange segments, palm fronds and Mayan temples, and has been poetically likened to nuns in a rugby scrum, a typewriter stuffed with scallop shells and the sexual congress of turtles. It's not until you get close that you realise that the seemingly solid expanse of white is actually composed of tiles – 1,056,000 self-cleaning cream-coloured Swedish tiles, to be exact.

The Opera House's construction was itself truly operatic – so much so, it was dramatised as *The Eighth Wonder,* performed here by Opera Australia in 1995. The predicted four-year construction started in 1959. After a tumultuous clash

ⓘ Need to Know

Map p50; ☑02-9250 7111, tour bookings
02-9250 7250; www.sydneyoperahouse.com;
Bennelong Point; tours adult/child $40/22;
⊗tours 9am-5pm; ␁Circular Quay

✕ Take a Break

Opera Bar (p64) has the best views in
the business.

★ Top Tip

Most events (more than 2400 of them
annually!) sell out quickly, but partial-
view tickets are often available on short
notice.

of egos, delays, politicking, death and cost
blow-outs, Utzon quit in disgust in 1966.
The Opera House finally opened in 1973.
Utzon and his son Jan were commissioned
for renovations in 2004, but Utzon died in
2008 having never seen his finished masterpiece in the flesh.

Tours

One-hour guided tours depart throughout the day: you're more likely to see
everything if you go early (some spaces
close for rehearsals). A highlight is the
Utzon Room, the only part of the Opera
House to have an interior designed by
the great man himself. The two-hour 7am
backstage tour ($165) includes the Green
Room, stars' dressing rooms, stage and
orchestra pit.

Performances

Dance, concerts, opera and theatre are
staged in the **Concert Hall**, **Joan Suth-
erland Theatre**, **Drama Theatre** and
Playhouse, while more intimate and left-of-
centre shows inhabit the **Studio**. Companies regularly performing here include:
Australian Ballet (☑1300 369 741; www.austral
ianballet.com.au)
Australian Chamber Orchestra (ACO; ☑02-
8274 3888; www.aco.com.au)
Bangarra Dance Theatre (p69)
Opera Australia (Map p50; ☑02-9318 8200;
www.opera.org.au; Sydney Opera House; ␁Circu-
lar Quay)
Sydney Symphony Orchestra (SSO; Map p50;
☑02-8215 4600; www.sydneysymphony.com; cnr
Harrington & Argyle Sts)
Sydney Theatre Company (p69)

The free monthly *What's On* brochure lists
upcoming events, including info on *Kids at
the House,* a pint-sized entertainment roster.

Sydney Harbour Bridge

Sydney's second-most-loved construction embodies both practicality and beauty. Views from the big steel rainbow are sublime, whether you're on foot or on a bridge climb.

Great For...

☑ Don't Miss

Walking across the 'coathanger' north to south, with Opera House views.

The Structure

At 134m high, 1149m long, 49m wide and 52,800 tonnes, the Sydney Harbour Bridge is the world's largest and heaviest (but not longest) steel arch. It links the Rocks with North Sydney, crossing the harbour at a narrow point.

The two halves of chief engineer JJC Bradfield's mighty arch were built outwards from each shore. In 1930, after seven years of merciless toil by 1400 workers, the two arches were centimetres apart when 100km/h winds set them swaying. The 'coathanger' hung tough, and the bridge finally opened to the public two years later.

The bridge is the centrepiece of Sydney's major celebrations, particularly the New Year's Eve fireworks.

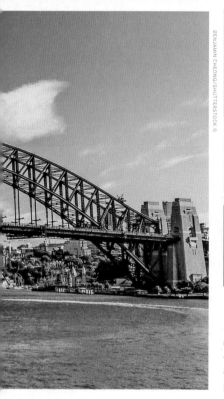

BENJAMIN CHEONG/SHUTTERSTOCK ©

❶ Need to Know

Map p50; 🚉Circular Quay, Milsons Point

✕ Take a Break

Try the rooftop at the Glenmore (p65) pub for a post-bridge beverage.

★ Top Tip

Suffer from vertigo? The track over the arch is wide enough for you to never see straight down.

BridgeClimb

Once only painters and daredevils scaled the Harbour Bridge – now anyone can do it. Make your way through the **BridgeClimb** (Map p50; ☎02-8274 7777; www.bridgeclimb. com; 3 Cumberland St; adult $263-388, child $183-278; 🚉Circular Quay) departure lounge and the extensive training session, don your headset, an umbilical safety cord and a dandy grey jumpsuit and up you go.

Tours last 2¼ to 3½ hours – a toilet stop before climbing is a smart idea. If you're uncertain whether your nerve or bladder will hold that long, a 90-minute sampler is available, but it only goes halfway and never reaches the summit. The priciest climbs are at dawn and sunset.

Crossing on Foot

The best way to experience the bridge is on foot – don't expect much of a view crossing by train or car (driving south there's a toll). Staircases access the bridge from both shores; a footpath runs along its eastern side and a cycleway along the west.

Pylon Lookout

The bridge's hefty pylons may look as though they're shouldering all the weight, but they're largely decorative – right down to their granite facing. There are awesome views from the top of the **Pylon Lookout** (Map p50; ☎02-9240 1100; www.pylonlook out.com.au; Sydney Harbour Bridge; adult/child $15/10; ⊙10am-5pm; 🚉Circular Quay), atop the southeast pylon, 200 steps above the bridge's footpath. Inside the pylon there are exhibits about the bridge's construction, in-cluding an eight-minute film, which screens every 15 minutes.

Sydney Harbour

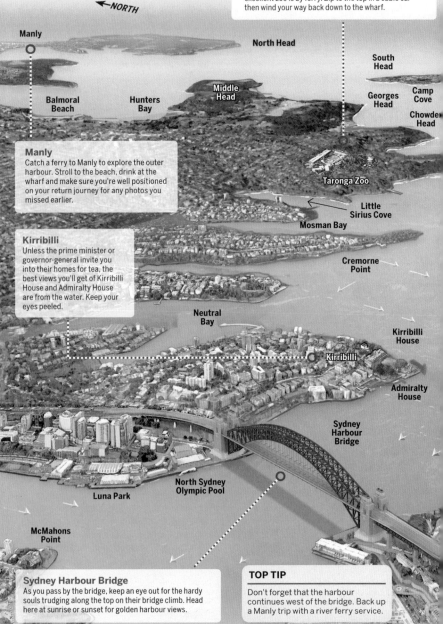

Taronga Zoo
Even if you've hired a car, the best way to reach this excellent zoo is by ferry. Zip to the top in a cable car then wind your way back down to the wharf.

← NORTH

Manly

North Head

South Head

Camp Cove

Georges Head

Chowder Head

Middle Head

Balmoral Beach

Hunters Bay

Taronga Zoo

Manly
Catch a ferry to Manly to explore the outer harbour. Stroll to the beach, drink at the wharf and make sure you're well positioned on your return journey for any photos you missed earlier.

Little Sirius Cove

Mosman Bay

Kirribilli
Unless the prime minister or governor-general invite you into their homes for tea, the best views you'll get of Kirribilli House and Admiralty House are from the water. Keep your eyes peeled.

Cremorne Point

Neutral Bay

Kirribilli House

Kirribilli

Admiralty House

Sydney Harbour Bridge

North Sydney Olympic Pool

Luna Park

McMahons Point

Sydney Harbour Bridge
As you pass by the bridge, keep an eye out for the hardy souls trudging along the top on their bridge climb. Head here at sunrise or sunset for golden harbour views.

TOP TIP
Don't forget that the harbour continues west of the bridge. Back up a Manly trip with a river ferry service.

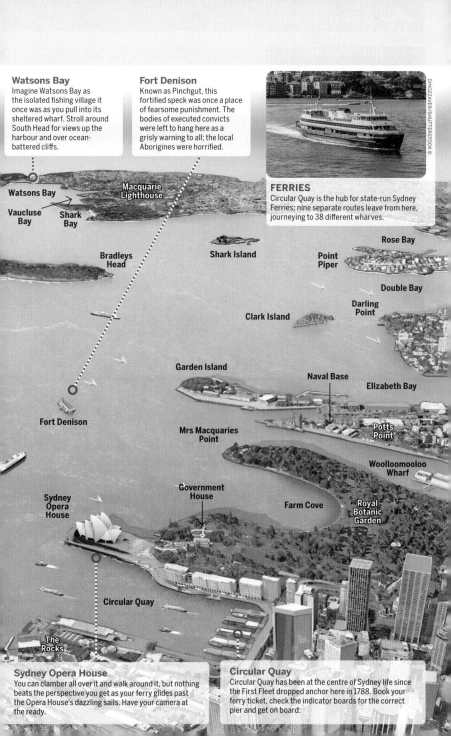

Watsons Bay
Imagine Watsons Bay as the isolated fishing village it once was as you pull into its sheltered wharf. Stroll around South Head for views up the harbour and over ocean-battered cliffs.

Fort Denison
Known as Pinchgut, this fortified speck was once a place of fearsome punishment. The bodies of executed convicts were left to hang here as a grisly warning to all; the local Aborigines were horrified.

DINOZZAVER/SHUTTERSTOCK ©

FERRIES
Circular Quay is the hub for state-run Sydney Ferries; nine separate routes leave from here, journeying to 38 different wharves.

Watsons Bay

Macquarie Lighthouse

Vaucluse Bay

Shark Bay

Rose Bay

Bradleys Head

Shark Island

Point Piper

Double Bay

Clark Island

Darling Point

Garden Island

Naval Base

Elizabeth Bay

Fort Denison

Mrs Macquaries Point

Potts Point

Woolloomooloo Wharf

Sydney Opera House

Government House

Farm Cove

Royal Botanic Garden

Circular Quay

The Rocks

Sydney Opera House
You can clamber all over it and walk around it, but nothing beats the perspective you get as your ferry glides past the Opera House's dazzling sails. Have your camera at the ready.

Circular Quay
Circular Quay has been at the centre of Sydney life since the First Fleet dropped anchor here in 1788. Book your ferry ticket, check the indicator boards for the correct pier and get on board.

Bondi Beach

Definitively Sydney, Bondi is one of the world's great beaches: ocean and land collide, the Pacific arrives in great foaming swells and all people are equal, as democratic as sand.

Great For...

☑ **Don't Miss**

A quick dip in the Bondi Icebergs Pool (p45).

A Day at the Beach

Bondi is the closest ocean beach to the city centre (8km away), has consistently good (though crowded) waves, and is great for a rough-and-tumble swim. Surfers carve up sandbar breaks at either end of the beach. Two surf clubs – Bondi and North Bondi – patrol the water between sets of red-and-yellow flags, positioned to avoid the worst rips and holes. Thousands of unfortunates have to be rescued from the surf each year (enough to make a TV show about it) – don't become a statistic! If the sea's angry or you have small children in tow, try the saltwater sea baths at either end of the beach.

North Bondi is a great place to learn to surf, and well-established surf school **Let's Go Surfing** (☑02-9365 1800; www.letsgosurf-ing.com.au; 128 Ramsgate Ave, North Bondi; board & wetsuit hire 1hr/2hr/day/week $25/30/50/200; 🕘9am-5pm; 🚌333) offers lessons catering to

Bondi Icebergs Pool

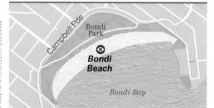

ⓘ Need to Know

Campbell Pde, Bondi Beach; 🚌333

✕ Take a Break

Grab a delicious bagel from **Lox, Stock & Barrel** (📞02-9300 0368; www.loxstock andbarrel.com.au; 140 Glenayr Ave, Bondi Beach; breakfast & lunch dishes $15-22, dinner mains $30-34; ⏰7am-3.30pm daily plus 6-10pm Wed & Thu, 6-11pm Fri & Sat; 🛜📶; 🚌379)

★ Top Tip

Swim between the red-and-yellow flags, indicating safe sections of beach patrolled by lifeguards.

practically everyone. There are classes for grommets aged seven to 16 (1½ hours, $49) and adults (two hours; $110, women-only classes available), or you can book a private tutor (1½ hours, $195/284 for one/two people). Prices drop outside summer.

Prefer wheels to fins? There's a **skate ramp** (Queen Elizabeth Dr, Bondi Beach; 🚌333) at the beach's southern end. If posing in your budgie smugglers (Speedos) isn't having enough impact, there's an outdoor **workout area** (Queen Elizabeth Dr, Bondi Beach; 🚌333) **FREE** near the North Bondi Surf Club. Coincidentally (or perhaps not), this is the part of the beach where the gay guys hang out.

What's Nearby?

Bondi Pavilion   Notable Building

(www.waverley.nsw.gov.au; Queen Elizabeth Dr, Bondi Beach; ⏰9am-5pm; 🚌333) **FREE** Built in

the Mediterranean Georgian Revival style in 1929, 'The Pav' is more a cultural centre than a changing shed. There's a free art gallery upstairs, a theatre out the back and various cafes and a bar lining the ocean frontage.

Bronte Beach   Beach

(Bronte Rd, Bronte; 🚌379) Half an hour's drive from Bondi, Bronte Beach is a winning family-oriented beach hemmed in by sandstone cliffs and a grassy park, which lays claims to the title of the oldest surf lifesaving club in the world (1903).

Bondi Icebergs Pool   Swimming

(📞02-9130 4804; www.icebergs.com.au; 1 Notts Ave, Bondi Beach; adult/child $8/5.50; ⏰6am-6.30pm Mon-Wed & Fri, from 6.30am Sat & Sun; 🚌333) Sydney's most famous pool (pictured above) commands the best view in Bondi and has a cute little cafe. It's a salt-water pool that's regularly doused by the bigger breakers. There's a more sheltered pool for kids.

Bondi to Coogee Clifftop Trail

Sydney's most scenic walk, this sublime coastal path is a must. Both ends are serviced by bus routes, and there are plenty of places to eat and swim en route.
Start Bondi Beach
Distance 6km
Duration Three hours

2 Small but perfectly formed, **Tamarama Beach** has a deep reach of sand, totally disproportionate to its width.

Bondi Rd

Old South Head Rd

Take a Break...
The best lunch option is Bronte's **Three Blue Ducks** (www.threeblueducks.com; 141-143 Macpherson St).

3 Descend from the clifftops onto **Bronte Beach** (p45) and take a dip, or head to a cafe for a caffeine hit.

Centennial Park

6 Beyond Cliffbrook Pde, take the steps down to **Gordons Bay**, one of Sydney's best dive spots.

Alison Rd

Alison Rd

7 The trail ends on glorious **Coogee Beach**. Swagger up to the rooftop of the **Coogee Pavilion** (www.merivale.com.au/coogeepavilion) and toast your efforts.

Randwick Racecourse

0 ———————— 1 km
0 ———————— 0.5 miles

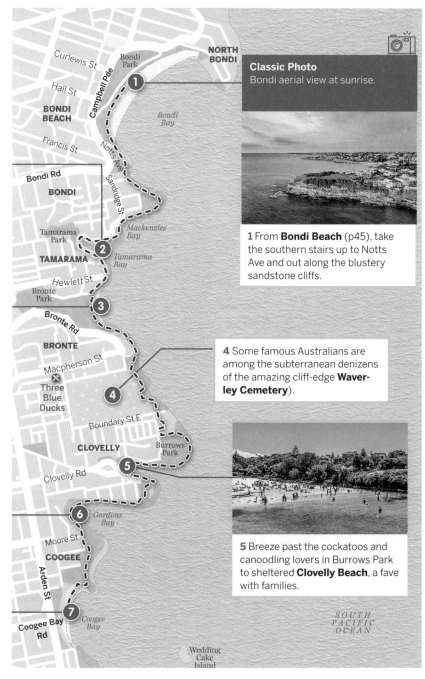

Classic Photo
Bondi aerial view at sunrise.

1 From **Bondi Beach** (p45), take the southern stairs up to Notts Ave and out along the blustery sandstone cliffs.

4 Some famous Australians are among the subterranean denizens of the amazing cliff-edge **Waverley Cemetery**).

5 Breeze past the cockatoos and canoodling lovers in Burrows Park to sheltered **Clovelly Beach**, a fave with families.

Curlewis St

Hall St

Campbell Pde

**BONDI
BEACH**

Bondi
Park

Bondi
Bay

Francis St

Notts Ave

Bondi Rd

BONDI

Sandridge St

Mackenzies
Bay

Tamarama
Park

TAMARAMA

Tamarama
Bay

Hewlett St

Bronte
Park

Bronte Rd

BRONTE

Macpherson St

**Three
Blue
Ducks**

Boundary St E

CLOVELLY

Burrows
Park

Clovelly Rd

Gordons
Bay

Moore St

COOGEE

Arden St

Coogee Bay
Rd

Coogee
Bay

Wedding
Cake
Island

*SOUTH
PACIFIC
OCEAN*

1 DARREN TIERNEY/SHUTTERSTOCK © 3 ANGELINA PILARINOS/SHUTTERSTOCK © 5 KEITMA/SHUTTERSTOCK ©

◎ SIGHTS
◎ Circular Quay & the Rocks

Join the tourist pilgrimage to the Opera House and Harbour Bridge then grab a schooner at a convict-era pub in the Rocks.

Royal Botanic Garden   Gardens

(Map p50; ☎02-9231 8111; www.rbgsyd.nsw.gov.au; Mrs Macquarie's Rd; ⊙7am-dusk; 🚇Circular Quay) ✔ FREE Southeast of the Opera House, this garden was established in 1816 and features plant life from around the world. Within the gardens are hothouses with palms and ferns, as well as the **Calyx** (Map p50; ⊙10am-4pm; 🤖; 🚇Martin Place) ✔, a striking exhibition space featuring a curving glasshouse gallery with a wall of greenery and temporary plant-themed exhibitions. Grab a park map at any main entrance.

Museum of Contemporary Art   Gallery

(MCA; Map p50; ☎02-9245 2400; www.mca.com.au; 140 George St; ⊙10am-5pm Thu-Tue, to 9pm Wed; 🚇Circular Quay) FREE The MCA is a showcase for Australian and international contemporary art, with a rotating permanent collection and temporary exhibitions. Aboriginal art features prominently. The art-deco building has had a modern space grafted on to it, the highlight of which is the rooftop cafe with stunning views. There are free guided tours daily, with several languages available.

Rocks Discovery Museum   Museum

(Map p50; ☎02-9240 8680; www.therocks.com; Kendall Lane; ⊙10am-5pm; 🚇Circular Quay) FREE Divided into four displays – Warrane (pre-1788), Colony (1788–1820), Port (1820–1900) and Transformations (1900 to the present) – this small, excellent museum, tucked away down a Rocks laneway, digs deep into the area's history on an artefact-rich tour. Sensitive attention is given to the Rocks' original inhabitants, the Gadigal (Cadigal) people, and there are interesting tales of early colonial characters.

Art Gallery of NSW

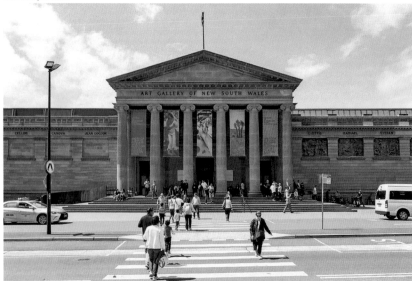

Sydney Observatory
Observatory

(Map p50; ☎02-9217 0111; www.maas.museum/
sydney-observatory; 1003 Upper Fort St; ⊙10am-
5pm; ⛴Circular Quay) **FREE** Built in the 1850s,
Sydney's copper-domed, Italianate sandstone observatory squats atop **Observatory Hill** (Map p50; Upper Fort St), overlooking the harbour. Inside is a collection
of vintage apparatus, including Australia's
oldest working telescope (1874), as well as
background on Australian astronomy and
transits of Venus. Also on offer (weekends
and school holidays) are child-focused
tours (adult/child $10/8), including a
solar telescope viewing and planetarium
show. Bookings are essential for night-time
stargazing sessions, which come in family-oriented (adult/child $22/17) and adult
(adult/child $27/20) versions.

◎ City Centre

Sydney's CBD features gracious colonial
buildings scattered among the skyscrap-
ers, with orderly parks providing breathing
space. Rambunctious Haymarket and
Chinatown are here too.

Art Gallery of NSW
Gallery

(Map p54; ☎1800 679 278; www.artgallery.nsw.
gov.au; Art Gallery Rd; ⊙10am-5pm Thu-Tue, to
10pm Wed; 🛈; ☒441, ⛴St James) **FREE** With
its neoclassical Greek frontage and modern
rear, this much-loved institution plays a
prominent and gregarious role in Sydney
society. Blockbuster international touring
exhibitions arrive regularly and there's
an outstanding permanent collection of
Australian art, including a substantial Indigenous section. The gallery also plays host
to lectures, concerts, screenings, celebrity
talks and children's activities. A range of
free guided tours is offered on different
themes and in various languages; enquire
at the desk or check the website.

Hyde Park
Barracks Museum
Museum

(Map p50; ☎02-8239 2311; www.sydneyliving
museums.com.au; Queens Sq, Macquarie St;
adult/child $24/16; ⊙10am-5pm; ⛴St James)
Convict architect Francis Greenway

👪 Sydney for Kids

Organised kids' activities ramp up during school holidays (December/January,
April, July and September); check www.
sydneyforkids.com.au, www.ellaslist.
com.au and www.childmags.com.au for
listings.

Most kids love the Sydney Sea Life
Aquarium (p52), Wild Life Sydney Zoo
(p52) and Australian National Maritime
Museum (p52) at Darling Harbour,
and the Powerhouse Museum (p52)
in neighbouring Ultimo. Also worth
investigating are the 'Tours for Tots' and
'Gallery Kids Sunday Performance' at
the Art Gallery of NSW – details are on
the gallery's website.

Elsewhere, Taronga Zoo (p55) and
Luna Park (p56) are sure to please. Or
just take them to the beach!

---

designed this squarish, decorously Georgian structure (1819) as convict quarters.
Fifty thousand men and boys sentenced
to transportation passed through here in
30 years. It later became an immigration
depot, a women's asylum and a law court.
These days it's a fascinating museum,
focusing on the barracks' history and the
archaeological efforts that helped reveal
it. At time of research the barracks was
closed until late 2019 as the exhibition was
rejigged.

Museum of Sydney
Museum

(MoS; Map p50; ☎02-9251 5988; www.sydney
livingmuseums.com.au; cnr Phillip & Bridge Sts;
adult/child $12/8; ⊙10am-5pm; 🛈; ⛴Circular
Quay) Built on the site of Sydney's first Government House, the MoS is a fragmented,
storytelling museum, which uses installations to explore the city's history. The
area's long Indigenous past is highlighted
throughout, plus there's interesting coverage of the early days of contact between
the Gadigal (Cadigal) people and the
colonists. Key figures in Sydney's planning

Central Sydney

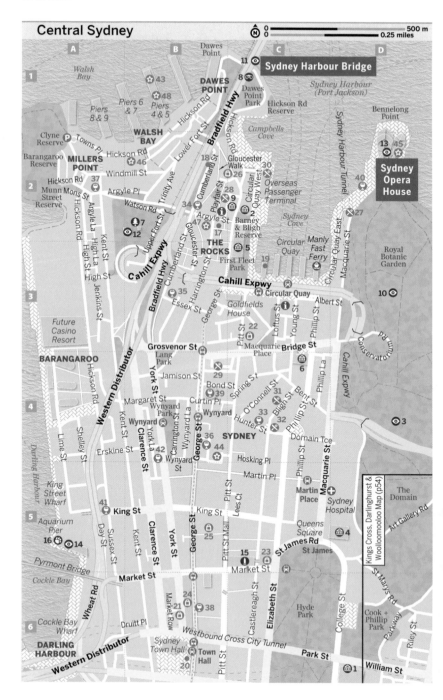

N

0 — 500 m
0 — 0.25 miles

A | B | C | D

1

Walsh
Bay

43

48

Piers 6
& 7

Piers
8 & 9

Piers
4 & 5

**DAWES
POINT**

Dawes
Point

11

8

Sydney Harbour Bridge

*Sydney Harbour
(Port Jackson)*

Dawes
Point
Park

Hickson Rd
Reserve

Bennelong
Point

13 45

**Sydney
Opera
House**

Clyne
Reserve

Towns Pl

Hickson Rd

**WALSH
BAY**

*Campbells
Cove*

Barangaroo
Reserve

**MILLERS
POINT**

46

Windmill St

18

Gloucester
Walk

30

26

Circular
Quay West

Overseas
Passenger
Terminal

40

2

Hickson Rd
Munn Mons
Street
Reserve

37

Argyle Pl

Watson Rd

34

Playfair St

28

9

2

*Sydney
Cove*

27

Royal
Botanic
Garden

7

12

Upper Fort St

Argyle St

47

17

Barney
& Bligh
Reserve

**THE
ROCKS**

5

Circular
Quay

Manly
Fast
Ferry

3

Cahill Expwy

35

Essex St

George St

Harrington St

First Fleet
Park

19

Cahill Expwy

Circular Quay

i

Albert St

10

Future
Casino
Resort

Goldfields
House

BARANGAROO

Western Distributor

Bradfield Hwy

Grosvenor St

Lang
Park

Pitt St

22

Loftus St

Young St

Phillip St

Macquarie
Place

Bridge St

6

Conservatory

29

Jamison St

Bond St

39

Spring St

O'Connell St

31

Bligh St

Bent St

Margaret St

Curtin Pl

Wynyard
Park

Wynyard

33

32

Phillip St

Hunter St

4

3

Erskine St

36

44

George St

SYDNEY

Domain Tce

Martin Pl

41

King St

King St

Martin
Place

**Sydney
Hospital**

4

Aquarium
Pier

16 14

Hosking Pl

Queens
Square

4

St James

5

Pyrmont Bridge

Cockle Bay

Market St

15

23

Market St

St James Rd

Hyde
Park

**DARLING
HARBOUR**

Cockle Bay
Wharf

Druitt Pl

24

21

38

Westbound Cross City Tunnel

Western Distributor

Sydney
Town Hall

20

**Town
Hall**

Park St

College St

6

1

William St

Kings Cross, Darlinghurst &
Woolloomooloo Map (p54)

The
Domain

Cook +
Phillip
Park

Central Sydney

and architecture are brought to life, while there's a good section on the First Fleet itself, with scale models.

Sydney Tower Eye   Tower

(Map p50; www.sydneytowereye.com.au; Level 5, Westfield Sydney, 188 Pitt St; adult/child $29/20; ☺9am-9pm, last entry 8pm; ⩗St James) The 309m-tall Sydney Tower (still known as Centrepoint by many Sydneysiders) offers unbeatable 360-degree views from the observation level 250m up. The visit starts with the 4D Experience, a short film giving you a bird's-eye view of city, surf, harbour and what lies beneath the water, accompanied by mist sprays and bubbles. Then it's up the lift to the viewing area. The **Skywalk**, where you can step onto glass-floored viewing platforms outside, was suspended at time of research.

Chinatown   Area

(www.sydney-chinatown.info; ⩗Paddy's Markets, ⩗Town Hall) Dixon St is the heart of Chinatown: a narrow, shady pedestrian mall with a string of restaurants and insistent spruikers. The ornate dragon gates (paifang) at either end have fake bamboo tiles, golden Chinese calligraphy and ornamental lions to keep evil spirits at bay. Chinatown in general (though not necessarily between the dragon gates) is a fabulous eating district, which effectively extends for several blocks north and south of here, and segues into Koreatown and Thaitown to the east.

⊙ Darling Harbour & Pyrmont

Dotted between the flyovers and fountains of Sydney's purpose-built tourist hub are some of the city's highest-profile attractions. In Pyrmont, on the harbour's western shore, the Star casino complex has had an expensive do-over.

Wild Life Sydney Zoo   Zoo

(Map p50; ☑1800 614 069; www.wildlifesydney. com.au; Aquarium Pier, Central Sydney; adult/ child $44/31; ⊙10am-5pm; ⓡTown Hall) Complementing its sister and neighbour, Sea Life, this surprisingly capacious complex houses an impressive collection of Australian native reptiles, butterflies, spiders, snakes and mammals (including koalas and a walk-through kangaroo area). The nocturnal section is particularly good, bringing out the extrovert in the quolls, potoroos, echidnas and possums. The up-close look at a sizeable saltwater croc is also memorable, while upstairs visitors queue up for cute koala selfies (from $25). Talks through the day fill you in on key species.

🗺 Kings Cross

Crowned by a huge illuminated **Coca-Cola Sign** (Map p54; Darlinghurst Rd, Kings Cross; ⓡKings Cross), the 'Cross' has long been the home of Sydney vice. Although once home to grand estates and stylish apartments, the suburb underwent a radical change in the 1930s, when wine-soaked intellectuals, artists and ne'er-do-wells rowdily claimed the streets. The neighbourhood's reputation was sealed during the Vietnam War, when American sailors based at nearby Garden Island flooded the Cross with a tide of drug-fuelled debauchery. The streets retain an air of seedy hedonism, although major building programs have accelerated gentrification.

It's a 15-minute walk to the Cross from the city, or you could hop on a train. Buses 311 and 323–6 from the city also pass through here.

Sydney Sea Life Aquarium   Aquarium

(Map p50; ☑1800 614 069; www.sydneyaquar ium.com.au; Aquarium Pier, Central Sydney; adult/child $46/33; ⊙10am-6pm; ⓡTown Hall) 🕭 As well as regular tanks, this impressive complex has large pools that you can walk through – safely enclosed in Perspex tunnels – as an intimidating array of sharks and rays pass overhead. Other highlights include a two-minute boat ride through a king and gentoo penguin enclosure, a dugong, disco-lit jellyfish, evolutionary throwbacks and the brilliant finale: the enormous Great Barrier Reef tank, which cycles you through different times of day in the life of coral, turtles, rare sharks and numerous fish.

Australian National Maritime Museum   Museum

(MU-SEA-UM; ☑02-9298 3777; www.sea. museum; 2 Murray St, Pyrmont; permanent collection free, temporary exhibitions adult/child $20/12; ⊙9.30am-5pm, to 6pm Jan; 🚌389, ⓡPyrmont Bay) **FREE** Beneath a soaring roof designed by architect Philip Cox, the Maritime Museum, sails through Australia's inextricable relationship with the sea. Exhibitions range from Indigenous canoes to surf culture, immigration to the navy. The worthwhile 'big ticket' (adult/child $32/20) includes entry to some of the vessels moored outside, including the atmospheric submarine HMAS *Onslow* and the destroyer HMAS *Vampire*. The high-production-value short film *Action Station*s sets the mood with a re-creation of a mission event from each vessel. Excellent guided tours explain each vessel's features.

Powerhouse Museum   Museum

(Museum of Applied Arts & Sciences/MAAS; ☑02-9217 0111; www.powerhousemuseum. com; 500 Harris St, Ultimo; adult/child $15/free; ⊙10am-5pm; 🛜; ⓡExhibition Centre) A short walk from Darling Harbour, this cavernous science and design museum whirs away inside the former power station for Sydney's defunct, original tram network. The collection and temporary exhibitions cover

Australian National Maritime Museum

everything from robots and life on Mars to steam trains to climate change to atoms to fashion, industrial design and avant-garde art installations. There are great options for kids of all ages but it's equally intriguing for adults. Grab a map of the museum once you're inside. Disabled access is good.

Sydney Fish Market — Market

(☑02-9004 1108; www.sydneyfishmarket.com.au; Bank St, Pyrmont; ⊙7am-4pm Mon-Thu, to 5pm Fri-Sun; ☐Fish Market) This piscatorial precinct on Blackwattle Bay shifts around 15 million kilograms of seafood annually, and has retail outlets, restaurants, sushi and oyster bars, delis and a highly regarded **cooking school** (☑02-9004 1111; www.sydney fishmarket.com.au/seafood-school; Sydney Fish Market, Pyrmont Bridge Rd, Pyrmont; 2/4hr courses $90/165; ☐Fish Market). Chefs, locals and overfed seagulls haggle over mud crabs, Balmain bugs, lobsters and salmon at the daily fish auction, which kicks off at 5.30am weekdays. Check it out on a behind-the-scenes tour (adult/child $45/20). A flash new market is being built a little further west, due to open in 2023.

◉ Surry Hills & Darlinghurst

Surry Hills is liberally scattered with corner pubs, fantastic eateries and quirky cafes and bars. Neighbouring Darlinghurst is synonymous with Sydney's gay community: the lower end of Oxford St is home to most of the city's gay bars.

Australian Museum — Museum

(Map p50; ☑02-9320 6000; www.australianmu seum.net.au; 6 College St, Darlinghurst; adult/child $15/free; ⊙9.30am-5pm; ☎; ☐Muse-um) Under ongoing modernisation, this museum, established just 40 years after the First Fleet dropped anchor, is brilliant. A standout is the section covering Aboriginal history and spirituality, from Dreaming stories to videos of the Freedom Rides of the 1960s. The elegant Long Gallery focuses on 100 objects (from a platypus-skin rug to an Egyptian death-boat to the 'Bone Ranger') and 100 key Australians. The excellent dinosaur gallery features enormous Jobaria as well as local bruisers like Muttaburrasaurus.

Kings Cross, Darlinghurst & Woolloomooloo

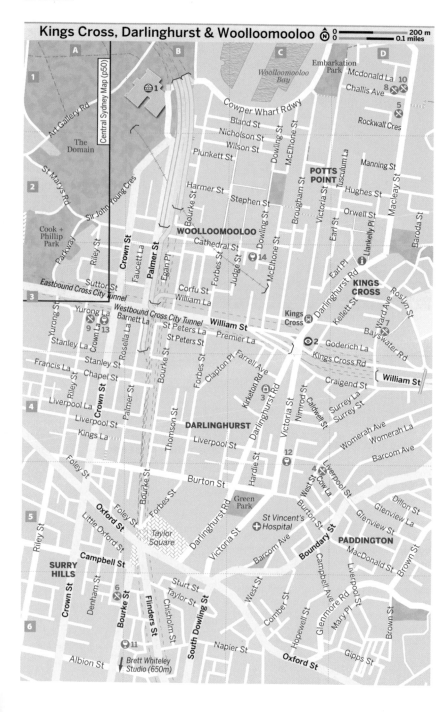

Kings Cross, Darlinghurst & Woolloomooloo

Brett Whiteley Studio   Gallery

(📞02-9225 1881; www.artgallery.nsw.gov.au/brett-whiteley-studio; 2 Raper St, Surry Hills; ⊙10am-4pm Fri-Sun; 🚌Surry Hills, 🚆Central) **FREE** Acclaimed local artist Brett Whiteley (1939–1992) lived fast and without restraint. His hard-to-find studio (look for the signs on Devonshire St) has been preserved as a gallery for some of his best work. Pride of place goes to his astonishing *Alchemy*, a giant multi-panel extravaganza that could absorb you for hours with its broad themes, intricate details and humorous asides. The studio room upstairs also gives great insight into the character of this masterful draughtsman and off-the-wall genius.

◎ Paddington & Centennial Park

Paddington, aka 'Paddo', is an upmarket residential suburb of restored Victorian-era terrace houses and jacaranda-lined streets. Visit on a Saturday to see the Paddington Markets (p56).

East of Paddington is the 220-hectare **Centennial Park** (📞02-9339 6699; www.centennialparklands.com.au; Oxford St; ⊙gates sunrise-sunset; 🚌Moore Park, 🚆Bondi Junction), which has running, cycling, skating and horse-riding tracks, duck ponds, BBQ sites and sports pitches.

◎ Manly & the North Shore

With both a harbour side and a glorious ocean beach, Manly is Sydney's only ferry destination with surf. It's worth visiting for the ferry ride alone.

Still on the North Shore, just east of the Harbour Bridge is stately Kirribilli, home to **Admiralty House** (www.gg.gov.au; Kirribilli Ave; 🚆Milsons Point) and **Kirribilli House** (Kirribilli Ave; 🚆Milsons Point), the Sydney residences of the governor-general and prime minister respectively.

Manly Beach   Beach

(⛴Manly) Sydney's second most famous beach (after Bondi, of course) is a magnificent strand that stretches for nearly two golden kilometres, lined by Norfolk Island pines and midrise apartment blocks. The southern end of the beach, nearest the Corso, is known as South Steyne, with North Steyne in the centre and Queenscliff at the northern end; each has its own surf lifesaving club.

Taronga Zoo Sydney   Zoo

(📞02-9969 2777; www.taronga.org.au; Bradleys Head Rd, Mosman; adult/child $47/27; ⊙9.30am-5pm Sep-Apr, to 4.30pm May-Aug; 🎫; 🚌M30, ⛴Taronga Zoo) 🚢 A 12-minute ferry ride from Circular Quay, this bushy harbour hillside is full of kangaroos, koalas and similarly hirsute Australians, plus numerous imported guests. The zoo's critters have million-dollar harbour views, but seem blissfully unaware of the privilege. Encouragingly, Taronga sets benchmarks in animal care and welfare. Highlights include the nocturnal platypus habitat, the Great Southern

Weekend Markets

Glebe Markets (www.glebemarkets.com.au; Glebe Public School, cnr Glebe Point Rd & Derby Pl; ⊘10am-4pm Sat; ⊟431, 433, ⊠Glebe) Inner-city hippies beat a hazy course to this crowded Saturday market. Once massaged, fuelled on lentil burgers and swathed in funky retro gear, they retreat to the lawns, pass the peace pipe and chill out to African drums.

Bondi Markets (www.bondimarkets.com.au; Bondi Beach Public School, Campbell Pde, Bondi Beach; ⊘10am-4pm Sun; ⊟333) While the kids are at the beach on Sunday while their school fills up with Bondi groovers rummaging through funky secondhand clothes and books, hippy jewellery, aromatherapy oils, candles and vinyl records.

Paddington Markets (⊘02-9331 2923; www.paddingtonmarkets.com.au; 395 Oxford St; ⊘10am-4pm Sat; ⊟333, 352, 440, M40) Join the throngs for a foot massage, a tarot reading or a funky clubbing shirt. Sydney's most well-attended weekend market coughs up everything from vintage clothes and hip fashions to jewellery, books, massage and palmistry.

The Rocks Market (Map p50; www.therocks.com/markets; George St; ⊘9am-3pm Fri, 10am-5pm Sat & Sun; ⊠Circular Quay) The 150 stalls here are a little on the tacky side (fossils, opals, faux Aboriginal art etc), but the quality is reasonably high and there are a few gems. The atmosphere is busy, and pubs are nearby for a quick beer.

Oceans section and the Asian elephant display. Feedings and encounters happen throughout the day, while in summer, twilight concerts jazz things up (see www.twilightattaronga.org.au).

North Head   National Park
(⊘1300 072 757; www.nationalparks.nsw.gov.au; North Head Scenic Dr, Manly; ⊘sunrise-sunset; ⊟135) **FREE** About 3km south of central Manly, spectacular North Head offers dramatic cliffs, lookouts, secluded beaches, pretty paths through the native scrub and sweeping views of the ocean, the harbour and the city. It's great to explore by bike or on foot. Grab a map and plot your own path through the headland, which takes in former military barracks, WWII gun emplacements, a quarantine cemetery and a **memorial walk** commemorating Australia's military. At the tip, **Fairfax Lookouts** offer dramatic clifftop perspectives.

Luna Park   Amusement Park
(⊘02-9922 6644; www.lunaparksydney.com; 1 Olympic Dr, Milsons Point; ⊘11am-4pm Mon-Thu, to 10pm Fri & Sat, 10am-6pm Sun; ⊠Milsons Point, ⊠Milsons Point) **FREE** A sinister chip-toothed clown face (50 times life-sized) forms the entrance to this old-fashioned amusement park overlooking Sydney Harbour. It's one of several 1930s features, including the Coney Island funhouse, a pretty carousel and the nausea-inducing Rotor. You can purchase a two-ride pass ($22), or buy a height-based unlimited-ride pass (adults $55, kids $25 to $45; cheaper if purchased online). Hours are complex, and extended during school and public holidays. It also functions as a concert venue.

✪ ACTIVITIES

Surf spots on the South Shore include Bondi, Tamarama, Coogee, Maroubra and Cronulla. The North Shore is home to a dozen surf beaches between Manly and Palm Beach, including Curl Curl, Dee Why, Narrabeen, Mona Vale and Newport. For updates on what's breaking where, see www.coastalwatch.com or www.magicseaweed.com.

There are 100-plus public swimming pools in Sydney, and many beaches have protected rock pools. Harbour beaches offer sheltered and shark-netted swimming.

Manly Scenic Walkway
Walking

(www.manly.nsw.gov.au; 🚢Manly) This marvellous coastal walk has two major components: the 10km western stretch between Manly and Spit Bridge, and the 9.5km eastern loop around North Head. Either download a map or pick one up from the information centre near the wharf.

Dive Centre Bondi
Diving

(📞02-9369 3855; www.divebondi.com.au; 198 Bondi Rd, Bondi; 2 guided dives incl equipment from shore/boat $155/195, PADI Open Water courses $495; ⏰9am-6pm Mon-Fri, from 8am Sat & Sun; 🚌333) Friendly and professional, this centre offers guided dives from shore or boat as well as equipment hire. It runs PADI Open Water courses as well as other certifications.

Manly Surf School
Surfing

(📞02-9932 7000; www.manlysurfschool.com; North Steyne Surf Club, Manly; surf lessons adult/child $70/60, surf safari $120; 🚌136, 139, 🚢Manly) Reliable and well established, this outfit offers two-hour surf lessons year-round, as well as private tuition. It's a fair bit cheaper if you book a multi-class package. You can also book classes at other beaches. They run good-value surf safaris up to the Northern Beaches, including two lessons, lunch, gear and city pick-ups; a fun day out.

Andrew (Boy) Charlton Pool
Swimming

(📞02-9358 6686; www.abcpool.org; 1c Mrs Macquaries Rd; adult/child $6.60/5; ⏰6am-7pm Sep & Apr, to 8pm Oct-Mar; 🚌441) One of Sydney's best saltwater pools – smack-bang next to the harbour – is a magnet for serious lap swimmers, who rule the roost (so maintain your lane). There's a cafe here looking across at the Garden Island base, great for some naval gazing. Wheelchair-accessible. **Yoga classes** (www.sydneyyogacollective.com; per class $12) are also available here, as well as other activities.

⊙ TOURS

Sydney Architecture Walks
Walking

(📞0403 888 390; www.sydneyarchitecture. org; adult walks $49-59, cycle not incl bike $90)

Luna Park

Captain Cook Cruises

These bright young archi-buffs run two 3½-hour cycling tours and six themed two-to-three-hour walking tours. There's an excellent focus on explaining modern architectural principles and urban design. It's cheaper if you book in advance.

Bonza Bike Tours
Cycling

(Map p50; ☎02-9247 8800; www.bonzabike tours.com; 30 Harrington St; tours from $99; ⊙office 9am-5pm; ⛴Circular Quay) These bike boffins run a 2½-hour Sydney Highlights tour (adult/child $99/79) and a four-hour Sydney Classic tour ($129/99). Other tours include the Harbour Bridge and Manly. It also hires out bikes ($15/30/40/130 per hour/half-day/day/week).

Captain Cook Cruises
Cruise

(Map p50; ☎02-9206 1111; www.captain cook.com.au; Wharf 6, Circular Quay; from $35; ⛴Circular Quay) As well as sightseeing ($35 to $55), lunch and dinner cruises, and whale watching, this crew offers an aquatic version of a hop-on, hop-off bus tour, with two main routes that include Watsons Bay, Taronga Zoo, Fort Denison, Shark Island

and Manly. It costs $49/27 per adult/child for two days and includes some commentary. Departures from Circular Quay, Darling Harbour and Barangaroo.

Sydney Harbour Kayaks
Kayaking

(☎02-9960 4389; www.sydneyharbourkayaks. com.au; Smiths Boat Shed, 81 Parriwi Rd, Mosman; kayaks/SUP per hour from $20/25, ecotours $125; ⊙9am-5pm Mon-Fri, from 7.30am Sat & Sun, closed Mon & Tue Jun-Sep; ⛴E66, E68, E71, E75, 76, 77) Rents kayaks and stand-up paddleboards (SUPs), and leads excellent four-hour ecotours from near the Spit Bridge.

I'm Free Walking Tours
Walking

(Map p50; ☎0405 515 654; www.imfree.com. au; 483 George St; walking tour by donation; ⊙10.30am & 2.30pm; ⛴Town Hall) Departing twice daily from the square off George St, between the Town Hall and St Andrew's Cathedral (no bookings taken – just show up), these three-hour tours are nominally free but are run by enthusiastic young guides for tips. The route takes in the Rocks, Circular Quay, Martin Place, Pitt St and Hyde Park. Group sizes can be quite large.

They also have a 90-minute Rocks tour, departing at 6pm outside **Cadman's Cottage** (Map p50; ☎02-9337 5511; www.national parks.nsw.gov.au; 110 George St; ℝCircular Quay) FREE.

🅐 SHOPPING

Queen Victoria Building
Shopping Centre

(QVB; Map p50; ☎02-9265 6800; www.qvb. com.au; 455 George St; ⊙9am-6pm Mon-Wed, Fri & Sat, to 9pm Thu, 11am-5pm Sun; 🛜; ℝTown Hall) The magnificent QVB takes up a whole block and boasts nearly 200 shops on five levels. It's a High Victorian neo-Gothic masterpiece – without doubt Sydney's most beautiful shopping centre.

Strand Arcade
Shopping Centre

(Map p50; ☎02-9265 6800; www.strandarcade. com.au; 412 George St; ⊙9am-5.30pm Mon-Wed & Fri, to 9pm Thu, to 4pm Sat, 11am-4pm Sun; ℝTown Hall) Constructed in 1891, the beautiful Strand rivals the QVB in the ornateness stakes. The three floors of designer fashions, Australiana and old-world coffee shops will make your shortcut through here considerably longer. Some of the top Australian designers and other iconic brands have stores here – chocolatiers included! Aesop, Haighs, Leona Edmiston, Dinosaur Designs and more are all present.

Australian Wine Centre
Wine

(Map p50; ☎02-9247 2755; www.australian winecentre.com; 42 Pitt St; ⊙9.30am-8pm Mon-Thu & Sat, to 9pm Fri, 10am-7pm Sun; ℝCircular Quay) This store, with multilingual staff, is packed with quality Australian wine, beer and spirits. Smaller producers are well represented, along with a staggering range of prestigious Penfolds Grange wines and other bottle-aged gems. Service is excellent and international shipping can be arranged.

David Jones
Department Store

(Map p50; ☎02-9266 5544; www.davidjones. com.au; 86-108 Castlereagh St; ⊙9.30am-7pm Sun-Wed, to 9pm Thu & Fri, from 9am Sat; ℝSt James) DJs is Sydney's premier depart-

ment store, with high-quality clothing and highbrow food court. A revamp has added a flashy new designer shoe floor on level 7, while a new kids' area and rooftop Champagne bar were also in the works at the time of research. David Jones also takes up a sizeable chunk of **Westfield Bondi Junction** (☎02-9947 8000; www.westfield.com.au; 500 Oxford St, Bondi Junction; ⊙9.30am-6pm Mon-Wed & Sat, to 9pm Thu, to 7pm Fri, from 10am Sun; 🛜; ℝBondi Junction).

Abbey's
Books

(Map p50; ☎02-9264 3111; www.abbeys.com. au; 131 York St; ⊙8.30am-6pm Mon-Wed & Fri, to 8pm Thu, 9am-5pm Sat, 10am-5pm Sun; ℝTown Hall) Easily central Sydney's best bookshop, Abbey's has many strengths. It's good on social sciences and has excellent resources for language learning, including a great selection of foreign films on DVD. There's also a big sci-fi and fantasy section. Staff are great and generally very experienced.

Artery
Art

(Map p54; ☎02-9380 8234; www.artery.com. au; 221 Darlinghurst Rd, Darlinghurst; ⊙10am-5pm; ℝKings Cross) ✿ Step into a world of mesmerising dots and swirls at this small gallery devoted to Aboriginal art. Artery's motto is 'ethical, contemporary, affordable', and while large canvases by more established artists cost in the thousands, small, unstretched canvases start at around $35. There's also a good range of giftware as well as an offbeat sideline in preserved insects.

Gannon House Gallery
Art

(Map p50; ☎02-9251 4474; www.gannon housegallery.com; 45 Argyle St; ⊙10am-6pm; ℝCircular Quay) Specialising in contemporary Australian and Aboriginal art, Gannon House purchases works directly from artists and Aboriginal communities. You'll find the work of prominent artists such as Gloria Petyarre here, alongside lesser-known names. There are always some striking and wonderful pieces.

⊗ EATING

⊗ Circular Quay & the Rocks

Fine Food Store   Cafe $

(Map p50; ☑02-9252 1196; www.finefoodstore.com; cnr Mill & Kendall Lanes; light meals $9-16; ⊗7am-4pm Mon-Sat, from 7.30am Sun; 🛜☑; ☒Circular Quay) The Rocks sometimes seems all pubs, so it's a delight to find this contemporary cafe that works for a sightseeing stopover or a better, cheaper breakfast than your hotel. Staff are genuinely welcoming, make very respectable coffee and offer delicious panini, sandwiches and other breakfast and lunch fare. The outside tables on this narrow lane are the spot to be.

Quay   Modern Australian $$$

(Map p50; ☑02-9251 5600; www.quay.com.au; Level 3, Overseas Passenger Terminal, Circular Quay West; 6/10 course degustation $210/275; ⊗6-9.30pm Mon-Thu, noon-1.30pm & 6-9.30pm Fri-Sun; ☒Circular Quay) What many consider to be Sydney's best restaurant matches a peerless bridge view with brilliant food. Chef Peter Gilmore never rests on his laurels, consistently delivering exquisitely crafted, adventurous cuisine. A shake-up of decor and menu in 2018 has left it better than ever. Book online well in advance.

⊗ City Centre

Mr Wong   Chinese $$

(Map p50; ☑02-9114 7317; www.merivale.com.au/mrwong; 3 Bridge Lane; mains $24-44; ⊗lunch noon-3pm Mon-Fri, 10.30am-3pm Sat & Sun, dinner 5.30-11pm Mon-Wed, to midnight Thu-Sat, to 10pm Sun; 🛜☑; ☒Wynyard) Classy but comfortable in an attractive, low-lit space on a CBD laneway, this has exposed-brick colonial warehouse chic and a huge team of staff and hanging ducks in the open kitchen. Lunchtime dim sum offerings bristle with flavour and the salad offerings are mouth-freshening sensations. Mains such as crispy pork hock are sinfully sticky, while Peking duck rolls are legendary.

Restaurant Hubert   French $$

(Map p50; ☑02-9232 0881; www.restauranthubert.com; 15 Bligh St; mains $20-50; ⊗4pm-1am Mon-Sat, plus noon-3pm Thu & Fri; ☒Martin Place) The memorable descent into the sexy old-time ambience plunges you straight from suity Sydney into a 1930s movie. Delicious French fare comes in old-fashioned portions – think terrine, black pudding or duck, plus a few more avant-garde creations. Candlelit tables and a long whisky-backed counter provide seating. No bookings for small groups, so wait it out in the bar area.

Rockpool Bar & Grill   Steak $$$

(Map p50; ☑02-8099 7077; www.rockpoolbarandgrill.com.au; 66 Hunter St; mains $37-68, bar mains $22-35; ⊗noon-3pm & 6-11pm Mon-Fri, 5.30-11pm Sat, 5.30-10pm Sun; ☒Martin Place) You'll feel like a 1930s Manhattan stockbroker when you dine at this sleek operation in the fabulous art-deco City Mutual Building. The bar is famous for its dry-aged, full-blood Wagyu burger (make sure you order a side of the hand-cut fat chips), but carnivores will be equally enamoured with the succulent steaks, stews and fish dishes served in the grill.

Tetsuya's   French, Japanese $$$

(☑02-9267 2900; www.tetsuyas.com; 529 Kent St; degustation menu $240, matching wines from $125; ⊗5.30-10pm Tue-Fri, noon-3pm & 6.30-10pm Sat; ☒Town Hall) Concealed in a villa behind a historic cottage amid the high-rises, this extraordinary restaurant is for those seeking a culinary journey rather than a simple stuffed belly. Settle in for 10-plus courses of French- and Japanese-inflected food from the genius of legendary Sydney chef Tetsuya Wakuda. It's all great, but the seafood is sublime. Great wine list. Book well ahead.

⊗ Inner West

Grounds of Alexandria   Cafe $$

(☑02-9699 2225; www.thegrounds.com.au; 2 Huntley St, Alexandria; lunch dishes $19-25; ⊗7am-4pm Mon-Fri, from 7.30am Sat & Sun; 🛜; ☒348, ☒Green Square) ✔ A quite extra-

Strand Arcade (p59)

ordinary Alexandria spot, the Grounds goes well beyond converted industrial chic. This former pie factory sports futuristic coffee technology, tip-top baking and delicious food, but it's the enormous garden setting that has the biggest impact: chickens, a waste-chewing pig and greenery all around. It's a real sight to behold. You won't behold it alone though...prepare to queue.

Also here is the **Potting Shed** (02-9699 2225; http://thegrounds.com.au; mains $24-37; 11.30am-9pm Mon-Thu, to 10pm Fri, 11am-10pm Sat, to 9pm Sun; 348, Green Square), another riot of plants open for evening drinks and food.

Boathouse on
Blackwattle Bay   Seafood $$$

(02-9518 9011; www.boathouse.net.au; 123 Ferry Rd, Glebe; mains $40-48; 6-10pm Tue-Thu, noon-2.45pm & 6-11pm Fri-Sun; Glebe) The best restaurant in Glebe, and one of the best seafood restaurants in Sydney. Offerings range from a selection of oysters so fresh you'd think you shucked them yourself, to a snapper pie that'll go straight to the top of your favourite-dish list. The views over the bay and Anzac Bridge are stunning. Arrive by water taxi for maximum effect.

Ester   Modern Australian $$$

(02-8068 8279; www.ester-restaurant.com. au; 46/52 Meagher St, Chippendale; share plates $18-50; 6-11pm Mon-Fri, from noon Sat, noon-4.30pm Sun; ; Central) Ester exemplifies Sydney's contemporary dining scene: informal but not sloppy; innovative without being overly gimmicky; hip, but never try-hard. The menu specialises in well-sourced Australian fish, molluscs and crustaceans prepared with a variety of global influences at play, but don't miss the blood-sausage sandwich either, or the excellent vegetarian creations. Desserts are well worth leaving room for too.

Surry Hills & Darlinghurst

Bourke Street Bakery   Bakery $

(02-9699 1011; www.bourkestreetbakery. com.au; 633 Bourke St, Surry Hills; items $5-14; 7am-6pm Mon-Fri, to 5pm Sat & Sun; ; 301, Surry Hills, Central) Queuing outside this teensy bakery is an essential

Mr Wong (p60)

Surry Hills experience. It sells a tempting selection of pastries, cakes, bread and sandwiches, along with near-legendary sausage rolls. There are a couple of spots to sit inside, but on a fine day you're better off on the street. Offshoots around town offer a bit more space.

Le Monde   Cafe $

(⌨02-9211 3568; www.lemondecafe.com. au; 83 Foveaux St, Surry Hills; dishes $10-18; ⊘6.30am-4pm Mon-Fri, 7.30am-2pm Sat; 🛜⚡; ⊠Central) Some of Sydney's best break-fasts are served between the demure dark wooden walls of this small street-side cafe. Top-notch coffee and a terrific selection of tea will gear you up to face the world, while dishes such as matcha hotcakes, truffled poached eggs, brilliant sandwiches or morning muffin specials make it worth walking up the hill for.

Dead Ringer   Modern Australian $$

(Map p54; ⌨02-9331 3560; www.deadringer.wtf; 413 Bourke St, Surry Hills; share plates $17-34; ⊘5-11pm Mon & Tue, from 4pm Wed, 4pm-midnight Thu & Fri, 10am-midnight Sat,

11am-11pm Sun; 🛜⚡; ⊠333, 440) This charcoal-fronted terrace is a laid-back haven of quality eating and drinking. Barstool it or grab an outdoor table and graze on the short, brilliant menu that changes slightly daily and runs from bar snacks through tapas to mains. Though well presented, the food's all about flavour combinations rather than airy artistry. There's always something interesting to accompany by the glass.

Marta   Italian $$

(⌨02-9361 6641; www.marta.com.au; 30 McLachlan Ave, Darlinghurst; mains $22-38; ⊘5.30-10pm Tue-Thu, to 10.30pm Fri & Sat, 9am-9pm Sun; ⊠Kings Cross) Set back from a showroom on its own sunny square – or should that be piazza? – this seductive spot focuses on traditional recipes from Rome and its region. Fairly priced and richly flavoured plates blend vernacular tradition with modern techniques to good effect. Daily specials are hearty favourites; pre-pare your palate with a drink of something sharp at the gleaming bar.

Firedoor   Grill $$$

(📞02-8204 0800; www.firedoor.com.au;
33 Mary St, Surry Hills; share plates $24-54,
degustation $90; ⏱5.30-11pm Tue, Wed & Sat,
noon-3pm & 5.30-11pm Thu & Fri; 🚆Central)
All the dishes in this moodily attractive
sunken space are produced over a blazing
fire, chef Lennox Hastie matching different
woods to the flavours of meat, seafood and
vegetables to create extraordinary dishes
with huge depth of flavour. The intriguing
menu changes on a daily basis. Look out
for the fleshy pipis (saltwater clams) with a
garlicky sauce that's perfect for mopping.

🔵 Bondi

Icebergs Dining Room   Italian $$$

(📞02-9365 9000; www.idrb.com; 1 Notts Ave,
Bondi Beach; mains $48-56; ⏱noon-3pm & 6.30-
11pm, from 10am Sun; 🚌333) Poised above
the famous swimming pool, Icebergs'
views sweep across the Bondi Beach arc
to the sea. Inside, bow-tied waiters deliver
fresh, sustainably sourced seafood and
steaks cooked with elan. There's also an
elegant cocktail bar. In the same building,
the Icebergs club has a bistro and bar with
simpler, cheaper fare.

❌ Kings Cross, Potts Point & Woolloomooloo

Cho Cho San   Japanese $$

(Map p54; 📞02-9331 6601; www.chochosan.com.
au; 73 Macleay St, Potts Point; dishes $12-33;
⏱5.30-11pm Mon-Thu, from noon Fri-Sun; 🚌311,
🚆Kings Cross) Glide through the shiny brass
sliding door and take a seat at the communal table that runs the length of this stylish
Japanese restaurant, all polished concrete
and blonde wood. The food is just as artful
as the surrounds, with tasty izakaya-style
bites emanating from both the raw bar
and the hibachi grill. There's a good sake
selection, too.

Fratelli Paradiso   Italian $$

(Map p54; 📞02-9357 1744; www.fratelliparadiso.
com; 12-16 Challis Ave, Potts Point; breakfast
$12-17, mains $25-39; ⏱7am-11pm Mon-Sat, to
10pm Sun; 🚌311, 🚆Kings Cross) This underlit

🍴 Sydney's Celebrity Chefs

Bill Granger Author of 10 cookbooks;
owner of the legendary **bills** (Map p54;
📞02-9360 9631; www.bills.com.au; 433
Liverpool St, Darlinghurst; mains $15-29;
⏱7.30am-3pm Mon-Sat, 8am-3pm Sun; 📶📷;
🚆Kings Cross).

Luke Nguyen Presents TV programs,
pens cookbooks and plates up Vietnamese delights at **Red Lantern on Riley**
(Map p54; 📞02-9698 4355; www.redlantern.
com.au; 60 Riley St, Darlinghurst; mains $38-
45; ⏱6-10pm Sun-Thu, noon-3pm & 6-11pm
Fri, 6-11pm Sat; 📷; 🚆Museum) ✏.

Matt Moran Boasting **Aria** (Map
p50; 📞02-9240 2255; www.ariasydney.
com.au; 1 Macquarie St; 2-/3-/4-course
dinner $115/145/170, degustation $205;
⏱noon-2.15pm & 5.30-10.30pm Mon-Fri,
noon-1.30pm & 5-11pm Sat, noon-1.45pm &
5.30-10pm Sun; 🚆Circular Quay), Chiswick
(p64) and Opera Bar (p64), Matt graces
the TV screen on *Master-Chef Australia*.

Neil Perry The city's original rock-star
chef (with ponytail) heads up Rockpool
Bar & Grill (p60) and **Spice Temple**
(Map p50; 📞02-8078 1888; www.rockpool.
com; 10 Bligh St; dishes $39-59; ⏱noon-3pm
& 6-10.30pm Mon-Wed, noon-3pm & 6-11pm
Thu & Fri, 5.30-11pm Sat, 5.30-10pm Sun;
📶📷; 🚆Martin Place).

Rockpool Bar & Grill
PAUL LOVELACE/ALAMY ©

trattoria has them queuing at the door
(especially on weekends). The intimate
room showcases seasonal Italian dishes
cooked with Mediterranean zing. Lots of

busy black-clad waiters, lots of Italian chatter, lots of oversized sunglasses. The streetside tables are the place to be, whether for morning espresso or night-time feasting. No bookings.

Farmhouse Modern Australian **$$**
(Map p54; ☑0448 413 791; www.farmhouse kingscross.com.au; 4/40 Bayswater Rd, Kings Cross; set menu $60; ◷sittings 6.30pm & 8.30pm Wed-Sat, 2pm & 6.30pm Sun; ℝKings Cross) Occupying a space between restaurant and supper club, this narrow sliver of a place has a tiny kitchen and charming hospitality. Diners sit at one long table and eat a set menu that features uncomplicated, delicious dishes from high-quality produce. There are good wines and a buzzy, fun atmosphere. Prebooking is essential.

Yellow Vegetarian **$$$**
(Map p54; ☑02-9332 2344; www.yellow sydney.com.au; 57 Macleay St, Potts Point; 5-/7-course degustation menu $80/100; ◷5-11pm Mon-Fri, 11am-2.30pm & 5-11pm Sat & Sun; ☑; ☐311, ℝKings Cross) This sunflower-yellow former artists' residence is now a top-notch contemporary vegetarian restaurant. Dishes are prepared with real panache, and excellent flavour combinations are present throughout. The tasting menus, which can be vegan, take the Sydney meat-free scene to new levels and the service is happily not too formal. Weekend brunch is also a highlight, as is the wine list.

😊 Paddington
Paddington Alimentari Deli **$**
(☑02-9358 2142; www.facebook.com/padding ton.alimentari; 2 Hopetoun St; light meals $5-15; ◷7am-5pm Mon-Fri, 7.30am-4pm Sat; ☐333, 352, 440, M40) Tucked away at the bottom of the William St boutiques, this is almost the soul of Paddington distilled into one friendly cafe-deli. Super coffee, tempting Italian products and a communal feel as well-heeled locals rub shoulders in friendly hedonism; quite a place.

Saint Peter Seafood **$$**
(☑02-8937 2530; www.saintpeter.com.au; 362 Oxford St, Paddington; mains $28-46; ◷5.30-10pm Tue-Thu, noon-2pm & 5.30-10pm Fri, 11am-3pm & 5.30-10pm Sat & Sun; ☐333, 352, 440, M40) Fish has sometimes been left behind in the race for nose-to-tailery, pulled meat and burgerisation of any land-based beast. It reclaims its deserved pre-eminence here, with an inspiring, innovative changing menu. Aged cuts of fish, impeccably sourced sustainable stock, and avant-garde creations makes this Sydney's finny tribe trailblazer. Check out their fish butchery a few doors up too.

Chiswick Modern Australian **$$**
(☑02-8388 8688; www.chiswickwoollahra.com.au; 65 Ocean St, Woollahra; mains $32-42; ◷noon-2.30pm & 6-10pm Mon-Thu, noon-3pm & 5.30-10pm Fri & Sat, noon-9pm Sun; ☎☑; ☐389) ✐ Though owned by celebrity chef Matt Moran, the real star of this show here is the kitchen garden that dictates what's on the menu. Meat from the Moran family farm and local seafood feature prominently too. The setting, an airy, light pavilion in a small park, is an especially lovely one and service strikes an agreeably casual note.

🍸 DRINKING & NIGHTLIFE
🍷 Circular Quay & the Rocks
Opera Bar Bar
(Map p50; ☑02-8587 5900; www.operabar.com.au; lower concourse, Sydney Opera House; ◷10.30am-midnight Mon-Thu, to 1am Fri, 9am-1am Sat, to midnight Sun; ☎; ℝCircular Quay) Right on the harbour with the Opera House on one side and the bridge on the other, this perfectly positioned terrace manages a very Sydney marriage of the laid-back and the sophisticated. It's an iconic spot for visitors and locals alike. There's live music or DJs most nights and really excellent food, running from oysters to fabulous steaks and fish.

Glenmore Hotel
Pub

(Map p50; 02-9247 4794; www.theglenmore.
com.au; 96 Cumberland St; 11am-midnight
Sun-Thu, to 1am Fri & Sat; ; Circular Quay)
Downstairs it's a predictably nice old Rocks
pub with great outdoor seating, but head
to the rooftop and the views are beyond
fabulous: Opera House (after the cruise
ship leaves), harbour and city skyline
all present and accounted for. It gets
crammed up here on the weekends, with
DJs and plenty of wine by the glass. The
food's decent too.

Lord Nelson Brewery Hotel
Brewery

(Map p50; 02-9251 4044; www.lordnelson
brewery.com; 19 Kent St; 11am-11pm Mon-Sat,
noon-10pm Sun; ; 311, Circular Quay)
This atmospheric boozer is one of three
claiming to be Sydney's oldest (all using
slightly different criteria). The on-site brewery cooks up its own natural ales; a pint of
dark, stouty Nelson's Blood is a fine way to
partake. Pub food downstairs is tasty and
solid; the upstairs brasserie is an attractive
space doing fancier food, including good
seafood choices.

Harts Pub
Pub

(Map p50; 02-9251 6030; www.hartspub.com;
cnr Essex & Gloucester Sts; noon-11pm Mon-Wed,
11.30am-midnight Thu, to 1am Fri & Sat, noon-10pm
Sun; ; Circular Quay) Pouring an excellent range of Sydney craft beers in a quiet
corner near the beginning of the Rocks, this
historical building has real character. The
dishes are quality pub food, with generous
salads, fish and steaks. At weekends, this is
enjoyably quieter than other Rocks boozers.
There are a few pleasant outdoor tables with
the Shangri-La hotel looming above.

City Centre
Uncle Ming's
Cocktail Bar

(Map p50; www.unclemings.com.au; 55 York St;
noon-midnight Mon-Thu, to 1am Fri, from 4pm
Sat; Wynyard) We love the dark romantic
opium-den atmosphere of this small bar se-
creted away in a basement by a shirt shop.
It's an atmospheric spot for anything from
a quick beer before jumping on a train to a
leisurely exploration of the cocktail menu. It
also does an excellent line in dumplings and,
usually, has very welcoming bar staff.

Opera Bar

Lord Nelson Brewery Hotel (p65)

Frankie's Pizza   Bar
(Map p50; www.frankiespizzabytheslice.com; 50
Hunter St; ⏰4pm-3am Sat-Thu, from noon Fri; 🚇;
🚆Martin Place) Descend the stairs and you'll
think you're in a 1970s pizzeria, complete
with plastic grapevines, snapshots covering
the walls and tasty pizza slices ($6). But
open the nondescript door in the corner
and an indie wonderland reveals itself.
Bands play here at least four nights a week
(join them on Tuesdays for live karaoke)
and there's another bar hidden below.

Slip Inn & Chinese Laundry   Club
(Map p50; 📞02-9114 7327; www.merivale.com.
au/chineselaundry; 111 Sussex St; club $28-43;
⏰11am-1am Mon-Thu, to 3am Fri, 2pm-3am Sat,
Chinese Laundry 9pm-3.30am Fri & Sat; 🚇; 🚆W-
ynyard) Slip in to this cheerfully colourful
atmospheric warren on the edge of Darling
Harbour and bump hips with the kids.
There are bars, pool tables, a pleasantly
packed beer garden and Mexican food,
courtesy of El Loco. On Friday and Saturday
nights the bass cranks up at the long-
running attached Chinese Laundry nightclub, accessed via Slip St below.

🌐 Inner West

Archie Rose
Distilling Co.   Bar
(📞02-8458 2300; www.archierose.com.au; 85
Dunning Ave, Rosebery; ⏰noon-10pm Sun & Mon,
to midnight Tue-Sat; 🚇; 🚌343, 🚆Green Square)
This distillery has made quite an impact
with its excellent gins – where better to try
them than the place itself? The bar is
appropriately industrial chic; the mezzanine is a great spot to sit and observe the
action. Try different gins in a flight, or pick
your perfect G&T combination or cocktail.
It also has some decent wine and beer.

Earl's Juke Joint   Bar
(www.facebook.com/earlsjukejoint; 407 King St,
Newtown; ⏰4pm-midnight Mon-Sat, to 10pm
Sun; 🚆Newtown) Swinging Earl's serves craft
beers and killer cocktails to the Newtown
hip-erati. It's hidden behind the down-at-
heel facade of the butcher's shop it used
to be, but once in, you're in downtown
New Orleans, with a bar as long as the
Mississippi.

Lazybones Lounge   Bar

(📞0450 008 563; www.lazyboneslounge.com.au; 294 Marrickville Rd, Marrickville; ⏰7pm-midnight Mon-Wed, 5pm-3am Thu-Sat, 5-10pm Sun; 📶; 🚃Marrickville) Roomy and extravagantly decorated, Lazybones is an excellent bar-lounge with live music nightly and a decent line in cocktails and food. At weekends it gets likeably louche, with a happy crowd dancing until late. Even the bouncers are friendly. There's a cover charge for the bands ($10 to $20); it's free later on. Enter on Illawarra Rd.

🍷 Surry Hills & Darlinghurst

Love, Tilly Devine   Wine Bar

(Map p54; 📞02-9326 9297; www.lovetillydevine.com; 91 Crown Lane, Darlinghurst; ⏰5pm-midnight Mon-Sat, to 10pm Sun; 🚃Museum) This dark and good-looking split-level laneway bar is pretty compact, but the wine list certainly isn't. It's an extraordinary document, with some exceptionally well-chosen wines and a mission to get people away from their tried-and-tested favourites and explore. Take a friend and crack open a leisurely bottle of something. Italian deli bites and fuller plates are on hand too.

Shakespeare Hotel   Pub

(📞02-9319 6883; www.shakespearehotel.com.au; 200 Devonshire St, Surry Hills; ⏰10am-midnight Mon-Sat, to 10pm Sun; 🚃Surry Hills, 🚃Central) This is a classic Sydney pub (1879) with art-nouveau tiled walls, scuzzy carpet, the horses on the TV and cheap bar meals. There are plenty of cosy hidey holes upstairs and a cast of local characters. It's a proper convivial all-welcome place that's the antithesis of the more gentrified Surry Hills drinking establishments.

Wild Rover   Bar

(📞02-9280 2235; www.thewildrover.com.au; 75 Campbell St, Surry Hills; ⏰4pm-midnight Mon-Sat; 🚃Central) Look for the unsigned wide door and enter this supremely cool brick-lined speakeasy, where a big range of craft beer is served in chrome steins and jungle animals peer benevolently from the green walls. The upstairs bar opens for trivia and

Swanky City Bars

Ivy (Map p50; 📞02-9240 3000; www.merivale.com/ivy; Level 1, 330 George St; ⏰noon-midnight Mon-Fri, to 3.30am Sat, plus pool party 1pm-midnight Sun Oct-Mar; 📶; 🚃Wynyard) Hidden down a lane off George St, Ivy is a fashionable complex of bars, restaurants – and even a swimming pool. It's also Sydney's most hyped venue; expect lengthy queues of suburban kids teetering on unfeasibly high heels on a Saturday for Sydney's hottest club night, run by Ministry of Sound.

Marble Bar (Map p50; 📞02-9266 2000; www.marblebarsydney.com.au; Basement, 488 George St; ⏰3.30pm-midnight Sun-Thu, to 2am Fri & Sat; 📶; 🚃Town Hall) Built for a staggering £32,000 in 1893 as part of the Adams Hotel on Pitt St, this ornate underground bar is one of the best places in town for putting on the Ritz (even if this is the Hilton). The over-the-top late-Victorian decor is staggering, and the atmosphere is great. Musos play anything from jazz to funk, Thursday to Saturday.

O Bar (Map p50; 📞02-9247 9777; www.obardining.com.au; Level 47, Australia Square, 264 George St; ⏰5pm-midnight Sat-Thu, noon-midnight Fri; 📶; 🚃Wynyard) The cocktails at this 47th-floor revolving bar aren't cheap, but they're still substantially cheaper than admission to Sydney Tower (p51) – and it's considerably more glamorous. The views are truly wonderful; get there for sunset. There's also smart food on offer.

live bands. Irish folk music at weekends get the place pumping.

Wyno   Wine Bar

(📞02-8399 1440; www.porteno.com.au; 4/50 Holt St, Surry Hills; ⏰noon-11pm Tue-Fri, 5pm-midnight Sat; 📶; 🚃Central) Run by **Porteño** (sharing plates $20-50; ⏰6pm-midnight Tue-Sat, plus noon-3pm Fri) next door, this

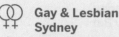

Gay & Lesbian Sydney

Gay and lesbian culture forms a vocal and vital part of Sydney's social fabric. Oxford St, Darlinghurst, has long been the locus of the gay scene, and every year tens of thousands line the street for the famous Sydney Gay & Lesbian Mardi Gras.

Free gay media includes *SX* (www.gaynewsnetwork.com.au), the *Star Observer* (www.starobserver.com.au) and *Lesbians on the Loose* (www.lotl.com).

Most hotels, restaurants and bars in Darlinghurst, Surry Hills and Newtown are very gay-friendly. For partying head to the following:

Beresford Hotel (Map p54; 02-9114 7328; www.merivale.com.au/theberesford hotel; 354 Bourke St, Surry Hills; noon-midnight Mon & Tue, to 1am Wed-Sun; ; 374, 397, 399) Always gay-friendly, but on Sundays play spot-the-straight.

Sly Fox (02-9557 2917; www.slyfox. sydney; 199 Enmore Rd, Enmore; 6pm-3am Wed & Thu, to 6am Fri & Sat; 423, 426, 428, M30) Working-class pub welcoming lesbians for many years.

Dolphin Hotel (02-9331 4800; www. dolphinhotel.com.au; 412 Crown St, Surry Hills; 11.30am-midnight Mon-Sat, to 10pm Sun; ; Central) Mixed as they come in the heart of Surry Hills.

Marlborough Hotel (02-9519 1222; www.marlboroughhotel.com.au; 145 King St, Newtown; 10am-4am Mon-Sat, to midnight Sun; Macdonaldtown) Home to Tokyo Sing Song, an underground hideout for the kooky and queer.

Green Park Hotel (Map p54; 02-9380 5311; www.greenparkhotel.com.au; 360 Victoria St, Darlinghurst; 11am-midnight Mon-Wed, 11am-2am Thu-Sat, noon-midnight Sun; ; Kings Cross) A proper local pub for all persuasions.

wine bar has its own character. Seat yourself at the long communal bar and ask the welcoming waitstaff to suggest delicious drops from their wine selection (ask the price to avoid a shock) and tasty snacks and larger plates to suit your inclinations. Juicy empanadas, cold cuts, crisp calamari or zingy salads regularly feature.

Kings Cross, Potts Point & Woolloomooloo

Old Fitzroy Hotel   Pub

(Map p54; 02-9356 3848; www.oldfitzroy. com.au; 129 Dowling St, Woolloomooloo; 11am-midnight Mon-Fri, noon-11pm Sat, 3-10pm Sun; ; Kings Cross) A gem hidden in the backstreets of Woolloomooloo, the totally unpretentious **Old Fitz Theatre** (Map p54; 0416 044 413; www.redlineproductions. au; tickets $25-48) is also a decent old-fashioned boozer in its own right, with a great variety of beers on tap and a convivial welcome. Prop up the bar, grab a seat at a street-side table or head upstairs to the bistro, pool table and couches.

Monopole   Wine Bar

(Map p54; 02-9360 4410; www.monopole sydney.com.au; 71a Macleay St, Potts Point; 5pm-midnight Mon-Fri, from noon Sat, noon-10pm Sun; ; 311, Kings Cross) Dark and sexy, Monopole seduces with its stylish interior, complete with hanging strips of black sound-absorption material and discreet front screen. A fabulous wine list of small Australian and international producers offers over 20 vintages by the glass or carafe, so an impromptu tasting session is easy. The food is great too, with house-cured charcuterie and intriguing cheeses a highlight.

Manly

Manly Wharf Hotel   Pub

(02-9977 1266; www.manlywharfhotel.com. au; East Esplanade, Manly; 11.30am-midnight Mon-Fri, 11am-1am Sat, 11am-midnight Sun; ; Manly) Just along the wharf from the ferry, this remodelled pub is all glass and water vistas, with loads of seating so you've a good chance of grabbing a share of the view. It's a perfect spot for sunny afternoon beers. There's good pub food, too (mains $22 to $30), with pizzas, fried fish and succulent rotisserie chicken all worthwhile.

⭐ ENTERTAINMENT

Sydney Theatre Company   Theatre

(STC; Map p50; ☑02-9250 1777; www.sydney theatre.com.au; Pier 4, 15 Hickson Rd; ⊗box office 9am-7.30pm Mon, to 8.30pm Tue-Fri, 11am-8.30pm Sat, 2hr before show Sun; ☑324, 325, ⓇCircular Quay) Established in 1978, the STC is Sydney theatre's top dog and has played an important part in the careers of many famous Australian actors (especially Cate Blanchett, co-artistic director from 2008 to 2013). Performances are also staged at the Opera House. Redevelopment of the Walsh Bay precinct means they will be in the nearby **Roslyn Packer Theatre** (Map p50; ☑02-9250 1999; www.roslynpackertheatre.com. au; 22 Hickson Rd) until 2020.

City Recital Hall   Classical Music

(Map p50; ☑02-8256 2222; www.cityrecital hall.com; 2 Angel Pl; ⊗box office 9am-5pm Mon-Fri; ⓇWynyard) Based on the classic configuration of the 19th-century European concert hall, this custom-built 1200-seat venue boasts near-perfect acoustics. Catch top-flight companies such as **Musica Viva** (☑1800 688 482; www.musicaviva.com.au), the **Australian Brandenburg Orchestra** (ABO; ☑02-9328 7581; www.brandenburg.com.au; tickets $70-170) and the Australian Chamber Orchestra (p39) here.

Metro Theatre   Live Music

(☑02-9550 3666; www.metrotheatre.com.au; 624 George St; ⓇTown Hall) The Metro is easily Sydney's best mid-sized venue for catching alternative local and international acts in intimate, well-ventilated, easy-seeing comfort. Other offerings include comedy, cabaret and dance parties.

Bangarra Dance Theatre   Dance

(Map p50; ☑02-9251 5333; www.bangarra.com. au; Pier 4, 15 Hickson Rd; ☑324, 325, ⓇCircular Quay) Bangarra is hailed as Australia's finest

Roslyn Packer Theatre

Spectator Sports

Sydneysiders are passionate about the **National Rugby League** (NRL; www.nrl.com). The season kicks off in March in suburban stadiums, with the grand final in early October.

Over the same period, home-town favourites the Sydney Swans and Greater Western Sydney Giants play in the **Australian Football League** (AFL; www.afl.com.au). The Swans play at the Sydney Cricket Ground and the Giants at the Sydney Showground Stadium in Sydney's Olympic Park.

The **cricket** (www.cricket.com.au) season runs from October to March, with the SCG hosting interstate Sheffield Shield and sell-out international Test, Twenty20 and One Day International matches.

Sydney Cricket Ground
SINGH_LENS/SHUTTERSTOCK ©

Aboriginal performance company. Artistic director Stephen Page conjures a fusion of contemporary themes, Indigenous traditions and Western technique. When not touring internationally, the company performs at the Opera House or at Walsh Bay. Redevelopment of the Walsh Bay precinct means they won't be found here again until 2020, however.

Moonlight Cinema   Cinema
(www.moonlight.com.au; Belvedere Amphi theatre, cnr Loch & Broome Aves, Centennial Park; adult/child $20/15; ⊙sunset Dec-Mar; ⊡333, 352, 440, M40; ⊠Bondi Junction) Take a picnic and join the bats under the stars

in magnificent Centennial Park; enter via the Woollahra Gate on Oxford St. A mix of new-release blockbuster, art-house and classic films is screened.

ⓘ INFORMATION

MEDICAL SERVICES

Hospitals with 24-hour accident and emergency departments include the following:

Royal Prince Alfred Hospital (RPA; ☑02-9515 6111; www.slhd.nsw.gov.au/rpa; Missenden Rd, Camperdown; ⊙24hr; ☎; ⊡412)

St Vincent's Hospital (Map p54; ☑02-8382 1111; www.svhs.org.au; 390 Victoria St, Darlinghurst; ⊠Kings Cross)

Sydney Children's Hospital (☑02-9382 1111; www.schn.health.nsw.gov.au; High St, Randwick; ⊡370)

Sydney Hospital (Map p50; ☑02-9382 7111; www.seslhd.health.nsw.gov.au/SHSEH; 8 Macquarie St; ⊠Martin Place)

TOURIST INFORMATION

○ Sydney's principal tourist office, **Sydney Visitor Centre – The Rocks** (Map p50; ☑02-8273 0000; www.sydney.com; cnr Argyle & Playfair Sts; ⊙9am-5.30pm; ⊠Circular Quay), is in the heart of the historic Rocks district

○ The city council operates a good tourist information desk in the **Customs House** (Map p50; www.cityofsydney.nsw.gov.au; Alfred St, Circular Quay; ⊙9am-8pm Mon-Sat, to 5pm Sun; ⊠Circular Quay) as well as kiosks in Martin Place, **Chinatown** (Dixon St, Haymarket; ⊙11am-7pm; ⊠Town Hall) and **Kings Cross** (Map p54; ☑0477 344 125; cnr Darlinghurst Rd & Springfield Ave, Kings Cross; ⊙9am-5pm; ⊠Kings Cross).

○ The helpful visitor centre **Hello Manly** (☑02-9976 1430; www.hellomanly.com.au; East Esplanade; ⊙9am-5pm Mon-Fri, 10am-4pm Sat & Sun; ⊠Manly), just outside the ferry wharf and alongside the bus interchange, has free pamphlets covering the Manly Scenic Walkway (p57) and other Manly attractions, plus loads of local bus information.

ℹ GETTING THERE & AWAY

AIR

Also known as Kingsford Smith Airport, **Sydney Airport** (Kingsford Smith Airport; Mascot Airport; 📞02-9667 6111; www.sydneyairport.com.au; Airport Dr, Mascot; 🚉Domestic Airport, 🚉International Airport), just 10km south of the centre, has separate international (T1) and domestic (T2 and T3) sections, 4km apart on either side of the runways. A free shuttle bus runs between the two terminals, taking around 10 minutes. They are also connected by train.

BUS

Long-distance coaches arrive at **Sydney Coach Terminal** (📞02-9281 9366; www.sydneycoach-terminal.com.au; Central Station; 🕐7am-6pm; 🚉Central) at Central Station. From here you can access the suburban train network, buses and light rail. The coach terminal office is upstairs in the main railway concourse.

TRAIN

Intercity trains pull into the old (Country Trains) section of Sydney's historic **Central Station** (Eddy Ave; 🚉Central), in the Haymarket area of the southern inner city. From here you can connect to the suburban train network, catch the light rail, or follow the signs to Railway Sq or Eddy Avenue for suburban buses.

ℹ GETTING AROUND

TO/FROM THE AIRPORT

Taxis to the city cost up to $55 and depart from the front of the terminals. Airport shuttles head to city hotels from $22. Trains depart from beneath the terminal, but charge a whopping $14.30 on top of the normal train fare for the short journey into the city.

PUBLIC TRANSPORT

Transport NSW (📞13 15 00; www.transportnsw.info) coordinates all of the state-run bus, ferry, train and light-rail services. You'll find a useful journey planner on its website.

BUS

Transport NSW has an extensive bus network, operating from around 5am to midnight, when less frequent NightRide services commence.

FERRY

Most Sydney ferries (see Transport NSW website for details) operate between 6am and midnight. The standard Opal card one-way fare for most harbour destinations is $6.01; ferries to Manly, Sydney Olympic Park and Parramatta cost $7.51.

Private company **Manly Fast Ferry** (Map p50; 📞02-9583 1199; www.manlyfastferry.com.au; Wharf 2, Circular Quay; adult one way $9.10) offers boats that blast from Circular Quay to Manly in 18 minutes.

LIGHT RAIL

Trams run between Central Station and Dulwich Hill, stopping at Chinatown, Darling Harbour, the Star casino, Sydney Fish Market, Glebe and Leichhardt en route.

TRAIN

Sydney Trains (📞13 15 00; www.transport.nsw.gov.au) has a large suburban railway web with relatively frequent services, although there are no lines to the northern or eastern beaches.

CAR & MOTORCYCLE

Avoid driving in central Sydney if you can: there's a confusing one-way street system, parking's elusive and expensive, and parking inspectors, tolls and tow-away zones proliferate. Conversely, a car is handy for accessing Sydney's outer reaches (particularly the beaches) and for day trips.

ℹ Online Resources

Destination NSW (www.sydney.com) Official visitors' guide.

Time Out (www.timeout.com/sydney) 'What's on' information and reviews.

Lonely Planet (www.lonelyplanet.com/sydney) Destination information, hotel bookings, traveller forum and more.

Opal Cards

Sydney's public transport network runs on a smartcard system called Opal (www.opal.com.au). The card can be obtained (for free) and loaded with credit (minimum $10) at numerous newsagencies and convenience stores across Sydney. When commencing a journey you'll need to touch the card to an electronic reader; these are located at the train station gates, near the doors of buses and light-rail carriages, and at the ferry wharves. You then need to touch a reader when you complete your journey so that the system can deduct the correct fare. You get a discount when transferring between services, and after a certain number of journeys in the week, and daily charges are capped at $15.80 ($2.70 on Sundays).

You can still buy single tickets (Opal single trip tickets) from machines at train stations, ferry wharves and light-rail stops, or from bus drivers. These are more expensive than the same fare using the Opal card.

Sydney bus in Martin Place
KASARP STUDIO/SHUTTERSTOCK ©

TOLL ROADS

There are hefty tolls on most of Sydney's motorways and major links (including the Harbour Bridge, Harbour Tunnel, Cross City Tunnel and Eastern Distributor). The tolling system is electronic, meaning that it's up to you to organise an electronic tag or visitors' pass through any of the following websites: www.roam.com.au,

www.linkt.com.au, www.tollpay.com.au or www.myetoll.com.au. Note that most car-hire companies supply e-tags.

TAXI

Metered taxis are easy to flag down in the central city and inner suburbs, except at changeover times (3pm and 3am). Flagfall is $3.60, with a $2.50 'night owl surcharge' after 10pm on a Friday and Saturday until 6am the following morning. After that the fare is $2.19 per kilometre, with an additional surcharge of 20% between 10pm and 6am.

The ride-sharing app Uber operates in Sydney and is very popular. Other apps such as GoCatch offer taxi bookings, which can be very handy on busy evenings. 13CABS is another nationwide taxi-booking app.

Legion Cabs (📞13 14 51; www.legioncabs.com.au)

Premier Cabs (📞13 10 17; www.premiercabs.com.au)

Silver Service (📞13 31 00; www.silverservice.com.au)

WATER TAXI

Water taxis are a fast way to shunt around the harbour (Circular Quay to Watsons Bay in as little as 15 minutes). Companies will quote on any pick-up point within the harbour and the river, including private jetties, islands and other boats. All have a quote generator on their websites; you can add in extra cruise time for a bit of sightseeing. It's much better value for groups than singles or couples.

Fantasea Yellow Water Taxis (📞1800 326 822; www.yellowwatertaxis.com.au; 🕐8am-9pm, prebooking required for service outside these hours)

H2O Maxi Taxis (📞1300 420 829; www.h2owatertaxis.com.au)

Water Taxis Combined (📞02-9555 8888; www.watertaxis.com.au)

Where to Stay

Sydney offers both a huge quantity and variety of accommodation, with solid options in every price range. Even so, the supply shrivels up under the summer sun, particularly around weekends and big events, so be sure to book ahead.

Neighbourhood	Atmosphere
Circular Quay & the Rocks	Big-ticket sights; vibrant nightlife; high-end hotels and restaurants; tourist central.
Sydney Harbour	Everywhere is a pleasant ferry journey from town; can be isolated.
City Centre & Haymarket	Good transport links; lots of sights, bars, fantastic Asian restaurants; can be noisy.
Darling Harbour & Pyrmont	Plenty to see and do; lively nightlife; top-end restaurants; not exactly soulful.
Glebe & Newtown	Bohemian; great coffee; interesting shops; priced for locals; thin on tourist sights.
Surry Hills & Darlinghurst	Sydney's hippest eating and drinking precinct; heart of the gay scene; few actual sights.
Kings Cross & Potts Point	Interesting and idiosyncratic; numerous hostels, bars and clubs; good transport links; sleazy strip clubs and dodgy alleyways.
Paddington & Centennial Park	Leafy and genteel, but not exactly thrilling; bus access to city and beaches; few sights.
Bondi to Coogee	Sand, surf and sexy bods; party bars; slow bus ride to the city.
Manly	Beautiful beaches; community feel; fair weather destination.

The Blue Mountains

On Sydney's back doorstep, the World Heritage–listed Blue Mountains are a must-see. A dense green canopy gives way to deep valleys, chiselled sandstone outcrops and quaint mountain towns.

Great For...

☑ **Don't Miss**

Echo Point's clifftop viewing platform, for killer views of the craggy Three Sisters.

Head for the Hills

The Blue Mountains' foothills begin 65km inland from Sydney, rising to an 1100m-high sandstone plateau riddled with valleys eroded into the stone. There are eight connected conservation areas in the region, offering truly fantastic scenery, excellent bushwalks (hikes), Aboriginal engravings and all the canyons and cliffs you could ask for.

Although it's possible to day-trip from Sydney, consider staying a night (or longer) so you can explore the towns, do at least one bushwalk and eat at some of the excellent restaurants.

Mountain Towns

In order of approach from Sydney, here's a rundown of the main Blue Mountain towns.

Three Sisters (p76)

MICHAEL W NZ/SHUTTERSTOCK ©

❶ Need to Know

Trains (📞13 15 00; www.transportnsw.
info) run hourly from Sydney's Central
Station to Katoomba (two hours). **Blue
Mountains Bus** (📞02-4751 1077; www.
cdcbus.com.au) also links towns.

✗ Take a Break

Katoomba's **Station Bar & Woodfired
Pizza** (📞02-4782 4782; www.stationbar.
com.au; 287 Bathurst Rd; pizzas $18-26;
⏰noon-midnight; 📶) has good things:
craft beer, pizza and live music.

★ Top Tip

The Blue Mountains can get surprisingly
chilly, even in summer: bring warm
clothes.

Glenbrook

From unassuming Glenbrook you can
drive or walk into the lower reaches of
Blue Mountains National Park (p77); this
is the only part of the park where vehicle
entry fees apply ($8). Six kilometres from
the park entrance gate is the **Mt Portal
Lookout**, with panoramic views into the
Glenbrook Gorge, over the Nepean River
and back to Sydney. **Red Hands Cave**
(www.nationalparks.nsw.gov.au) houses an
Aboriginal rock art gallery: it's an easy 7km
walk from **Glenbrook Information Centre**
(📞1300 653 408; www.bluemountainscitytour
ism.com.au; Great Western Hwy; ⏰8.30am-4pm
Mon-Sat, to 3pm Sun; 📶).

Wentworth Falls

As you head into Wentworth Falls, you'll get
your first real taste of Blue Mountains scenery: views to the south open out across the
majestic Jamison Valley. The village itself is
pleasant for a short potter along the main
street. The **falls** (Falls Rd; 🚉Wentworth Falls)
that lend the town its name launch a plume
of spray over a 300m drop.

Leura

The Blue Mountains' prettiest town is fash-
ioned around undulating streets, well-tended
gardens and sweeping Victorian verandas.
Leura Mall, the tree-lined main street, offers
rows of country craft shops and cafes for
the daily tourist influx. Southeast of Leura,
a sharp, triangular outcrop narrows to the
dramatic **Sublime Point** (Sublime Point Rd)
lookout with sheer cliffs on each side.

Katoomba

Swirling, otherworldly mists, steep streets
lined with art-deco buildings, astonishing

valley views, and a quirky miscellany of restaurants, buskers, artists, bawdy pubs and classy hotels – Katoomba, the biggest town in the mountains, manages to be bohemian and bourgeois, embracing and distant all at once. The must-see **Echo Point** lookout and **Three Sisters** rock formation are here (both on Echo Point Rd). **Echo Point Visitors Centre** (1300 653 408; www.bluemountainscitytourism.com. au; Echo Point Road; ⊙9am-5pm) has the local low-down.

The natural history exhibits at the **Blue Mountains Cultural Centre** (02-4780 5410; www.bluemountainsculturalcentre.com.au; 30 Parke St; adult/child $5/free; ⊙10am-5pm Mon-Fri, to 4pm Sat & Sun) are also worth a look. On the edge of town is the Blue Mountains' most touristy attraction, **Scenic World** (02-4780 0200; www.scenicworld.com. au; Violet St; adult/child $43/23; ⊙9am-5pm), a cable car offering spectacular views.

Blackheath

The crowds and commercial frenzy fizzle out considerably 10km north of Katoomba in neat, petite Blackheath. The town measures up in the scenery stakes, and it's an excellent base for visiting the Grose and Megalong Valleys. Memorable lookouts around town include **Evans Lookout** (Evans Lookout Rd) and **Govetts Leap Lookout** (Govetts Leap Rd), plus there are trailheads for some top hikes; contact the Blue Mountains Heritage Centre for info.

Blackheath is also the gastronomic centre of the region, with some excellent restaurants. For Blackheath's best coffee,

Jenolan Caves

head to **Anonymous** (www.anonymouscafe blackheath.com.au; 237 Great Western Hwy; meals $15-20; ⊘7am-3pm Mon, Wed & Thu, to 4pm Fri & Sat, from 7.30am Sun; 🛜), then take a journey around the culinary world at **Cinnabar** (📞02-4787 7269; www.cinnabar.kitchen; 246 Great Western Hwy; share plates $26-38; ⊘5.30-11pm Wed-Sat; 🔌). **Fumo** (📞02-4787 6899; www.fumorestaurant.com.au; 33 Govetts Leap Rd; mains $35-38; ⊘noon-3pm & 5.30-10.30pm Fri-Sun) combines Australian meats with Japanese sauces to memorable effect with a range of creative flavours.

🚗 **Worth a Trip**

An hour beyond Blackheath are the amazing Jenolan Caves (www.jenolan caves.org.au), one of the most extensive, accessible and complex limestone cave systems in the world.

MINA RYAD/SHUTTERSTOCK ©

Blue Mountains National Park

What is known as the Blue Mountains is actually a sandstone plateau riddled with steep gullies eroded by rivers over thousands of years.

Initially thought to be impenetrable, the mountains were first crossed by European explorers in 1813. On this epic quest, Gregory Blaxland, William Wentworth and William Lawson followed the mountain ridges up over the top; today their route is pretty much traced by the Great Western Hwy.

More than three million visitors a year visit the scenic lookouts and waterfalls of **Blue Mountains National Park** (www.nationalparks.nsw.gov.au), the most popular and accessible section of the Greater Blue Mountains World Heritage Area. There are bushwalks for everyone, from those with limited fitness to the downright intrepid, lasting from a few minutes to several days.

Bushwalking

For tips on walks to suit your level of experience and fitness, call the National Parks' **Blue Mountains Heritage Centre** (📞02-4787 8877; www.nationalparks.nsw.gov.au; Govetts Leap Rd; ⊘9am-4.30pm; 🛜) in Blackheath, or the information centres in Glenbrook (p75) or Katoomba (p76). All three sell a variety of walk pamphlets, maps and books.

As you'd expect in such rugged terrain, there are hazards: walkers get lost, bushfires flare up and there are definitely snakes in the grass. Emergencies are relatively rare, but it pays to get some up-to-date advice from the visitor centres before you propel yourself into the wilderness. The Katoomba police and the national parks and information centres all offer free personal locator beacons and it's strongly suggested you take one with you, especially for longer hikes. Whatever you do, take plenty of water; it can get powerfully hot here, and the steep gradients can dehydrate you fast.

The two most popular bushwalking areas are the Jamison Valley, south of Katoomba, and the Grose Valley, northeast of Katoomba and east of Blackheath. Top choices include the **Golden Stairs Walk** (Glenraphael Dr) in Katoomba and the **Grand Canyon Walk** (Evans Lookout Rd) at Blackheath.

One of the most rewarding long-distance walks is the 45km, three-day **Six Foot Track** from Katoomba along the Megalong Valley to Cox's River and on to the Jenolan Caves. It has campsites along the way.

Tours

Blue Mountains Adventure Company Adventure

(☎02-4782 1271; www.bmac.com.au; 84a Bathurst Rd, Katoomba; abseiling from $185, canyoning $275; ⊘8am-6pm Oct-Mar, 9am-5pm Apr-Sep) Opposite Katoomba station, this competent and very welcoming set-up offers year-round abseiling, canyoning, bushwalking and rock climbing. They'll leave any day with bookings of two or more people. Good lunches are included on full-day trips.

Blue Mountain Bikes Mountain Biking

(☎0432 699 212; www.bluemountainbikes.com. au; 207 Katoomba St, Katoomba; half-day routes $98, bike hire 2/4/7 days $165/250/350; ⊘8am-8pm) Good-quality mountain-bike hire for a variety of set routes, including a friendly pre-ride set-up and briefing session. Options range from beginner-appropriate ridge-top jaunts between Katoomba and other towns to serious downhill runs. You can also take bikes for set periods and explore your own paths. Bookings essential, and not all options are available every day.

Aboriginal Blue Mountains Walkabout Cultural

(☎0408 443 822; www.bluemountainswalkabout.com; tour $95) This full-day Indigenous-owned and -guided bushwalk starts and finishes at Faulconbridge train station. The walk (there are some potentially slippery descents, so bring decent shoes) takes in some sacred sites and delves into Aboriginal spirituality and creation stories. There's also good information on various plants and their edible and medicinal uses.

High 'n' Wild Australian Adventures Adventure

(☎02-4782 6224; www.highandwild.com.au; 207 Katoomba St, Katoomba; abseiling $150-260, canyoning $250-290, rock climbing $190-250) ⚐ Based at the Blue Mountains YHA, this outfit runs daily tours, offering abseiling, rock climbing, canyoning and various bushwalking and survival courses.

Blue Mountains Explorer Bus Bus

(☎1300 300 915; www.explorerbus.com.au; 283 Bathurst Rd, Katoomba; adult/child $50/25; ⊘departures 9.15am-4.15pm) Significantly better than its average city equivalents, this is a useful way to get around the most popular attractions. It offers a hop-on, hop-off service on a Katoomba–Leura loop. Buses leave from Katoomba station every 30 minutes and feature entertaining live

Wentworth Falls (p75), Blue Mountains National Park

commentary. Various packages include admission to attractions.

Tread Lightly Eco Tours
Tours

(📞0414 976 752; www.treadlightly.com.au; most walks $145 per person) 🌿 Has a wide range of guided bushwalks and 4WD tours that emphasise the region's ecology. The company makes an effort to be sustainable and also operates some night walks to see glow-worms.

Bells Line of Road

This stretch of road between North Richmond and Lithgow is the most scenic route across the Blue Mountains and is highly recommended if you have the time and your own transport. It's far quieter than the main highway and offers bountiful views.

Bilpin, at the base of the mountains, is known for its apple orchards. The Bilpin Markets are held at the district hall every Saturday from 10am to noon.

Midway between Bilpin and Bell, the **Blue Mountains Botanic Garden Mount Tomah** (📞02-4567 3000; www.bluemountains botanicgarden.com.au; ⏰9am-5.30pm Mon-Fri, from 9.30am Sat & Sun) 🌿 **FREE** is a cool-climate annexe of Sydney's Royal Botanic Garden where native plants cuddle up to exotic species, including some magnificent rhododendrons.

> ℹ️ **Did You Know?**
> The purple haze that gives the Blue Mountains their name comes from a fine mist of oil exuded by eucalyptus trees.

CHRISTIAN B/SHUTTERSTOCK ©

CANBERRA

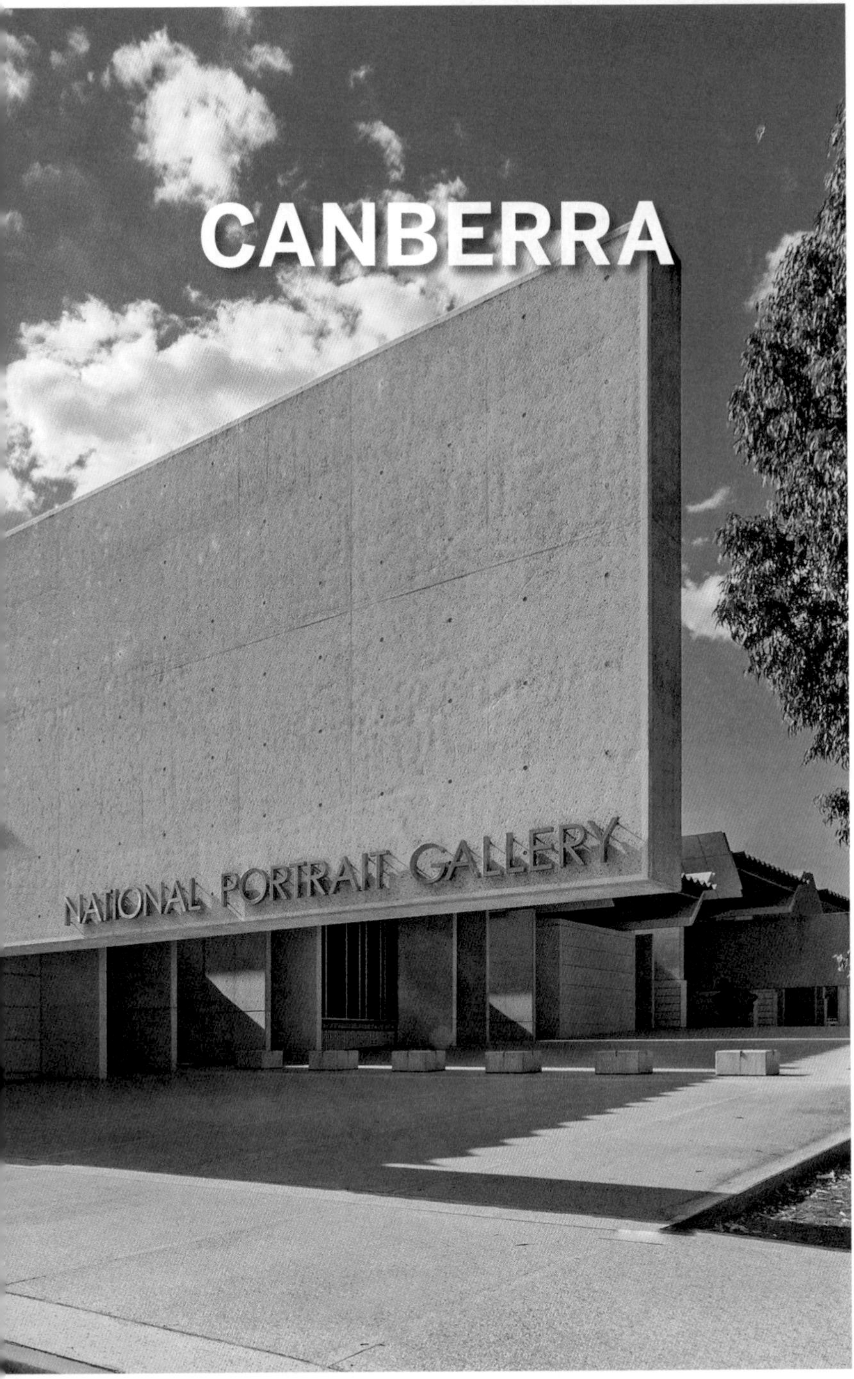

NATIONAL · PORTRAIT · GALLERY

Canberra at a Glance...

Canberra is a wonderfully green little city, with a lively and sophisticated dining and bar scene, interesting architecture and a smorgasbord of major institutions to keep even the most avid culture vulture engrossed for days on end.

Canberra was laid out by visionary American architect Walter Burley Griffin and his wife Marion Mahony Griffin following an international design competition. The city features expansive open spaces, broad boulevards and a seamless alignment of built and natural elements...and of course, the buzz of national politics.

Canberra in Two Days

Begin your Canberra jaunt at the **National Gallery of Australia** (p84). In the afternoon, attend Question Time at **Parliament House** (p86), if it's a sitting week, continuing the debate over dinner in the Civic district.

Next day, head to the **National Museum of Australia** (p84) then explore the **Australian National Botanic Gardens** (p86). Dine on the Kingston Foreshore among the city's movers and shakers.

Canberra in Four Days

On day three, check out the faces at the **National Portrait Gallery** (p85), then cycle around impressive **Lake Burley Griffin** (p86). Drinks at the **Capital Brewing Co** (p93) await.

On day four, hit the Lonsdale St cafes in Braddon, then pay your respects at the haunting **Australian War Memorial** (p85).

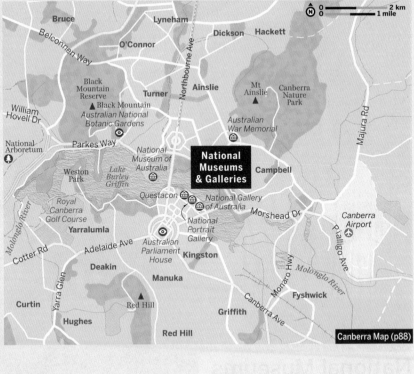

National Museums & Galleries

Canberra Map (p88)

Arriving in Canberra

Canberra Airport (p94) is 10 minutes' drive from the city centre. A taxi into the city costs around $50. Bus routes 11 and 11A run regularly into the city between 6am and 6pm (adult/child $5/2.50, 20 to 40 minutes).

Alternatively, the drive from Sydney is a little over three hours, four hours by train, or five hours by bus.

Where to Stay

Canberra is totally geared towards the car: nobody walks anywhere. Wherever you stay, you'll be driving, bussing or cabbing it to your daily destinations. Stay in Civic, Kingston or Griffith for eating options; or New Acton, the Kingston Foreshore or Braddon if you're feeling hip. Accommodation gets busy and pricey during parliamentary sitting days (mid-week); rates cool off on weekends.

National Museums & Galleries

You don't have to go far in Canberra to find a world-class museum or gallery. The city features some of Australia's best collections of art and artefacts.

Great For...

☑ Don't Miss

The National Museum's introductory film, shown in the small rotating Circa Theatre.

National Gallery of Australia   Gallery

(✆02-6240 6502; www.nga.gov.au; Parkes Pl, Parkes; temporary exhibition prices vary; ☉10am-5pm) **FREE** The nation's extraordinary art collection is showcased in a suitably huge purpose-built gallery within the parliamentary precinct. Almost every big name you could think of from the world of Australian and international art, past and present, is represented. Famous works include one of Monet's *Waterlilies,* several of Sidney Nolan's *Ned Kelly* paintings, Salvador Dali's *Lobster Telephone,* an Andy Warhol *Elvis* print and a triptych by Francis Bacon.

National Museum of Australia   Museum

(✆02-6208 5000; www.nma.gov.au; Lawson Cres, Acton Peninsula; ☉9am-5pm) **FREE** As well as telling Australia's national story,

ALEX CIMBAL/SHUTTERSTOCK ©

this museum, stunningly designed by architects Ashton Raggatt McDougall and Robert Peck von Hartel Trethowan, hosts blockbuster touring exhibitions. Don't miss the 12-minute introductory film, shown in the small rotating Circa Theatre before you dig in. The exhibition jam-packed with Aboriginal artefacts is a highlight. However, the disjointed layout of the displays means that the museum doesn't quite gel in the way that Canberra's other national cultural institutions do.

National Portrait Gallery   Gallery

(📞02-6102 7000; www.portrait.gov.au; King Edward Tce, Parkes; ⊗10am-5pm) **FREE** Occupying a flash new purpose-built building designed by architect Richard Johnson, this wonderful gallery tells the story of Australia through its faces – from wax cameos of Indigenous Australians to colonial portraits of the nation's founding families, to Howard Arkley's Day-Glo portrait of musician Nick Cave. There is a good cafe for post-exhibition coffee and reflection.

Australian War Memorial   Museum

(📞02-6243 4211; www.awm.gov.au; Treloar Cres, Campbell; ⊗10am-5pm) **FREE** Canberra's glorious art-deco war memorial, designed by Emil Sodersten and John Crust, is a highlight in a city filled with interesting architecture. Built to commemorate 'the war to end all wars', it opened its doors in 1941 when the next world war was already in full swing. Attached to it is a large, exceptionally well-designed museum devoted to the nation's military history.

Questacon   Museum

(National Science & Technology Centre; 📞02-6270 2800; www.questacon.edu.au; King Edward Tce, Parkes; adult/child $23/17.50; ⊗9am-5pm; 👶) This kid-friendly science centre has educational and fun interactive exhibits. Explore the physics of sport, athletics and fun parks; cause tsunamis; and take shelter from cyclones and earthquakes. Exciting science shows, presentations and puppet shows are all included.

⊙ SIGHTS

Australian
Parliament House   Notable Building

(☎02-6277 5399; www.aph.gov.au; ⊙9am-5pm)
FREE Designed by Romaldo Giurgola and
built in 1988, Australia's national parliament building is a graceful and deeply
symbolic piece of architecture. Sitting atop
Capital Hill, the building is crossed by two
axis, north–south and east–west, representing the historical progression and legis-
lative progression of Australian democracy.
There's plenty to see inside, whether the
politicians are haranguing each other in the
chambers or not.

Australian National
Botanic Gardens   Gardens

(☎02-6250 9588; www.nationalbotanicgardens.
gov.au; Clunies Ross St; ⊙8.30am-5pm) **FREE**
On the lower slopes of Black Mountain,
these sprawling gardens showcase
Australian floral diversity over 35 hectares
of cultivated garden and 50 hectares of
remnant bushland. Various themed routes
are marked out, with the best introduction

being the main path (45 minutes return),
which takes in the eucalypt lawn, rock
garden, rainforest gully and Sydney Region
garden. A 3.2km bushland nature trail leads
to the garden's higher reaches.

Museum of
Australian Democracy   Museum

(MoAD; ☎02-6270 8222; www.moadoph.gov.
au; Old Parliament House, 18 King George Tce,
Parkes; adult/child/family $2/1/5; ⊙9am-5pm)
The seat of government from 1927 to 1988,
this elegantly proportioned building offers
visitors a taste of the political past. Displays
cover Australian prime ministers, the roots
of democracy and the history of local
protest movements. You can also visit the
old Senate and House of Representative
chambers, the parliamentary library and
the prime minister's office.

Lake Burley Griffin   Lake

This ornamental lake was created in 1963
when the 33m-high Scrivener Dam was
built across the Molonglo River. It's lined
with important institutions and monu-

Australian Parliament House

ments, including the **National Carillon**
(www.nca.gov.au; Aspen Island) and **Captain
Cook Memorial Water Jet** (Captain Cook's
Fountain). You can cycle the entire 28km
perimeter in two hours or walk it in seven.
Alternatively, you can make a smaller 'loop'
by making use of the two bridges – the
popular central loop is 5km and can be
walked in one to 1½ hours.

National Film &
Sound Archive   Library
(☑02-6248 2000; www.nfsa.gov.au; McCoy Circuit; ☺9am-5pm Mon-Thu, to 8pm Fri, noon-5pm
Sat & Sun) FREE Set in a delightful art-
deco building (look for the stained-glass
platypus in the foyer dome), this archive
preserves Australian moving-picture and
sound recordings. The gallery space stages
free temporary exhibitions on Australian
film history. There's also a cute little theatre
where documentaries are played and the
larger Arc Cinema, used for special screenings and film festivals; check the website
for show times.

National Library
of Australia   Library
(☑02-6262 1111; www.nla.gov.au; Parkes Pl,
Parkes; ☺10am-8pm Mon-Thu, to 5pm Fri & Sat,
1.30-5pm Sun, galleries 10am-5pm daily) FREE
This institution has accumulated more than
10 million items since being established in
1901 and has digitised more than nine bil-
lion files. You can pop by the **Main Reading
Room** at any time to browse newspapers
and magazines by the large windows. Don't
miss the **Treasures Gallery**, where artefacts such as Captain Cook's *Endeavour*
journal and Captain Bligh's list of mutineers
are among the regularly refreshed displays;
free 30-minute tours of the gallery are held
at 11.30am daily.

National Arboretum   Park
(☑02-6207 8484; www.nationalarboretum.act.
gov.au; Forest Dr, Weston Creek; ☺6am-8.30pm
Oct-Mar, 7am-5.30pm Apr-Sep, village centre
9am-4pm; P) FREE Canberra's National
Arboretum is an ever-developing showcase

🚲 Cycling
Canberra

Canberra's streets are perfect for
cycling, and the city has an extensive
network of dedicated cycle paths. The
visitor centre (p94) is a good source
of information, as is Pedal Power ACT
(www.pedalpower.org.au).

Cyclists at Lake Burley Griffin
MEGAPIXELES.ES/SHUTTERSTOCK ©

of trees from around the world, with 94 forests of different species currently on-site. It
is early days for many of the plantings, but
it's still worth visiting for the spectacular
visitor centre and the excellent views over
the city. Regular guided tours are informative, and there is a brilliant adventure
playground for kids.

National Capital
Exhibition   Museum
(☑02-6272 2902; www.nationalcapital.gov.au;
Barrine Dr, Commonwealth Park; ☺9am-5pm)
FREE This small but fascinating museum
tells the story of how Canberra came to
be Australia's capital. Displays include
reproductions of the drawings entered in
the international competition to design the
city, including the exquisite watercolour
renderings of the winning design created
by Marion Mahony Griffin, the often over-
looked wife and creative partner of Walter
Burley Griffin.

The glass pavilion offers lovely views
over the lake and Capital Hill, so you can
see the real-life outcomes of the plans
you're perusing.

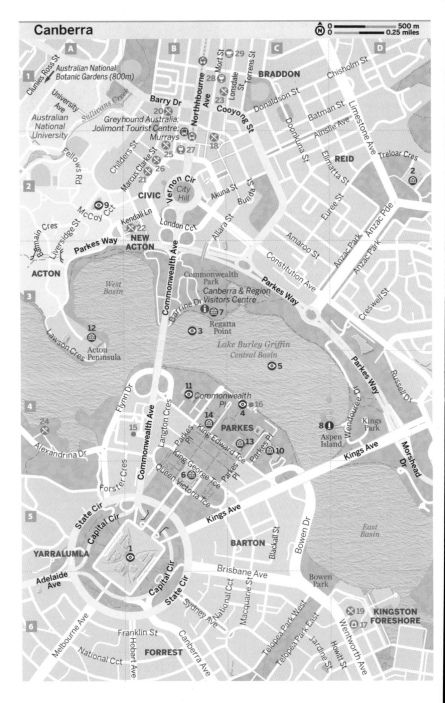

Canberra

◉N 0 ————— 500 m
0 ————— 0.25 miles

Australian National
Botanic Gardens (800m)

Clunies Ross St

University Ave

Australian National University

Fellows Rd

Sullivans Creek

Barry Dr

Greyhound Australia;
Jolimont Tourist Centre;
Murrays

Childers St

Marcus Clarke St

Mort St

Northbourne Ave

29

28

23

Cooyong St

Lonsdale St

Torrens St

BRADDON

Chisholm St

Donaldson St

Batman St

Doonkuna St

Ainslie Ave

Limestone Ave

Treloar Cres

20

25 27

18

26

21

Vernon Cir

City Hill

CIVIC

Akuna St

Bunda St

Elimatta St

Euree St

REID

2

McCoy Cct

Batman Cres

Liversidge St

9

Kendall Ln

22

London Cct

NEW ACTON

Parkes Way

ACTON

West Basin

Amaroo St

Constitution Ave

Anzac Park

Anzac Pde

Parkes Way

Creswell St

Commonwealth Ave

Barrine Dr

Commonwealth Park

Canberra & Region
Visitors Centre

7

3

Regatta Point

Lake Burley Griffin
Central Basin

5

12

Acton Peninsula

Lawson Cres

Flynn Dr

11

Commonwealth Pl

16

4

14

PARKES

15

Langton Cres

Commonwealth Ave

24

Alexandrina Dr

Forster Cres

Parkes Pl

King Edward Tce

13

Parkes Pl

10

King George Tce

6

Queen Victoria Tce

8

Aspen Island

Kings Park

Wendouree Dr

Kings Ave

Parkes Way

Russell Dr

Morshead Dr

State Cir

Capital Cir

1

YARRALUMLA

Adelaide Ave

Kings Ave

BARTON

Blackall St

Bowen Dr

East Basin

Bowen Park

Capital Cir

State Cir

Brisbane Ave

Sydney Ave

National Cct

Macquarie St

Telopea Park West

Telopea Park East

19

17

KINGSTON FORESHORE

Wentworth Ave

Howitt St

Jardine St

Franklin St

Melbourne Ave

Hobart Ave

National Cct

Canberra Ave

FORREST

Canberra

TOURS

Balloon Aloft
Ballooning

(☏02-6249 8660; www.balloonaloftcanberra. com.au; 120 Commonwealth Ave, Yarralumla; adult/child from $330/240) Meet in the foyer of the Hyatt for an early-morning flight over Canberra – the ideal way to understand the city's unique design.

Lake Burley Griffin Cruises
Cruise

(☏0419 418 846; www.lakecruises.com.au; Queen Elizabeth Tce, Parkes; adult/child $20/9; ⊙mid-Sep–May) Informative one-hour lake cruises depart from the wharf in front of the **International Flag Display** (Queen Elizabeth Tce, Parkes).

SHOPPING

Bison Home
Ceramics

(☏02-6128 0788; www.bisonhome.com; 14/27 Lonsdale St, Braddon; ⊙10am-5pm Mon-Fri, to 4pm Sat & Sun) A Braddon outpost of Pialligo-based ceramics label Bison, this aesthetically pleasing store will have you re-thinking every object in your kitchen, from mugs to mixing bowls. Smaller items – like

tiny ceramic milk bottles in a rainbow of colours – make lovely souvenirs or gifts.

Old Bus Depot Markets
Market

(☏02-6295 3331; www.obdm.com.au; 21 Wentworth Ave, Kingston; ⊙10am-4pm Sun) A Sunday institution, this bustling market has one hall completely devoted to food and another to crafts. Self-caterers and picnickers will delight in the freshly baked goods, cheese, charcuterie and produce; come at lunch to take full advantage of the 'international' food court, with cuisine from Thailand, Ethiopia, Jordan and the USA, as well as the usual pancakes and coffee.

National Library Bookshop
Books

(☏02-6262 1424; http://bookshop.nla.gov.au; Parkes Pl, Parkes; ⊙10am-5pm) Specialises in Australian books, but also has a good selection of recent titles and giftware.

EATING

Snappers

Fish & Chips $

(☏02-6273 1784; www.cscc.com.au/snapper; Mariner Pl, Yarralumla; fish & chips $14; ⊙11am-8pm Sep-May, to 3pm Mon-Fri, to 8pm Sat & Sun

Jun-Aug) This tasty fish-and-chip shop in the bottom floor of the yacht club does a roaring trade on summer evenings. There is some seating available, but you may want to BYO picnic rug and find your own slice of lake view.

Two Before Ten   Cafe $

(www.twobeforeten.com.au; 1 Hobart Pl, Acton; mains $11-18; ⊙7am-4pm Mon-Fri, 8am-2pm Sat & Sun) Breaking from the Australian tradition that says good cafes should be bohemian and battered looking, this airy place brings a touch of Cape Cod to the centre of a city block. The excellent coffee comes from its own roastery in Aranda, where there is also another outpost of the cafe.

Morning Glory   Cafe $$

(☑02-6257 6464; www.morning-glory.com.au; 2/15 Edinburgh Ave, New Acton; dishes $12-27; ⊙6am-3pm; ❄🤍) Nestled in the heart of the New Acton complex, this sprawling cafe has a sleek, contemporary vibe and is a popular coffee stop for local office workers. The menu offers modern cafe dishes with

an Asian twist, like black sesame and milk-tea pancake waffles at breakfast, or soba salad with wakame seaweed and enoki mushrooms at lunch.

Cupping Room   Cafe $$

(☑02-6257 6412; www.thecuppingroom.com. au; 1 University Ave, Civic; mains $11-25; ⊙7am-4pm Mon-Fri, 8am-3pm Sat & Sun; 🖊) Queues often form outside this airy corner cafe, drawn by the prospect of Canberra's best coffee and an interesting menu, including great vegetarian and vegan options. The seasonal chia pudding is extraordinary, but if you prefer something a little more familiar, the burgers are equally as delicious. Choose your coffee blend from the tasting notes; we recommend the filter coffee.

Rye   Cafe $$

(☑02-6156 9694; www.ryecafe.com.au; 9 Lonsdale St, Braddon; breakfast $14-17, lunch $7-22; ⊙6.30am-4pm) Charming, Scandi-inspired Rye is all blonde wood, bright lights and modish furniture, with a menu to match. Danish *smørrebrød* (open sandwiches on

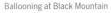
Ballooning at Black Mountain

dark rye bread) are a popular choice at lunch, while breakfast options are variations on cafe faves like poached eggs and avocado with Danish feta and broad beans. Great coffee.

Lazy Su   Asian $$

(☑02-5105 3812; www.lazy-su.com.au; 9 Lonsdale St, Braddon; dishes $12-29; ☉5-11pm Mon, from noon Tue-Thu & Sun, to 1am Fri & Sat) Lazy Su's playful Asian vibe is obvious as you enter past the wall of lucky cats. You can't go far wrong with the menu, but if you can't decide between the pork-belly *bao-ger* and the yellowfin tuna tataki, opt for the seven-dish 'People's Banquet' ($49 per person).

Terra   Australian $$

(☑02-6230 4414; www.terracanberra.com. au; Shop G2, No Name Lane, 40 Marcus Clarke St; mains breakfast & lunch $10-16, dinner $18-30, set menu per person $58; ☉7.30am-4pm Mon-Wed, to late Thu & Fri, 10.30am-late Sat) By day this atmospheric, contemporary space churns out delectable seasonal brunch dishes and fabulous coffee. At night the rotisserie takes centre stage, with six-hour roasted meats on offer, alongside innovative sides like fried cauliflower or baked potatoes with miso. The best option, though, is the 'Feed Me' set menu (minimum two people) – trust us, you won't go home hungry.

Akiba   Asian $$

(☑02-6162 0602; www.akiba.com.au; 40 Bunda St; noodle & rice dishes $10-21, share plates $16-33; ☉11.30am-midnight Sun-Wed, to 2am Thu-Sat) A high-octane vibe pervades this superslick pan-Asian place, fuelled by a lively young crew that effortlessly splashes together cocktails, dispenses food recommendations and juggles orders without breaking a sweat. A raw bar serves delectable sashimi, freshly shucked oysters and zingy ceviche. Salt-and-Sichuan-pepper squid and pork-belly buns are crowd pleasers, and we love the Japanese-style eggplant.

📖 Canberra History

Canberra is built on Ngunnawal country. The Ngunnawal people are the Indigenous Australian nation that lived on the land around Canberra at the time of European settlement, along with the Gundungurra to the north, the Ngarigo to the south, the Yuin to the west, and the Wiradjuri to the east. Rock paintings found in nearby Tharwa indicate that Indigenous Australians have lived in this region for at least 20,000 years, though evidence from nearby regions suggests an even longer duration.

The Ngunnawal people called this place Kanberra, believed to mean 'Meeting Place'. The name was probably derived from huge intertribal gatherings that happened annually when large numbers of bogong moths – a popular food source – appeared in the region. The Ngunnawal way of life was violently disrupted following the arrival of Europeans in 1820, when settlers began to move into the Canberra basin, bringing sheep and other introduced species.

In 1901 Australia's separate colonies were federated and became states. The rivalry between Sydney and Melbourne meant neither could become the new nation's capital, so a location between the two cities was carved out of southern New South Wales (NSW) as a compromise. This new city was officially named Canberra in 1913, and replaced Melbourne as the national capital in 1927.

Lake Burley Griffin (p86)

From left: Old Bus Depot Markets (p89); fountain, Lake Burley Griffin (p86); National Arboretum (p87)

Agostini's   Italian $$

(☎02-6178 0048; www.easthotel.com.au/agos itinis; 69 Canberra Ave, Kingston; pizzas $21-25, mains from $25; ☺noon-3pm & 5.30pm-late) Wood-fired pizza, rosé on tap and house-made gelato are just some of the charms of this cool, millennial-pink bistro, set in the ground floor of **East Hotel** (☎02-6295 6925; www.easthotel.com.au; apt from $180; P❄@☎). Holidaying families rub shoulders with Canberra's glitterati along the plush, window seating; for a real show, however, request a seat at the bar with a view of the pizza oven. Reservations recommended.

Pilot   Modern Australian $$$

(☎02-6257 4334; www.pilotrestaurant.com; 5/6 Wakefield Gardens, Ainslie; mains $25-45, set menu per person $90, with paired drinks non-alcoholic/alcoholic $120/150; ☺6pm-late Wed-Sat, noon-3.30pm Sun) Elegant, seasonal dishes are the highlight at this classy fine-dining restaurant in suburban Ainslie. The menu changes daily but features local produce and interesting flavour combinations. À la carte options are available, but for

the full experience try the 'prix fixe' tasting menu, available paired with either alcoholic or nonalcoholic beverages. There's also a Sunday 'long lunch' ($60 per person).

Courgette   Modern Australian $$$

(☎02-6247 4042; www.courgette.com.au; 54 Marcus Clarke St; 3-course lunch $66, 4-course dinner $88; ☺noon-3pm & 6-11pm Mon-Sat) With its crisp white linen, impeccable service and discreet but expensive ambience, Courgette is the kind of place to bring someone you want to impress, like a date, or perhaps the Finnish ambassador. The exacting standards continue with the precisely prepared, exquisitely plated and flavour-laden food.

Aubergine   Modern Australian $$$

(☎02-6260 8666; www.aubergine.com.au; 18 Barker St, Griffith; 4-course menu per person $98; ☺6-10pm Mon-Sat) You'll need to travel out to the southern suburbs to find Canberra's top-rated restaurant. While the location may be unassuming, the same can't be said for the menu, which is exciting, innovative and seasonally driven. Although only a four-course menu is offered, you can

CHAMELEONSEYE/SHUTTERSTOCK ©

choose between a handful of options for most courses. Service and presentation are assured.

🍸 DRINKING & NIGHTLIFE

Kyō Coffee Project — Coffee

(www.kyocoffeeproject.com; 5/27 Lonsdale St, Braddon; ⊙7am-4pm Tue-Sat, 7.30am-3.30pm Sun) In a little courtyard just off Lonsdale St, achingly hip Kyō serves coffee just as good as its slick, minimalist fit-out promises. Options are limited to black, white or a batch brew. There's a petite, mildly Japanese-inspired menu if you're peckish.

Capital Brewing Co — Brewery

(☎02-5104 0915; www.capitalbrewing.co; Bldg 3, 1 Dairy Rd, Fyshwick; ⊙11.30am-late) It's worth seeking out this Fyshwick brewery offering straight-from-the-tap local craft beers in a stylishly fitted-out tap room. Get your bearings with a tasting paddle that includes the popular Coast Ale. Outside, the green is great for kids and dogs (who can sample the nonalcoholic dog brew). Hungry? The original **Brodburger** (☎02-6162 0793; www.brodburger.com.au; Glassworks Bldg, 11 Wentworth Ave, Kingston; burgers $14-21; ⊙noon-3pm & 5.30pm-late Tue-Sat, noon-4pm Sun; ☛) van serves burgers, hot dogs and snacks.

Bar Rochford — Wine Bar

(☎02-6230 6222; www.barrochford.com; 1st fl, 65 London Circuit; ⊙5pm-late Tue-Thu, 3pm-1am Fri, from 5pm Sat) Bearded barmen concentrate earnestly on their cocktail constructions and wine recommendations at this sophisticated but unstuffy bar in the Melbourne Building. Dress up and hope for a table by one of the big arched windows.

Molly — Bar

(www.molly.bar; Odgers Lane; ⊙4pm-midnight Mon-Wed, to 2am Thu-Sat, 5pm-late Sun) The doorway to this little gem, hidden away down quiet Odgers Lane, is illuminated only by a light bulb. It may take some courage to push through the unmarked wooden door, but have faith; inside you'll find an atmospheric 1920s-style speakeasy, with dim lighting, cosy booths and a very impressive whisky selection. Try the cocktails.

Knightsbridge
Penthouse
Cocktail Bar

(☑02-6262 6221; www.knightsbridgepenthouse. com.au; 34 Mort St, Braddon; ☺5pm-midnight Tue & Wed, to late Thu-Sat) Just behind the main Braddon strip, this quirky place offers good DJs, excellent cocktails and a mellow ambience. Come on Fridays before 8pm for 'Happy Friday' cheap cocktails ($10) and house wine ($5).

ℹ INFORMATION

Canberra & Region Visitors Centre (☑02-6205 0044; www.visitcanberra.com.au; Regatta Point, Barrine Dr, Commonwealth Park; ☺9am-5pm Mon-Fri, to 4pm Sat & Sun) Staff at this exceptionally helpful centre can dispense masses of information and brochures, including the free quarterly *Canberra Events* brochure.

Canberra Hospital (☑02-5124 0000; www. health.act.gov.au; Yamba Dr, Garran; ☺24hr) Has a 24-hour emergency department.

ℹ GETTING THERE & AWAY

AIR

Canberra Airport (☑02-6275 2222; www.can berraairport.com.au; Terminal Ave, Pialligo) is only 7km southeast of Civic.

Daily domestic flights service most Australian capital cities and some regional destinations. Qantas (www.qantas.com) flies to/from Adelaide, Brisbane, Melbourne, Perth and Sydney. Virgin Australia (www.virginaustralia. com.au) flies to/from Adelaide, Brisbane, Gold Coast, Melbourne and Sydney. Tigerair Australia (www.tigerair.com.au) also heads to Melbourne.

BUS

The interstate bus terminal is in the centre of Civic at the **Jolimont Centre** (67 Northbourne Ave,; ☺5am-10.30pm), where you'll find booking desks for the major bus companies.

Greyhound Australia (☑02-6211 8545; www. greyhound.com.au; 65 Northbourne Ave) has daily coaches to Sydney (from $39, 3½ hours),

Old Bus Depot Markets (p89)

Albury (from $62, 4½ hours) and Melbourne (from $69, eight hours), along with seasonal buses to the ski resorts.

Murrays (☐13 22 51; www.murrays.com.au; 65 Northbourne Ave; ☺3.30am-6pm) offers express services to Sydney (from $39, 3½ hours), Wollongong ($49, 3¼ hours), Batemans Bay ($38, 2½ hours), Moruya ($41, 3¼ hours) and Narooma ($49, 4½ hours), as well as the ski fields.

CAR & MOTORCYCLE

The Hume Hwy connects Sydney and Melbourne, passing 50km north of Canberra. The Federal Hwy runs north to connect with the Hume near Goulburn, and the Barton Hwy (Rte 25) meets the Hume near Yass.

Driving possibilities include Sydney (290km, three hours) and Melbourne (670km, seven hours).

TRAIN

NSW TrainLink (☐13 22 32; www.nswtrainlink. info) has services from Sydney ($28, 4¼ hours) which pull into Kingston's **Canberra Railway Station** (☐13 22 32; Burke Cres) three times daily.

V/Line (☐1800 800 007; www.vline.com. au) has a daily service combining a train from Melbourne to Wodonga with a bus to Canberra (from $67, nine hours), terminating at the Jolimont Centre.

❶ GETTING AROUND

TO/FROM THE AIRPORT

A taxi to the city centre costs from $30 to $40.

Bus routes 11 and 11A run between city platform 9 and the airport at least hourly between 6am and 6pm (adult/child $5/2.50, 20 to 40 minutes).

PUBLIC TRANSPORT

The bus network, operated by **Transport Canberra** (☐13 17 10; www.transport.act.gov.au;

Lake Burley Griffin

Though it might seem at first glance that Canberra was built around the sparkling waters of Lake Burley Griffin, the reality is actually the other way around. The concept of an artificial lake was part of the original design of the nation's capital as early as 1909, however it wasn't until 1961, with the excavation of the lake floor and the damming of the Molonglo River at Scrivener Dam, that Lake Burley Griffin finally came into existence. Even then, the final stages of construction were hampered by a prolonged period of drought, which meant that the lake did not reach its planned water level until 1964, when it was officially inaugurated by then Prime Minister Sir Robert Menzies. A statue of Menzies, who championed the lake project throughout his prime ministership, can be seen strolling along the lake shore near Nerang Pool.

single adult/child $5/2.50, day pass $9.60/4.80), will get you to most places of interest in the city.

Travellers can use the MyWay smart-card system, but if you're only here for a week or so you're better off paying the driver in cash, as a card costs a nonrefundable fee of adult/child $5/2.50. A day pass costs less than two single tickets, so purchase one on your first journey of the day.

Canberra's new light-rail line from Civic to Gungahlin via Dickson began taking passengers in April 2019.

TAXI

Cabxpress (☐02-6181 2700; www.cabxpress. com.au)

Canberra Elite Taxis (☐02-6126 1600; www. canberraelite.com.au)

BYRON BAY

Byron Bay at a Glance...

The reputation of this famous beach town on the New South Wales north coast precedes it – as they say in Byron, it's got a great vibe! Come to surf epic breaks at dawn, paddle through hazy beach afternoons and sigh at the enchanting sunsets. Come to do reiki, refine your yoga practice, do a raw fast and hang with the fire-twirlers by the beach at sunset. Idle at the town's excellent restaurant tables, then kick on with backpackers, musicians, models, young entrepreneurs, ageing hippies and property developers at one of its beery, shouty pubs. Do it all, then repeat!

Byron Bay in Two Days

Don't muck around: down an excellent cafe breakfast then book a surf lesson. Take your pick of excellent dinner options, then hit Byron's bars: everyone seems to end up at **Railway Friendly Bar** (p106).

Next day, ignore your hangover and head for **Cape Byron Lighthouse** (p102) to see the sunrise. A day of alt therapies awaits: yoga, massage, meditation...

Byron Bay in Four Days

Book a hinterland day tour to check out waterfalls and hippy, smoke-hazed Nimbin. Back in Byron, catch a live band at the **Great Northern** (p107).

Thursday? Don't miss **Byron Farmers Market** (p104). Otherwise, get a different take on Byron via a kayaking tour in Cape Byron Marine Park (exhibitionist dolphins guaranteed).

Previous page: View from Fisherman's Lookout, Byron Bay
DAVID ANTON ANDERSON/SHUTTERSTOCK ©

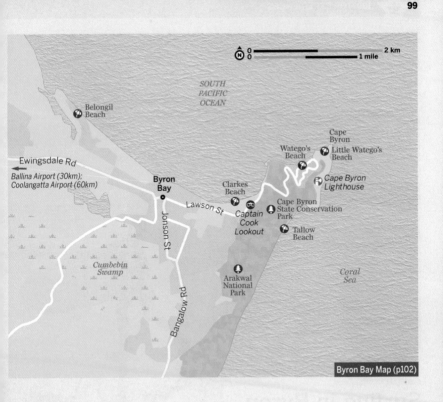

SOUTH PACIFIC OCEAN

Belongil Beach

Cape Byron

Watego's Beach
Little Watego's Beach

Ewingsdale Rd

Ballina Airport (30km); Coolangatta Airport (60km)

Byron Bay

Clarkes Beach

Cape Byron Lighthouse

Lawson St

Captain Cook Lookout

Cape Byron State Conservation Park

Jonson St

Tallow Beach

Cumbebin Swamp

Bangalow Rd

Arakwal National Park

Coral Sea

Byron Bay Map (p102)

Arriving in Byron Bay

Byron's train service is no more, so you'll either be arriving here under your own steam (surfing road trip!), rolling into town on a bus, or catching a flight to the nearby **Ballina Airport** (p107) or **Gold Coast Airport** (p107) in Coolangatta. Shuttles service both airports. Qantas flies from Sydney; Jetstar and Virgin also service Melbourne.

Where to Stay

Byron beds are expensive, and the whole town does book out. But if you're in the market for 'barefoot luxury' – relaxed but stylish – you're in luck. Book well in advance for January, during festival times (eg Bluesfest at Easter) and school holidays. If you're not on the edge of 17 years old, avoid Schoolies Week in mid-November.

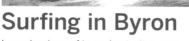

Surfing in Byron

Learning to surf is an Australian rite of passage – if you feel like joining in, Byron Bay has plenty of good learn-to-surf schools and waves for beginners through to pros.

Surf Culture in Australia

Australia has been synonymous with surfing ever since the Beach Boys effused about 'Australia's Narrabeen', one of Sydney's northern beaches, in 'Surfin' USA'. Other surfing hotspots such as Bells Beach, Margaret River, the Pass at Byron Bay, the heavy-breaking Shipstern Bluff in Tasmania and Burleigh Heads on the Gold Coast also resonate with international wave addicts. Iron Man and Surf Lifesaving competitions are also held on beaches around the country, attracting dedicated fans to the sand.

More than a few Australian surfers have attained 'World Champion' status. In the men's competition, legendary surfers include Mark Richards, Tom Carroll, Joel Parkinson and 2013 champ (and shark survivor) Mick Fanning. On the women's

Great For

☑ **Don't Miss**

The Ben King Memorial Surf Classic competition in June, running for 40-plus years.

Surfer at The Pass, Byron Bay

CAMAC/ALAMY ©

the waves and, with a bit of hard work and natural ability kicking in, have you standing up and barrelling towards the shore after a lesson or two. Tip: it ain't as easy at it looks!

Surf schools all provide wetsuits and boards. Afterwards, once you've worked up a bit of confidence, most hostels provide free boards to guests, or you can rent all the requisite gear from local surf shops.

Black Dog Surfing   Surfing

(☏02-6680 9828; www.blackdogsurfing.com; 11 Byron St; 3½hr group lesson $65, 3hr private lesson $140) One of four Byron Bay–based surf schools that can hold lessons at a Byron Bay beach, rather than further afield. They offer intimate (seven people maximum) group lessons, including women's and kids' courses. Highly rated.

Soul Surf School   Surfing

(☏1800 089 699; www.soulsurfschool.com. au; 14 Bay St; 4hr group lesson $69) Offers half-day to five-day courses for beginners with small groups of up to six people, or you can opt for a private lesson ($160 for 2½ hours).

side, iconic Aussie surfers include Wendy Botha, seven-time champion Layne Beachley, 2018 champ (and seven-time winner) Stephanie Gilmore and 2016 winner Tyler Wright.

The Pass

Byron's famous break is the Pass, a long, lusciously peeling right-hander formed by waves refracting around Cape Byron and running almost at right angles to the shore. It's surfable even when it's small, but gets mighty crowded when the swell picks up. It's not really beginners' terrain: cut your teeth over at Main Beach instead.

Surf Schools

There are plenty of surfing instructors in Byron Bay who can get you safely out into

⊙ SIGHTS

Cape Byron State Conservation Park
State Park

(www.nationalparks.nsw.gov.au/cape-byron-state-conservation-area; ⊘8.30am-sunset) The Cape Byron State Conservation Park is home to the **Cape Byron lighthouse** (www.nationalparks.nsw.gov.au; Lighthouse Rd; ⊘museum 10am-4pm) **FREE**, plenty of stunning lookouts (including from the most eastern point of the Australia mainland) and the excellent Cape Byron Walking Track (p103). There is parking available at the lighthouse ($8).

⊙ Beaches

Northwest of the town centre, wild **Belongil Beach** with its high dunes avoids the worst of the crowds and is clothing-optional in parts. At its eastern end lies the **Wreck**, a powerful right-hand surf break.

Immediately in front of town, lifesaver-patrolled **Main Beach** is busy from sunrise to sunset with yoga classes, buskers and, occasionally, fire dancers. As it stretches east it merges into **Clarkes Beach**. The most popular surf break is at the **Pass** near the eastern headland.

Around the rocks is gorgeous **Watego's Beach**, a wide crescent of white sand surrounded by rainforest that fringes Byron's most affluent enclave. A further 400m walk brings you to secluded **Little Watego's** (inaccessible by car, but accessible by steps leading down from the lighthouse), another lovely patch of sand directly under rocky Cape Byron. Head here at sunset for an impressive moonrise (depending on your timing). Tucked under the south side of the Cape (entry via Tallow Beach Rd) is **Cosy Corner**, which offers a decent-sized wave and a sheltered beach when the northerlies are blowing elsewhere.

Tallow Beach is an incredible, deserted sandy stretch that extends for 7km south from Cape Byron. This is the place to flee the crowds. **Kings Beach** is a popular

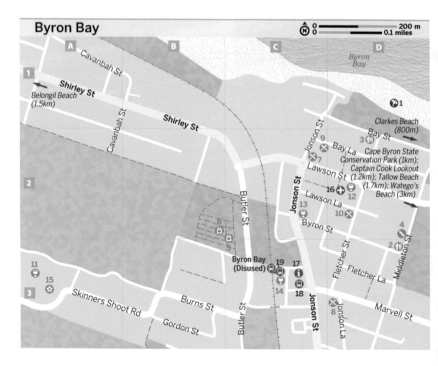

gay-friendly beach, just off Seven Mile Beach Rd past the Broken Head Holiday Park.

🏃 ACTIVITIES

Cape Byron Walking Track   Walking
(www.nationalparks.nsw.gov.au/things-to-do/walking-tracks/cape-byron-walking-track) Spectacular views reward those who climb up from the **Captain Cook Lookout** (Lighthouse Rd) on the Cape Byron Walking Track. Ribboning around the headland and through rainforest, the track dips and (mostly) soars its way to the lighthouse. Look out for dolphins (year-round) and migrating whales (June to November). Allow about two hours for the entire 3.7km loop.

Gaia Retreat & Spa   Spa
(☎02-6687 1670; www.gaiaretreat.com.au; 933 Fernleigh Rd, Brooklet; massage & treatments $140-520) 🌿 Sure, Byron is packed with places for pampering, but none quite like Gaia, famously co-owned by Olivia Newton John. This luxurious retreat, consistently topping world's best lists, is tucked away in the verdant hinterland in Bundjalung country. If you don't have the cash to overnight here, a visit to the day spa is the next best thing.

Go Sea Kayaks   Kayaking
(☎0416 222 344; www.goseakayakbyronbay.com.au; adult/child $75/50) 🌿 Reputable 2½-hour sea-kayak tours in Cape Byron Marine Park are led by a team of local surf lifesavers daily at 9.30am and 2pm. Whale, dolphin or turtle sightings are guaranteed; otherwise you can book again for free.

Sundive   Diving, Snorkelling
(☎02-6685 7755; www.sundive.com.au; Shop 8, 9-11 Byron St; dives from $110, snorkelling tours $75) Two to three expeditions to Julian Rocks daily, plus various courses. Office entrance is on Middleton St.

🎯 TOURS

Aboriginal Cultural Concepts   Cultural
(☎0405 654 280; www.aboriginalculturalconcepts.com; half-/full-day tours $95/190; ☺tours run Wed-Sat) Heritage tours led by Lois Cook, a traditional custodian of Nyangbul country in the region, explore cultural and mythological sights, and sample bush tucker along the Bundjalung coast.

Vision Walks   Wildlife
(☎0405 275 743; www.visionwalks.com; full-day tours adult/child $145/110) See all manner of creatures in their natural habitat, including nocturnal animals (on the Night Vision Walk) and hippies (on the Hippy Hinterland Trail that takes you to Nimbin).

Underwater Byron

About 3km offshore, Julian Rocks Marine Reserve is a meeting point for cold southerly and warm northerly currents, attracting a profusion of marine species including three types of turtle. You might also spot leopard sharks and manta rays in summer, and grey nurse sharks in winter. Operators such as **Byron Bay Dive Centre** (02-6685 8333; www.byronbaydivecentre.com.au; 9 Marvell St; h9am-5pm; dives incl gear from $100, snorkelling tours $75) and Sundive (p103) offer guided dives and snorkelling trips.

Stingray, Byron Bay
NICO FARAMAZ/SHUTTERSTOCK ©

🛍 SHOPPING

Byron Farmers Market　　　Market
(www.byronfarmersmarket.com.au; Butler Street Reserve; ⊘8-11am Thu) Both a market and a symbol of the strength of the local community, this weekly market has a wide variety of mainly organic stalls, with both fresh produce and all manner of local products. Come early and hang with the locals for great coffee and breakfast, then linger for live music.

Byron Community Market　　　Market
(www.byronmarkets.com.au; Butler St Reserve; ⊘8am-3pm 1st Sun of month) The biggest market in the region, with more than 300 stalls covering over a hectare of land. Organic farmers and foodies meet alternative therapists, craftspeople and musicians at this monthly extravaganza.

🍴 EATING

Top Shop　　　Cafe $
(65 Carlyle St; mains $10-17; ⊘6.30am-4pm) High up on the hill east of town, Top Shop has long been the choice of local surfers. Today it's a casually upmarket version of the old-school takeaway, with diners ripping into acai bowls, steak sandwiches and burgers while lazing on the lawn.

Three Blue Ducks at the Farm　　　Cafe, Australian $$
(02-6684 7888; www.thefarmbyronbay.com.au; 11 Ewingsdale Rd, Ewingsdale; breakfast $18-25, lunch & dinner $27-36; ⊘7am-3pm Mon-Thu, to 10pm Fri-Sun) The legendary Sydney team behind Three Blue Ducks moved up north to showcase its paddock-to-plate food philosophy. Their rustic barn cafe and restaurant forms the beating heart of **The Farm** (tours adult/child $20/15; ⊘7am-4pm) **FREE**. Breakfast features typical Byron healthy fare, as well as a streaky bacon and egg roll, and slow-roasted brisket, while the lunch and dinner menus step it up with a gentle sophistication to the menu.

Il Buco Cafe & Pizzeria　　　Pizza $$
(02-6680 9186; www.ilbucobyronbay.com; 4/4 Bay Lane; pizza $15-28; ⊘5.30pm-late) The best pizza in town comes thanks to a group of friends from Tuscany who've set up shop in Byron. Authentic thin-crust wood-fired pizzas are sparingly topped with outstanding flavours using as much local produce as possible. The delicious prosciutto funghi features Bangalow sweet pork ham, while the simple margherita is made with a deliciously slurpable homemade passata and *fior di latte* mozzarella. BYO (no corkage!). Also does takeaway.

St Elmo　　　Spanish $$$
(02-6680 7426; www.stelmodining.com; cnr Fletcher St & Lawson Lane; dishes $16-29; ⊘5-11pm Mon-Sat, to 10pm Sun) Perch on a stool at this moody modern tapas restaurant, where bar staff can whip up inventive cocktails or pour you a glass of wine from the largely Australian and Spanish list (including natural and minimal intervention

Cafe in Byron Bay

drops). The solidly Iberian menu is bold and broad, with traditional favourites mixing it up with contemporary flourishes.

Bay Leaf Café   Cafe $$

(www.facebook.com/bayleafcoffee; 2 Marvell St; mains $17-24; ⊙7am-2pm) There's a raft of Byron clichés on offer at this hip, busy cafe (golden lattes, kombucha, a '70s psych rock soundtrack), but everything is made with remarkable attention to detail and a passion for produce. Breakfasts are fantastic, from the granola or Bircher muesli to the poached eggs with house-made dukkah or young Australia's national dish: avocado on sourdough.

Balcony Bar   International $$

(☑02-6680 9666; www.balcony.com.au; cnr Lawson & Jonson Sts; mains $22-32; ⊙noon-11pm Mon-Thu, to late Fri, 9am-late Sat & Sun; 🛜) The eponymous architectural feature here wraps around the building and gives you tremendous views of the passing Byron parade (and the ever-busy traffic circle). Decor is an appealing postcolonial pastiche, while the food is a great mix of

tasty tapas-style dishes, Med-inflected warm-weather-appropriate salads and sophisticated main meals from chilli crab linguine to a dry-aged beef burger on brioche.

Rae's Dining Room   Seafood $$$

(☑02-6685 5366; www.raesonwategos.com; 8 Marine Pde, Watego's Beach; mains $36-44; ⊙noon-3pm & 6-11pm) The sound of the surf perfectly sets off the excellent Mediterranean-influenced dishes at this exclusive little retreat overlooking Watego's Beach. Headed up by chef Jason Barratt, formerly at Melbourne's acclaimed Attica (p165) restaurant, seafood features heavily on the menu with a strong focus on sourcing local produce from the Northern Rivers region.

🍷 DRINKING & NIGHTLIFE

Treehouse on Belongil   Pub

(☑02-6680 9452; www.treehouseonbelongil. com; 25 Childe St; ⊙7.30am-11pm) A homespun beach bar where wooden decks spill out among the trees, afternoons are for drinking, and live, original music is played Thursday to Sunday. Soak up the beer with a menu of well-made pizzas, burgers, steaks and seafood.

Locura   Bar, Club
(02-6675 9140; www.locura.com.au; 6 Lawson St; 5pm-late) No strangers to Byron's hospitality scene, the guys from Three Blue Ducks (p104) are weaving their magic on the town's bar scene with the opening of Locura, a sleek and sophisticated bar. The decor leans towards minimalist/industrial, while the menu is Latin American inspired, with plenty of tequila and mezcal paired with shredded pork tacos, oysters with hot sauce, and ceviche.

Railway Friendly Bar   Pub
(The Rails; 02-6685 7662; www.therailsbyron bay.com; 86 Jonson St; 11am-midnight, from noon Sun) 'The Rails' indoor-outdoor mayhem draws everyone from lobster-red British tourists to high-on-life earth mothers and babyboomer tourists. The front beer garden – conducive to long, beery afternoons – has free live music, while the kitchen pumps out excellent burgers, with variants including roo, grilled fish and pork belly with slaw.

Stone & Wood   Brewery
(02-6685 5173; www.stoneandwood.com.au; 100 Centennial Circuit; tasting room 10am-5pm Mon-Fri, noon-6pm Sat & Sun) This independent and proudly local brewery – with a core family of ales, experimental pilot batches and seasonal beers – upgraded to a huge new space in late 2018 where you can still drop by for a paddle and to pick up a few beers or a carton; or book online for a 1½-hour in-depth tour (three daily, except Tuesdays; $25 per person).

Byron Bay Brewery   Brewery
(02-6639 6100; www.byronbaybrewery.com.au; 1 Skinners Shoot Rd; noon-late Wed-Sun) At this old piggery turned booze barn you can drink frosty glasses of house pale ale or lager in a light, louvred space by the brewing vats or outside in the tropical courtyard shaded by a giant fig tree. Free brewery tour and tastings run at 2pm on weekends. There's a pub-snack menu, and entertainment includes live music, DJs and open-mic nights.

Balcony Bar (p105)

ANDREW HOLT/ALAMY ©

⭐ ENTERTAINMENT

Northern Hotel   Pub

(📞02-6685 6454; www.thenorthern.com.au;
35-43 Jonson St; ⊙noon-late) This live-music
stalwart is as grungy and boozy as it ever
was, and has played host to everyone from
Billy Bragg and Dizzee Rascal to Dinosaur
Jr and PJ Harvey. The front bar is a prime
spot for people-watching with a cold drink
out the open windows or on a street-side
table, and does $10 burger-and-chip deals
for lunch daily.

Pighouse Flicks   Cinema

(📞02-6685 5828; www.pighouseflicks.com.au;
1 Skinners Shoot Rd; tickets adult/child $15/5)
Part of the Byron Bay Brewery complex,
this atmospheric lounge-cinema shows
classic reruns and art-house flicks.

ℹ️ INFORMATION

Byron Visitor Centre (📞02-6680 8558; www.
visitbyronbay.com; Old Stationmaster's Cottage,
80 Jonson St; ⊙9am-5pm Mon-Sat, 10am-4pm
Sun; 🛜) is the place for accurate tourist information, and last-minute accommodation and
bus bookings.

The website www.byron-bay.com is a helpful
resource.

Bay Centre Medical (📞02-6685 6206; www.
byronmed.com.au; 6 Lawson St; ⊙8am-5.30pm
Mon-Thu, to 5pm Fri, to noon Sat)

Byron Central Hospital (📞02-6639 9400;
https://nnswlhd.health.nsw.gov.au/about/
hospitals/byron-central-hospital; 54 Ewingsdale Rd; ⊙24hr)

ℹ️ GETTING THERE & AWAY

AIR

The closest airport is in **Ballina** (📞02-6681
1858; www.ballinabyronairport.com.au; Southern
Cross Dr), 30 minutes south. Byron Easy Bus,
Steve's Airport Transfers (📞0414 660 031;
https://stevestransport.com.au; one way/return

> 📖 **John Byron,
> not Lord Byron**
>
> James Cook named Cape Byron, main-
> land Australia's most easterly point,
> after renowned navigator John Byron,
> grandfather of the poet Lord Byron. Lat-
> er bureaucrats mistakenly planned out
> streets named after fellow poets such
> as Jonson, Burns and Shelley.

$20/35) and **Xcede** (📞02-6620 9200; https://
byronbay.xcede.com.au) all serve Ballina airport
($20, 20 minutes).

Gold Coast Airport (www.goldcoastairport.
com.au; Eastern Ave, Bilinga), 40 minutes away in
Coolangatta, has more services. **Skybus** (www.
skybus.com.au/byron-bay-express; one way
adult/child $28/14) runs daily services between
Byron Bay and Gold Coast Airport ($28, 55
minutes), as does Byron Easy Bus ($32) and
Xcede ($40).

BUS

Coaches stop on **Jonson St** near the Byron Visitor Centre. Operators include **Premier** (📞13 34
10; www.premierms.com.au), **Greyhound** (📞1300
473 946; www.greyhound.com.au) and **NSW
TrainLink** (📞13 22 32; www.nswtrainlink.info).

Blanch's (📞02-6686 2144; www.blanchs.com.
au) Regular buses to/from Ballina Byron Gateway Airport ($7.40, one hour), Ballina ($9.60,
55 minutes), Lennox Head ($5, 25 minutes),
Bangalow ($5, 25 minutes) and Mullumbimby
($5, 25 minutes).

Byron Bay Express (www.byronbayexpress.
com.au; one way/return $30/55) Four buses
daily to/from Gold Coast Airport (45 minutes)
and Surfers Paradise (1½ hours) for $30/55 one
way/return.

Byron Easy Bus (📞02-6685 7447; www.byron
bayshuttle.com.au; adult/child $20/12) Minibus
service to Brisbane ($44, three hours).

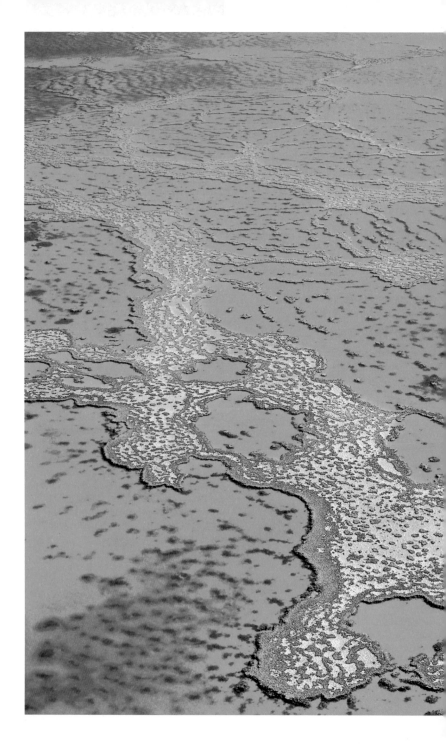

GREAT BARRIER
REEF &
THE DAINTREE

Great Barrier Reef & the Daintree at a Glance...

Tropical, touristy Cairns is unmissable. Experienced divers and first-time toe-dippers swarm to the steamy city for its easy access to the Great Barrier Reef, while the more party-prone are well served by a barrage of bars and clubs.

The winding road north hugs the ludicrously scenic shoreline en route to Port Douglas. North of here, the profuse Daintree Rainforest stretches to Cape Tribulation and beyond, tumbling onto long swaths of white-sand beach.

The Great Barrier Reef & the Daintree Rainforest in Two Days

The 'GBR' and Daintree are VAST: with just two days, do one or the other! For the reef, fly into Cairns, explore the **Esplanade, Boardwalk & Lagoon** (p123) and visit **Reef Teach** (p123) ahead of your reef trip the next day. For the Daintree, chill in **Port Douglas** (p126) for a day then day-trip into the jungle.

The Great Barrier Reef & the Daintree Rainforest in Four Days

Four days affords a little flexibility. Either base yourself around the southern reef islands and really get a feel for these tropical climes (Heron Island has some of the world's best diving); or launch into a Cairns–Great Barrier Reef–Port Douglas–Daintree four-day extravaganza.

Previous page: Hardy Reef, Great Barrier Reef

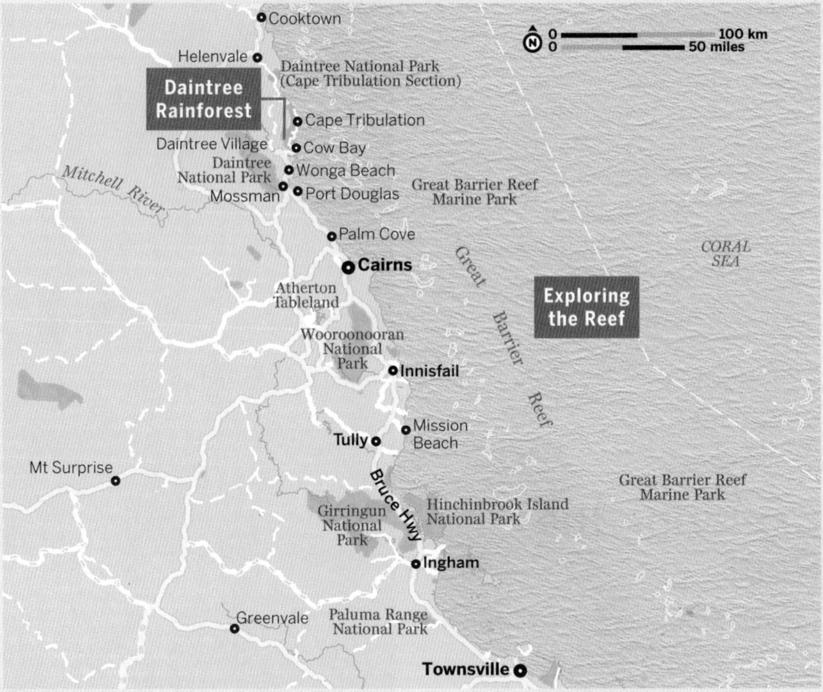

Cooktown

Helenvale

Daintree Rainforest

Daintree National Park
(Cape Tribulation Section)

Cape Tribulation

Daintree Village

Cow Bay

Daintree
National Park

Wonga Beach

Mossman

Port Douglas

Great Barrier Reef
Marine Park

Mitchell River

Palm Cove

Cairns

Atherton
Tableland

*CORAL
SEA*

**Exploring
the Reef**

Wooroonooran
National
Park

Innisfail

Mt Surprise

Tully

Mission
Beach

Bruce Hwy

Girringun
National
Park

Hinchinbrook Island
National Park

Great Barrier Reef
Marine Park

Ingham

Greenvale

Paluma Range
National Park

Townsville

100 km
50 miles

Arriving in the Great Barrier Reef & the Daintree Rainforest

Cairns is the main base for exploring the northern reef. **Cairns Airport** (p125) is 6km north of town: shuttles meet all flights, or a taxi will cost about $30. Bundaberg, Gladstone and Town of 1770 offer boat and air connections to the southern reef islands. Port Douglas, an hour's drive north of Cairns, is the natural jumping-off point for Daintree adventures.

Where to Stay

Cairns has myriad accommodation for all budgets; Port Douglas too, though businesses here are a little more geared towards the 'luxe' traveller. Most reef island resorts are distinctly high-end, though some (eg Lady Elliot Island) won't break a midrange traveller's bank. Daintree accommodation includes hostels (Cape Tribulation) and jungle B&Bs and lodges around Cape Tribulation and Cow Bay.

Exploring the Reef

There are many ways to approach this massive undersea wonder: join an organised tour from a gateway town; take a multiday sailing or diving trip; or fly to a remote island.

Great For...

❶ Need to Know

June to November is the best time to visit: not too hot, with good underwater visibility.

★ **Top Tip**
Skies grey? The reef is exponentially more colourful and glorious on a sunny day.

Picking Your Spot

Given the reef's size, it follows that there are many popular spots from which to access it – but bear in mind that the qualities of individual areas do change over time, depending on the weather, tidal shifts or recent cyclone or coral-bleaching damage.

Mainland Gateways

The major mainland reef access points all offer slightly different experiences or activities. This list is organised from south to north.

- Bundaberg
- Agnes Water & Town of 1770
- Gladstone
- Airlie Beach
- Cairns
- Port Douglas

Island Gateways

Rising above the waterline throughout the Reef are hundreds of islands and cays, offering instant access to the undersea marvels. Some of our favourite islands include lady Elliot Island and Heron Island.

Island Resorts

The Great Barrier Reef is home to over a dozen island resorts, offering varying levels of comfort and style. Where to stay depends not only on your budget, but also what sort of activities you have in mind. Some resorts are small and secluded (and don't allow children), which can be ideal for a tropical getaway doing little more than

Snorkeller in jellyfish stinger suit

sipping tropical cocktails. If this sounds ideal, try Orpheus Island. Other resorts have a busier vibe and offer a wide range of activities, from sailing and kayaking to helicopter joy rides, plus restaurants and even some nightlife.

Boat Excursions

Unless you're staying on a coral-fringed island, you'll need to join a boat excursion to experience the reef's real beauty. Day trips leave from many places along the coast, as well as from island resorts, and typically include the use of snorkelling gear, snacks and a buffet lunch, with scuba

> ## ★ Top Tip
>
> Remember never to walk on the coral: not only can it cut you badly, but it's also very fragile.

CHAMELEONSEYE/SHUTTERSTOCK ©

diving an optional extra. On some boats, naturalists or marine biologists present talks on the reef's ecology.

Boat trips vary dramatically in passenger numbers, type of vessel and quality – which is reflected in the price – so it's worth getting all the details before committing. When selecting a tour, consider the vessel (motorised catamaran or sailing ship), the number of passengers (from six to 400), what extras are offered and the destination. The outer reefs are usually more pristine. Inner reefs often show signs of damage from humans and coral-eating crown-of-thorns starfish. Coral bleaching is a major issue in far northern sections of the reef. Some operators offer the option of a trip in a glass-bottomed boat or semi-submersible.

Many boats have underwater cameras for hire, although you can save money by hiring these on land (or using your own waterproof camera or underwater housing). Some boats also have professional photographers on board who will dive and take high-quality shots of you in action.

Diving & Snorkelling the Reef

Much of the diving and snorkelling on the reef is boat-based, although there are some excellent reefs accessible by walking straight off the beach of some islands. Free use of snorkelling gear is usually part of any day cruise to the reef – you can typically fit in around three hours of underwater wandering. Overnight or live-aboard trips obviously provide a more in-depth experience and greater coverage of the reefs.

If you don't have a diving certificate, many operators offer the option of an introductory dive, where an experienced diver conducts an underwater tour. A lesson in safety and procedure is given beforehand and you don't require a five-day Professional Association of Diving Instructors (PADI) course or a 'buddy'.

Top Reef Dive Spots

The Great Barrier Reef is home to some of the world's best diving sites. Here are a few of our favourite spots to get you started:

SS Yongala A sunken shipwreck that has been home to a vivid marine community for more than 90 years.

Cod Hole Go nose-to-nose with a potato cod.

Heron Island Join a crowd of colourful fish straight off the beach.

Lady Elliot Island With 19 highly regarded dive sites.

Wheeler Reef Massive variety of marine life, plus a great spot for night dives.

Top Snorkelling Sites

Some non-divers may wonder if it's really worth going to the Great Barrier Reef 'just to snorkel'. The answer is a resounding 'Yes!' Much of the rich, colourful coral lies just underneath the surface (as coral needs bright sunlight to flourish) and is easily accessible. Here's a round-up of what we think are the top snorkelling sites:

- Fitzroy Reef Lagoon (Town of 1770)
- Heron Island (Capricorn Coast)
- Great Keppel Island (Capricorn Coast)
- Lady Elliot Island (Capricorn Coast)
- Lady Musgrave Island (Capricorn Coast)
- Lizard Island (Cairns)
- Michaelmas Reef (Cairns)
- Hastings Reef (Cairns)
- Norman Reef (Cairns)
- Saxon Reef (Cairns)
- Green Island (Cairns)

Trips from Cairns

Reef trips generally include transport, lunch, stinger-suits and snorkelling gear. When choosing a tour, consider the vessel type, its capacity, inclusions and destination: outer reefs are more pristine but further afield; inner reefs can be patchy and show signs of decay. Some prefer smaller, less-crowded vessels, while others go for the wide range of inclusions bigger boats promise.

Vendors with their own pontoon offer all-round value: pontoons are a great way for families to experience the reef – those who aren't keen on getting in the water can enjoy the pontoon's facilities, or a trip in a glass-bottomed boat or semi-submersible.

Almost all boats depart from the Marlin Wharf (with check in and booking facilities located inside the Reef Fleet Terminal) around 8am, returning around 6pm. Smaller operators may check-in boat-side at their berth on the wharf itself; check with your operator.

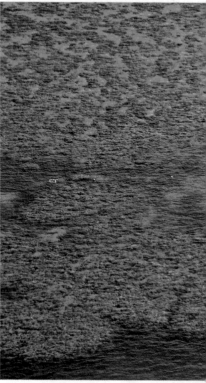

Tour boat docked on a pontoon, Great Barrier Reef

Recommended operators include the following:

Tusa Dive (📞07-4047 9100; www.tusadive.com; cnr Shields St & Esplanade; adult/child day trips from $215/140, introductory dive $285/210) 🐟 A maximum of 60 passengers aboard the custom-designed reef vessel (the *T6*), a roving outer-reef permit and a high staff-to-passenger ratio make this operator an excellent choice for day trips.

Reef Magic (📞07-4031 1588; www.reefmagic-cruises.com; Reef Fleet Terminal; adult/child/family day trips from $220/110/557; 👪) A long-time family favourite, Reef Magic's high-speed cat sails to its all-weather Marine World pontoon moored on the edge of the outer reef. If you're water shy, try a glass-bottomed boat ride, chat with the marine biologist or have a massage!

Great Adventures (📞07-4044 9944; www.greatadventures.com.au; Reef Fleet Terminal; adult/child/family day trips from $236/125/597; 👪) Great Adventures runs trips to Green Island and the outer Great Barrier Reef aboard its fast catamaran. Diving add-ons, and glass-bottomed boat, semi-submersible and Scuba Doo underwater scooter tours are also available.

❶ Did You Know?

The Great Barrier Reef is approximately 8000 years old and is around the size of Germany.

Daintree Rainforest

The impossibly lush Daintree represents many things: World Heritage–listed rainforest, a river, a reef, laid-back villages and the home of its traditional custodians, the Kuku Yalanji people.

Great For...

☑ Don't Miss

A long beach-combing amble along Cape Tribulation Beach or Myall Beach at Cape Trib.

An Amazing Rainforest

Upon entering the forest, you'll be enveloped by a cacophony of birdsong, frog croaking and the buzz of insects. Continue exploring the area via wildlife-spotting night tours, mountain treks, interpretive boardwalks, canopy walks, self-guided walking trails, 4WD trips, horse riding, kayaking, croc-spotting cruises, tropical-fruit orchard tours and tastings...Whew! If you're lucky, you might even spot a cassowary.

History, Controversy & Control

The greater Daintree Rainforest is protected as part of Daintree National Park, but this protection is not without controversy. In 1983, despite conservationist blockades, what's now the Bloomfield Track was bulldozed through lowland rainforest from Cape Tribulation to the Bloomfield River.

Aerial walkway at the Daintree Discovery Centre (p128)

❶ Need to Know

Daintree Rainforest (www.daintreerain forest.com)

✕ Take a Break

Mason's Store & Cafe (p129) in Cape Tribulation is a one-stop-shop for food, booze and info.

★ Top Tip

The water of the Daintree River looks inviting: the resident saltwater crocodiles agree.

Ensuing publicity led to the federal government nominating Queensland's wet tropical rainforests for World Heritage listing, generating state government and timber industry opposition. In 1988 the area was inscribed on the World Heritage List and commercial logging here was banned.

Unesco World Heritage listing (www.whc. unesco.org) doesn't affect ownership rights or control. Since the 1990s the Queensland government and conservation agencies have attempted to buy back and rehabilitate freehold properties in the area, adding them to the Daintree National Park. Sealing the road to Cape Tribulation in 2002 triggered the buy-back of even more land, which, coupled with development controls, now bears the fruits of forest regeneration. Check out Rainforest Rescue (www.rainforestrescue. org.au) for more information.

Daintree Tours

Cape Tribulation Wilderness Cruises
Boating

(📞0457 731 000; www.capetribcruises.com; Cape Tribulation Rd; adult/child from $34/24) This is the only tour boat permitted in the Cape Trib section of the Daintree National Park, cruising Cooper Creek in search of crocs. Book ahead.

Cooper Creek Wilderness
Walking

(📞07-4098 9126; www.coopercreek.com.au; 2333 Cape Tribulation Rd; guided walks $70-185) Book ahead for expert guided rainforest walks that include a dip in Cooper Creek. A variety of itineraries are available.

Tony's Tropical Tours
Tours

(📞07-4099 3230; www.tropicaltours.com.au) 🍃 This luxury, small-group (eight to 10 passengers) tour operator, based in Port Douglas, specialises in trips to out-of-the-way sections of the Mossman Gorge and Daintree Rainforest (adult/child $185/160).

For more on the Daintree see p128.

Southern Reef Islands

While much fuss is made about the Great Barrier Reef's northern splendour, the Southern Reef Islands are the place of 'castaway' dreams: tiny coral atolls fringed with sugary white sand and turquoise-blue seas, and hardly anyone within flipper-flapping reach. From beautiful Lady Elliot Island, 80km northeast of Bundaberg, secluded and uninhabited coral reefs and atolls dot the ocean for about 140km up to Tryon Island. Access is from Town of 1770 and Gladstone.

Lady Elliot Island

Set on the southern rim of the Great Barrier Reef, Lady Elliot is a 40-hectare vegetated coral cay populated with nesting sea turtles and an impressive number of seabirds. It's considered to have the best snorkelling in the southern Great Barrier Reef and the diving is good too.

Lady Elliot Island is not a national park, and camping is not allowed; your only option is the low-key **Lady Elliot Island Eco**

Resort (☏1800 072 200; www.ladyelliot.com.au; r with half board & activities $185-450, child $130).

The only way to reach the island is in a light aircraft. Resort guests are flown in from Bundaberg, the Gold Coast and Hervey Bay. The resort also manages fantastic, great-value day trips for around $365, including a scenic flight, a snorkelling tour and lunch.

Lady Musgrave Island

Wannabe castaways look no further. This tiny, 15-hectare cay, 100km northeast of Bundaberg, sits on the western rim of a stunning, turquoise-blue reef lagoon renowned for its safe swimming, snorkelling and diving. A squeaky, white-sand beach fringes a dense canopy of pisonia forest brimming with roosting bird life, including terns, shearwaters and white-capped noddies. Birds nest from October to April while green turtles nest from November to February.

Day trips ($205) to Lady Musgrave depart from Bundaberg as part of the **Lady Musgrave Experience** (☏0427 009 922; www.ladymusgraveexperience.com.au; Shop 5,

Heron Island

GEKKO GALLERY/SHUTTERSTOCK ©

15-17 Marina Drive, Burnett Heads, Bundaberg Port Marina; adult/child/family $218/118/599; 🚗)

Heron Island

Part of the smaller Capricornia Cays group, Heron Island is ranked among the finest scuba diving spots in the world, particularly in terms of ease of access. Visitors to Heron generally know what they are coming for – underwater paradise – but the island's rugged beauty is reason enough to stay above the surface. There's **Heron Island Resort** (📞1800 875 343; www.heronisland.com; d/ste from $347/589; ❄) and a research station on the northeastern third of the island; the remainder is national park.

The Heron Islander (📞1800 875 343; www.heronisland.com; one way adult/child $64/32) departs Gladstone daily at 2pm (adult/child one way $62/31, 2½ hours).

For a more glamorous approach, take a **seaplane** (📞1800 875 343; www.heronisland. com; one way $349).

ⓘ GETTING THERE & AWAY

Depending on their remoteness, the Southern Reef Islands are accessible from mainland by boat (from Town of 1770) or plane or helicopter (from Bundaberg, Gladstone or Hervey Bay).

ⓘ GETTING AROUND

Once on the islands, boats organised by the resorts or local operators are the only means of transport.

Agnes Water & Town of 1770

Happily tucked away a decent distance from Bundaberg or Gladstone, on gorgeous coastal lands owned traditionally by the Gureng Gureng people, these two idyllic little beach towns retain an unfussy charm that is seaside Australia at its best.

Agnes Water has the east coast's most northerly surf beach, a sleepy commercial centre, and some excellent hostels. Just 8km up the road is the site of Captain Cook's first landing in Queensland, in 1770.

🤿 Looking After the Reef

The Great Barrier Reef is incredibly fragile: it's worth taking some time to educate yourself on responsible practices to minimise the impact of your visit. It is an offence to damage or remove coral in the marine park.

○ If you touch or walk on coral, you'll damage it (and probably get some nasty cuts).

○ Don't touch or harass marine animals, and don't enter the water near a dugong.

○ If you have a boat, be aware of the rules in relation to anchoring around the reef, including 'no anchoring areas' to avoid coral damage.

○ If you're diving, check that you are weighted correctly before entering the water and keep your buoyancy control well away from the reef. Ensure that equipment such as secondary regulators and gauges aren't dragging over the reef.

○ Hire a wetsuit or a 'rashie' rather than slathering on sunscreen, which can damage the reef.

○ Watch where your fins are – try not to stir up sediment or disturb coral.

○ Note that there are limits on the amount and types of shells that you can collect.

MYRIAM B/SHUTTERSTOCK ©

Kuranda Scenic Railway

Winding 34km from Cairns to Kuranda through picturesque mountains, the track used by the **Kuranda Scenic Railway** (☑07-4036 9333; www.ksr.com.au; adult/child one way from $50/25, return from $76/38; 🎫) was completed in 1891: workers dug tunnels by hand, battling sickness, steep terrain and venomous creatures. The two-hour pleasure trip includes seating in heritage-style carriages, audio commentary, souvenir trip guide and a stop at the Barron Falls viewing platform.

Trains depart Cairns Central Railway Station (p125) at 8.30am and 9.30am daily, returning from Kuranda station at 2pm and 3.30pm. Kuranda Scenic Railway and **Skyrail Rainforest Cableway** (☑07-4038 5555; www.skyrail.com.au; cnr Cook Hwy & Cairns Western Arterial Rd, Smithfield; adult/child one way from $53/26.50, return from $79/39.50; 🕘9am-5.15pm; 🎫) ✏ offer combination tickets (adult/child from $112.50/56.25): take the railway up and the cableway back down.

Kuranda Scenic Railway Station
ADRIANOK/SHUTTERSTOCK ©

🏃 ACTIVITIES

1770 Liquid Adventures   Kayaking
(☑0428 956 630; www.1770liquidadventures.com.au) This experienced outfit makes the most of 1770's delightful surrounds on its sunset tours (from $55). You'll be guided around the usually placid waters off Eurimbula National Park, before retiring to Bustard Bay beach for drinks and snacks in the gloaming – keep an eye out for dolphins. You can also rent kayaks for self-directed fun ($20/25 single/double kayaks per hour).

🍴 EATING

Getaway Garden Café   Cafe $$
(☑07-4974 9323; www.1770getaway.com.au; 303 Bicentennial Dr, Agnes Water; breakfast & lunch mains $18-20, dinner per person $28; 🕘8am-2.30pm Sun-Fri, with booking 5.30-7.30pm Wed & Sun; 🍴) This open-sided, teak-doored pavilion, set in restful tropical gardens popular with local wildlife, is the venue for some of the best food in Agnes. Dealing primarily in breakfast and lunch (eggs Benedict with brisket on brioche will set you up; a vibrant salad with grilled halloumi will keep you going), it also does a mean coffee and cake.

ℹ️ INFORMATION

Agnes Water Visitor Information Centre
(☑07-4902 1533; www.visitagnes1770.com.au; 71 Springs Rd, Agnes Water; 🕘8.30am-4.30pm Mon-Fri, 9am-4pm Sat, to 1pm Sun)

Discover 1770 (☑07-4974 7557; www.discover1770.com.au; cnr Round Hill Rd & Captain Cook Dr, Agnes Water; 🕘8.30am-5.30pm)

ℹ️ GETTING THERE & AWAY

Greyhound (☑1300 473 946; www.greyhound.com.au) buses detour off the Bruce Hwy to Agnes Water; daily services include Bundaberg ($29, 1½ hours) and Cairns ($244, 22½ hours).

Cairns

Cairns (pronounced 'cans') has come a long way since its humble beginnings as a boggy swamp and rollicking goldfields port. As the number-one base for Far North Queensland and the Great Barrier Reef, today Cairns heaves under the weight of an ever-growing number of resorts, tour agencies, souvenir shops, backpacker bars and reef boats. This is a tourist town, and unashamedly so.

The city centre is more boardshorts than briefcases. There's no beach in town, but spend time at the Esplanade lagoon or the Pier marina and you'll understand why many travellers fall for Cairns.

The Cairns region is the traditional land of the Yirrganydji and Yidinji peoples.

◎ SIGHTS & ACTIVITIES

Cairns Esplanade, Boardwalk & Lagoon Waterfront
(www.cairns.qld.gov.au/esplanade; ◷lagoon 6am-9pm Thu-Tue, noon-9pm Wed; ⊕) FREE Sunseekers and fun-lovers flock to Cairns Esplanade's spectacular **swimming lagoon** on the city's reclaimed foreshore. The artificial, sandy-edged, 4800-sq-metre saltwater pool with its Woven Fish sculptures, is lifeguard patrolled and illuminated nightly. The adjacent 3km foreshore **boardwalk** has picnic areas, birdwatching vantage points, free BBQs and fitness equipment. Follow the signposts for the excellent **Muddy's** (www.cairns.qld.gov.au; Esplanade; ⊕) FREE, which has playgrounds and water fun for little kids, and the skate ramp, beach volleyball courts, bouldering park and Fun Ship playground.

Tjapukai Aboriginal Cultural Park Cultural Centre
(☏07-4042 9999; www.tjapukai.com.au; Cairns Western Arterial Rd; adult/child/family $62/42/166; ◷9am-4.30pm & 7-9.30pm; ⊕) ⊘ Managed by the area's original custodians, this award-winning cultural extravaganza tells the story of creation using giant holograms and actors. There's a dance theatre, a gallery, boomerang- and spear-throwing demonstrations and turtle-spotting canoe rides. The **Nightfire** dinner-and-show package (adult/child/family $123/75/321, from 7pm to 9.30pm) culminates in a fireside corroboree.

Reef Teach Cultural Centre
(☏07-4031 7794; www.reefteach.com.au; 2nd fl, Mainstreet Arcade, 85 Lake St; adult/child/family $23/14/60; ◷lectures 6.30-8.30pm Mon, Wed, Fri) ⊘ Take your knowledge to new depths

at this fun, informative centre, where marine experts explain how to identify specific species of fish and coral, and how to approach the reef respectfully.

ⓐ SHOPPING

Rusty's Markets Market
(☏07-4040 2705; www.rustysmarkets.com.au; 57-89 Grafton St; ◷5am-6pm Fri & Sat, to 3pm Sun) No weekend in Cairns is complete without a visit to this busy and vibrant multicultural market. Weave (and taste) your way through piles of seasonal tropical fruits, veggies and herbs, plus farm-fresh honey, locally grown flowers, excellent coffees, curries, cold drinks, antiques and more.

⊗ EATING

Ganbaranba Japanese $
(☏07-4031 2522; 14 Spence St; mains $10-14; ◷11.30am-2.30pm & 5.30-8.30pm) Ganbaranba is a cult joint, and without a doubt the best place for ramen noodles and gyoza in Cairns. Slurpers can watch the chefs making noodles; if the view proves too tempting, you can ask for a refill for a mere $1.50. Absolutely worth the wait.

Fusion Art Bar & Tapas Tapas $$
(☏07-4051 3888; www.fusionartbar.com.au; 12 Spence St; tapas $9-20, mains $19-35; ◷3-10pm Tue-Thu, 11am-11pm Fri & Sat; ☜) Everything in this crazy-cool cafe is a piece of art and there's a real eclectic charm to everything from the furniture to the thoughtfully designed tapas menu of cured kangaroo tartare or pumpkin ravioli. Share plates feature vegan paella and pork ribs with mash and pineapple. Good wine list and coffee.

Perrotta's at the Gallery Mediterranean $$
(☏07-4031 5899; 38 Abbott St; mains $13-29; ◷6.30am-10pm; ⊘) This unmissable eatery, attached to the **Cairns Art Gallery** (☏07-4046 4800; www.cairnsregionalgallery.com.au; cnr Abbott & Shields Sts; ◷9am-5pm Mon-Fri,

Cairns Esplanade (p123)

10am-5pm Sat, 10am-2pm Sun) FREE, tempts you onto its covered deck with splendid gourmet breakfasts (6.30am to 3pm), fresh juices, barista coffee and an inventive Mediterranean-inspired lunch and dinner menu. It's a chic spot with an interesting crowd and ideal people-watching perches.

Ochre Modern Australian $$$
(☑07-4051 0100; www.ochrerestaurant.com. au; Marlin Pde; mains $20-42; ☺11.30am-3pm & 5.30-9.30pm) The menu at this innovative waterfront restaurant utilises native Aussie fauna (such as salt and native pepper-leaf crocodile and prawns or wallaby fillet) and flora (wattle-seed, lemon myrtle or Davidson plum glaze). Tablelands steaks are cooked to perfection. Can't decide? Order a tasting plate (six courses from $105) or a platter ($30 to $76).

🍷 DRINKING & NIGHTLIFE

Green Ant Cantina Microbrewery
(☑07-4041 5061; www.greenantcantina.com; 183 Bunda St; ☺4pm-late Tue-Sat) Behind the train station, this grungy, rockin' Tex-Mex

bar is an ace and arty alternative hangout. Smothered in bright murals, the Green Ant brews its own beers (seven varieties, including a strong brown ale) and hosts regular music events. It also does fab food, including pulled-pork quesadillas, jambalaya and the infamous, blistering Wings of Death.

Salt House Bar
(☑07-4041 7733; www.salthouse.com.au; 6/2 Pierpoint Rd; ☺6.30am-2am) On the waterfront by the yacht club, Cairns' coolest, classiest bar caters to a hip and happy crowd. With killer cocktails, tremendous views, live music and DJs, and a superb Mod-Oz nibbles-and-mains menu, the Salt House is absolutely not to be missed. The pizzeria here is justifiably popular.

ℹ️ INFORMATION

The Cairns Regional Council's website (www. cairns.qld.gov.au/region/tourist-information) has tonnes of details on events, activities and transport in the region.

The government-run but volunteer-staffed visitor centre has surprisingly closed. That leaves the many private information and booking offices around town; they all book the same trips at similar prices, but you can usually get better deals booking through your accommodation, especially at backpacker hostels.

There are several medical centres in Cairns; the **Cairns 24 Hour Medical Centre** (☑07-4052 1119; cnr Grafton & Florence Sts; ⏱24hr) never closes and accepts walk-ins. There are pharmacies (chemists) on almost every corner of the city.

❶ GETTING THERE & AWAY

AIR

Qantas (☑13 13 13; www.qantas.com.au), **Virgin Australia** (☑13 67 89; www.virginaustralia.com) and **Jetstar** (☑13 15 38; www.jetstar.com.au), and a handful of international carriers, arrive at and depart from **Cairns Airport** (☑07-4080 6703; www.cairnsairport.com; Airport Ave), approximately 6km from the city centre, with direct services to all Australian capital cities except Canberra and Hobart.

BUS

Long-distance buses arrive at and depart from the **Interstate Coach Terminal** (Reef Fleet Terminal), Cairns Central Railway Station and the **Cairns Transit Mall** (Lake St). Operators include the following:

Greyhound Australia (☑1300 473 946; www.greyhound.com.au)

Premier Motor Service (☑13 34 10; www.premierms.com.au)

Sun Palm (☑07-4087 2900; www.sunpalmtransport.com.au; Cairns Airport)

CAR & MOTORCYCLE

Major car-rental companies have airport and city (usually on Sheridan St) branches.

TRAIN

The Kuranda Scenic Railway (p122) runs daily; the **Savannahlander** (☑07-4053 6848; www.savannahlander.com.au; tours adult/child from $380/260) offers a miscellany of rail journeys into the outback from **Cairns Central Railway Station** (Bunda St).

Queensland Rail (☑1300 131 722; www.queenslandrailtravel.com.au) operates services between Brisbane and Cairns.

❶ GETTING AROUND

TO/FROM THE AIRPORT

Many hotels and hostels offer courtesy pick-up. Sun Palm meets incoming flights until about 6.30pm and runs a shuttle (adult/child $15/7.50) directly to your accommodation; its **Airport Connect Shuttle** ($6) runs between the airport and a stop on Sheridan St just north of town. **Cairns Airport Shuttle** (☑0432 488 783; www.cairnsairportshuttle.com.au) is a good option for groups; the more passengers, the cheaper the fare. Taxis to the city centre cost around $25 (plus $4 airport surcharge).

TAXI

Cairns Taxis (☑13 10 08, 07-4048 8333; www.cairnstaxis.com.au)

Mossman Gorge

In the southeast corner of Daintree National Park, 5km west of Mossman town (itself 20km north of Port Douglas), Mossman Gorge forms part of the traditional lands of the Kuku Yalanji people. The gorge is a boulder-strewn valley where sparkling water washes over ancient rocks. It's 3km by road from the **visitor centre** (☑07-4099 7000; www.mossmangorge.com.au; ⏱8am-6pm) to a viewpoint and refreshing swimming hole – take care as the currents can be swift. Walk the 3km or take the shuttle bus.

Port Douglas

Welcome to your holiday. Port Douglas (Port or PD) is equal parts flash and fun, from the million-dollar marina to the dreamy Four Mile Beach and the five-star resorts big enough to warrant their own postcode. A growing number of flashpackers, cashed-up couples and fiscally flush families choose Port Douglas over Cairns as their Far North base, and for good reason.

The peninsula was the traditional home of the Yirrganydji people.

◉ SIGHTS

Wildlife Habitat
Port Douglas   Zoo
(📞07-4099 3235; www.wildlifehabitat.com.au; Port Douglas Rd; adult/child/family $36/18/90; ⏰8am-5pm; 🚼) 🌿 This sanctuary endeavours to keep and showcase native animals in enclosures that mimic their natural environment, while allowing you to get up close to koalas, kangaroos, crocs, cassowaries and more. Tickets are valid for three days.

For an extra special experience book for **Breakfast with the Birds** (www.wildlife habitat.com.au; Wildlife Habitat Port Douglas, Port Douglas Rd; breakfast incl admission $56; ⏰9-10.30am; 🚼) or **Lunch with the Lorikeets** (www.wildlifehabitat.com.au; Wildlife Habitat Port Douglas, Port Douglas Rd; adult incl admission $58; ⏰noon-2pm; 🚼). The latest addition is the Predator Plank – a walkway across the saltwater croc enclosure. It's 5km from town ($5 by shuttle bus).

Four Mile Beach   Beach
(🚼) Fringed by lazy palms, this broad stretch of squeaky sand reaches as far as you can squint. There's a patrolled swimming area in front of the surf life-saving club (with a stinger net in summer) and sun loungers available for hire.

Trinity Bay Lookout   Viewpoint
(Island Point Rd) FREE Head up to Flagstaff Hill for sensational views over Four Mile Beach and the Coral Sea. Drive or walk up via Wharf St, or there's a walking path leading up from the north end of Four Mile Beach.

❸ ACTIVITIES

Wind Swell   Water Sports
(📞0427 498 042; www.windswell.com.au; Barrier St; lessons from $50) Kitesurfing and stand-up paddleboarding for everyone from beginners to high-flyers. Kitesurfing lessons and paddleboarding tours from the beach start at $50, but there are also plenty of advanced options. Find them in action at the southern end of Four Mile Beach.

❺ TOURS

Quicksilver   Cruise
(📞07-4087 2100; www.quicksilver-cruises. com; Crystalbrook Marina; adult/child/family $257/132/625) Major operator with fast cruises to its private pontoon on Agincourt Reef. Additional activities include an 'ocean walk' helmet dive ($170) on a submerged platform, introductory diving ($172), certified dive ($124) or snorkelling with a marine biologist (from $64). Also offers 10-minute scenic helicopter flights ($189, minimum two passengers).

Reef Sprinter   Snorkelling
(📞07-4099 6127; www.reefsprinter.com.au; Shop 3, Crystalbrook Marina; adult/child from $130/110; 🚼) The fastest way to the reef, this 2¼-hour snorkelling trip gets to the Low Isles in just 15 minutes for one to 1½ hours in the water. Half-day outer reef trips are also available (from $200).

Tony's
Tropical Tours   Tours
(📞07-4099 3230; www.tropicaltours.com.au; day tours adult/child from $198/178) 🌿 This luxury, small-group (eight to 10 passengers) tour operator specialises in trips to out-of-the-way sections of the Mossman Gorge and Daintree Rainforest ($185/160 adult/child).

🔒 SHOPPING

Port Douglas Markets   Market
(Anzac Park, Macrossan St; ⊘8am-2pm Sun)
PD's Sunday market is legendary for its
locally made crafts and jewellery, health-
care products, local tropical fruits and fresh
produce.

✖ EATING

Yachty   Modern Australian **$$**
(⍾07-4099 4386; www.portdouglasyachtclub.
com.au; 1 Spinnaker Close; mains $20-32;
⊘noon-2.30pm & 5.30-8pm) One of the
best-value nights out is the local yacht club,
where well-crafted meals, from seafood pie
to Thai green curry, are served nightly with
sunset views over Dickson Inlet. The lunch
menu is similar but cheaper.

**Flames of
the Forest**   Modern Australian **$$$**
(⍾07-4099 3144; www.flamesoftheforest.com.
au; dinner with show, drinks & transfers per
person $192-220; ⊘Tue, Thu & Sat) This unique
experience goes way beyond the traditional
concept of 'dinner and a show', with diners
escorted deep into the rainforest for a
truly immersive night of theatre, culture
and gourmet cuisine. Transport provided
from Port Douglas or Cairns (no self-drive).
Bookings essential.

**Harrisons
Restaurant**   Modern Australian **$$$**
(⍾0455 594 011; www.harrisonsrestaurant.
com.au; Sheraton Grand Mirage; mains $38-54;
⊘4pm-midnight) Marco Pierre White–trained
chef-owner Spencer Patrick whips up culi-
nary gems that stand toe to toe with Aus-
tralia's best. Fresh, locally sourced produce
is turned into dishes such as smoked duck
breast and tamarind beef cheeks. Originally
on Wharf St, Harrisons is now ensconsed in
the flash Sheraton Grand Mirage.

🍷 DRINKING & NIGHTLIFE

Hemingway's   Microbrewery
(⍾07-4099 6663; www.hemingwaysbrewery.
com; Crystalbrook Marina, 44 Wharf St) Hem-
ingway's makes the most of a fabulous
location at the marina with a broad deck,

Port Douglas

Daintree Village

For wildlife lovers and birdwatchers, it's well worth taking the 20km each-way detour from the Mossman-Daintree Rd to tiny Daintree Village, set on a plateau of farmland on the Upper Daintree River. Croc-spotting cruises are the main event.

Try long-running **Crocodile Express** (☑07-4098 6120; www.crocodileexpress.com; 1hr cruises adult/child/family $28/14/65; ⏱cruises 8.30am; 🐾), **Daintree River Wild Watch** (☑0447 734 933; www.daintree riverwildwatch.com.au; 2hr cruises adult/child $60/35; 🐾), which has informative sunrise birdwatching cruises and sunset photography nature cruises, or **Daintree River Cruise Centre** (☑07-4098 6115; www.daintreerivercruisecentre.com.au; 2914 Mossman-Daintree Rd; adult/child $30/15/80; ⏱9.30am-4pm; 🐾).

Cassowary, Daintree National Park
TORSTEN PURSCHE/SHUTTERSTOCK ©

a long bar and Dickson Inlet views. There are usually six brews on tap, including Hard Yards dark lager and Pitchfork Betty's pale ale. Naturally, food is available, but this is one for the beer connoisseurs. A tasting paddle is $15.

🛈 INFORMATION

There's no official government-accredited visitor information centre in Port Douglas, but there are lots of private bookings agents, such as **Port Douglas Tourist Information Centre** (☑07-4099 5599; www.infoportdouglas.com.au; 23 Macrossan St; ⏱8am-6.30pm).

🛈 GETTING THERE & AWAY

Port Douglas Bus (☑07-4099 5665; www.port douglasbus.com.au; 53-61 Macrossan St) and Sun Palm (p125) operate daily between Port Douglas, Cairns and Cairns airport.

Trans North (☑07-4095 8644; www.transnorth bus.com.au) picks up in Port Douglas on the coastal drive between Cairns and Cooktown.

The Daintree

The Daintree represents many things: Unesco World Heritage–listed rainforest (p118), a river, a reef, laid-back villages and the home of its traditional custodians, the Kuku Yalanji people.

Part of the Wet Tropics World Heritage Area, the spectacular region from the Daintree River north to Cape Tribulation features ancient rainforest, sandy beaches and rugged mountains. North of the Daintree River, electricity is supplied by generators or, increasingly, solar power. Shops and services are limited, and mobile-phone reception is patchy at best. The **Daintree River Ferry** (www.douglas.qld. gov.au/community/daintree-ferry; car one way/return $16/28, motorcycle $6/11, pedestrian & bicycle $1/2; ⏱6am-midnight), one of the few cable ferries of its kind in Australia, carries wanderers and their wheels across the river every 15 minutes or so.

Cow Bay & Around

Tiny Cow Bay is the first community you reach after the Daintree ferry crossing. The white-sand and mostly deserted **Cow Bay Beach**, 5km east of the main road at the end of Buchanan Creek Rd, rivals any coastal paradise.

⊙ SIGHTS

Daintree Discovery Centre Nature Reserve
(☑07-4098 9171; www.discoverthedaintree. com; Tulip Oak Rd; adult/child/family $35/16/85; ⏱8.30am-5pm; 🐾) 🍃 This award-winning attraction's **aerial walkway**, which includes

a 23m tower used to study carbon levels, takes you high into the forest canopy. A theatre screens films on cassowaries, crocodiles, conservation and climate change. An excellent audio-guide tour and interpretive booklet is included in the admission fee; tickets are valid for re-entry for seven days.

EATING

Daintree Ice Cream
Company   Ice Cream $

(☑07-4098 9114; www.daintreeicecream.com.au; Lot 100, Cape Tribulation Rd; ice-cream tasting cup $7.50; ☺11am-5pm) We dare you to drive past this all-natural ice-cream producer with a range of flavours that changes daily. The tasting cup includes four flavours – you might get macadamia, black sapote, wattleseed or soursop, but they're all delicious.

Cape Tribulation

Cape Trib is at the end of the winding sealed road from the Daintree River and, with its two magnificent beaches, **Myall** and **Cape Tribulation**, laid-back vibe and rainforest walks, it's a little slice of tropical paradise.

TOURS

Ocean Safari   Snorkelling

(☑07-4098 0006; www.oceansafari.com.au; Cape Tribulation Rd; adult/child/family $149/97/447; ☺8am & noon) Ocean Safari leads small groups (25 people maximum) on morning and afternoon snorkelling cruises to the Great Barrier Reef, just half an hour offshore by fast inflatable. Swimming with sea turtles is a highlight. Wetsuit hire ($8) available.

Jungle Surfing
Canopy Tours   Outdoors

(☑07-4098 0043; www.junglesurfing.com.au; Cape Tribulation Rd; zip lines $105, night walks $45; ☺8am-5.30pm, night walks 7.30pm) Get right up into the rainforest on an exhilarating two-hour flying-fox (zip-line) surf through the canopy. Guided night walks follow biologist-guides who shed light on the rainforest after dark. Rates include pick-up from Cape Trib accommodation (self-drive not permitted).

EATING

Mason's Store & Cafe   Cafe $

(☑07-4098 0016; 3781 Cape Tribulation Rd; mains $9-18, tasting plates from $29; ☺10am-4pm) Everyone calls into Mason's for **tourist info** (☑07-4098 0070; ☺8am-5pm), the liquor store (open until 5.30pm), or to dine out on exotic meats. Pride of place on the menu at this laid-back al fresco cafe goes to the croc burger, but you can also try camel, emu and kangaroo in burgers or tasting plates. A short walk away is a crystal-clear, croc-free swimming hole ($1).

Whet   Australian $$

(☑07-4098 0007; www.whet.net.au; 1 Cape Tribulation Rd; lunch $16-20, dinner $20-35; ☺11am-3pm & 6-8pm) ✒ Whet is regarded as Cape Trib's most sophisticated place to eat, with a loungey cocktail-bar feel and romantic, candlelit, al fresco dining. Tempura wild barramundi and house chicken curry grace the menu; all lunch dishes are under $20. You'll often find locals at the bar and the owners pride themselves on fresh produce and eco-friendly processes.

GETTING THERE & AWAY

The road to Cape Trib is sealed so it's suitable for any hire vehicle.

Trans North (☑07-4095 8644; www.transnorthbus.com; Cairns Central Railway Station) runs buses from Cairns to Cape Tribulation three times a week year-round.

THE
WHITSUNDAYS

The Whitsundays at a Glance...

Seen from above, the Whitsundays archipelago resembles an organism under a microscope: a mesmerising mosaic of indigo, aqua, yellow and bottle-green blobs. Sheltered by the Great Barrier Reef, these waters are perfect for sailing – any of the 74 islands will hypnotise on approach and leave you giddy with your good fortune.

Five islands here have resorts, but most are uninhabited. Whitehaven Beach is the finest beach in the Whitsundays and, many claim, the world. Airlie Beach, on the mainland, is the major gateway to the islands, where you can book myriad tours and activities, or just party.

The Whitsundays in Two Days

Get your bearings (then forget where you put them) in **Airlie Beach** (p136), one of Queensland's great party towns. Shake off your efforts the next day with a day trip out to see the sea – perhaps to **Daydream Island** (p139), where hair-of-the-dog bars entice. Alternatively, **Ocean Rafting** (p137) runs excellent high-speed day trips to Whitehaven Beach.

The Whitsundays in Four Days

With four days to play with, book yourself onto a longer sailing jaunt, perhaps a two-nighter taking in **Whitehaven Beach** (p138) on Whitsunday Island, and **Hook Island** (p140) with lots of snorkelling and wildlife-spotting. Or, just check yourself into the flashy **Hayman Island Resort** (p141) and chill to the absolute max.

Arriving in the Whitsundays

The two main entry points for the Whitsundays are Airlie Beach, on the mainland, and the resort island of Hamilton Island, which has a major domestic airport, with connections to Sydney, Melbourne, Brisbane and Cairns. Airlie Beach is on Queensland's major coastal bus route between Brisbane and Cairns.

Sleeping

Airlie Beach is a backpacker haven, but hostel standards vary wildly. There is also a remarkable variety of midrange accommodation here, which is particularly suitable for families. For a more top-end experience, head to the swish island resort of your choice: Hamilton, Daydream and Hayman islands top the list. You can also camp on some islands: see www.npsr.qld.gov.au.

Sailing in the Whitsundays

The Whitsundays are the place to skim across fantasy-blue waters on a tropical breeze. Most sailing trips offer snorkelling on colourful fringing reefs; diving and other activities are often optional extras.

Great For

☑ Don't Miss

The staggeringly photogenic Whitehaven Beach, often acclaimed as Australia's finest.

Day Trip or Overnighter?

Other than super-fast boat trips run by the likes of Ocean Rafting (p137) and **Big Fury** (☎0418 782 266; www.magicwhitsundays.com; adult/child/family $170/105/510), most yachts can't reach Whitehaven Beach on day trips from Airlie. Instead, they usually go to the lovely Langford Reef and Hayman Island; check before you book.

Most overnight sailing packages are for three days and two nights, or two days and two nights – plenty of time to see the best bits of the archipelago.

Crewing

In return for a free bunk, meals and a sailing adventure, crewing will see you hoisting the mainsail and cleaning the head. Look for

Whitehaven Beach (p138)

AUTAUJ/SHUTTERSTOCK ©

ℹ Need to Know

Sailing here is best between August and October (mild weather, calm seas).

✕ Take a Break

Daydream Island Resort (p139) has a clutch of bars and restaurants open to non-residents.

★ Top Tip

If you're aboard a smaller boat without a bar, you can usually BYO bottles.

offers the least expensive, yet consistently good, sailing tours to the islands.

Prima Sailing   Boating

(☑1800 550 751; www.primasailing.com.au; 2-day, 2-night tours from $499) Fun tours with a 12-person maximum. Ideal for couples chasing style and substance.

Booking Your Boat

If you're flexible with dates, last-minute stand-by rates can considerably reduce costs. Many travellers hang out in Airlie for a few days for this exact purpose (just don't blow your savings in the pub!).

Book your boat via one of the many booking agencies in Airlie Beach, including the following:

Whitsundays Central Reservation Centre
(Whitsundays Central Reservation Centre; ☑1800 677 119; www.airliebeach.com; 259 Shute Harbour Rd; ⊗8am-7pm Mon-Fri, to 6pm Sat & Sun)

Whitsunday Sailing Adventures (☑1300 653 100, 07-4940 2000; www.whitsundayssailing adventures.com.au; 402 Shute Harbour Rd; ⊗7am-5pm)

Explore Whitsundays (☑07-4967 7555; www.ex plorewhitsundays.com; Suite 1, 4 Airlie Esplanade; tours adult/child from $55/39)

'Crew Wanted' signs around the marina, at restaurants and hotels. Your experience will depend on the vessel, skipper, other crew members (if any) and your own attitude. Be sure to let someone know where you're going, with whom and for how long.

Tours

Derwent Hunter   Boating

(☑1800 334 773; www.tallshipadventures.com. au; day trips adult/child $195/99) A deservedly popular sailing safari on a beautiful timber gaff-rigged schooner. A good option for couples and those more keen on wildlife than the wild life.

Illusions 2   Boating

(☑0455 142 021; www.illusions-whitsundays. com.au; day tours $165) A 12m catamaran that

Airlie Beach

Sitting on lovely undulating coastline traditionally owned by the Ngaro and Gia peoples, Airlie is the gateway to the unparalleled Whitsunday Islands and an essential stop on most east-coast road trips. Its multiple hostels, sprawling beer gardens and myriad tour operators are strung along Shute Harbour Rd, separated from Pioneer Bay by a lovely lawn-fringed swimming lagoon.

Those looking to avoid the party scene – families especially – will have no trouble finding quieter lodgings close enough to the centre of town. And if that's still too hectic, the forests and walking trails of Conway National Park lie just south and east of town.

🟢 ACTIVITIES

Lagoon   Swimming
(Shute Harbour Rd) 𝗙𝗥𝗘𝗘 Take a dip year-round in the stinger-, croc- and tropical-nasties-free lagoon in the centre of town.

Salty Dog
Sea Kayaking   Kayaking
(📞07-4946 1388; www.saltydog.com.au; Shute Harbour; half-/full-day trips $90/145) Based in Shute Harbour, Salty Dog offers guided day tours to South Molle Island, kayak rental (half-/full-day $60/90) and longer kayak-and-camping missions, including a wonderful six-day expedition ($1850). It's a charming and healthy way to see the islands, with the chance to spot sea turtles, dolphins, vividly patterned fish and (between July and September) even humpback whales.

Skydive
Airlie Beach   Skydiving
(📞1300 585 224; www.skydive.com.au/airlie-beach; 1/265 Shute Harbour Rd; skydives from $199; ⏰7am-9pm) With operations in four Australian states, this organised-but-relaxed outfit offers tandem jumps from 2134m and 4572m at Airlie Beach, and 4572m at Whitehaven Beach, with free return shuttles from their office in central Airlie.

Airlie beach

🅖 TOURS

Cruise Whitsundays   Cruise

(☑07-4846 7000; www.cruisewhitsundays.com; Port of Airlie, 24 The Cove Rd; half-day cruise adult/child from $115/45) Cruise Whitsundays offers trips to various Whitsunday Islands and Barrier Reef locations, including Hamilton island, Whitsunday Island and Hardy Reef. A particularly delightful option is overnighting on the company's pontoon at spectacular Hardy Reef, 39 nautical miles offshore (from $525 per person). Also memorable are day trips around Whitsunday Island on the catamaran *Camira* (adult/child $209/145).

Red Cat Adventures   Boating

(☑07-4946 4444; www.redcatadventures.com.au; tours from $179) Excellent family-owned operation with three distinct crafts and tours. Our pick is the Ride to Paradise (one/two nights $309/599), which takes in several Whitsunday highlights before overnighting in Paradise Cove, a 16.2-sq-km resort north of Airlie. Departures are from Abell Point Marina.

Whitsunday
Crocodile Safari   Safari

(☑07-4948 3310; www.crocodilesafari.com.au; adult $129, child $39-69) This day-long tour heads out to the Proserpine River, Goorganga Plains wetlands and coastal mangroves in all weathers, getting gawping visitors close to the 150-odd estuarine crocodiles that live here. Guides are knowledgeable, and lunch and bus transfers to Airlie are provided.

Air Whitsunday Seaplanes   Tours

(☑07-4946 9111; www.airwhitsunday.com.au; Terminal 1, Whitsunday Airport; tours from $295) Air Whitsunday offers a range of tours aboard Cessna and de Havilland seaplanes, from flyovers of the Outer Reef, where you don't leave the aircraft (which nonetheless performs a 'touch-n-go' water landing en route, just for thrills), to excursions landing at Whitehaven Beach and Heart Reef, where passengers disembark to snorkel, sightsee and bliss out.

🚢 High-Speed Boat Trips from Airlie Beach

Ocean Rafting (☑07-4946 6848; www. oceanrafting.com.au; Abell Point Marina, Shingley Dr; adult/child/family $159/102/476; 🚐) The best way to see the Whitsundays' top attractions in a single day is on Ocean Rafting's Northern Exposure or Southern Lights trips (the former is best for snorkelling; the latter for blissing out on the beach). The iconic yellow semi-rigid boats zoom to Whitehaven Beach, and buffet lunch ($16 per person) and drinks can be bought on board.

Pioneer Jet Whitsundays (☑1800 335 975; www.pioneerjet.com.au; South Village, Abell Point Marina, Shingley Dr; adult/child $69/49) The Ultimate Bay Blast is a thunderous 30-minute spin around Pioneer Bay aboard the 6.5m jetboat *Cheeky Bee,* which can clock 38 knots even with a full load. Fun and informative guides round off the experience. Expect to get very wet.

🅧 EATING

Wisdom Cafe   Cafe $

(☑07-4946 5199; 1b/273 Shute Harbour Rd; snacks $5-8; ☺7.30am-4pm; 🅿) This deservedly busy corner cafe does takeaway and dine-in at indoor and outdoor tables. It serves healthy toasties, sandwiches, veggie, vegan and gluten-free food, and a huge array of fresh smoothies and juices.

Fish D'vine   Seafood $$

(☑07-4948 0088; www.fishdvine.com.au; 303 Shute Harbour Rd; mains $30-33; ☺5-11pm) The nautical staples of seafood and rum are the fortes of this bustling, upmarket cornerside restaurant in central Airlie. Locally caught barramundi, red emperor and other fish star in the more elaborate mains, while fish and chips and seafood pasta maintain the high standards. Plus, the rum bar has an absurd 560-plus cane distillations to experience.

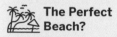

The Perfect Beach?

One of of Australia's most photogenic and hyped beaches, **Whitehaven**, on Whitsunday Island, is a pristine 7km-long stretch of blinding sand (at 98% pure silica, some of the whitest in the world) framed by lush vegetation and a brilliant blue sea. From Hill Inlet at the northern end of the beach, the swirling pattern of dazzling sand through the turquoise and aquamarine water paints a magical picture. Also offering good snorkelling, it's on the day-tour itineraries of nearly all Airlie-based operators.

Camping is the only sleeping option on the island. The Queensland Parks & Wildlife Service in Airlie Beach issues permits and can advise on transport. Alternatively, take a boat tour or contact Scamper (p140).

Whitehaven beach
TOMAS LESA/SHUTTERSTOCK ©

Denmans
Beer Cafe   Pub Food $$

(☑07-4990 6701; www.denmans.com.au; Shop 15, 33 Port of Airlie Dr; mains $24-27; ☺kitchen 11.30am-8.30pm Mon & Thu, 4-8.30pm Tue & Wed, 11.30am-9pm Fri-Sun) Regular live music and a convivial mood are found in this bar, which stocks more craft beers than the rest of town combined. The food – such as a shared paella ($55), or grilled local fish with sweet-potato puree ($27) – is decent, with 'tapas' including soft-shelled crab tacos and chicken-leek croquettes available as drinking food.

☻ DRINKING & NIGHTLIFE

Northerlies Beach Bar & Grill   Bar

(☑1800 682 277; www.northerlies.com.au; 116 Pringle Rd, Woodwark; ☺10am-8.30pm Sun-Thu, to 9pm Fri & Sat) Tucked away on a lovely tranquil shore-front in Woodwark, facing Airlie across Pioneer Bay, Northerlies is just the place for a sundowner. The broad, timber-floored bar and restaurant, open-sided to get the most of the views and the bay breezes, is set up to linger over craft beers, cocktails and well-chosen wines from Australia, New Zealand and Europe.

❶ GETTING THERE & AWAY

AIR

The closest major airports, **Whitsunday Coast** (Proserpine Airport; www.whitsundaycoastairport.com.au; Lascelles Ave, Gunyarra) at Proserpine and Hamilton Island (p141), aka Great Barrier Reef Airport, have regular connections with Sydney, Melbourne and Brisbane.

BOAT

Transfers between the **Port of Airlie** (☑1800 676 526; www.portofairlie.com.au; 13 The Cove Rd) and Hamilton and Daydream Islands ($55 per person) are provided by Cruise Whitsundays (p137).

BUS

Greyhound (☑1300 473 946; www.greyhound.com.au) and **Premier Motor Service** (☑13 34 10; www.premierms.com.au) buses detour off the Bruce Hwy, connecting Airlie Beach to all of the major centres along the coast.

Whitsunday Transit (☑07-4946 1800; www.whitsundaytransit.com.au) connects Proserpine (for Whitsunday Coast Airport), Cannonvale, Abell Point Marina, Airlie Beach and Shute Harbour.

Long Island

Long Island has secluded, pretty white beaches and lots of adorable, wild rock wallabies. The beaches here are among the best in the Whitsundays, and there is 13km of walking tracks with some fine lookouts.

South Molle Island

Long Island has seen its two major resorts close down in recent years. The **Palm Bay Resort** (☑1300 655 126; www.palmbay resort.com.au; villas/bures/bungalows from $269/299/370; ☀)t fills a void at the high end, while campers are adequately served at Long Island National Park Camp Site.

The **Queensland Parks & Wildlife Service** (☑07-4946 1480, 13 74 68; http://parks. des.qld.gov.au; cnr Shute Harbour & Mandalay Rds; ☺9am-4.30pm Mon-Fri) in Airlie Beach can offer advice on getting to the island.

Two water taxis run scheduled services to Long Island's Palm Bay Resort: **Island Transfers** (☑0488 022 868; www.islandtrans-fers.com) from Proserpine, Airlie and Shute Harbour, and **Mars Charters** (☑1800 202 909; www.marscharters.com.au) from Hamilton Island.

South Molle Island

The largest of its group, South Molle is virtually joined to its reef-fringed siblings, Mid and North Molle Islands. Hit hard by Cyclone Debbie in March 2017, its resort in Bauer Bay was yet to reopen at the

time of writing. Beyond this, the island is all national park and is criss-crossed by 15km of walking tracks, with some superb lookout points. The Queensland Parks campgrounds at Sandy and Paddle Bays are the only places to overnight.

Buy camping permits (adult/family $6.55/26 per night) online from Queens-land Parks & Wildlife before visiting. Day trippers and campers can get to South Molle with Scamper (p140) for $65 return.

Daydream Island

Just 5km from Shute Harbour, the rainforest-cloaked, reef-fringed Daydream Island is only 1km long and 200m wide, allowing it to be explored in an hour or two. For most visitors, the natural port of call is the 277-room **Daydream Island Resort & Spa** (☑07-3259 2350; www.daydreamisland. com; d from $392; ☀☎☀). **Cruise Whitsundays** (☑07-4846 7000; www.cruisewhitsundays. com) ferries stop here on their way between Shute Harbour and Hamilton Island ($55 one-way per person).

Hook Island

The 53-sq-km Hook Island, the second-largest island in the Whitsunday group, is predominantly national park and rises to 450m at Hook Peak. There is a number of good beaches dotted around the island, and some of the region's best diving and snorkelling locations. There are Queensland Parks campgrounds at Maureen's Cove, Steen's Beach, Curlew Beach and Crayfish Beach. Although basic, they provide some wonderful back-to-nature opportunities.

Buy camping permits (adult/family $6.55/26 per night) online from Queensland Parks & Wildlife (p139) before visiting. **Scamper** (✆0487 226 737, 07-4946 6285; www.whitsundaycamping.com.au) carries passengers from Shute Harbour, 10km east of Airlie Beach, to the campgrounds at Maureen's Cove and Steen's and Crayfish Beaches on the island (return $160 per person).

Hamilton Island

Welcome to a little slice of resort paradise, where the road is ruled by golf buggies, the forested interior is criss-crossed by steep, rocky walking trails, and the white beaches are buzzing with water-sports action. Though such an all-sufficing resort experience is not for everyone, it's hard not to be impressed by the selection of high-end accommodation, restaurants, bars and activities – if you've got the cash, there's something for everyone. Our pick is **Qualia** (✆1300 780 959; www.qualia.com.au; 20 Whitsunday Blvd; villas from $1250; ❄ @ 🛜 🌊), an ultraluxe resort set on 12 secluded hectares, with modern villas materialising like heavenly tree houses in the leafy hillside.

🏃 ACTIVITIES

You can hire stand-up paddleboards, kayaks, windsurfers, catamarans, jet

Hamilton Island

BEACHY PHOTOGRAPHY/SHUTTERSTOCK ©

skis and other equipment from centrally located **Catseye Beach**, or go parasailing or waterskiing. Non-motorised equipment costs around $15 for half-hour rental, $30 for an hour.

⊗ EATING

The main resort complex has a number of restaurants, which you can peruse in advance at www.hamiltonisland.com.au. The marina also offers plenty of choices, including a good bakery-deli, **Bob's** (☑07-4946 8281; 137 Front St; sandwiches from $9, pies from $4.90; ⊘7am-4pm), a fish and chip shop, **Popeye's** (☑07-4946 9999; Front St; fish & chips $12; ⊘10am-9pm), a **tavern** (☑07-4946 9999; 172 Front St; ⊘11am-late) and a supermarket-cum-general-store for self-caterers.

ⓘ GETTING THERE & AWAY

AIR

Hamilton Island Airport (Great Barrier Reef Airport; ☑07-4946 8620; www.hamiltonisland. com.au; Airport Dr), the main arrival centre for the Whitsundays, is serviced by **Qantas** (☑13 13 13; www.qantas.com.au) to/from Sydney, Melbourne, Brisbane and Cairns, **Virgin** (☑13 67 89; www.virginaustralia.com) to/from Sydney, Melbourne and Brisbane, and **Jetstar** (☑13 15 38; www.jetstar.com.au) to/from Sydney.

BOAT

Cruise Whitsundays (☑07-4846 7000; www. cruisewhitsundays.com) connects Hamilton Island Airport and the marina with the Port of Airlie in Airlie Beach (adult/child one way $62/40).

Hayman Island

The most northerly of the Whitsunday group, little **Hayman Island** is just 4 sq km in area and rises to 250m above sea level. It has forested hills, valleys and beaches, and a luxury five-star resort – Australia's most celebrated, and long a stage for the lifestyles of the rich and famous.

 Top Five Beaches

If the Whitsundays have some of Australia's finest beaches, and Australian beaches are some of the best in the world, then beach connoisseurs have hit the jackpot. Although there are plenty of secluded, postcard-perfect, sandy bays in this tropical paradise, the following are reasonably accessible for most tour companies:

Whitehaven Beach (p138) With azure-blue waters lapping the pure-white silica sand, Whitehaven on Whitsunday Island is absolutely stunning.

Chalkies Beach Opposite Whitehaven Beach, on Haslewood Island, this is another idyllic, white-sanded beach. It's not on the usual tourist circuit, though some operators do stop there. Otherwise, charter a boat yourself.

Langford Island At high tide, Langford is a thin strip of sand on the rim of a ludicrously picturesque, coral-filled turquoise lagoon. More a sandbank than a beach, but surreally beautiful nonetheless.

Butterfly Bay On the northern side of Hook Island is this protected bay, which flutters with butterfly song each winter. It's popular with discerning bareboat-charter-goers, who snorkel in the shallows and lob on the sand like happy beached whales.

Catseye Beach Hamilton Island was chosen for development for good reason. Catseye Beach is a busy-ish spot by Whitsunday standards, but its palm-shaded sand and turquoise waters are social-media ready. Plus you can rent kayaks and buy a drink!

Badly hit by Cyclone Debbie in March 2017, the resort was under redevelopment at the time of writing but will be open by the time you read this.

MELBOURNE

Melbourne at a Glance...

Stylish, arty Melbourne is dynamic, sports-mad and cosmopolitan. Its stately architecture and multicultural make-up reflect the city's history; edgy street art, top museums and sticky-carpeted band venues point to its present-day personality.

The city's character is defined by its inner-city neighbourhoods. Despite a long-standing north–south divide (flashy St Kilda versus hipster Fitzroy), there's a coolness about its bars, cafes, restaurants, festivals and inhabitants that transcends the borders. The city centre has meanwhile reinvented itself, with chic eateries and rooftop bars.

Melbourne in Two Days

Check out the galleries at Federation Square, then join **Melbourne by Foot** (p159) to see the city's streetscapes or just chill in a rooftop bar. On day two, stroll along **Birrarung Marr** (p154) and into the **Royal Botanic Gardens** (p159), then shop your way to the **Queen Victoria Market** (p149). Head to the **St Kilda** for an afternoon stroll along the foreshore and catch a gig at the **Prince Bandroom** (p168) in the evening.

Melbourne in Four Days

Day three, visit the **Melbourne Museum** (p158), then revive with coffee on bohemian Brunswick St, Fitzroy. Back in the CBD, check the street art in **Hosier Lane** (p155), explore **Chinatown** (p154) and see Ned Kelly's armour at the **State Library** (p155). On day four, catch a footy game or take a tour at the **MCG** (p151). Wind up with dinner on Smith St, Collingwood, then head to the **Tote** (p168) for more live tunes.

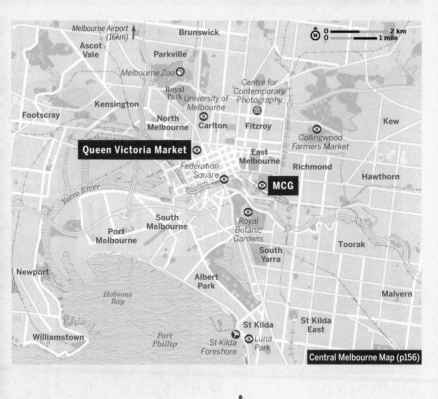

Melbourne Airport (16km)

Brunswick

Ascot Vale

Parkville

Melbourne Zoo

Royal Park

University of Melbourne

Centre for Contemporary Photography

Kensington

Footscray

North Melbourne

Carlton

Fitzroy

Kew

Queen Victoria Market

Collingwood Farmers Market

East Melbourne

Richmond

Federation Square

Yarra River

Hawthorn

MCG

South Melbourne

Royal Botanic Gardens

Port Melbourne

South Yarra

Toorak

Newport

Hobsons Bay

Albert Park

Malvern

Williamstown

Port Phillip

St Kilda Foreshore

St Kilda

Luna Park

St Kilda East

0 ——— 2 km
0 ——— 1 mile

Central Melbourne Map (p156)

Arriving in Melbourne

Most travellers to Melbourne arrive at **Melbourne Airport** (p169) 22km north of the city, with city connections via **Skybus** (p169) shuttle ($18) and taxi (around $65). Interstate trains and buses arrive at **Southern Cross Station** in the CBD. There's also the **Spirit of Tasmania** (p169) vehicle ferry to/from Tasmania, that docks in Port Melbourne.

Where to Stay

Carlton and Fitzroy, north of the CBD, have lots of midrange accommodation, plus great drinking and eating. Central Melbourne is studded with apartments, swish hotels and budget hostels. Down on the bay, raffish St Kilda has both budget and boutique options, while East Melbourne is somewhat refined and removed from the hubbub.

Melbourne Galleries

Melbourne takes seriously its claim to being the arts capital of the country, from big-ticket, city-centre galleries to dynamic spaces for contemporary art elsewhere across the city.

Great For...

☑ Don't Miss

Rembrandt's self-portrait and Picasso's *Weeping Woman* in the NGV International.

NGV International
Gallery

(National Gallery of Victoria International; ✆03-8620 2222; www.ngv.vic.gov.au; 180 St Kilda Rd, Southbank; ⊙10am-5pm; ☎; ⌂Flinders St) **FREE** Housed in a vast, brutally beautiful, bunker-like building, the international branch of NGV has an expansive collection, from ancient artefacts to the bleeding edge. Blockbuster exhibitions draw crowds, and there are free 50-minute tours from 11am to 2pm daily. It's a rite of passage to touch the water wall at the entrance.

Ian Potter Centre: NGV Australia
Gallery

(✆03-8620 2222; www.ngv.vic.gov.au; Federation Sq, Melbourne; ⊙10am-5pm; ☎; ⌂Flinders St) **FREE** The National Gallery of Victoria's impressive Fed Sq offshoot showcases its extraordinary collection of Australian works. Set over three levels, it's a mix of

KEITMA/ALAMY ©

WELCOME TO
**THE IAN POTTER CENTRE:
NGV AUSTRALIA**

NOW SHOWING

**BALDESSIN/
WHITELEY:
PARALLEL VISIONS**

POLLY BORLAND
POLYVERSE

**RIGG DESIGN
PRIZE 2018**

DESI
STOR
THE WO
BROACH

KEN
TRULY,

FRON
INDIGEN
NGV CO

ⓘ Need to Know

Art galleries have free admission, but you pay for big-name temporary exhibitions.

✕ Take a Break

Genre-defining MoVida (p163) is just over Flinders St from the Ian Potter Centre.

★ Top Tip

Avoid NGV International blockbuster exhibitions at weekends when queues are long.

permanent and temporary exhibitions, comprising paintings, decorative arts, photography, prints, sculpture and fashion. Free daily tours.

Ian Potter Museum of Art   Gallery

(📞03-8344 5148; www.art-museum.unimelb. edu.au; Melbourne University, 800 Swanston St, Parkville; 🕙10am-5pm Tue-Fri, from noon Sat & Sun; 🚊1, 3, 5, 6, 16, 64, 67, 72) **FREE** Manages Melbourne University's extensive art collection – the largest university collection in the country – over three levels. It ranges from antiquities and Indigenous art to contemporary Australian work. Check the website for panel discussions, public talks or film screenings.

Buxton Contemporary   Gallery

(📞03-9035 9339; www.buxtoncontemporary. com; cnr Southbank Blvd & Dodds St, South-

bank; 🕙11am-5pm Wed & Fri-Sun, to 8pm Thu; 📶; 🚊1, 3, 5, 6, 16, 64, 67, 72) **FREE** Weird, wonderful and thought-provoking Buxton Contemporary, located at the University of Melbourne's art school, opened in 2018, powered by the Michael Buxton Collection of contemporary Australian art. The four public galleries contain various exhibitions with works along a spectrum from contemporary to creepy. Check online for talks and lectures.

Centre for Contemporary Photography   Gallery

(CCP; 📞03-9417 1549; www.ccp.org.au; 404 George St, Fitzroy; 🕙11am-5pm Wed-Fri, from noon Sat & Sun; 🚊86) **FREE** This not-for-profit centre has contemporary photography exhibitions across five galleries. Shows traverse traditional techniques and the highly conceptual, and change every six weeks or so. There's a focus work involving video projection, including a nightly after-hours screening in a window, seen at the corner of George and Kerr Sts.

Queen Victoria Market

With more than 600 traders, effervescent Queen Vic Market is the largest open-air market in the southern hemisphere and attracts thousands of shoppers.

Great For...

☑ Don't Miss

Stallholders spruiking discounted meat and seafood (still perfectly fresh) just before closing time.

Food, Glorious Food

This is where Melburnians sniff out fresh produce among the booming cries of spruiking fishmongers and fruit-and-veg vendors. The wonderful deli hall (with art-deco features) is lined with everything from soft cheeses, wines and Polish sausages to Greek dips, truffle oil and kangaroo biltong.

The market has been here for more than 130 years; before that, from 1837 to 1854, it was the old Melbourne Cemetery (remarkably, around 9000 bodies remain buried here, from underneath Shed F to the car park leading to Franklin St). There's a small memorial on the corner of Queen and Therry Sts.

As well as the deli hall, make sure you check out the food court, the shops on Elizabeth and Victoria streets, and the latest

JIA1Q289/SHUTTERSTOCK ©

❶ Need to Know

☎9320 5822; www.qvm.com.au; cnr Elizabeth & Victoria Sts, Melbourne; ⊙6am-2pm Tue & Thu, to 5pm Fri, to 3pm Sat, 9am-4pm Sun; Ⓟ; 🚌19, 57, 58, 59, 🚃Flagstaff

✕ Take a Break

An outpost of the **Padre Coffee Empire** (www.padrecoffee.com.au; L Shed, String Bean Alley, Queen Victoria Market; ⊙7am-3pm Fri-Sun; 🚃Flagstaff) is the perfect pit stop.

★ Top Tip

Check the website for heritage, cultural and foodie tours.

addition to the market, String Bean Alley, a series of shipping containers housing artisans and traders (open Friday, Saturday and Sunday).

Join the thronging locals and snatch up some classic Vic Market treats:

- A bratwurst from the Bratwurst Stall (with German mustard and sauerkraut).

- Terrine from the French Shop (with French butter and cornichons).

- African hot-smoked blue-eye cutlets from Tribal Tastes (or biltong, or *shitto* – Ghanaian smoked fish and chilli sauce)..

- Superb 'wedding sausage', ham, brawn or bacon from the Polish deli (and perhaps a Polish doughnut).

- A perfectly blended *ras el hanout* spice mix from Gewürzhaus.

What's On

Saturday morning is particularly buzzing, with market-goers breakfasting to the sounds and shows of buskers. Clothing and knick-knack stalls dominate on Sunday; they're big on variety, but don't come looking for style. (If you're in the market for sheepskin moccasins or cheap T-shirts, you'll be in luck.)

On Wednesday evenings from mid-November to the end of February, the **Summer Night Market** takes over. It's a lively social event featuring hawker-style food stalls, bars, and music and dance performances. There's also a **Winter Night Market** each Wednesday evening from June to August.

Melbourne Cricket Ground

With a capacity of 100,000 people, the MCG is one of the world's great sports venues, hosting cricket in the summer, and AFL footy in the winter. Hallowed ground!

Great For...

☑ **Don't Miss**

The Indigenous Round in the AFL – a celebration of Aboriginal footballers' sublime skills.

History

In 1858 the first game of 'Aussie Rules' football was played where the MCG and its car parks now stand, and in 1877 it was the venue for the first Test cricket match between Australia and England. The MCG was the central stadium for the 1956 Melbourne Olympics and the 2006 Commonwealth Games. It was also used as army barracks during WWII.

MCG Dreaming

Where did Australian Rules football come from? There's plenty of evidence to suggest that Aboriginal men and women played a form of football (called 'marngrook') prior to white settlement. Did they play it at the MCG site pre-settlement? The MCG has two scar trees from which bark was removed by Aboriginal people to make

Need to Know

MCG; 03-9657 8888; www.mcg.org.au; Brunton Ave, East Melbourne; tour adult/child/family $25/14/60, incl museum $35/18/76; tours 10am-3pm; Jolimont

Take a Break

Crowd-favourite **Top Paddock** (03-9429 4332; www.toppaddockcafe.com; 658 Church St, Richmond; dishes $17-24; 7am-4pm Mon-Fri, from 8am Sat & Sun; 78) is industrial-chic.

★ Top Tip

Never try to drive to 'the G' on a big match day: you'll surely regret it.

canoes. These reminders make it clear that Melbourne's footy fans (and perhaps players) were not the first to gather at the site of the MCG.

Visiting 'the G'

Make it to a game if you can (highly recommended). On non-match-days, **tours** take you through the stands, media and coaches' areas, change rooms and out onto the ground.

Sports fans can also visit the **National Sports Museum** (03-9657 8879; www.nsm.org.au; Gate 3, MCG; adult/child/family $25/14/60; 10am-5pm) in the bowels of the ground, focusing on Australia's favourite sports and historic sporting moments. Kids will love the interactive section where they can test their footy, cricket or netball skills. There's even a hologram of cricketer Shane Warne.

Objects on display include the handwritten rules of Australian Rules football from 1859; a collection of baggy green caps worn by Australian cricket legends (including Don Bradman); olive branches awarded to Edwin Flack, Australia's first Olympic medallist (1886); various Olympic medals; and sprinter Cathy Freeman's famous Sydney Olympics swift suit.

MCG Events

AFL Grand Final   Sports

(www.afl.com.au; Sep) Grand Final tickets are next to impossible to procure. But pubs across the city buzz with finals fever.

Boxing Day Test   Sports

(www.mcg.org.au; 26 Dec) Boxing Day is day one of Melbourne's hugely popular annual Test cricket matches..

Arcades & Lanes

Central Melbourne is a warren of 19th-century arcades and gritty-turned-hip cobbled bluestone lanes featuring street art, basement restaurants, boutiques and bars.

Start Campbell Arcade
Distance 3km
Duration 2½ hours

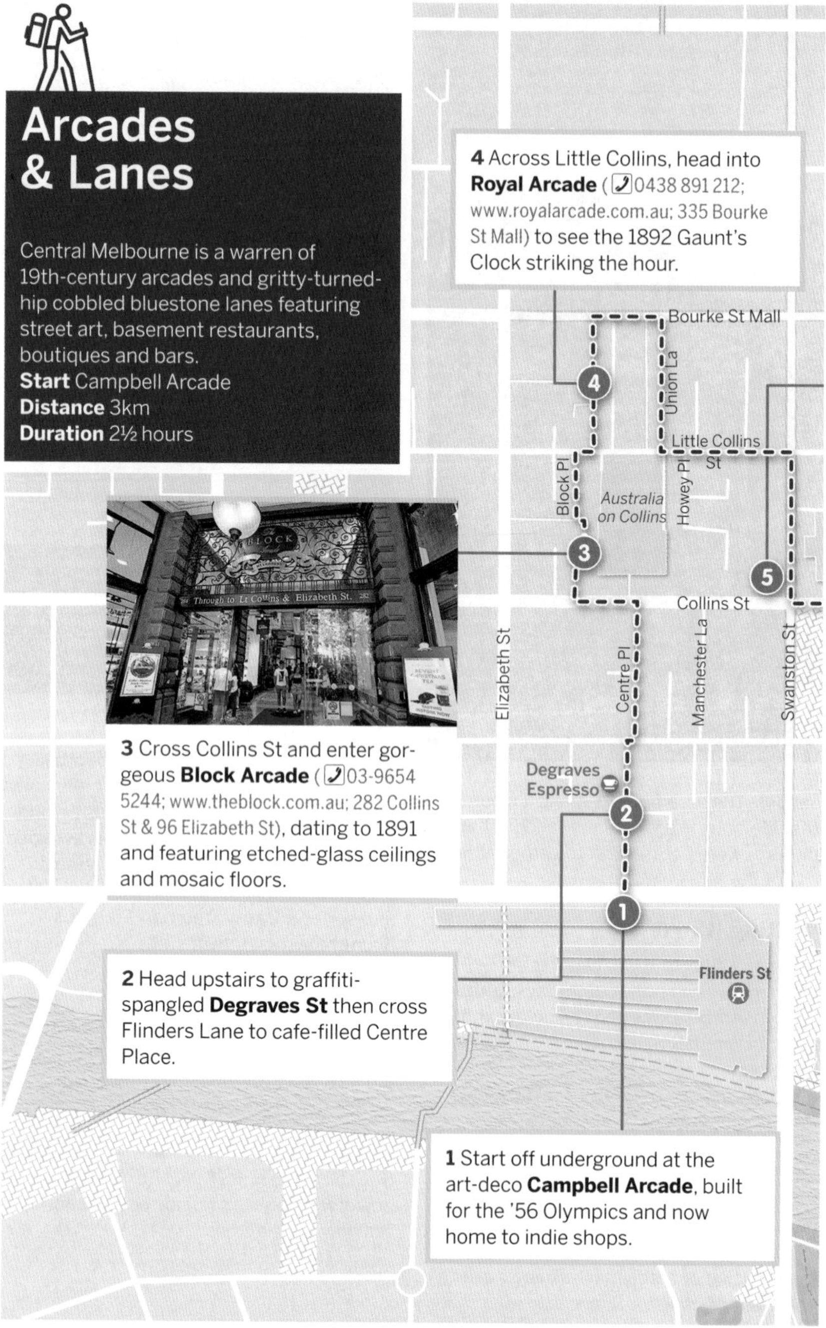

4 Across Little Collins, head into **Royal Arcade** (☎0438 891 212; www.royalarcade.com.au; 335 Bourke St Mall) to see the 1892 Gaunt's Clock striking the hour.

3 Cross Collins St and enter gorgeous **Block Arcade** (☎03-9654 5244; www.theblock.com.au; 282 Collins St & 96 Elizabeth St), dating to 1891 and featuring etched-glass ceilings and mosaic floors.

2 Head upstairs to graffiti-spangled **Degraves St** then cross Flinders Lane to cafe-filled Centre Place.

1 Start off underground at the art-deco **Campbell Arcade**, built for the '56 Olympics and now home to indie shops.

Bourke St Mall

Union La

Little Collins St

Block Pl

Howey Pl

Australia on Collins

Collins St

Elizabeth St

Centre Pl

Manchester La

Swanston St

Degraves Espresso

Flinders St

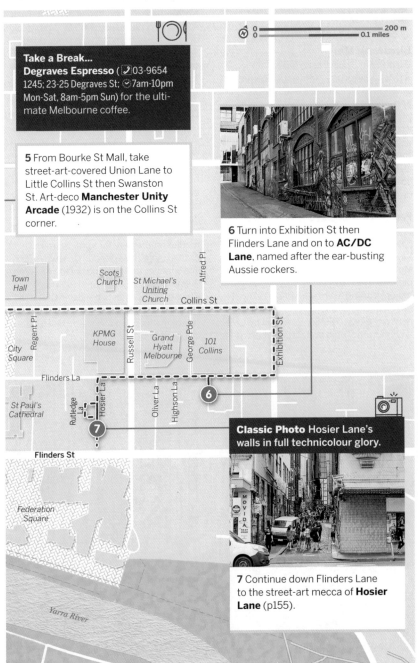

Take a Break...
Degraves Espresso (☎03-9654 1245; 23-25 Degraves St; ☉7am-10pm Mon-Sat, 8am-5pm Sun) for the ultimate Melbourne coffee.

5 From Bourke St Mall, take street-art-covered Union Lane to Little Collins St then Swanston St. Art-deco **Manchester Unity Arcade** (1932) is on the Collins St corner.

6 Turn into Exhibition St then Flinders Lane and on to **AC/DC Lane**, named after the ear-busting Aussie rockers.

Town Hall

Scots Church

St Michael's Uniting Church

Alfred Pl

Collins St

City Square

Regent Pl

KPMG House

Russell St

Grand Hyatt Melbourne

George Pde

101 Collins

Exhibition St

Flinders La

St Paul's Cathedral

Rutledge La

Hosier La

Oliver La

Highson La

6

Flinders St

Federation Square

Yarra River

Classic Photo Hosier Lane's walls in full technicolour glory.

7 Continue down Flinders Lane to the street-art mecca of **Hosier Lane** (p155).

3 KEITMA/SHUTTERSTOCK © 6 COLIN E WINGTON/ALAMY © 7 KITSADA WETCHKASART/SHUTTERSTOCK ©

⊙ SIGHTS

⊙ Central Melbourne

Birrarung Marr   Park

(Batman Ave; ℝFlinders St) **FREE** Multi-terraced Birrarung Marr is a welcome addition to Melbourne's patchwork of parks and gardens, featuring grassy knolls, river promenades, thoughtful planting of Indigenous flora and great viewpoints of the city and the river. There's also a scenic route to the MCG (p151) via the 'talking' William Barak Bridge – listen out for songs, words and sounds representing Melbourne's cultural diversity as you walk.

Federation Square   Square

(☏03-9655 1900; www.fedsquare.com; cnr Flinders & Swanston Sts; ☎; ℝFlinders St) **FREE** Whether they love or hate the architecture, Melburnians embrace Federation Sq as a place to meet, celebrate, protest, watch major sporting events or simply hang out on deckchairs. Occupying a prominent city block, 'Fed Sq', designed by LAB architecture studio and Bates Smart, is far

from square: its undulating and patterned forecourt is paved with 460,000 hand-laid cobblestones from the Kimberley region in Western Australia, with sight lines to important landmarks. Its buildings are clad in a fractal-patterned reptilian-like skin. Check the website to see what's on.

Chinatown   Area

(www.chinatownmelbourne.com.au; Little Bourke St, btwn Swanston & Exhibition Sts; ℝMelbourne Central, Parliament) **FREE** For more than 150 years this section of central Melbourne, now flanked by five traditional arches, has been the focal point for the city's Chinese community. It remains a vibrant neighbourhood of historic buildings filled with Chinese and other restaurants. A must-visit for foodies, come here for yum cha (dim sum) or to explore the attendant laneways for late-night dumplings and cocktails. Some restaurants stay open until the wee hours. Chinatown also hosts the city's **Chinese New Year** (www.melbournechinesenew year.com; Little Bourke St; ◷Jan/Feb) **FREE** celebrations.

Chinatown

State Library of Victoria   Library

(🎫03-8664 7000; www.slv.vic.gov.au; cnr Russell & La Trobe Sts; ⓦ10am-9pm Mon-Thu, to 6pm Fri-Sun, galleries 10am-6pm Thu-Tue, to 9pm Wed; 🛜; 🚋1, 3, 5, 6, 16, 30, 35, 64, 67, 72, 🚉Melbourne Central) **FREE** This grand neoclassical building has been at the forefront of Melbourne's literary scene since 1856. When its epicentre, the octagonal **La Trobe Reading Room**, was completed in 1913, the six-storey-high, reinforced-concrete dome was the largest in the world; its natural light illuminates ornate plasterwork and studious Melburnians. At the time of writing the library's original reading room, **Ian Potter Queen's Hall**, and the **Dome Galleries** were set to open late 2019. Free 45-minute tours depart daily at 11am from Readings bookshop at the rear of the library on Russell St.

Flinders Street
Station   Historic Building

(cnr Flinders & Swanston Sts; 🛜; 🚉Flinders Street) Turning 100 years old in 2010, Melbourne's first train station is also its most iconic building. You'd be hard-pressed to find a Melburnian who hasn't uttered the phrase, 'Meet me under the clocks' – the popular rendezvous spot at the front entrance. Stretching along the Yarra, the neoclassical building crowned with a striking octagonal dome contains an abandoned ballroom, closed to the public.

Koorie
Heritage Trust   Cultural Centre

(🎫03-8662 6300; www.koorieheritagetrust. com; Level 1 & 3, Yarra Building, Federation Sq, cnr Swanston & Flinders Sts; tours adult/child $30/15; ⓦ10am-5pm; 🚉Flinders St) **FREE** Devoted to southeastern Aboriginal culture, this centre houses interesting artefacts and oral history recordings. There's a shop and gallery downstairs; upstairs, carefully preserved significant objects can be viewed in display cases and drawers. It also runs hour-long tours along the Yarra (subject to weather conditions) led by Koorie guides that evoke the history and memories that lie beneath the modern city. You can book online or in person.

Street Art
Hotspots

Hosier Lane (Hosier Lane, Melbourne; ⓦ24h; 🚉Flinders St) is Melbourne's most celebrated laneway for street art. It's cobbled length draws camera-wielding crowds and wannabe Instagram models, posing in front of and snapping edgy graffiti, stencils and art installations (watch them from the comfort of the window seats at **Bar Tini**). Subject matter runs to the mostly political and countercultural, spiced with irreverent humour. Be sure to see **Rutledge Lane**, which horseshoes around Hosier.

   Blender Lane (🎫03-9328 5556; www. melbournestreettours.com; 110 Franklin St; 🚉Melbourne Central) is an unsigned laneway off Franklin St, showcasing the work of underground artists, that features some of Melbourne's best street art. It's named after the influential, since-relocated Blender Studios. One of the most informed ways to explore the lane is through the studio's highly recommended Melbourne Street Art Tours (🎫03-9328 5556; www.melbournestreettours.com; tours adult/child $69/34.50; ⓦcity centre 1.30pm Tue, Thu & Sat, Fitzroy 11am Sat), run by street artists.

Hosier Lane
TOOYKRUB/SHUTTERSTOCK ©

◉ Southbank & Docklands

Eureka Skydeck   Viewpoint

(🎫03-9693 8888; www.eurekaskydeck.com.au; 7 Riverside Quay, Southbank; adult/child $23/19, Edge extra $12/8; ⓦ10am-10pm; 🚉Flinders St) Melbourne's tallest building, the 297m-high

Central Melbourne

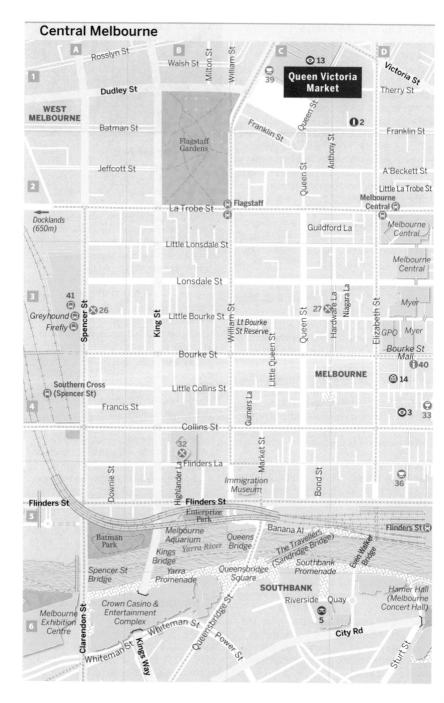

Rosslyn St

A 1

WEST
MELBOURNE

Dudley St

Walsh St

B

Milton St

William St

C

◉ 13
🚊 39

Queen Victoria Market

Victoria St

D

Therry St

Batman St

Jeffcott St

Flagstaff
Gardens

Franklin St

Queen St

❶ 2

Anthony St

Franklin St

A'Beckett St

Little La Trobe St

La Trobe St

🚇 Flagstaff

Melbourne
Central 🚇

2

Docklands
(650m)

Little Lonsdale St

Guildford La

Melbourne
Central

Melbourne
Central

Lonsdale St

41

Greyhound 🚌
Firefly 🚌

Spencer St

✕ 26

King St

Little Bourke St

William St

Lt Bourke
St Reserve

Queen St

27 ✕

Hardware La

Niagara La

Elizabeth St

Myer

Myer

GPO

3

Southern Cross
🚉 (Spencer St)

Bourke St

Little Collins St

Francis St

Gurners La

Little Queen St

MELBOURNE

Bourke St
Mall

❶ 40

🏛 14

◉ 3

🏧 33

Collins St

4

Market St

32
✕

Flinders La

Immigration
Museum

Bond St

🏧 36

Downie St

Highlander La

Flinders St

Flinders St

Flinders St 🚉

5

Enterprize
Park

Batman
Park

Melbourne
Aquarium

Kings
Bridge

Yarra River

Queens
Bridge

Banana Al

The Travellers
(Sandridge Bridge)

Evan Walker
Bridge

Spencer St
Bridge

Yarra
Promenade

Queensbridge
Square

Queensbridge
Promenade

Southbank
Promenade

Hamer Hall
(Melbourne
Concert Hall)

SOUTHBANK

Melbourne
Exhibition
Centre

Clarendon St

Crown Casino &
Entertainment
Complex

Whiteman St

Kings Way

Whiteman St

Queensbridge St

Power St

Riverside Quay

🚲
5

City Rd

Sturt St

6

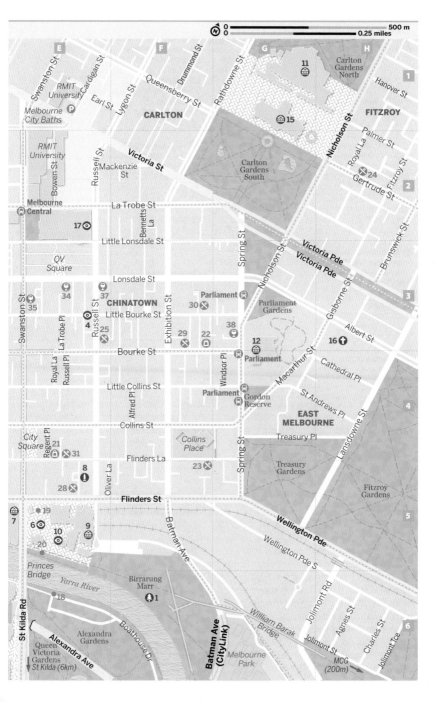

Central Melbourne

Eureka Tower was erected in 2006, and a wild elevator ride takes you to its 88th floor in less than 40 seconds (check out the photo on the elevator floor if there's time). The Edge – a slightly sadistic glass cube – cantilevers you out of the building; you have no choice but to look down.

◎ Fitzroy & Around

Collingwood Children's Farm   Farm
(☑03-9417 5806; www.farm.org.au; 18 St Heliers St, Abbotsford; adult/child/family $12/7/25; ☺9.15am-4.45pm; ☐200, 207, ☐Victoria Park) The inner city melts away at this rustic riverside retreat that's much beloved, and not just by children. There are frolicking farm animals that kids can help feed, as well as cow milking and guinea-pig cuddles. The fantastic, open-air **cafe** (☑03-9415 6581; www.farmcafe.com.au; dishes $13-21; ☺9am-3pm Mon-Fri, to 4pm Sat & Sun; ☑)

opens at 9am and can be visited without entering the farm itself, while the monthly **farmers market** (www.mfm.com.au/markets/collingwood-childrens-farm; adult/child $2/free; ☺8am-1pm 2nd Sat of month) is a local highlight.

◎ Carlton & Around

Melbourne Museum   Museum
(☑13 11 02; www.museumvictoria.com.au; 11 Nicholson St, Carlton; adult $15, child & student free, exhibitions extra; ☺10am-5pm; ☐Tourist Shuttle, ☐City Circle, 86, 96, ☐Parliament) This museum provides a grand sweep of Victoria's natural and cultural histories, incorporating dinosaur skeletons, a 600-species-strong taxidermy hall, 3D volcano and an open-air forest atrium of Victorian flora. There's a children's gallery, and the excellent **Bunjilaka** on the ground floor presents Indigenous Australian history told

through objects and Aboriginal voices with state-of-the-art technology. There's also an **IMAX cinema**.

Royal Exhibition Building
Historic Building

(📞13 11 02; www.museumvictoria.com.au/reb; 9 Nicholson St, Carlton; tours adult/child $10/7; 🚌Tourist Shuttle, 🚋City Circle, 86, 96, 🚆Parliament) Built for the 1880 International Exhibition, this Victorian edifice in Carlton Gardens symbolises the glory days of 19th-century Melbourne's economic supremacy. It was the first Australian building to fly the country's flag, to house an aquarium, to hold parliament (in 1901) and to receive Unesco World Heritage Status (in 2004). Tours of the building leave from Melbourne Museum (p158) at 2pm; call to confirm.

Melbourne Zoo
Zoo

(📞1300 966 784; www.zoo.org.au; Elliott Ave, Parkville; adult/child $37/19, child weekends & holidays free; ⏱9am-5pm, from 8am summer holidays; 🚌58, 🚆Royal Park) 🏊 Established in 1862, this compact zoo is the oldest in Australia and the third oldest in the world. It remains one of the city's most popular attractions and continues to innovate, becoming the world's first carbon-neutral zoo. Set in prettily landscaped gardens, the enclosures aim to simulate the animals' natural habitats and give them the option to hide if they want to (the gorillas and tigers are particularly good at playing hard to get).

⊚ South Yarra
Royal Botanic Gardens
Gardens

(Melbourne Gardens; 📞03-9252 2300; www.rbg.vic.gov.au; Birdwood Ave, South Yarra; ⏱7.30am-sunset; 🚌Tourist Shuttle, 🚋1, 3, 5, 6, 16, 64, 67, 72) **FREE** From the air, these stunning, 38-hectare gardens evoke a giant green lung in the middle of the city. Drawing nearly two million visitors annually, they're considered one of the finest examples of Victorian-era landscaping in the world. Here you'll find global plantings and a range of Australian flora. Mini ecosystems, a herb

garden and an Indigenous rainforest are set amid vast, picnic-friendly lawns and black-swan-spotted ponds. Be sure to book the **Aboriginal Heritage Walk** (📞03-9252 2429; adult/child $35/12; ⏱tours from 11am Sun-Fri) 🏊.

⊚ St Kilda
Luna Park
Amusement Park

(📞03-9525 5033; www.lunapark.com.au; 18 Lower Esplanade, St Kilda; single ride adult/child $11/10, unlimited rides $50/40; ⏱hours vary; 🚌3, 16, 96) Luna Park opened in 1912 and still has an old-style amusement-park feel, with creepy Mr Moon's gaping mouth swallowing you up as you enter. There's a heritage-listed scenic railway (the oldest wooden roller coaster in the world – it stayed in operation during WWI when the rest of the park was closed); a beautiful baroque carousel with hand-painted horses, swans and chariots; and the full complement of gut-churning rides, with something for all ages and levels of adrenaline-seeker.

🎫 TOURS
Rentabike
Cycling

(📞0417 339 203, 03-9654 2762; www.rentabike.net.au; Vault 14, Federation Wharf, Federation Sq, Melbourne; rental per hour/day $15/40, 4hr tour incl lunch adult/child $120/79; ⏱10am-5pm; 🚆Flinders St) 🏊 Renting out bikes for more than 40 years, this outfit also runs **Real Melbourne Bike Tours**, offering a local's insight into the city with a foodie focus. Tours max out at eight people. Electric bikes are also available.

Melbourne By Foot
Walking

(📞1300 311 081; www.melbournebyfoot.com; departs Federation Sq, Melbourne; tours $50; ⏱1pm; 🚆Flinders St) Take a few hours out and experience a mellow, informative three-hour walking tour that covers laneway art, politics, Melbourne's history and diversity – highly recommended. There's even a Beer Lovers tour ($90). Book online.

🍷 Yarra Valley Wineries

The lush Yarra Valley, about an hour's drive northeast of Melbourne, has more than 80 wineries and 50 cellar doors scattered around its rolling hills. Cool-climate chardonnay and pinot noir are why you're here.

The pick of the bunch are:

Domain Chandon (☏03-9738 9200; www.chandon.com; 727 Maroondah Hwy, Coldstream; tastings $12; ⊘10.30am-4.30pm; P) This slick operation is worth a visit for the free guided tours (11am, 1pm and 3pm).

Oakridge (☏03-9738 9900; www.oakridgewines.com.au; 864 Maroondah Hwy, Coldstream; 2-/3-course menus $70/85; ⊘cellar door 10am-5pm, restaurant 11.30am-3pm Thu-Mon; 🔊) Awesome vineyard views and a chic restaurant.

Yering Station (☏03-9730 0100; www.yering.com; 38 Melba Hwy, Yering; ⊘10am-5pm Mon-Fri, to 6pm Sat & Sun; P) Taste wines in the original 1859 winery. Modern fine-dining restaurant too.

Domain Chandon
OLIVER FOERSTNER/SHUTTERSTOCK ©

Hidden Secrets Tours   Walking

(☏03-9663 3358; www.hiddensecretstours.com; tours from $49) Get oriented with a variety of walking tours covering lanes and arcades, history, architecture and cafe culture. There are also tailored accessible tours and others for travellers with visual impairments, because 'cities are for everyone', as they say at Hidden Secrets HQ.

Kayak Melbourne   Kayaking

(☏0418 106 427; www.kayakmelbourne.com.au; Community Hub at The Dock, 912 Collins St, Docklands; tours $75-110; 🚃11, 48) ✎ Ninety-minute City Sights tours paddle past Southbank to Docklands, while two-hour River to Sky tours include entry to the Eureka Skydeck (p155). You can start your day saluting the sun on a two-hour Yoga Sunrise tour or end it with a 2½-hour Moonlight tour starting from Docklands. Other tours start at Boathouse Dr, directly across the Yarra River from Federation Sq.

🛍 SHOPPING

Readings   Books

(☏03-9347 6633; www.readings.com.au; 309 Lygon St, Carlton; ⊘9am-11pm Mon-Sat, 10am-9pm Sun; 🚃Tourist Shuttle, 🚃1, 6) A potter around this defiantly prosperous indie bookshop can occupy an entire afternoon, if you're so inclined. There's a dangerously loaded (and good-value) specials table and switched-on, helpful staff. Just next door is its speciality children's shop.

Polyester Records   Music

(☏03-9419 5137; www.polyesterrecords.com; 387 Brunswick St, Fitzroy; ⊘11am-7pm Mon-Wed, to 10pm Thu-Sat, to 5pm Sun; 🚃11) Opening in 1981, this popular record shop has been selling independent music for decades, with a great range of local stuff. The knowledgeable staff will help you find what you're looking for and can offer suggestions, while there are often free gigs (check their social media). In-house bar **Crazy Arms** is open 4pm to 10pm Thursday to Saturday.

Craft Victoria   Arts & Crafts

(☏03-9650 7775; www.craft.org.au; Watson Pl, off Flinders Lane, Melbourne; ⊘11am-6pm Mon-Fri, to 5pm Sat; 🚃Parliament) This retail arm of Craft Victoria showcases goods handmade exclusively by Victorian artists and artisans. Its range of jewellery, textiles, accessories, glass and ceramics bridges the art–craft divide and makes for some wonderful Melbourne mementos. There are also a few galleries with changing exhibitions; admission is free. Pop in for a guide to the **Craft Cubed Festival** in August.

Melbournalia — Gifts & Souvenirs

(📞03-9663 3751; www.melbournalia.com.au; Shop 5/50 Bourke St, Melbourne; ⊙10am-7pm Mon-Thu, to 8pm Fri, 11am-6pm Sat & Sun; 🚇Parliament) This is the place to stock up on interesting souvenirs by more than 100 local designers – prints featuring city icons, tram socks, native Aussie-inspired earrings and great books on Melbourne, as well as maps and guides, gift cards, postcards and more. The friendly staff can help you send excess shopping home. Extended December hours.

St Kilda Esplanade Market — Market

(www.stkildaesplanademarket.com.au; Esplanade, St Kilda; ⊙10am-4pm Sun May-Sep, to 5pm Oct-Apr; 🚋3, 12, 16, 96) Fancy a Sunday shop by the seaside? This is the place, with a kilometre of trestle tables joined end to end. Pick up everything from local ceramics, sculpture, glassware and woodwork to photographic prints, organic soaps, jewellery and tongue-in-cheek tea towels.

✦ EATING
Central Melbourne

Hakata Gensuke — Ramen $

(📞03-9663 6342; www.gensuke.com.au; 168 Russell St, Melbourne; ramen $13.50-15; ⊙11.30am-10pm Mon-Thu, 11.30am-1am Fri, noon-1am Sat, to 10pm Sun; 🚇Parliament) The original of four shops, Gensuke only does one thing and does it extraordinarily well: *tonkotsu* (pork broth) ramen. Choose from four types (signature, garlic and sesame-infused 'black' broth, spicy 'god fire' or the lighter *shio*) and then order extra toppings like marinated *cha shu* pork, egg, seaweed and black fungus. Worth queuing for.

Pellegrini's Espresso Bar — Italian $

(📞03-9662 1885; 66 Bourke St, Melbourne; mains $18; ⊙8am-11.30pm Mon-Sat, noon-8pm Sun; 🚇Parliament) The Italian equivalent of a diner, locally famed Pellegrini's has remained unchanged since 1954. There's no menu; staff tell you what's available. Expect Italian comfort food: sloppy lasagne, spaghetti bolognese, watermelon granita and big slabs of cake. Service can be brusque, but that's

Royal Exhibition Building (p159)

From left: Luna Park (P159); Pellegrini's Espresso Bar (p161); Federation Square (p154)

all part of the experience. A photo under the neon sign outside is a rite of passage.

Miznon
Israeli $

(☑03-9670 2861; www.miznonaustralia.com; 99 Hardware Lane, Melbourne; gourmet pitas $12-19, dinner share plates $6-19; ☺noon-10pm Mon-Sat; ☑; 🚊86, 96) Originating in Tel Aviv, Miznon is as fun and as fresh as it gets. Book seats on iconic Hardware Lane, sit on the 'steps' inside or up at the mezzanine level. Order pitas stuffed with everything from hot chickpeas to ocean trout belly and share roasted whole cauliflower. Help yourself to the pita, tahini and pickle bar while you wait.

Higher Ground
Cafe $$

(☑03-8899 6219; www.highergroundmelbourne. com.au; 650 Little Bourke St, Melbourne; mains day $16.50-28.50, night $27-45; ☺7am-4pm Mon-Wed, 8am-11pm Thu-Sat, 8am-4pm Sun; 🛜; 🚉Southern Cross) Melbourne's most impressive cafe looks more like an industrial designer hotel as it's housed in a former power station. Within 15m-high ceilings are nooks, crannies and a mezzanine level – all flooded with light from arched windows.

Diners queue to order from the innovative brunch menu, but it's also open for dinner Thursday to Saturday.

Sunda
Asian $$

(☑03-9654 8190; www.sunda.com.au; 18 Punch Lane, Melbourne; set menu $85, share dishes $22-42; ☺6pm-late Mon-Thu, noon-3pm & 5.30pm-late Fri, 5.30pm-late Sat; 🚉Parliament) This contemporary Southeast Asian restaurant is in a former car park down a laneway. Slick with metal scaffolding, raw brick, a long communal table and mezzanine level, the calm kitchen plates modern Indonesian, Vietnamese and Malaysian dishes spiked with native Australian ingredients. Bar seats are best, while the off-menu roti with Vegemite curry is essential – and far better than it sounds.

Supernormal
Asian $$

(☑03-9650 8688; www.supernormal.net.au; 180 Flinders Lane, Melbourne; dishes $14-36; ☺11am-11pm Sun-Thu, to midnight Fri & Sat; 🚉Flinders St) From the man behind **Cumulus Inc** (☑03-9650 1445; www.cumulusinc.com.au; 45 Flinders Lane, Melbourne; breakfast $14-18, mains $36-44; ☺restaurant 7am-11pm Mon-Fri, from

8am Sat & Sun, wine bar 5pm-late Tue-Thu, from 4pm Fri & Sat; ☒Parliament), Andrew McConnell, comes this creative selection of pan-Asian sharing dishes, from dumplings to raw seafood to slow-cooked Sichuan lamb. The New England lobster roll is famous, but we prefer the lunchtime *tonkatsu* sandwich special. No dinner bookings after 5.30pm, so arrive early to put your name on the list. Look for the neon cherries.

MoVida   Tapas $$

(☎03-9663 3038; www.movida.com.au; 1 Hosier Lane, Melbourne; tapas $3.80-9.50, raciones $16.50-30; ☺noon-10pm Sun-Tue, to 10.30pm Wed-Sat; ☒Flinders St) MoVida's location in graffitied Hosier Lane is about as Melbourne as it gets. Line up by the bar, cluster around little window tables or, if you've booked, take a seat in the dining area for Spanish tapas and *raciones*. **MoVida Next Door** – yes, right next door – and newer **Bar Tini** are the perfect place for pre-show drinks and tapas.

Vue de Monde   Modern Australian $$$

(☎03-9691 3888; www.vuedemonde.com.au; 55th fl, Rialto, 525 Collins St, Melbourne; set menu $275-310; ☺reservations from midday & 6-9pm Thu-Sun, 6-9pm Mon-Wed; ☒Southern Cross) Surveying the world from the old observation deck of the Rialto tower, Melbourne's favoured spot for occasion dining has views to match its storied reputation. Visionary chef Shannon Bennett, when he's not mentoring on *MasterChef,* produces sophisticated and theatrical set menus showcasing the very best Australian ingredients. Book months ahead.

🍴 Fitzroy

Lune Croissanterie   Bakery $

(☎03-9419 2320; www.lunecroissanterie.com; 119 Rose St; pastries $5.90-12.50; ☺7.30am-3pm Mon-Fri, from 8am Sat & Sun; ☒11) Good things come to those who queue, and here they come in the form of unrivalled pastries, from innovative cruffins to plain croissants often dubbed the world's best. In the centre of this warehouse space is a glass, climate-controlled cube where the magic happens. Book well in advance for the Lune Lab experience, an innovative three-course pastry flight ($65).

Industry Beans — Cafe $$

(📞03-9417 1034; www.industrybeans.com; 3/62 Rose St; mains $18-25; ⏰7am-4pm Mon-Fri, from 8am Sat & Sun; 🛜; 🚋96, 11) With something for both food and coffee lovers, this warehouse cafe tucked down a side street offers a coffee guide that takes you through speciality styles roasted on-site and an innovative, all-day menu. Dishes like brioche with tonka bean ice cream, maple peanuts, blackberry coulis, manuka sherbert and coffee caviar are commonplace. Try a coffee bubble cup.

Cutler & Co — Modern Australian $$$

(📞03-9419 4888; www.cutlerandco.com.au; 55-57 Gertrude St; mains $46-54; ⏰6pm-late Tue-Sun, lunch from noon Sun; 🚋86) Hyped for all the right reasons, this is Andrew McConnell's flagship Melbourne restaurant and its attentive, informed staff and joy-inducing dishes make it one of Melbourne's top places for fine dining. The menu incorporates the best seasonal produce across the à la carte offering, degustation menu (from $170), and casual Sunday lunch designed for sharing ($75).

🚫 Carlton & Around

D.O.C. Espresso — Italian $$

(📞03-9347 8482; www.docgroup.net; 326 Lygon St, Carlton; pasta $19-26, focaccia & piadina $12-16; ⏰7am-9.30pm Mon-Thu, to 10pm Fri & Sat, 8am-9.30pm Sun; 🚌Tourist Shuttle, 🚋1, 6) Run by third-generation Italian Australians, D.O.C. is one of the best casual Italian options at the Carlton end of Lygon St. The espresso bar specialises in homemade pasta and sells microbrewery beers from Italy. During *aperitivo* (4pm to 7pm), you can enjoy a complimentary nibble board with your negroni.

King and Godfrey — Deli, Italian

(📞03-9347 1619; www.kingandgodfree.com.au; cnr Faraday & Lygon Sts, 293-297 Lygon St, Carlton; ⏰rooftop & restaurant noon-late, deli 8am-8pm, espresso bar 7am-late; 🚋1, 6) It took three years to transform King and Godfrey, an Italian grocer since 1884, into this multi-venue wonder. There's **Johnny's Green Room** with 360-degree rooftop views and a glitterati cocktail vibe; a deli with cold cuts, cheese and food to take away; **Agostino**

St Kilda Esplanade Market (p161)

wine bar and restaurant; and the all-day espresso bar for coffee, panini, pasta or a negroni or two.

Hellenic Republic   Greek $$

(☑03-9381 1222; www.hellenicrepublic.com.au; 434 Lygon St, Brunswick East; starters $7-17, shared mains $19-48; ⊙5.30-9.30pm Mon-Thu, noon-4pm & 5.30-late Fri-Sun; ☐1, 6) The ironbark charcoal grill at George Calombaris' northern outpost works overtime as long-time staff serve and chat with ease. The slow-roasted lamb shoulder is the signature here, but taramasalata (white cod roe dip) and grilled saganaki with sticky figs make an unbelievably good start. Wash it all down with ouzo from the long list.

Rumi   Middle Eastern $$

(☑03-9388 8255; www.rumirestaurant.com.au; 116 Lygon St, Brunswick East; small plates $9-16.50, large plates $15-29; ⊙6-10pm; ☐1, 6) A well-considered place that mixes traditional Lebanese cooking with contemporary interpretations of old Persian dishes. The *sigara boregi* (cheese and pine-nut pastries) are a local institution, and generous mains from the charcoal BBQ are balanced by an interesting selection of vegetable dishes.

🌟 St Kilda & Around

Penta   Cafe $

(☑03-9523 0716; www.pentaelsternwick.com.au; 28 Riddell Pde, Elsternwick; dishes $17.50-22.50; ⊙7am-4pm Mon-Fri, from 7.30am Sat, from 8am Sun; 🛜; ☒Elsternwick) Pumping Penta might be all polished concrete and muted tones inside, but the food here is a rainbow of colours, textures and technique usually reserved for dinner. The Nutella panna cotta must be one of Melbourne's most Instagrammed brunches, planted in a flowerbed of toasted marshmallows, edible blooms and banana slices coated in nut butter.

Stokehouse   Seafood $$$

(☑03-9525 5555; www.stokehouse.com.au; upstairs, 30 Jacka Blvd, St Kilda; mains $39-55; ⊙noon-2.30pm & 6pm-late; ☐3a, 16, 96) After a devastating fire, lauded Stokehouse rebuilt better and brighter. Striking contemporary

architecture and floor-to-ceiling bay views set the tone for modern, seafood-centric dishes and a devilishly good bombe. This is one of Melbourne's most-loved occasion restaurants, so book ahead. For a cheaper view, watch the sunset from adjoining **Stokebar** with a cocktail and snacks.

Attica   Modern Australian $$$

(☑03-9530 0111; www.attica.com.au; 74 Glen Eira Rd, Ripponlea; tasting menu $295; ⊙6pm-late Tue-Sat; ☐67, ☒Ripponlea) Award-winning Attica is one of the top restaurants in Australia. Here Ben Shewry creates contemporary dishes with native ingredients, like saltwater crocodile rib glazed with soured honey and peppermint gum, and dessert served in emu eggs. Even more popular since starring in Netflix's *Chef's Table;* reservations are taken on the first Wednesday of the month for the following three months.

🍷 DRINKING & NIGHTLIFE

🍸 Central Melbourne

Heartbreaker   Bar

(☑03-9041 0856; www.heartbreakerbar.com.au; 234a Russell St; ⊙3pm-3am Mon-Thu, from noon Fri & Sat, noon-1am Sun; ☒Melbourne Central) Black walls, red lights, skeleton handles on the beer taps, random taxidermy, craft beer, a big selection of bourbon, a jukebox and tough-looking sweethearts behind the bar – it's always a good time at Heartbreaker. Cocktails are pre-batch only. Order **Connie's Pizza** slices from the bar and pick up behind the pool table.

Bar Americano   Cocktail Bar

(www.baramericano.com.au; 20 Presgrave Pl; ⊙5pm-1am Mon-Sat; ☒Flinders St) A hideaway bar in a lane off Howey Pl, Bar Americano is a teensy standing-room-only affair with black-and-white chequered floors complemented by classic 'do not spit' subway-tiled walls and a subtle air of speakeasy. Once it hits its 14-person max, the grille gets pulled shut. The cocktails here don't come cheap, but they do come classic and superb.

🍾 Rooftop Drinking

If you like your brew with a view, swing up to these excellent Melbourne rooftop bars.

Siglo (☎03-9654 6631; www.siglobar.com.au; 2nd fl, 161 Spring St, Melbourne; ⊙5pm-3am; ☒Parliament) Siglo's sought-after terrace comes with Parisian flair, wafting cigar smoke and serious drinks. It fills with suits on Friday night, but any time is good to mull over a classic cocktail and admire the 19th-century vista over Parliament (www.parliament.vic.gov.au) and St Patrick's Cathedral (www.stpatrickscathedral.org.au). With Melbourne's strict smoking laws, food is limited to snacks. Entry is via the similarly unsigned **Supper Club** (☎03-9654 6300; www.melbournesupperclub.com.au; 1st fl, 161 Spring St, Melbourne; ⊙5pm-4am Sun-Thu, to 6am Fri & Sat).

Rooftop Bar (☎03-9654 5394; www.rooftopbar.co; 7th fl, Curtin House, 252 Swanston St, Melbourne; ⊙noon-1am Apr-Nov, from 11am Dec-Mar; ☒Melbourne Central) This bar sits atop happening Curtin House. In summer (December to March) there are daily DJs and it transforms into an outdoor cinema with striped deckchairs and a calendar of new and classic favourite flicks. Hit up the burger shack, order a cocktail jug and make some new friends.

Naked for Satan (☎03-9416 2238; www.nakedforsatan.com.au; 285 Brunswick St, Fitzroy; ⊙noon-midnight Sun-Thu, to 1am Fri & Sat; ☒11) Reviving an apparent Brunswick St legend (a man nicknamed Satan who would get naked because of the heat in an illegal vodka distillery under the shop), this place is packed with travellers vying for a seat on the roof terrace with wrap-around balcony, **Naked in the Sky**. Food is disappointing compared with nearby options, but the view is a standout.

Lui Bar   Cocktail Bar
(☎03-9691 3888; www.luibar.com.au; 55th fl, Rialto, 525 Collins St; ⊙5.30pm-midnight Mon-Wed, 11.30am-1am Thu, 11.30am-3am Fri & Sat, 11.30am-midnight Sun; ☒Southern Cross) Some people are happy to shell out $27 for the view from the 120m-high Melbourne Star, but we'd much rather spend $25 on a cocktail at this sophisticated bar perched 236m up the Rialto tower. Beside and owned by Vue de Monde (p163), it's Vue's view and liquid creativity without the price tag. Arrive early (and nicely dressed) for a table.

Cookie   Bar
(☎03-9663 7660; www.cookie.net.au; 1st fl, Curtin House, 252 Swanston St; ⊙noon-3am; ☒Melbourne Central) Part bar, part Thai restaurant, this kooky-cool venue with grand bones is one of the more enduring rites of passage of the Melbourne night. The bar is unbelievably well stocked with fine whiskies, wines and plenty of craft beers, with more than 200 brews on offer. The staff also know how to make a serious cocktail.

Boilermaker House   Bar
(☎03-8393 9367; www.boilermakerhouse.com.au; 209-211 Lonsdale St; ⊙4pm-3am Mon-Wed, from 3pm Thu & Sun, from noon Fri & Sat; ☒Melbourne Central) A real surprise on busy, workaday Lonsdale St, this dimly lit haven of urbanity has a phenomenal 900 whiskies on its list, along with 12 craft beers on tap and a further 30 by the can and bottle. Snack on cheese and charcuterie as you make your way through them, or order a wallaby burger (yes, we eat them).

⊙ Fitzroy

Black Pearl   Cocktail Bar
(☎03-9417 0455; www.blackpearlbar.com.au; 304 Brunswick St; ⊙5pm-3am, Attic Bar 7pm-1am Thu, to 3am Fri & Sat; ☒11) After more than 15 years in the game, Black Pearl goes from strength to strength, winning awards and receiving global accolades. Low lighting, leather banquettes and candles set the mood downstairs. Prop at the bar to study the extensive cocktail list or let the

Rooftop Bar, Curtin House

expert bartenders concoct something to your tastes. Upstairs is table-service **Attic Bar**; book ahead.

Everleigh
Cocktail Bar

(☎03-9416 2229; www.theeverleigh.com; Upstairs, 150-156 Gertrude St; ☺5pm-1am; ☒86) Sophistication is off the charts at this hidden, upstairs nook. Settle into a leather booth in the intimate setting with a few friends for conversation and classic cocktails, or sidle up to the bar for a solo martini. The Bartender's Choice is encouraged: state your flavour and alcohol preferences and a tailored cocktail will appear soon after.

Napier Hotel
Pub

(☎03-9419 4240; www.thenapierhotel.com; 210 Napier St; ☺3-11pm Mon-Thu, noon-1am Fri, to 11pm Sat, 1-11pm Sun; ☒11, 86) The friendly Napier has stood on this corner for more than a century. Worm your way around the central bar to the boisterous dining room for an iconic Bogan burger. Lesser known is that this place is the biggest seller of kangaroo in Victoria, thanks to a pepper-crust-ed steak. There's a fireplace for winter and beer garden for summer.

🅒 Carlton

Jimmy Watson's
Wine Bar

(☎03-9347 3985; www.jimmywatsons.com.au; 333 Lygon St; ☺restaurant & wine bar 11.30am-late; ☒Tourist Shuttle, ☒1, 6) If this Robin Boyd–designed midcentury building had ears, there'd be a few generations of writers and academics in trouble. There's something for all ages, whether a bottle of something special in the handsome indoor space to accompany a long lunch, in the sunny courtyard or at the **Wolf's Lair** rooftop, a great spot for cocktails.

🅢 St Kilda & Around

Bar Di Stasio
Wine Bar

(☎03-9525 3999; www.distasio.com.au; 31 Fitzroy St, St Kilda; ☺11.30am-midnight; ☒3, 12. 16, 96) Within red Pompidou-style scaffolding – the work of artist Callum Morton – lies this buzzing, sophisticated spot, dominated by a grand marble bar and plaster-chipped walls behind lit glass. Waiters seemingly plucked from Venice's Caffè Florian mix perfect spritzes while dishing out bites, from lightly fried local seafood to elegant pastas (available until 11pm). You'll want to book as it's extremely popular.

⭐ ENTERTAINMENT

Esplanade Hotel   Live Music
(☏03-9534 0211; www.hotelesplanade.com. au; 11 The Esplanade, St Kilda; ⏰11am-late) You could spend a day going from room to room now the beloved 'Espy' is back, following a $15 million renovation. Antiques complement its Victorian bones and there are three food and beverage offerings, plus about 10 bars, including the **Ghost of Alfred Felton**. There's also the **Espy Kitchen**; modern Cantonese restaurant **Mya Tiger**; a podcasting studio; and band rooms.

Prince Bandroom   Live Music
(☏03-9536 1168; www.princebandroom.com. au; 29 Fitzroy St, St Kilda; 🚋12, 16, 96) The

Prince is a legendary St Kilda venue, with a solid line-up of local and international acts spanning hip-hop, dance, rock and indie. It's been going for more than 75 years with an eclectic mix of guests, from Lenny Kravitz and Coldplay to UK rapper Tinie Tempah and Nordic hardcore-punk outfit Refused.

The Tote   Live Music
(☏03-9419 5320; www.thetotehotel.com; cnr Johnston & Wellington Sts, Collingwood; ⏰4pm-1am Wed, to 3am Thu-Sat, to 11pm Sun; 🚋86) One of Melbourne's most iconic live-music venues, this divey pub has been hosting a roster of local and international punk, heavy metal and hardcore bands since the '80s. It has one of the best jukeboxes in the universe and its temporary closure in 2010 saw people fiercely protest against the liquor-licensing laws that were blamed for the closure.

Cinema Nova   Cinema
(☏03-9347 5331; www.cinemanova.com.au; 380 Lygon St, Carlton; adult/student/child $21/16/13;

Naked for Satan (p166)

🚋Tourist Shuttle, 🚋1, 6) See the latest in art-house, docos and foreign films at this cinema, a locals' favourite. Cheap Monday screenings ($7/10 before/after 4pm).

ℹ️ INFORMATION

Melbourne Visitor Booth (https://whatson. melbourne.vic.gov.au; Bourke St Mall; ⏰9am-5pm) Official city booth dispensing free tourist information.

Royal Children's Hospital (📞03-9345 5522; www.rch.org.au; 50 Flemington Rd, Parkville; ⏰7.30am-5.30pm Mon-Fri, 10am-2pm Sat, emergency 24hr; 🚌57)

Royal Melbourne Hospital (📞03-9342 7000; www.thermh.org.au; 300 Grattan St, Parkville; ⏰24hr; 🚌19, 58, 59)

ℹ️ GETTING THERE & AWAY

AIR

Melbourne Airport (MEL; 📞03-9297 1600; www. melbourneairport.com.au; Departure Rd, Tullamarine; 🛜) is the city's only international and main domestic airport, located 22km northwest of the city centre in Tullamarine.

Dozens of airlines fly here from destinations in the South Pacific, Asia, the Middle East and the Americas. The main domestic airlines are **Qantas** (📞131 313; www.qantas.com), **Jetstar** (📞131 538; www.jetstar.com), **Virgin Australia** (📞13 67 89; www.virginaustralia.com) and **Tigerair** (📞1300 174 266; www.tigerair.com.au).

BOAT

The **Spirit of Tasmania** (📞1800 634 906, 03-6419 9320; www.spiritoftasmania.com.au; Station Pier, Port Melbourne; adult/car one way from $89/99; 🛜) ferry crosses Bass Strait from Melbourne to Devonport, Tasmania, at least nightly; there are also day sailings during peak season. The crossing takes between nine and 11 hours.

BUS

The main terminus for long-distance buses is in the northern half of Southern Cross train station.

Firefly (📞03-8318 0318, 1300 730 740; www. fireflyexpress.com.au; Southern Cross station, 99 Spencer St, Coach Terminal) has overnight coaches to and from Sydney ($70, 12 hours), Albury ($70, 3½ hours), Ballarat ($65, 1¾ hours) and Adelaide ($60, 9¾ hours).

Greyhound (📞1300 473 946; www.greyhound. com.au) has coaches to Albury (from $56, 3½ hours), Sydney (from $113, 12 hours) and Canberra (from $65, eight hours).

V/Line services destinations within Victoria, including Korumburra ($15.60, two hours), Mansfield ($30.40, three hours) and Echuca ($30.40, three hours).

TRAIN

Southern Cross station is the terminus for intercity and interstate trains.

Great Southern Rail (📞1800 703 357; www. greatsouthernrail.com.au) Runs the *Overland* between Melbourne and Adelaide ($164, 10 to 11 hours, twice weekly).

NSW TrainLink (📞bookings 13 22 32; www. nswtrainlink.info) Twice-daily services to and from Sydney ($89, 11½ hours).

V/Line (📞1800 800 007; www.vline.com.au) Operates the Victorian train and bus networks, including direct services to Geelong (one hour) with bus connections to the Great Ocean Road.

ℹ️ GETTING AROUND

TO/FROM THE AIRPORT

There are no direct trains or trams to Melbourne Airport. Taxis charge $55-75 for the trip to the CBD, or you can catch the **SkyBus** (📞1300 SKY-BUS, 03-9335 2811; www.skybus.com.au; Southern Cross Station, 99 Spencer St, Docklands; adult/child one way $19.75/10, return $38/20; 🚉Southern Cross), which departs regularly and connects the airport to Southern Cross station 24 hours a day.

BUS

Melbourne has an extensive bus network. Most routes run from 6am to 9pm weekdays, 8am to 9pm Saturdays and 9am to 9pm Sundays. You'll

Myki Cards

Melbourne's buses, trams and trains use myki, a 'touch on, touch off' travel-pass system. It's not particularly convenient for short-term visitors as it requires you to purchase a $6 plastic myki card and then add credit before you travel.

Note that myki cards are not needed within the cbd's free tram zone. See www.ptv.vic.gov.au for details, and listen out for announcements on the tram.

Travellers should consider buying a myki Explorer ($15), which includes the card, one day's travel and discounts on various sights; it's available from SkyBus terminals, PTV hubs and some hotels. Otherwise, standard myki cards can be purchased at 7-Elevens, newsagents and major train stations.

The myki can be topped up at 7-Eleven stores, machines at most train stations, and at some tram stops in the city centre; online top-ups take some time to process.

For travel within metropolitan Melbourne (zones 1 and 2), the pay-as-you-go fare is $4.40 for two hours, capped at $8.80 for the day ($6.40 on weekends and public holidays).

There are large fines for travelling without having touched on a valid myki card; ticket inspectors are vigilant, unforgiving and sometimes undercover.

For more information, see PTV.

need a myki card to use the buses; **PTV** (Public Transport Victoria; 1800 800 007; www.ptv. vic.gov.au) has timetables, maps and a journey planner on its website.

CAR & MOTORCYCLE

CAR HIRE

Most car and campervan hire places have offices at Melbourne Airport and in the city or central suburbs.

TOLL ROADS

Both drivers and motorcyclists will need to purchase a Melbourne Pass ($5.50 start-up fee, plus tolls and a 55c or 30c vehicle-matching fee per trip, depending on the toll road) if planning on using one of the two toll roads: **CityLink** (13 33 31; www.citylink.com.au), from Tullamarine Airport to the city and eastern suburbs, or **EastLink** (03-9955 1400; www.eastlink.com. au), which runs from Ringwood to Frankston. Pay online or via phone – but pay within three days of using the toll road to avoid a fine.

TAXI

Melbourne's taxis are metered and require an estimated prepaid fare when hailed between 10pm and 5am. Toll charges are added to fares. Two of the largest taxi companies are **Silver Top** (131 008; www.silvertop.com.au) and **13 Cabs** (13 22 27; www.13cabs.com.au). **Uber** (www. uber.com) also operates in Melbourne.

TRAIN

Flinders St Station is the main city hub for Melbourne's 17 train lines, which run from around 5am weekdays until midnight Sunday to Thursday, and all night on Friday and Saturday nights.

Payment is via myki card; PTV (p170) has timetables, maps and a journey planner on its website.

TRAM

Melbourne's extensive tram network covers the city. They run roughly every 10 minutes during the day, and every 20 minutes in the evening.

The city centre is a free tram zone. Beyond this, pay with a myki card (available at 7-Elevens, newsagents and major train stations). PTV (p170) has timetables, maps and a journey planner on its website.

Where to Stay

While you'll have no trouble finding a place to stay that suits your taste and budget, for a city that's big on style Melbourne has only a handful of small, atmospheric hotels. Prices peak for major sporting events and over the summer.

Neighbourhood	Atmosphere
Carlton	Midrange places aimed at the university and hospital crowd.
Central Melbourne	Lots of places across all price ranges; in the heart of the action.
East Melbourne	Takes you out of the action; walking distance from the city; ready access to the MCG.
Fitzroy	Vibrant area; plenty of attractions; a walk away from the city.
North Melbourne	Has a few budget options.
St Kilda	A budget traveller enclave but there are some stylish options a short walk from the beach.

GREAT OCEAN ROAD

In This Chapter

Great Ocean Road at a Glance...

The Great Ocean Road is an epic Australian road trip and rite-of-passage for surfers. The drive takes you past world-class beach breaks, through pockets of rainforest and becalmed seaside towns, and under koala-filled tree canopies. Along the way are sheer limestone cliffs, dairy farms and heathlands, with the crashing waves of the Southern Ocean an ever-present soundtrack.

Day-tripping tourists from Melbourne rush in and out in less than 12 hours, but in a perfect world (and along this stretch of coast, it seems that way), you'd spend at least a week here.

The Great Ocean Road in Two Days

The Great Ocean Road officially begins at **Torquay** (p178). A slight detour takes you to famous **Bells Beach** (p178), the powerful point break that is part of international surfing folklore.

Take a **surf lesson** (p179) in Anglesea, stop for a night in stylish **Lorne** (p181), then continue west to **Apollo Bay** (p182), a tight-knit community of fisherfolk, artists, musicians and sea changers.

The Great Ocean Road in Four Days

Day three go koala spotting around **Cape Otway** (p182), then continue west to **Port Campbell National Park** (p184), home to the much-photographed Twelve Apostles. Count them from the clifftops, then roll into Port Campbell itself for a night.

Further west is endearing maritime **Port Fairy** (p185), home of Australia's best folk festival and your final destination along the Great Ocean Road.

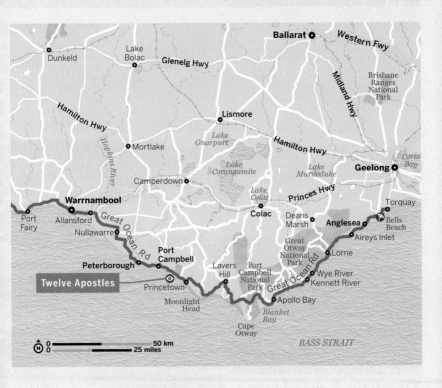

Arriving at the Great Ocean Road

Public transport can get you here (take the train from Melbourne to Geelong, then the bus), but to best explore this gorgeous coastline, bring your own wheels. If you're in a rush, bypass Geelong and take the Princess Hwy via Colac directly to the Twelve Apostles... but the lure here is in the slow and scenic coastal route.

Sleeping

Historic hotels, lighthouse cottages and boutique beach houses are just some of the memorable places to stay along the Great Ocean Road. Most towns have a hostel, as well as caravan parks.

Things book out solidly come the summer holidays, Easter and long weekends, so reserve well ahead if visiting during peak periods.

Twelve Apostles

The Great Ocean Road's iconic sight, the Twelve Apostles rock stacks rise spectacularly from the ocean, seemingly abandoned to the sea by the retreating headland.

Great For

☑ **Don't Miss**

Snaring the classic Twelve Apostles photo from atop the cliffs.

The Approach

East of the Otways, the Great Ocean Road levels out and enters narrow, flat scrubby escarpment lands that fall away to sheer, 70m-high cliffs along the coast between Princetown and Peterborough – a distinct change of scene. This is Port Campbell National Park, home to the Twelve Apostles, and the most famous and most photographed stretch of the Great Ocean Road.

How Many Apostles?

The Twelve Apostles are not 12 in number and, from all records, never have been. From the viewing platform you can clearly count seven Apostles, but maybe some obscure others? We consulted widely with Parks Victoria officers, tourist-office staff and even the cleaner at the lookout, but it's

TARAS VYSHNYA/SHUTTERSTOCK ©

ℹ Need to Know

The Apostles are 15km from Port Campbell. Unless you're taking a tour, driving here is your best option.

✕ Take a Break

The **Twelve Apostles Visitor Centre Kiosk** (⊙10am-5pm Sun-Fri, to 5.30pm Sat) serves sandwiches and fast food.

★ Top Tip

Visit at sunset: optimum photographic conditions, no tour-bus crowds and little penguins returning ashore.

still not clear. Locals tend to say 'It depends where you look from', which really is true.

The Apostles are called 'stacks' in geologic parlance, and the rock formations were originally called the 'Sow and Piglets'. Someone in the 1960s (nobody can recall who) thought they might attract some tourists with a more venerable name, so they were renamed 'the Apostles'. Since apostles tend to come by the dozen, the number 12 was added sometime later. The two stacks on the eastern (Otway) side of the viewing platform are not technically Apostles – they're Gog and Magog.

The soft limestone cliffs are dynamic and changeable, with constant erosion from the unceasing waves – one 70m-high stack collapsed into the sea in 2005 and the Island Archway lost its archway in 2009.

Guided Tours

12 Apostles Helicopters

Scenic Flights

(☑03-5598 8283; www.12apostleshelicopters.com.au; 15min flights per person $145) For the undisputed best views, head up into the skies for a chopper tour of the Twelve Apostles and surrounding sights. This operator is based at Twelve Apostles Visitor Centre (p177).

Go West Tours

Bus

(☑03-9485 5290; www.gowest.com.au; $135) Melbourne-based company offering full-day tours taking in Bells Beach, koalas in the Otways, the Twelve Apostles and around, returning to Melbourne.

Torquay

In the 1960s and '70s Torquay was just another sleepy seaside town. Back then, surfing in Australia was a decidedly countercultural pursuit, its devotees crusty hippy dropouts living in clapped-out Kombis, smoking pot and making off with your daughters. These days it's become unabashedly mainstream, and the town's proximity to world-famous Bells Beach and its status as the home of two iconic surf brands – Rip Curl and Quiksilver, both initially wetsuit makers – ensure Torquay's place as the undisputed capital of the country's surf industry.

◎ SIGHTS & ACTIVITIES

Bells Beach   Surfing

(Bells Beach Rd) The powerful point break at Bells Beach is part of international-al surfing folklore and is the site of a world-championship surfing contest (www.worldsurfleague.com) that's been held every Easter since 1973. When the right hander is working, it's one of the longest rides in the country, but it's a wave for experienced surfers only.

Australian National Surfing Museum   Museum

(☑03-5261 4606; www.australiannationalsurf-ingmuseum.com; Surf City Plaza, 77 Beach Rd; adult/child/family $12/8/25; ☺9am-5pm) The perfect starting point for those embarking on a surfing safari, this superbly curat-ed museum pays homage to Australian surfing. Here you'll see Simon Anderson's ground-breaking 1981 thruster, Mark Richard's awesome airbrushed board-art collection and, most notably, Australia's Surfing Hall of Fame. It's full of great mem-orabilia (including Duke Kahanamoku's wooden longboard), videos and displays on surf culture from the 1960s to the '80s. Its themed shows throughout the year are always quality, too.

⊗ EATING

Bomboras Torquay   Pizza $

(☑03-5264 7881; www.bomboras.com.au; 37 The Esplanade; pizzas $12-21; ☺6am-late) Catch

Bells Beach

RICHARD CARTARWICK/SHUTTERSTOCK ©

the sea breeze while digging into authentic thin-crust pizzas, washed down by a craft beer, and enjoying ocean views from the front terrace. There's a heap of modern Australian dishes and sharing plates, plus cafe-style breakfasts, and top-notch coffee by Padre in Melbourne.

ℹ️ INFORMATION

Torquay Visitor Information Centre (www.torquaylife.com.au; Surf City Plaza, Beach Rd; ◷9am-5pm) The well-resourced tourist office next to the Australian National Surfing Museum makes a good starting point along the Great Ocean Road to fine-tune your itinerary.

ℹ️ GETTING THERE & AWAY

Torquay is 15 minutes' drive south of Geelong on the B100.

McHarry's Buslines (☎03-5223 2111; www.mcharrys.com.au) Bus 51 runs hourly from 9am to 8pm (around 5pm weekends) between Geelong and Torquay ($3.40, 40 minutes).

V/Line (☎1800 800 007; www.vline.com.au; Geelong Station, Gordon Ave) Buses run four times daily from Geelong to Torquay ($3.40, 25 minutes).

Anglesea

Mix sheer orange cliffs falling into the ocean with hilly, tree-filled 'burbs and a population that booms in summer and you've got Anglesea, where sharing fish and chips with seagulls by the Anglesea River is a decades-long family tradition for many.

🎯 ACTIVITIES

Go Ride a Wave   Surfing
(☎03-5263 2111, 1300 132 441; www.gorideawave.com.au; 143b Great Ocean Rd; 2hr lesson adult/child from $72/62, 2hr board hire from $25; ◷9am-5pm) Long-established surf school that runs lessons and hires out boards, stand-up paddleboards and kayaks.

🍴 Brae at Birregurra

Located a 40-minute drive from Lorne is the picturesque town of Birregurra, known affectionately as 'Birrie'. It features an attractive 19th-century streetscape and is famous among Melburnian foodies, who come here on pilgrimage to its restaurant Brae.

Regarded as one of Australia's best restaurants, **Brae** (☎03-5236 2226; www.braerestaurant.com; 4285 Cape Otway Rd; 8-course tasting plates per person $275, matched wines additional $175; ◷from 6pm Thu, noon-3pm & from 6pm Fri & Sat, noon-3pm Sun & Mon) 🍴 was established by acclaimed chef Dan Hunter – who made his name at Dunkeld's Royal Mail Hotel – in 2012. The restaurant mostly uses whatever's growing in its 12 hectares of organic gardens to create delightful gastronomic concoctions, all masterfully presented and with plenty of surprises.

COLIN PAGE/BRAE ©

Anglesea Golf Club Kangaroo Tours   Wildlife Watching
(☎03-5263 1582; www.angleseagolfclub.com.au; Golf Links Rd, Anglesea Golf Club; 20min kangaroo tours adult/child/family $12.50/5/30, 9/18 holes from $30/50, club hire 9/18 holes $25/35; ◷10am-4pm) Get up close to eastern grey kangaroos on a tour of Anglesea's golf course, famous for its mob of resident roos that have lived here for many a year. Tours are informative and offer good photo ops.

From left: Anglesea Golf Club (p179); diners at Lorne; Erskine Falls

🍴 EATING

Hot Chicken Project
Chicken $

(📞03-5263 1365; www.thehotchickenproject.
com; 143a Great Ocean Rd; mains $18; ⊙noon-
9pm) Anglesea's dining scene just got a little
hotter with the arrival of this spicy-chicken
joint from **Geelong** (📞03-5221 8977;www.
thehotchickenproject.com; 84a Little Malop St;
mains from $18; ⊙noon-10pm). Opening in late
2018, its speciality is authentic Nashville
chicken: hot wings, tenders or dark meat
(along with fish and tofu), with a side of
fries, coleslaw or turnip greens. There are
also burgers, craft beers on tap and natural
wines.

Captain Moonlite
Australian $$

(📞03-5263 2454; www.captainmoonlite.com.
au; 100 Great Ocean Rd; breakfast $8-16, lunch
& dinner from $26; ⊙8am-10pm Fri-Sun, to 3pm
Mon, 5.30-10pm Thu) Sharing space with
the life-saving club – and with unbeatable
beach views – Moonlite is Anglesea's first
restaurant to earn a Good Food Guide

chef's hat. It mixes an unpretentious
atmosphere with a quality menu it de-
scribes as 'coastal European'. Expect tasty
breakfasts such as ocean trout on rye with
a soft-boiled egg, meze-style plates, and
mains such as slow-roasted lamb and fresh
seafood.

ℹ️ INFORMATION

Anglesea Visitor Information Centre (www.
visitgreatoceanroad.org.au; Great Ocean Rd;
⊙9am-5pm; 📶) Located at the lake, this tiny
volunteer-run information centre has a heap of
brochures on the area, including walks in the
surrounding Great Otway National Park.

ℹ️ GETTING THERE & AWAY

Anglesea is around a 1½-hour drive from
Melbourne.

There are four to six daily V/Line buses
between Geelong and Anglesea ($6.80, 45
minutes).

ANYA NEWRCHA/SHUTTERSTOCK ©

Lorne

One of the Great Ocean Road's original resort towns, Lorne may be a tad overdeveloped these days, but it retains all the charms that have lured visitors here since the 19th century. Beyond its main strip it has an incredible natural beauty: tall old gum trees line its hilly streets, and Loutit Bay gleams irresistibly.

⊙ SIGHTS & ACTIVITIES

Great Ocean Road Story   Museum
(15 Mountjoy Pde; ⊗9am-5pm) **FREE** Inside Lorne Visitor Centre (p182), this permanent exhibition of displays, videos and books offers informative background to the Great Ocean Road's construction. There are multimedia displays, and the opportunity to get yourself superimposed into a picture of an old automobile chugging along the magnificent Great Ocean Road.

Qdos Art Gallery   Gallery
(☑03-5289 1989; www.qdosarts.com; 35 Allenvale Rd; ⊗9am-5pm Thu-Mon, daily Jan, Fri-Mon

winter) **FREE** Set amid the lush forest behind Lorne, Qdos always has something interesting showing at its contemporary gallery, to go with its open-air sculpture garden. There's also a lovely little cafe doing wood-fired pizzas and *ryokan*-style **accommodation** (r incl breakfast $325-495; ☎).

Erskine Falls   Waterfall
(Erskine Falls Access Rd) Head out of town to see this lovely 30m waterfall. It's an easy walk from the Erskine Falls car park to the viewing platform (15 minutes return) or 300, often slippery, steps down to its base (30 minutes return), from where you can explore further or head back up.

⊗ EATING

**Lorne Beach
Pavilion**   Australian $$
(☑03-5289 2882; www.lornebeachpavilion. com.au; 81 Mountjoy Pde; breakfast $8-24, mains $18-45; ⊗9am-5pm Mon-Thu, to 9pm Fri, 8am-9pm Sat & Sun) With its unbeatable foreshore location, at the pavilion life is a beach, especially with a cold drink in hand.

 Cape Otway

Cape Otway is the second-most-southerly point of mainland Australia (after Wilsons Promontory) and one of the wettest parts of the state. This coastline is particularly beautiful, rugged and historically treacherous for passing ships. The turn-off for Lighthouse Rd, which leads 12km down to 1848 **Cape Otway Lightstation** (🖉03-5237 9240; www.lightstation.com; Lighthouse Rd; adult/child/family $19.50/7.50/49.50; ☺9am-5pm), is 21km from Apollo Bay. It's a beautiful forested road with towering trees, which are home to a sizeable population of koalas.

Cape Otway Lightstation
RUBEN MARTINEZ BARRICARTE/SHUTTERSTOCK ©

Cafe-style breakfasts and lunches hit the spot, while a more upmarket Modern Oz menu of seafood and rib-eye steaks is on for dinner. Come at happy hour (3pm to 6pm) for $7 pints, or swing by at sunset for a bottle of prosecco.

Movida Lorne   Spanish $$$
(🖉03-5289 1042; www.movida.com.au; 176 Mountjoy Pde; tapas $4-8.50, raciones $15-70; ☺noon-3pm & 5.30-10pm) One of Melbourne's hottest restaurants has gone for a sea change, setting up on the ground floor of the **Lorne Hotel** (🖉03-5289 1409; www.lorne-hotel.com.au; 1r $160-300; ❄🛜), Movida has brought its authentic Spanish cuisine to the Great Ocean Road. The menu features a mix of classic dishes made with flair using regional produce.

ℹ INFORMATION

Lorne Visitor Centre (🖉1300 891 152, 03-5289 1152; www.lovelorne.com.au; 15 Mountjoy Pde; ☺9am-5pm; 🛜) Stacks of information (including heaps of ideas for walks in the area), helpful staff, fishing licences, bus tickets and accommodation referrals. Also has a gift shop, internet access, free wi-fi and a charger out the front for electric cars.

ℹ GETTING THERE & AWAY

If you're driving from Melbourne allow just under two hours for the 143km journey. Birregurra and Forrest, inland, are both around a 45-minute drive away.

V/Line buses pass through daily from Geelong ($12.40, 1½ hours) en route to Apollo Bay ($5.40, from 65 minutes).

Apollo Bay

One of the larger towns along the Great Ocean Road, Apollo Bay has a tight-knit community of fisherfolk, artists, musicians and sea changers. Rolling hills provide a postcard backdrop to the town, while broad, white-sand beaches dominate the foreground. It's an ideal base for exploring magical Cape Otway and the adjoining national park. There are some decent restaurants and several lively pubs, and it's one of the best towns on the Great Ocean Road for budget travellers, with numerous hostels and ready transport access.

The Gadubanud people are the traditional custodians of Apollo Bay and the Otways region.

◉ SIGHTS & ACTIVITIES

Marriners Lookout   Viewpoint
(155 Marriners Lookout Rd) Located 1.5km from town back towards Cape Patton, this scenic walk offers wonderful panoramic views over town and the ocean. If you have a car it's a steep five-minute walk from the lookout car park; otherwise, it's around a 45-minute walk (one way) from the centre of town.

Apollo Bay Surf & Kayak   Adventure
(📞0405 495 909, 03-5237 1189; www.apollobay
surfkayak.com.au; 157-159 Great Ocean Rd; 2hr
kayak tours $75, 1½hr SUP/surfing lesson $70/75)
For a cool wildlife encounter, grab a paddle
and head out by kayak to visit an Australian
fur-seal colony on these well-run tours.
They depart from Marengo Beach (south of
the town centre); children need to be over
12 years old. Also offers surfing and stand-
up paddleboarding lessons, plus board and
mountain-bike hire ($35 per half-day).

Otway Eco Tours   Canoeing
(📞0419 670 985; www.platypustours.net.au;
adult/child $85/50) While you may have
been lucky enough to spot a bunch of
native wildlife on your journey, the elusive
platypus is the one that often gets away.
Fortunately, here you can sign up for a
dawn or dusk guided canoe trip on Lake
Elizabeth, where you have a reasonable
chance of encountering this truly unique
animal. On the dusk trip you'll also see
glow-worms.

🍴 EATING

**Chris's Beacon
Point Restaurant**   Greek $$$
(📞03-5237 6411; www.chriss.com.au; 280
Skenes Creek Rd; breakfast $13-21, mains from
$42-55; ⊙8.30-10.40am & 6pm-late daily, plus
noon-2pm Sat & Sun; 🅿) Feast on memorable
ocean views, deliciously fresh seafood and
Greek-influenced dishes at Chris's hilltop
fine-dining sanctuary among the treetops.
Reservations recommended. You can also
stay in its wonderful **stilted villas** (📞03-
5237 6218; www.beaconpoint.com.au; r incl
breakfast $170-370; ❄🅿). It's accessed via
Skenes Creek.

ℹ INFORMATION

Great Ocean Road Visitor Centre (📞1300 689
297; www.visitapollobay.com; 100 Great Ocean
Rd; ⊙9am-5pm) Modern and professional tourist
office with a heap of info on the area. Has free
wi-fi and can book bus tickets too.

Marriners Lookout

Loch Ard Gorge

ⓘ GETTING THERE & AWAY

Driving to Apollo Bay along the Great Ocean Road from Melbourne is a 4½-hour drive. Alternatively, catch a train to Geelong then transfer to a connecting bus ($30.40, 3¾ hours).

Port Campbell & Port Campbell National Park

This small, windswept town is poised on a dramatic, natural bay, eroded from the surrounding limestone cliffs, and almost perfectly rectangular in shape. It's a friendly place with some great bargain accommodation options, and makes an ideal spot for debriefing after the Twelve Apostles (p176) within Port Campbell National Park, 12km from the town.

◎ SIGHTS

Loch Ard Gorge   Beach
Close to the Twelve Apostles, Loch Ard Gorge is where the Shipwreck Coast's most famous and haunting tale unfolded when

two young survivors of the wrecked iron clipper *Loch Ard* made it to shore. There are several walks in the area, the most popular being the path down to the picturesque beach and cave where the pair took shelter. Further trails from here lead to scenic viewpoints, a cemetery, a blowhole and a rugged beach.

Gibson Steps   Beach
Follow 86 steps, hacked by hand into the cliffs by 19th-century landowner Hugh Gibson (and more recently replaced by concrete ones), down to wild Gibson Beach. You can walk along the beach, but be careful not to get stranded by high tides. It's a 50m walk from the car park, or a 2.2km return walk along a trail that sets out from the Twelve Apostles Visitor Centre (p177).

✕ EATING

Forage on the Foreshore   Cafe $$
(☏03-5598 6202; www.forageontheforeshore. com.au; 32 Cairns St; dishes $12-32; ⊙9am-4pm; 🛜) In the old post office is this seafront cottage cafe with wooden floorboards, art on

the walls, an open fireplace and a vintage record player spinning vinyl. There's an all-day breakfast menu, gourmet sandwiches, burgers, duck-fat-fried chips, and items featuring fresh abalone and regional produce.

🛈 INFORMATION

Port Campbell Visitor Centre (☏1300 137 255; www.visit12apostles.com.au; 26 Morris St; ⊙9am-5pm) Stacks of regional and accommodation information and interesting relics from various shipwrecks – the anchor from the *Loch Ard* is out the front. Offers free use of binoculars, stargazer telescopes, cameras and GPS equipment, and runs scavenger hunts for kids.

🛈 GETTING THERE & AWAY

V/Line buses leave Geelong on Monday, Wednesday and Friday and travel through to Port Campbell ($35.60, 5¼ hours), but you'll need to transfer to a different bus in Apollo Bay (two hours and 15 minutes), which generally leaves 30 minutes later. There's also a bus from Port Campbell to Warrnambool ($8.40, 1¼ hours) that leaves on the same days.

West of Port Campbell

The Great Ocean Road continues west of Port Campbell passing more rock stacks. The next one is the **Arch**, offshore from Point Hesse. Nearby is **London Bridge** (fallen down!) and the **Grotto**. The **Bay of Islands** is 8km west of tiny Peterborough. A short walk from the car park takes you to magnificent lookout points.

The Great Ocean Road ends near here where it meets the Princes Hwy, which

---

Hard Yakka

The first sections of the Great Ocean Road were constructed by hand (using picks, shovels and crowbars) by returned WWI soldiers. Work began in September 1919 and the road between Anglesea and Apollo Bay was completed in 1932.

---

continues through the traditional lands of the Gunditjmara people into South Australia.

Port Fairy

Settled in 1833 as a whaling and sealing station, Port Fairy – 20 minutes west of Warrnambool – retains its historic 19th-century charm with a relaxed, salty feel, heritage bluestone and sandstone buildings, whitewashed cottages, colourful fishing boats and wide, tree-lined streets.

Australia's premier folk-music festival, **Port Fairy Folk Festival** (www.portfairy-folkfestival.com; tickets $290-310, free events in town) is held on the Labour Day long weekend in early March. Book accommodation early.

Port Fairy Visitor Centre (☏1300 656 564; www.portfairyaustralia.com.au; Railway Pl, Bank St; ⊙9am-5pm; 🛜) provides the usual swath of brochures, including the *Maritime & Shipwreck Heritage Walk*. Architecture buffs will want to buy a copy of *Historic Buildings of Port Fairy*. You can buy V/Line tickets here too, or hire a bike (half-/full day $15/25).

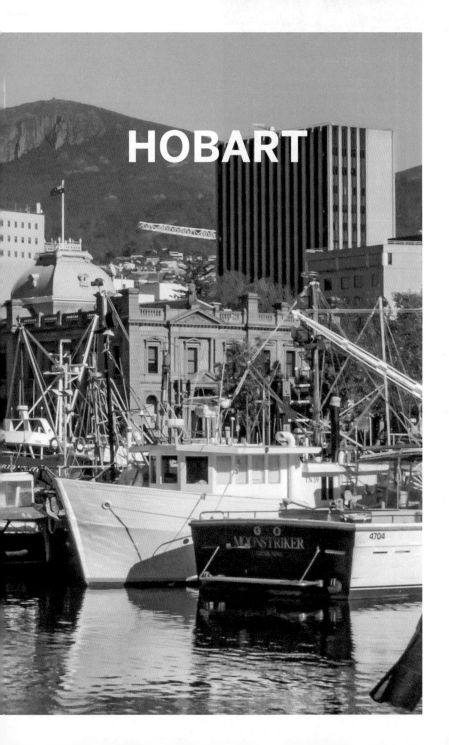

HOBART

Hobart at a Glance...

No doubt about it, Hobart's future is looking rosy. Tourism is booming and the old town is brimming with new-found self-confidence.

Riding high above the city is kunanyi/Mt Wellington, a rugged monolith seemingly made for mountain biking and bushwalking. Down on the waterfront, the Salamanca Place cafes, bars and restaurants showcase the best of Tassie produce. There's more great eating and boozing along Elizabeth St in bohemian North Hobart. And don't miss Battery Point, Hobart's first neighbourhood, which oozes historic charm.

Hobart in Two Days

Get your head into history mode with an amble around **Battery Point** (p196). Afterwards, wander down Kelly's Steps to **Salamanca Place** (p192) and check out the craft shops and restaurants, and chug a few ales. On day two, catch the ferry to **MONA** (p191), with dinner and some live music afterwards in North Hobart.

Hobart in Four Days

Blow out the cobwebs with a mountain-bike ride on the **Mt Wellington Descent** (p199). In the foothills of the mountain is the legendary **Cascade Brewery** (p197): take a tour and sip a few, before dinner back on the waterfront. On day four, hit the museums: top of your list should be the **Tasmanian Museum & Art Gallery** (p196) and **Mawson's Huts Replica Museum** (p199).

Previous page: Victoria Dock (p197), Hobart
CRBELLETTE/SHUTTERSTOCK ©

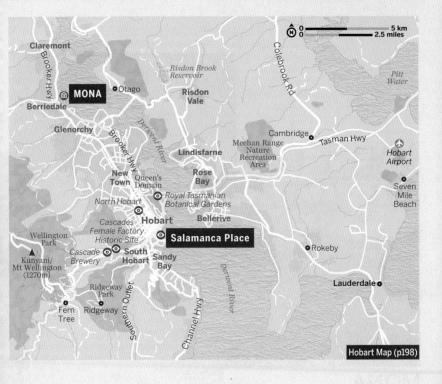

Hobart Map (p198)

Arriving in Hobart

Hobart Airport (p204) is at Cambridge, 19km east of the city. Many visitors to Hobart rent a car: rental desks proliferate in the airport terminal. There's no public transport to the airport, so grab a cab ($50, 20 minutes) or pre-book a seat on a shuttle bus (adult/child $19/14).

Sleeping

The most pumping areas to stay in Hobart are the waterfront and Salamanca Place (apartments and boutique hotels aplenty), though prices here are usually sky-high and vacancy rates low. If you're visiting in January, book as far in advance as humanly possible. The CBD has less atmosphere, but most of the backpacker hostels, pubs with accommodation and midrange hotels are here.

MONA

*No matter what your expectations –
arresting architecture, exquisite
artefacts, confronting installations,
quirky festivals or fab food and wine –
MONA delivers.*

The MONA Effect

Twelve kilometres north of Hobart's city
centre, occupying a saucepan-shaped
peninsula jutting into the Derwent River,
MONA is so darn popular it has almost
single-handedly dragged Hobart onto the
world stage. The so-called 'MONA effect'
has elevated the city's hospitality and
business standards in kind. The brainchild
of Hobart philanthropist and eccentric
gambling multi-millionaire David Walsh and
designed by architect Nonda Katsalidis, the
$75 million MONA is arrayed across three
underground levels abutting sheer rock
faces. Described by Walsh as 'a subversive
adult Disneyland', the museum features
ancient antiquities showcased next to
contemporary works: the experience is
sexy, provocative, disturbing and deeply
engaging.

Great For...

☑ Don't Miss

bit.fall: Julius Popp's two-storey installation dripping random phrases from
news websites.

ARCHITECT: NONDA KATSALIDIS. IMAGE BY: CHAMELEONSEYE/SHUTTERSTOCK ©

ⓘ Need to Know

Museum of Old & New Art; ☑03-6277 9900; www.mona.net.au; 655 Main Rd, Berriedale; adult/child $28/free, Tasmanian residents free; ⊙10am-6pm Jan, 10am-6pm Wed-Mon Feb-Apr & Dec, to 5pm Wed-Mon May-Nov

✕ Take a Break

The outstanding **Source** (☑03-6277 9904; www.mona.net.au/eat-drink/the-source-restaurant; mains $22-40; ⊙7.30-10am & noon-2pm Wed-Mon, 6pm-late Fri & Sat) restaurant is on site.

★ Top Tip

Catch the ferry here, sitting in the 'Posh Pit' (champagne and canapes!).

Monanism

'Monanism' is the name given to the broad collection of art here, numbering upwards of 1900 pieces. Some works are so big and/or important that the museum was designed around them, including *Snake,* a 46m-long array of images exploring the connections between myth and modernity; and the *Chamber of Pausiris,* containing the coffin and mummy of a 2000-year-old Egyptian. Other must-sees include the room dedicated solely to the worship of Madonna; the fabulous programmed waterfall *bit.fall;* and every kid's favourite, the impressive poo machine *Cloaca Professional,* which recreates (with alarmingly accurate waste products) the human digestive system.

Moorilla

As well as the gallery, MONA is home to the cellar door for **Moorilla** (☑03-6277 9960; www.moorilla.com.au; tastings/tours $10/20; ⊙tastings 9.30am-5pm Mon-Wed, tours 3.30pm Wed-Mon), a winery established here in the 1950s; duck in for a wine or a beer tasting.

Dark MOFO Festival

Dark MOFO (www.darkmofo.net.au) broods in the half-light of June's winter solstice. Expect live music, installations, readings, film noir, bonfires, red wine and midnight feasts, all mainlining Tasmania's Gothic blood flow.

Note the wonderfully eclectic festival of music and arts, Mona Foma, which used to be held on the grounds of MONA, has relocated to Launceston.

Salamanca Place

A gorgeous row of 1830s stone warehouses, Salamanca Place hosts myriad restaurants, cafes, bars and shops, and Saturday's unmissable Salamanca Market.

Great For...

☑ Don't Miss

Behind Salamanca Place is Salamanca Square, a former quarry lined with cafes, bars and shops.

Eating & Drinking

Interesting fact for the day: Salamanca Place takes its name from the Spanish province of Salamanca, where the Duke of Wellington claimed victory in the Battle of Salamanca in 1812. Something to discuss over a meal or an evening drink, perhaps – eating and drinking being the prime reasons you're here! So popular is the Salamanca scene that the Hobart City Council recently widened the footpath in front of the warehouses, to allow restaurants and bars more space for street-side tables and chairs. Wander along and see what grabs you.

Salamanca Market

What started out as a couple of hippies selling raspberries in 1972 has evolved

Need to Know

Salamanca Place is in Sullivans Cove, on Hobart's waterfront, a five-minute walk from the city centre.

Take a Break

Keep Retro Cafe (p202) at the top of your Salamanca Place cafe list.

★ Top Tip

Salamanca Place is closed to traffic on market days, and parking anywhere nearby is hell. Walk instead!

---

into a kilometre-long frenzy of food and commerce that consumes *all* of Salamanca Place every Saturday morning. With thousands of people here every week, **Salamanca Market** (☎03-6238 2843; www. salamancamarket.com.au; Salamanca Pl; ⊙8am-3pm Sat) is something to behold: make a slow-shuffling circuit down one side of the stalls then back down the other. The cafes overflow, the buskers are in fine voice and (even in winter) the vibe is downright convivial.

Salamanca Arts Centre

As with many of Tasmania's architectural relics, the Salamanca Place warehouses only survived the 20th century because no one here had the money to knock them down. Thank goodness! Indeed, these chunky stone walls would take some

shifting: step into the **Salamanca Arts Centre** (SAC; ☎03-6234 8414; www.salarts. org.au; 65-77 Salamanca Pl; ⊙shops & galleries 9am-5pm) for a close-up look...oh, and to check out the dozens of artists' studios, retail spaces, performance venues, cafes and galleries that comprise this progressive art co-op, running since 1975.

Friday Night Fandango

Live music doesn't come more atmospheric than Friday nights at the Salamanca Arts Centre Courtyard (p204). There's no cover charge and, if you're lucky, you'll get to hear the reason behind the unusual, if rather catchy name 'Rektango' – the band of the same name sometimes takes the stage here. Most genres are welcome from Afrobeat or Latino to rockabilly.

Hobart's Harbour & History

Catch Hobart's historic vibe with a walk from the city centre, through historic Battery Point and down to Salamanca Place on the waterfront.

Start Franklin Square
Distance 3km
Duration Three hours

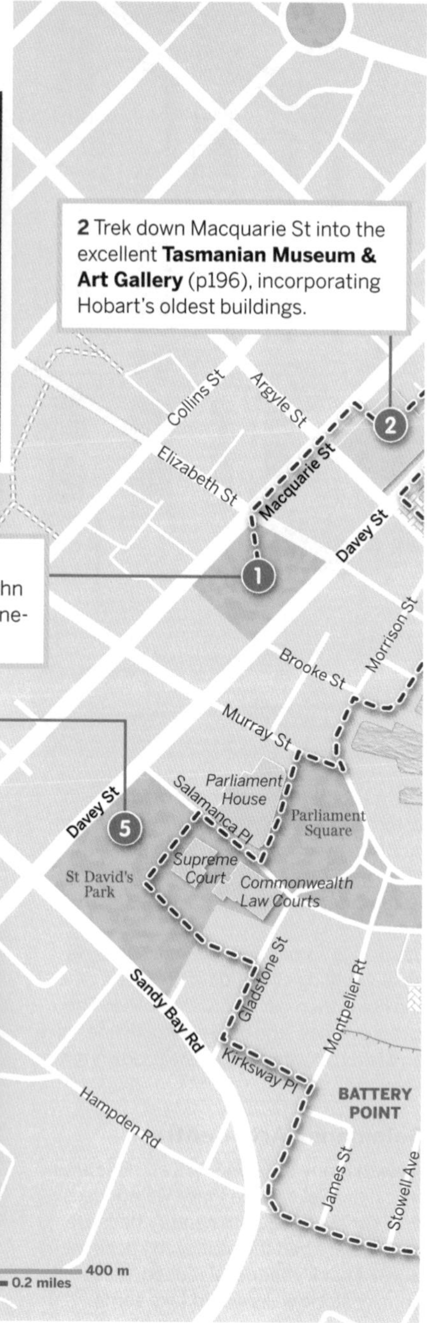

2 Trek down Macquarie St into the excellent **Tasmanian Museum & Art Gallery** (p196), incorporating Hobart's oldest buildings.

1 Launch your expedition at **Franklin Sq**, named after Sir John Franklin, Van Diemen's Land's one-time lieutenant-governor.

5 Skirt around Constitution Dock and the broad Sullivans Cove waterfront to **St David's Park**, Hobart Town's original cemetery.

Classic Photo Arthur Circus is an improbably quaint roundabout lined with Georgian cottages.

0   400 m
0   0.2 miles

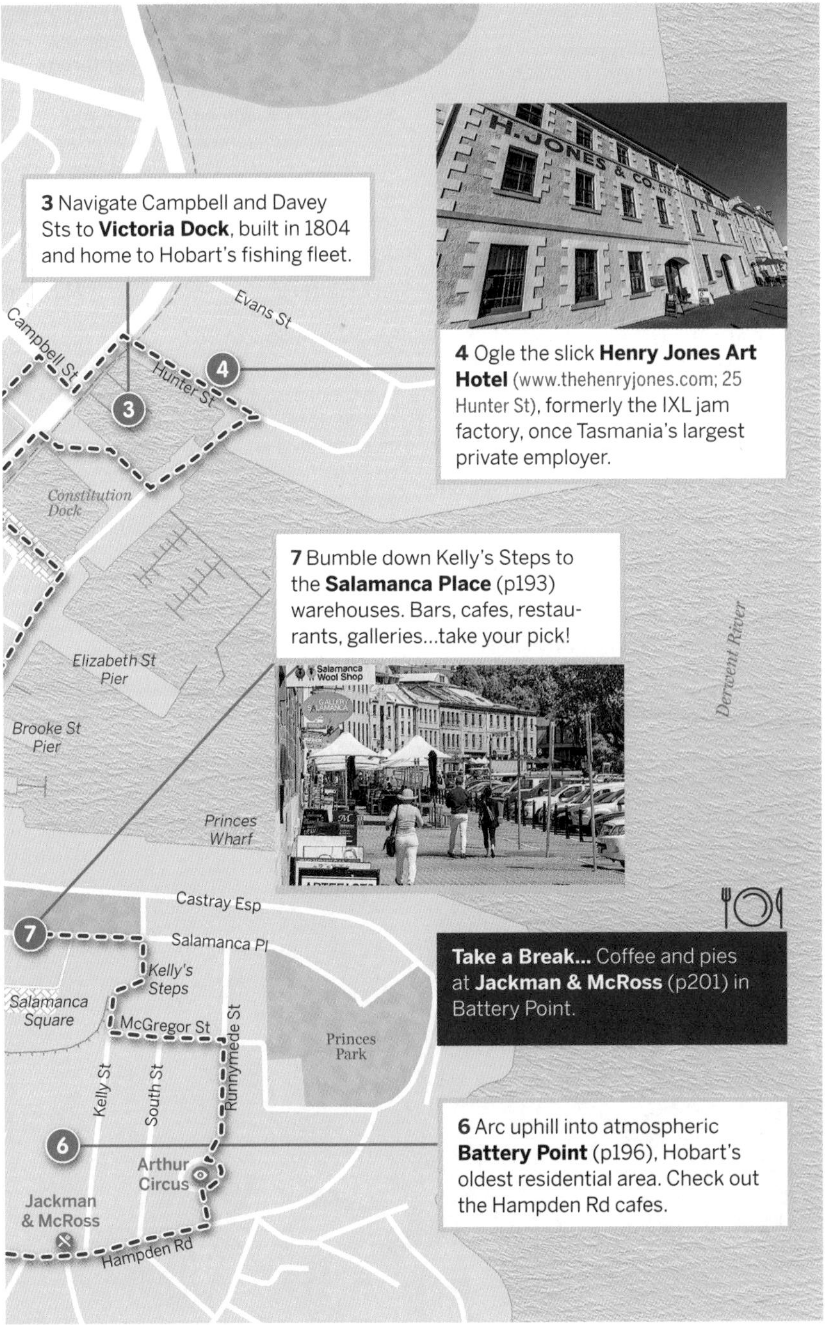

3 Navigate Campbell and Davey Sts to **Victoria Dock**, built in 1804 and home to Hobart's fishing fleet.

4 Ogle the slick **Henry Jones Art Hotel** (www.thehenryjones.com; 25 Hunter St), formerly the IXL jam factory, once Tasmania's largest private employer.

7 Bumble down Kelly's Steps to the **Salamanca Place** (p193) warehouses. Bars, cafes, restaurants, galleries...take your pick!

Evans St

Campbell St

Hunter St

Constitution Dock

Elizabeth St Pier

Brooke St Pier

Derwent River

Princes Wharf

Castray Esp

Salamanca Pl

Kelly's Steps

Salamanca Square

McGregor St

Kelly St

South St

Runnymede St

Princes Park

Arthur Circus

Jackman & McRoss

Hampden Rd

Take a Break... Coffee and pies at **Jackman & McRoss** (p201) in Battery Point.

6 Arc uphill into atmospheric **Battery Point** (p196), Hobart's oldest residential area. Check out the Hampden Rd cafes.

◉ SIGHTS

Kunanyi/Mt Wellington   Mountain

(www.wellingtonpark.org.au; Pinnacle Rd, via Fern Tree) Ribbed with its striking Organ Pipes cliffs, kunanyi/Mt Wellington (1271m) towers over Hobart like a benevolent overlord. The view from the top stretches over Hobart and much of the state's south, and the slopes are laced with walking trails. Mountain bikers come for the **North South Track**, descending from the Springs to Glenorchy, while you can also coast down the sealed summit road on a bike with Mt Wellington Descent (p199). The Hobart Shuttle Bus Company (p205) runs daily two-hour tours to the summit and the Explorer Bus (p205) also runs this route.

Battery Point   Historic Site

Tucked in behind Salamanca Pl, the old maritime village of Battery Point is a tight nest of lanes and 19th-century cottages. Spend an afternoon exploring: stumble up **Kelly's Steps** (Kelly St) from Salamanca Pl and wander through **Princes Park**, where the gun battery of the suburb's name stood, protecting Hobart Town from nautical threats both real and imagined. Spin around picturesque **Arthur Circus**, refuel in Hampden Rd's cafes, then ogle **St George's Anglican Church** (☑03-6223 2146; www.stgeorgesbatterypoint.org; 30 Cromwell St; ⊘office 9.15am-2.15pm Mon-Thu, services 8am & 10am Sun) – the tower was designed by a convict architect.

Tasmanian Museum & Art Gallery   Museum

(TMAG; ☑03-6165 7000; www.tmag.tas.gov.au; Dunn Pl; ⊘10am-4pm, closed Mon Apr-Dec) **FREE** Incorporating Tasmania's oldest surviving public building, the Commissariat Store (1808), TMAG features Aboriginal and colonial relics and an excellent Antarctic and Southern Ocean display. The gallery curates a collection of Tasmanian colonial and modern art, and there are changing temporary exhibitions. Free guided tours run at 1pm and 2pm from Wednesday to Sunday, plus special themed tours at 11am; check the website to see what's on. There's a cool courtyard cafe and shop, too.

Tourists at Kunanyi/Mt Wellington

Waterfront   Area

Hobartians flock to the city's waterfront like seagulls to chips. Centred on **Victoria Dock** (a working fishing harbour) and **Constitution Dock** (full of floating fish punts and the odd wayward seal), it's a brilliant place to explore. The obligatory Hobart experience is to sit in the sun, munch some fish and chips and watch the harbour hubbub. If you'd prefer something with a knife and fork, there are some superb restaurants here, too – head for **Elizabeth Street Pier** or Mures (p202).

Cascade Brewery   Brewery

(✆03-6212 7801; www.cascadebrewery.com.
au; 140 Cascade Rd, South Hobart; brewery
tour adult/child 16-18yr $30/15, Beer School
adult/child $15/10) Standing in startling, Gothic isolation next to the clean-running Hobart Rivulet, Australia's oldest brewery (1824) is still pumping out great beers. The daily one-hour tours involve plenty of history, with tastings at the end. Note that under-16s aren't permitted on the main brewery tour (take the family-friendly Beer School tour instead), and that brewery machinery might not be running if you're here on a weekend (brewers have weekends, too). To get here, take bus 446, 447 or 449.

Cascades Female Factory
Historic Site   Historic Site

(✆03-6233 6656, 1800 139 478; www.female
factory.org.au; 16 Degraves St, South Hobart;
adult/child/family $8/5/20, Heritage Tour
$18/12/45; ☺9.30am-4pm, tours 10am, 11am,
1pm, 2pm & 3pm) This World Heritage Site was where Hobart's female convicts were incarcerated and put to work. Around 12,500 women were transported to Tasmania, and at its height the Cascades Female Factory held 1200 women – more convicts than Port Arthur ever held at a time. You can explore the hauntingly spare yards with their interpretive installations independently, or take a guided Heritage Tour or the excellent **Her Story** (✆03-6233
6656; www.livehistoryhobart.com.au/her-story;
adult/child/family $25/15/70) dramatisation.

👪 Hobart for Children

The free Friday-night Rektango (p204) music event in the courtyard at the Salamanca Arts Centre is a family-friendly affair, while the street performers and buskers at Saturday's Salamanca Market (p193) captivate. There's always something going on around the waterfront – fishing boats chugging in and out, yachts tacking in Sullivans Cove...and you can feed the tribe on a budget at the floating fish punts on Constitution Dock.

Rainy-day attractions to satisfy your child (or inner child) include the Tasmanian Museum & Art Gallery and the excellent Mawson's Huts Replica Museum (p199).

Hobart is an active kinda town: take a boat cruise up or down the river; assail the heights of kunanyi/Mt Wellington; or hire a bike and explore the cycling paths.

Constitution Dock
JAX10289/SHUTTERSTOCK ©

To get here by public transport, take bus 446, 447 or 449.

North Hobart   Area

Hobart at its most bohemian, the Elizabeth St strip in North Hobart (aka NoHo) is lined with dozens of cafes, restaurants, bars and pubs – enough to keep you coming back meal after drink after meal. Also here is the excellent art-house State Cinema (p204), and Hobart's staunchest live-music room, the Republic Bar & Café (p204). Must-do Hobart!

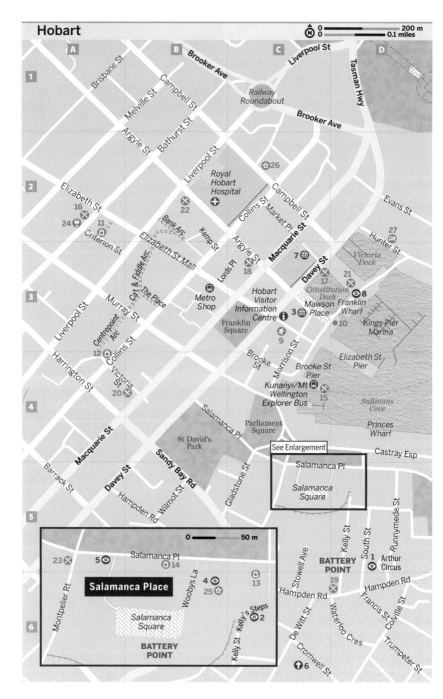

Hobart

◉N 0 ___ 200 m
    0 ___ 0.1 miles

Brisbane St

Brooker Ave

Liverpool St

Melville St

Campbell St

Railway Roundabout

Tasman Hwy

Bathurst St

Argyle St

Brooker Ave

Liverpool St

Royal Hobart Hospital ✚

☆26

Campbell St

Evans St

Elizabeth St

16

24

11

Criterion St

22

Bank Arc

Kemp St

Elizabeth St Mall

Collins St

Market Pl

Macquarie St

Hunter St

27

Victoria Dock

Cat & Fiddle Arc

The Place

Lords Pl

Argyle St

7

Davey St

17

21

8

Metro Shop

18

Hobart Visitor Information Centre ℹ

Constitution Dock

Mawson Place

Franklin Wharf

Murray St

Centrepoint Arc

3

Franklin Square

10

Kings Pier Marina

Liverpool St

12

Collins St

Brooke St

9

Morrison St

Elizabeth St Pier

Harrington St

Victoria St

20

Brooke St Pier

Brooke St

Kunanyi/Mt Wellington Explorer Bus

15

Sullivans Cove

Macquarie St

Salamanca Pl

Parliament Square

Princes Wharf

St David's Park

Gladstone St

See Enlargement

Castray Esp

Sandy Bay Rd

Salamanca Pl

Barrack St

Davey St

Salamanca Square

Hampden Rd

Wilmot St

Runnymede St

0 ___ 50 m

23

5

Salamanca Pl

14

Kelly St

South St

BATTERY POINT

1

Arthur Circus

Woobys La

4

25

13

Montpelier Rt

Salamanca Place

Stowell Ave

19

Hampden Rd

Salamanca Square

Kelly's Steps

2

De Witt St

Waterloo Cres

Francis St

Colville St

BATTERY POINT

Cromwell St

6

Trumpeter St

Hobart

Mawson's Huts Replica Museum
Museum

(☏03-6231 1518, 1300 551 422; www.maw
sons-huts-replica.org.au; cnr Morrison & Argyle
Sts; adult/child/family $15/5/35; ☺9am-6pm
Oct-Apr, 10am-5pm May-Sep) This excellent
waterfront installation is an exact model
of one of the huts in which Sir Douglas
Mawson's Australasian Antarctic Expedition team, which set sail from Hobart,
hunkered down from 1911 to 1914. The
replica is painstakingly exact (Mawson's
tiny keyboard, a sledge and an ice axe are
actually originals) and a knowledgeable
guide is on hand to answer your Antarctic
enquiries. Imagine 18 men living here,
dining on penguin stew...

Royal Tasmanian Botanical Gardens
Gardens

(☏03-6166 0451; www.rtbg.tas.gov.au; Lower
Domain Rd, Queen's Domain; ☺8am-6.30pm Oct-
Mar, to 5.30pm Apr & Sep, to 5pm May-Aug) **FREE**
On the eastern side of the Queen's Domain
park, these beguiling 200-year-old gardens
feature more than 6000 exotic and native
plant species. Picnic on the lawns, check
out the Subantarctic House or grab a bite
at the restaurant or cafe. Call to ask about

guided tours. Down the hill from the main
entrance, opposite Government House,
is the site of the former **Beaumaris Zoo**,
where the last captive Tasmanian tiger died
in 1936; a couple of dilapidated enclosures
remain.

⭐ ACTIVITIES

Roaring 40s Kayaking
Kayaking

(☏0455 949 777; www.roaring40skayaking.com.
au; Marieville Esplanade, Sandy Bay; adult/child
$90/60; ☺10am Oct-Apr, 10am & 4pm Nov-Mar)
Hobart looks its prettiest from the water.
Take a safe, steady, 2½-hour guided paddle
with Roaring 40s, named after the prevail-
ing winds at these latitudes. You'll cruise
from Sandy Bay, rounding Battery Point
and heading into Constitution Dock for
some fish and chips while you float, before
returning to Sandy Bay.

⭐ TOURS

Mt Wellington Descent
Cycling

(☏1800 444 442; www.underdownunder.com.
au/tour/mount-wellington-descent; adult/child
$85/65; ☺10am & 1pm year-round, plus 4pm

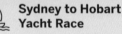

Sydney to Hobart Yacht Race

Arguably the world's greatest and most treacherous open-ocean yacht race, the **Sydney to Hobart Yacht Race** (www.rolexsydneyhobart.com; ⊘Dec) has Hobart's Constitution Dock as its finish line, with many yachts finishing some time around New Year's Eve. As the sometimes storm-battered yachts limp across the finish line, Champagne corks pop and weary sailors turn the town upside down. On New Year's Day, find a sunny spot by the harbour, munch some lunch from the Taste of Tasmania food festival and count spinnakers on the river. New Year's resolutions? What New Year's resolutions?

Sydney to Hobart Yacht Race
SLOW WALKER/SHUTTERSTOCK ©

Dec-Feb) Take a van ride to the summit of kunanyi/Mt Wellington, and follow with 21km of downhill cruising on a mountain bike. It's terrific fun, with minimal energy output and maximum views. If you want to up the adventure, there's an off-road option. Tours start and end on Elizabeth St, opposite the visitor centre, and last 2½ hours. No kids under eight.

Pennicott Wilderness Journeys   Boating
(☑03-6234 4270; www.pennicottjourneys.com. au; Dock Head Bldg, Franklin Wharf; tours adult/ child from $125/100; ⊘7am-6.30pm) Pennicott offers several outstanding boat trips around key southern Tasmanian sights, including trips along Bruny Island, the Tas-

man Peninsula and the Iron Pot Lighthouse south of Hobart. The 7½-hour Tasmanian Seafood Seduction trip, replete with a Neptune's bounty of abalone, lobster, oysters and salmon, is a winner for fans of all things fishy.

Hobart Historic Tours   Walking
(☑03-6234 5550; www.hobarthistorictours. com.au; tours $33-50) Informative, entertaining walking tours of Hobart and historic Battery Point. There's a 1½-hour Old Hobart Pub Tour (5pm Thursday to Saturday), which sluices through some waterfront watering holes, a 1½-hour Historic Walk and a three-hour Grand Hobart Walk (both 2pm Wednesday to Sunday).

Gourmania   Food & Drink
(☑0419 180 113; www.gourmaniafoodtours.com. au; tours $129-139) Fabulous, flavour-filled walking tours run by passionate local foodies, taking in Salamanca Pl and central Hobart. Expect plenty of tasting opportunities and chats with restaurant, cafe and shop owners. Saturday sees a two-hour Salamanca Market tour ($95).

🔒 SHOPPING
Fullers Bookshop   Books
(☑03-6234 3800; www.fullersbookshop.com.au; 131 Collins St; ⊘8.30am-6pm Mon-Fri, 9am-5pm Sat, 10am-4pm Sun) Hobart's best bookshop has a great range of literature and travel guides, plus regular book launches, signings and readings, and the writerly **Afterword Café** in the corner. Fullers has been a true hub of the Hobart literary scene for almost a century.

Handmark Gallery   Art
(☑03-6223 7895; www.handmark.com.au; 77 Salamanca Pl; ⊘10am-5pm Mon-Fri, to 4pm Sat & Sun) A key tenant at the Salamanca Arts Centre (p193), Handmark has been here for 30 years, displaying unique ceramics, glass, woodwork and jewellery, plus paintings and sculpture – 100% Tasmanian, 100% exquisite.

Cool Wine
Wine

(☏03-6231 4000; www.coolwine.com.au; Shop 8, MidCity Arcade, Criterion St; ☉9.30am-6.30pm Mon-Sat) Offers an excellent selection of Tasmanian wine, spirits and craft beers (plus a few global interlopers, if they're up to scratch), as well as regular tastings and the likes of gin master classes. Freight available.

🗙 EATING
Bury Me Standing
Cafe $

(☏0424 365 027; www.facebook.com/bury mestandinghobarttown; 83-85 Bathurst St; bagels $5-13; ☉6am-4pm Mon-Fri, 7am-2pm Sat & Sun) Stepping into this brilliant little coffee-and-bagel joint, run by a chipper Minnesotan who ended up in Hobart accidentally, is like waking into an old-time curiosity shop – skeleton wallpaper one side, bright swatches of paisley wrapping paper on the other. Seats are few and bagels are pot-boiled in the traditional method – don't go past the meat-free bagel dogs.

Burger Haus
Burgers $

(☏03-6234 9507; www.theburgerhaus.com.au; 364a Elizabeth St, North Hobart; burgers $13-16; ☉11.30am-late) Boasting big beefy burgers, a little outdoor terrace, craft beers and ciders, and a view that combines a concrete car park with the moody hues of kunanyi/ Mt Wellington, this back-lane burger bar has it all! The Haus Burger (with bacon, onion rings, caramelised pineapple and mustard mayo) reigns supreme.

Jackman & McRoss
Bakery $

(☏03-6223 3186; 57-59 Hampden Rd, Battery Point; items $4-14, breakfast $6-15; ☉7am-5pm) Make sure you stop by this enduring Hobart favourite, even if it's just to gawk at the display cabinet full of delectable pies, tarts, baguettes and pastries. Breakfasts involve scrambled egg, bacon and avocado panini or potato, asparagus and brie frittatas, or perhaps just grab a duck, cranberry and walnut sausage roll.

There's also a city **branch** (☏03-6231 0601; 4 Victoria St; ☉7am-4.30pm Mon-Fri).

Royal Tasmanian Botanical Gardens (p199)

Retro Cafe
Cafe $

(📞03-6223 3073; 31 Salamanca Pl, Hobart; mains $11-20; ⏲7.30am-5pm Mon-Fri, 8am-5pm Sat & Sun) So popular it hurts, funky Retro is ground zero for Saturday brunch among the market stalls (or any day, really). Masterful breakfasts, bagels, salads and burgers interweave with laughing staff, chilled-out jazz and the whirr and bang of the coffee machine. A classic Hobart cafe.

Pigeon Hole
Cafe $$

(📞03-6236 9306; www.pigeonholecafe.com. au; 93 Goulburn St, West Hobart; mains $12-22; ⏲7.30am-4pm Mon-Fri, 8am-3.30pm Sat & Sun) This compact bakery-cafe is the kind of place every inner-city neighbourhood should have. The love-child of a family farm at Hobart's edge, its menu is filled with farm produce that merges into the likes of whipped sweet corn tofu with roasted asparagus, or potato and smoked eel rösti covered in abundant greens.

Flippers
Fish & Chips $

(📞03-6234 3101; www.flippersfishandchips. com.au; 1 Constitution Wharf; fish & chips $12-17; ⏲9am-9.30pm; 👪) There are four floating fish punts moored in Constitution Dock, selling fresh-caught seafood either uncooked or cooked. Our pick is Flippers, an enduring favourite with a voluptuous fish-shaped profile. Fillets of flathead and curls of calamari come straight from the deep blue sea and into the deep fryer. The local seagulls will adore you.

Templo
Italian $$

(📞03-6234 7659; www.templo.com.au; 98 Patrick St; plates $14-32; ⏲6pm-late Thu & Fri, noon-2.30pm & 6pm-late Sat-Mon) Unpretentious little Templo, on a nondescript reach of Patrick St, is a Hobart dining treasure. With only 20 seats (bookings essential), most of them around a communal table, and only three or four Italian-inspired mains to choose from, it's an exercise in selectivity and sharing (your personal space, and your food). Survey the pricey-but-memorable wine list at the cute bar.

Mures
Seafood $$

(📞Lower Deck 03-6231 2009, Upper Deck 03-6231 1999; www.mures.com.au; Victoria Dock;

Mures

mains Lower Deck $15-29, Upper Deck $36-42; ⏰Lower Deck 7am-10pm, Upper Deck 11am-late; 🛜) The big fish in Hobart's seafood scene, the bottle-green Mures has a **Lower Deck** with fishmonger, a fish-and-chip shop and ice cream, while the **Upper Deck** is a sassier, bookable affair, with silvery dockside views and à la carte seafood dishes. The fresh seafood comes direct from Mures' own boat.

Myu Asian $$

(📞03-6228 7777; www.facebook.com/Myu. easybites; 2/93 New Town Rd, New Town; mains $19-28; ⏰5.30-8.30pm Tue-Sat) Let yourself in on a little Hobart secret at this unsigned, unadulterated dining room in an unprepossessing strip of shops where the ever-changing menu rolls straight off the home printer each night. Expect a pan-Asian journey – the night's menu might include beef rendang, Hainanese chicken, bao and momos.

Franklin Modern Australian $$$

(📞03-6234 3375; www.franklinhobart.com.au; 30 Argyle St; shared plates $16-40; ⏰5pm-late Tue-Sat) Regularly on lists of Australia's top restaurants, Franklin fills a lofty industrial space (the former *Hobart Mercury* newspaper printing room) and is all concrete, steel beams, cowhide and curtains. Everything is on show in the central kitchen, as the likes of wood-roasted octopus and Littlewood Farm lamb slip in and out of the 10-tonne oven.

Aløft Modern Australian $$$

(📞03-6223 1619; www.aloftrestaurant.com; Brooke St Pier; plates $14-36, banquets from $80; ⏰6pm-late Tue-Sat; 🍴) Boldly claiming itself as Hobart's top restaurant, angular Aløft occupies a lofty eyrie atop the floating Brooke St Pier. Menu hits include silken tofu with burnt onion and baby leeks, and crispy duck leg with kimchi. If you can drag your gaze away from the view, service and presentation are both excellent, in an unpretentious Hobart kinda way.

🍸 DRINKING & NIGHTLIFE

New Sydney Hotel Pub

(📞03-6234 4516; www.newsydneyhotel.com.au; 87 Bathurst St; ⏰noon-10pm Mon, to midnight Tue-Sat, 4-9pm Sun) This low-key pub is the best boozer in the CBD, with open fires, creative pub food (such as trout Kiev, or hazelnut and beetroot gnocchi; mains $15 to $38) and more than a dozen island craft beers and ciders on tap. No poker machines or TVs!

Glass House Cocktail Bar

(📞03-6223 1032; www.theglass.house; Brooke St Pier; ⏰noon-late) The very fancy Glass House sits in the prow of the floating Brooke St Pier, sandwiched between Aløft and Brooke St Larder, with a huge window-wall affording uninterrupted views across the Derwent River. Put on your best duds, order a martini with sheep-whey vodka and soak it all in. Fab bar food, too (small plates $12 to $36).

Hobart Brewing Company Craft Beer

(📞03-6231 9779; www.hobartbrewingco.com. au; 16 Evans St; ⏰3-10pm Wed & Thu, to 11pm Fri, 2-11pm Sat, 2-5.30pm Sun) In a big red shed on Macquarie Point, fronted by the Red Square community space (fancy a haircut from a caravan hair salon?), Hobart Brewing Company is doing good things with craft beer. There are up to a dozen creative brews on tap, plus regular live music and the **Hobart Blues, Brews and Barbecues festival** around February or March.

Shambles Brewery Craft Beer

(📞03-6289 5639; www.shamblesbrewery.com. au; 222 Elizabeth St, North Hobart; ⏰4pm-late Wed & Thu, from noon Fri-Sun) An excellent brewery just south of the NoHo strip, with minimalist interiors and a concrete-block bar. Head out the back to drink among the vats (and have a hit of table tennis). Tasting paddles are $14, or refill your 'growler' (1.9L bottle) to take home and savour. Terrific beery bar food, too: burgers, wallaby drumsticks, fried chicken and the like.

The Winston   Pub

(☎03-6231 2299; www.thewinstonbar.com; 381 Elizabeth St, North Hobart; ⊙4pm-late) The grim old art-deco Eaglehawk pub has been transformed into the Winston, a craft-beery, US-style alehouse. Grab a pint of the house stout from one of the beardy guys behind the bar and check out the wall of US registration plates near the pool table. The food flavours – buffalo wings, grilled corn, brisket – match the setting.

⭐ ENTERTAINMENT

Republic Bar & Café   Live Music

(☎03-6234 6954; www.republicbar.com; 299 Elizabeth St, North Hobart; ⊙3pm-late Mon & Tue, from noon Wed-Sun; 🎵) The Republic is a raucous art-deco pub hosting live music every night (often with free entry). It's the number-one live-music pub around town, with an always interesting line-up, including international acts. Loads of different beers and excellent food (mains $20 to $33; try the Jack Daniel's–marinated rump steak). Just the kind of place you'd love to call your local.

State Cinema   Cinema

(☎03-6234 6318; www.statecinema.com.au; 375 Elizabeth St, North Hobart; tickets adult/child $20/16) Saved from the wrecking ball in the 1980s, the 11-screen State (built in 1913) shows independent and art-house flicks. There's a great cafe and bar on-site, plus a summertime rooftop screen (with another bar!), a browse-worthy **bookshop** (☎03-6169 0720; www.statecinemabookstore.com.au; ⊙9.30am-7pm Sun & Mon, to 9pm Tue-Sat) and the foodie temptations of North Hobart's restaurants right outside. Magic.

Theatre Royal   Theatre

(☎03-6233 2299, box office 03-6146 3300; www.theatreroyal.com.au; 29 Campbell St; ⊙box office 10am-4pm Tue-Sun) This venerable old stager is Australia's oldest continuously operating theatre, with actors first treading the boards here back in 1837 (the foundation stone says 1834, but it took them a few years to finish it). Theatregoers can expect an eclectic range of music plus ballet, theatre, opera, comedy and university revues.

Rektango   Live Music

(☎03-6234 8414; www.salarts.org.au/rektango; Salamanca Arts Centre Courtyard, Salamanca Pl; ⊙5.30-7.30pm Fri) Some of Hobart's best live tunes get an airing every Friday night in the Salamanca Arts Centre Courtyard, best reached off Woobys Lane. It's a free community event that started with the current millennium, adopting its name from a band that sometimes graces the stage. Acts vary month to month – expect anything from African beats to rockabilly, folk and gypsy-Latino.

ℹ️ INFORMATION

MEDICAL SERVICES

Royal Hobart Hospital (☎03-6166 8308; www.dhhs.tas.gov.au; 48 Liverpool St; ⊙24hr) Accident and emergency, running round the clock.

TOURIST INFORMATION

Hobart Visitor Information Centre (☎03-6238 4222; www.hobarttravelcentre.com.au; 20 Davey St; ⊙8.30am-5pm Mon-Fri, from 9am Sat & Sun) Poised perfectly between the CBD and the waterfront. Information, maps, and statewide tour, transport and accommodation bookings.

ℹ️ GETTING THERE & AWAY

Hobart's 'international' **airport** (☎03-6216 1600; www.hobartairport.com.au; 6 Hinkler Rd, Cambridge) has only domestic flights, with services operated by Qantas, Virgin Australia, Jetstar and Tiger Air. Direct flights arrive from Melbourne, Sydney, Brisbane and (less regularly) Adelaide, Perth and Gold Coast. The airport is in Cambridge, 19km east of the city.

ℹ️ GETTING AROUND

BICYCLE

There are a number of bike-hire outlets around the city: it's a handy, affordable option if the

Cascade Brewery (p197)

weather is looking good and you don't mind sweating it out on a hill or three.

BUS

The local bus network is operated by **Metro Tasmania** (☑13 22 01; www.metrotas.com.au), which is reliable but infrequent outside of business hours. The **Metro Shop** (☑13 22 01; www.metrotas.com.au; 22 Elizabeth St; ☺8am-5.30pm Mon-Fri) handles ticketing and enquiries: most buses depart from this section of Elizabeth St, or from nearby Franklin Sq.

Alternatively, the **Hobart Shuttle Bus Company** (☑0408 341 804; www.hobartshuttle-bus.com) has minibus transfers and tours from Hobart to Richmond and the summit of kunanyi/ Mt Wellington, while the **kunanyi/Mt Wellington Explorer Bus** (☑03-6236 9116; www.mtwelling-tonexplorer.com.au; Brooke St Pier; one way pass adult/child $25/15, all-day pass $35/25; ☺9am, 10am, 11am, 1pm, 2pm & 3pm Nov-Apr, 9.30am, 11.30am & 2.30pm May-Oct) can also haul you (and your bike) up the mountain.

CAR

The big-boy rental firms have airport desks and city offices. Cheaper local firms offer daily rental rates from as low as $30.

Timed, metered parking predominates in the CBD and tourist areas such as Salamanca Place and the waterfront. For longer-term parking, large CBD car parks (clearly signposted) offer reasonable rates.

TAXI

Ride-share operator Uber also operates in Hobart.

131008 Hobart (☑13 10 08; www.131008hobart.com) Standard taxis.

Hobart Maxis (☑13 32 22; www.hobartmaxitaxi.com) Wheelchair-accessible vehicles, and taxis for groups.

Yellow Cab Co (☑13 19 24; http://hobart.yellow-cab.com.au) Standard cabs (not all of which are yellow).

ADELAIDE & SOUTH AUSTRALIA'S WINE REGIONS

Adelaide & South Australia's Wine Regions at a Glance...

Restrained, dignified, neat-casual – this is the staid self-image Adelaide has tradi-tionally projected, a nod to the days of free colonisation without the 'penal colony' taint. These days, things are much hipper in this Unesco 'City of Music', with multi-cultural restaurants, pumping arts and live-music scenes, savvy laneway bars and a packed festival calendar.

Day trip to the world-class Barossa Valley and McLaren Vale wine regions (superb shiraz), plus the utterly photogenic Adelaide Hills – a rolling landscape of cool-climate wineries, cosy pubs and historic stone villages.

Adelaide & South Australia's Wine Regions in Two Days

Head to Adelaide's **Central Market** (p216) early for breakfast, then take a tour – a **RoofClimb** (p219) or at ground-level – of **Adelaide Oval** (p216). Wander through the estimable **Art Gallery of South Australia** (p216), then hit the bars around Peel St. On day two, day-trip into the **Adelaide Hills**: wineries, historic villages, koalas and viewpoints.

Adelaide & South Australia's Wine Regions in Four Days

On day three, broaden your SA adven-ture with a visit to either the **McLaren Vale** (p212) or **Barossa Valley** (p210) wine regions, both an hour or less from the city. On day four, take the tram to **Glenelg** for some beach time and sun-set fish-and-chips by the sea. Drinks on Rundle St back in the city await.

Arriving in Adelaide & South Australia's Wine Regions

Adelaide Airport (p223) is 7km west of the CBD; taxis, shuttles and buses are on hand. The main **bus station** (p223) is in the city centre; the interstate **train station** (p223) is 1km southwest. From the city, it's a day-trip drive or tour to the Adelaide Hills and wine regions.

Sleeping

Most Adelaide accommodation is in the city centre, but in a grid-town this easy to navigate, staying outside the CBD is viable. North Adelaide is under the flight path, but it's otherwise low-key. For beachside accommodation, try Glenelg. In the Barossa and McLaren Vale you'll find B&Bs and luxe stays; the Adelaide Hills have slick pub rooms and yet more B&Bs.

Barossa Valley Wine Region

With hot, dry summers and cool, moderate winters, the Barossa is one of the world's great wine regions – an absolute must for anyone keen on a good drop.

Great For...

☑ **Don't Miss**

The view over the valley from Mengler's Hill Lookout (p225).

Big Reds, Aromatic Whites

The Barossa is best known for shiraz, with riesling the dominant white. There are around 80 vineyards here and 60 cellar doors, ranging from boutique wine rooms to monstrous complexes. The long-established 'Barossa Barons' hold sway – big, brassy operators – while spritely young boutique wineries are harder to sniff out. Here's the pick of the bunch.

Penfolds   Winery

(☎08-8568 8408; www.penfolds.com; 30 Tanunda Rd, Nuriootpa; ⊙9am-5pm) If you don't know the name, Penfolds is a Barossa legend. Book ahead for the Make Your Own Blend tour ($65) or the Taste of Grange tour ($150).

Rockford Wines

MILLEFLORE IMAGES/SHUTTERSTOCK ©

Barossa Valley
Wine Region

Adelaide
Airport ⊙ Adelaide

ℹ Need to Know

Just 65km northeast of Adelaide, the Barossa makes an easy day trip from the city.

✕ Take a Break

Fino Seppeltsfield (p227) is one of the best restaurants in Australia.

★ Top Tip

Cycling is a great way to see the valley: roll into the Barossa Cycle Hub (p228).

riesling vintages here are probably the most consistent and affordable Barossa wines.

St Hallett   Winery

(☑08-8563 7070; www.sthallett.com.au; 100 St Hallett Rd, Tanunda; ☺10am-5pm) Unpretentious St Hallett produces reasonably priced but consistently good whites (try the Poacher's Blend) and the excellent Old Block Shiraz.

Rockford Wines   Winery

(☑08-8563 2720; www.rockfordwines.com.au; 131 Krondorf Rd, Tanunda; ☺11am-5pm) Our favourite boutique Barossa winery, this 1850s cellar door sells traditionally made, small-range wines, including sparkling reds.

Henschke   Winery

(☑08-8564 8223; www.henschke.com.au; 1428 Keyneton Rd, Keyneton; ☺9am-4.30pm Mon-Fri, to noon Sat) Detour 10km southeast of Angaston to the Eden Valley, where old-school Henschke bottles its iconic Hill of Grace red.

Peter Lehmann   Winery

(☑08-8565 9555; www.peterlehmannwines. com; Para Rd, Tanunda; ☺9.30am-5pm Mon-Fri, 10.30am-4.30pm Sat & Sun) The shiraz and

Guided Tours

Wine-flavoured day tours departing either Adelaide or locally are bountiful; the Barossa Visitor Information Centre (p228) can help with bookings. Operators include the following:

Taste the Barossa (☑08-8357 1594; www. tastethebarossa.com.au; full day from $139)

Barossa Wine Lovers Tours (p226)

Barossa Taste Sensations (p226)

McLaren Vale Wine Region

Most people come to McLaren Vale – just a 40-minute drive south of Adelaide – to cruise the 80-plus wineries here: you could spend days doing nothing else!

Great For...

☑ **Don't Miss**

Nosing your way into some sublime shiraz at McLaren Vale's many cellar doors.

Seriously Good Wineries

If the Barossa Valley is SA wine's old school, then McLaren Vale is the upstart teenager smoking cigarettes behind the shed and stealing nips from mum's sherry bottle. The luscious vineyards around here have a Tuscan haze in summer, rippling down to a calm coastline that's positively Ligurian. This is shiraz country – solid, punchy and seriously good. Quaff some at five of the region's best.

d'Arenberg   Winery

(☏08-8329 4888; www.darenberg.com.au; 58 Osborn Rd; ☺10am-5pm) The wine labels are part of the character of this place: the Dead Arm shiraz and the Broken Fishplate sauvignon blanc are our faves.

d'Arenberg

COURTESY OF D'ARENBERG ©

Adelaide Airport ✈ ◉ **Adelaide**

⦿ **McLaren Vale Wine Region**

❶ Need to Know

Pick up a map of winery cellar doors at the McLaren Vale & Fleurieu Visitor Information Centre (p229).

✗ Take a Break

Duck into Blessed Cheese (p228) for a coffee, burger, pastry or...some cheese!

★ Top Tip

Saturday morning? The effervescent, rootsy **Willunga Farmers Market** (📞08-8556 4297; www.willungafarmers market.com; Willunga Town Sq, Willunga; ⊙8am-12.30pm Sat) is just 6km south of McLaren Vale.

your plonk? This barnlike, 1894 cellar door has a grassy picnic area, and there's a roaring fire inside in winter.

Alpha Box & Dice
Winery

(📞08-8323 7750; www.alphaboxdice.com; 8 Olivers Rd; ⊙11am-5pm Mon-Fri, 10am-6pm Sat & Sun) One out of the box, this refreshing little gambler wins top billing for interesting blends, funky retro furnishings, quirky labels and laid-back staff.

Coriole
Winery

(📞08-8323 8305; www.coriole.com; Chaffeys Rd; ⊙10am-5pm Mon-Fri, 11am-5pm Sat & Sun) Take your regional tasting platter out into the garden of this beautiful cottage cellar door (1860), made lovelier by a swill of the flagship chenin blanc.

Wirra Wirra
Winery

(📞08-8323 8414; www.wirrawirra.com; cnr McMurtrie & Strout Rds; ⊙10am-5pm Mon-Sat, 11am-5pm Sun) Fancy some *pétanque* with

SC Pannell
Winery

(📞08-8323 8000; www.pannell.com.au; 60 Olivers Rd; ⊙11am-5pm) With one of the best views in the business, SC Pannell (Steve, to his mates) produces excellent reds you can drink young.

Guided Tours

Most tours can be taken from Adelaide, or, for a few dollars less, from McLaren Vale itself. Operators include the following:

Adelaide's Top Food & Wine Tours (📞08-8386 0888; www.topfoodandwinetours.com.au)

Chook's Little Winery Tours (📞0414 922 200; www.chookslittlewinerytours.com.au; per person incl lunch $120-160)

McLaren Vale Wine Tours (📞0414 784 666; www.cellardoortours.com.au)

Adelaide Hills Wine Region

The Hills make a brilliant day trip from Adelaide: hop from town to town, passing stone pubs, old cottages, olive groves and wineries along the way.

Great For...

☑ Don't Miss

The view over the Adelaide Plains from Mt Lofty Summit (p230).

Cool-climate Wineries

With night mists and reasonable rainfall, the Adelaide Hills' mid-altitude slopes sustain one of SA's cooler climates – perfect for producing some complex and truly top-notch white wines, especially chardonnays and sauvignon blancs. There are dozens of wineries in the Hills (see www.adelaide hillswine.com.au for details, or pick up the *Adelaide Hills Cellar Door Guide* brochure); January's Crush festival and Winter Reds in July celebrate this rich bounty. The pick of the bunch:

Shaw & Smith (✆08-8398 0500; www. shawandsmith.com; 136 Jones Rd, Balhannah; wine-flight tastings from $20; ⊗11am-5pm)

Bird in Hand (✆08-8389 9488; www.birdinhand. com.au; cnr Bird in Hand & Pfeiffer Rds, Woodside; ⊗10am-5pm Mon-Fri, 11am-5pm Sat & Sun)

Bird in Hand

ANDREW HUANG/ALAMY ©

❶ Need to Know

Autumn is particularly atmospheric here: cool, misty weather and deciduous colours.

✕ Take a Break

Seasonal Garden Cafe (📞08-8388 7714; www.facebook.com/theseasonalgardencafe; 100 Main St, Hahndorf; mains $8-20; ⊙7am-5pm; 🅿) 🍴 is the pick of Hahndorf's myriad options.

★ Top Tip

For a tailored Hills experience, take a day trip with **Ambler Touring** (📞0414 447 134; www.ambler.net.au; half-/full day per person from $99/155) or Tour Adelaide Hills (p231).

Deviation Road (📞08-8339 2633; www.deviationroad.com; 207 Scott Creek Rd, Longwood; ⊙10am-5pm; 🍴)

The Lane (📞08-8388 1250; www.thelane.com.au; 5 Ravenswood Lane, Hahndorf; ⊙10am-4pm)

Pike & Joyce (📞08-8389 8102; www.pikeandjoyce.com.au; 730 Mawson Rd, Lenswood; ⊙11am-4pm Mon-Fri, 11am-5pm Sat & Sun)

Cheeky Overnighter?

Most travellers tackle the Adelaide Hills as a day trip from Adelaide – it's barely 15 minutes away. But if you want to stay the night, you'll find ritzy renovated pub rooms, historic hotels and some good B&Bs. If you feel like staying the night, both the **Stirling Hotel** (📞08-8339 2345; www.stirlinghotel.com.au; 52 Mt Barker Rd, Stirling; d from $230; 🅿❄🛜) and **Crafers Hotel** (📞08-8339 2050; www.crafershotel.com.au; 8 Main St, Crafers; d

from $250; 🅿❄🛜) have stylish boutique rooms upstairs, while **Mt Lofty House** (📞08-8339 6777; www.mtloftyhouse.com.au; 74 Mt Lofty Summit Rd, Crafers; d/ste/cottage from $299/399/499; 🅿❄🛜🏊) is an 1850s stone mansion with show-stopping valley views.

Fab Hills Festivals

Crush   Wine
(www.crushfestival.com.au; ⊙Jan) Celebrating all things good about life in the Adelaide Hills, with food and wine to the fore. Lots of cellar-door events and tastings.

Winter Reds   Wine
(www.winterreds.com.au; ⊙Jul) 'Brrr, it's chilly. Pour me another shiraz.' Winter Reds celebrates the cold season in the Adelaide Hills, with winery tastings, hearty food and lots of open fires.

Adelaide

◉ SIGHTS

Central Market   Market

(☑08-8203 7494; www.adelaidecentralmarket.
com.au; 44-60 Gouger St, Adelaide; ⊙7am-
5.30pm Tue & Thu, 9am-5.30pm Wed, 7am-9pm
Fri, 7am-3pm Sat) **FREE** A tourist sight, or
a shopping op? Either way, satisfy your
deepest culinary cravings at the 250-odd
stalls in superb Adelaide Central Market. A
sliver of salami from the Mettwurst Shop,
a crumb of English Stilton from the Smelly
Cheese Shop, a tub of blueberry yoghurt
from the Yoghurt Shop – you name it, it's
here. Good luck making it out without
eating anything. Adelaide's Chinatown is
right next door. Adelaide's Top Food & Wine
Tours (p220) offers guided tours.

Adelaide Oval   Landmark

(☑08-8205 4700; www.adelaideoval.com.au;
King William Rd, North Adelaide; tours adult/child
$25/15; ⊙tours 10am, 11am & 2pm daily, plus
1pm Sat & Sun) Hailed as the world's prettiest
cricket ground, the Adelaide Oval hosts
interstate and international cricket matches in summer, plus national AFL football
and state football matches in winter. A
wholesale redevelopment has boosted
seating capacity to 53,000 – when they're
all yelling, it's a serious home-town advantage! Guided 90-minute tours run on non-
game days, departing from the Riverbank
Stand (south entrance), off War Memorial
Dr: call for bookings or book online.

Art Gallery of
South Australia   Gallery

(☑08-8207 7000; www.artgallery.sa.gov.
au; North Tce, Adelaide; ⊙10am-5pm) **FREE**
Spend a few hushed hours in the vaulted,
parquetry-floored gallery that represents
the big names in Australian art. Permanent
exhibitions include Australian, Aboriginal
and Torres Strait Islander, Asian, European
and North American art (20 bronze Ro-
dins!). Progressive visiting exhibitions occupy the basement. There are free guided
tours (11am and 2pm daily) and lunchtime
talks (12.30pm every day except Tuesday).
There's a lovely cafe out the back too.

Adelaide Oval

South Australian Museum
Museum

(☎08-8207 7500; www.samuseum.sa.gov.au; North Tce, Adelaide; ☺10am-5pm) **FREE** Dig into Australia's natural history with the museum's special exhibits on whales and Antarctic explorer Sir Douglas Mawson. Over two levels, the amazing Australian Aboriginal Cultures gallery is one of the largest collections of Aboriginal artefacts in the world. Elsewhere, the giant squid and the lion with the twitchy tail are definite highlights. Free one-hour tours depart at 11am. The cafe here is a handy spot for lunch/recaffeination.

National Wine Centre of Australia
Winery

(☎08-8313 3355; www.wineaustralia.com.au; cnr Botanic & Hackney Rds, Adelaide; ☺9am-6pm) **FREE** Check out the free self-guided, interactive Wine Discovery Journey exhibition at this very sexy wine centre (doubling as a research facility for the University of Adelaide, as well as a visitor centre). It's a great way to understand the issues winemakers contend with, and you can even have your own virtual vintage rated. Explore the Cellar Door (the largest in Australia!) and get stuck into some cleverly automated tastings (from $2.50). Free guided tours run at 11.30am daily.

Adelaide Zoo
Zoo

(☎08-8267 3255; www.zoossa.com.au/adelaidezoo; Frome Rd, Adelaide; adult/child/family $36/20/91.50; ☺9.30am-5pm) Around 1800 exotic and native mammals, birds and reptiles roar, growl and screech at Adelaide's wonderful zoo, dating from 1883. There are free walking tours half-hourly (plus a slew of longer and overnight tours), feeding sessions and a children's zoo. Wang Wang and Fu Ni are Australia's only giant pandas and always draw a crowd (panda-monium!). Other highlights include the nocturnal and reptile houses. You can take a river cruise to the zoo on **Popeye** (☎08-8232 7994; www.thepopeye.com.au; Elder Park, Adelaide; return adult/child $15/8, one way $10/5; ☺10am-4pm, reduced hours winter).

✳ Mad March

Adelaide hosts a string of world-class festivals...but why do most of them have to be in March?

Adelaide Festival (www.adelaidefestival.com.au; ☺Mar) Top-flight international and Australian dance, drama, opera, literature and theatre performances in March. Arguably Australia's best performing arts festival. Don't miss the Northern Lights along North Tce – old sandstone buildings ablaze with lights – and the hedonistic late-night club.

Adelaide Fringe (www.adelaidefringe.com.au; ☺Feb/Mar) This annual independent arts festival in February and March is second only to the Edinburgh Fringe. Funky, unpredictable and downright hilarious, with hundreds of events over a very entertaining month – a world-class festival. There's a handy ticket booth in Rundle Mall. Get into it!

WOMADelaide (www.womadelaide.com.au; ☺Mar) One of Australia's best live-music events, with more than 300 musicians and performers from around the globe, doing their thing over a warm autumn weekend. Food, wine and wholesome fun. Perfect for families and those with a new-age bent. Attracts almost 100,000 folks over the weekend – fantastic!

Adelaide Fringe
GREYBOOTS40/SHUTTERSTOCK ©

Adelaide Botanic Gardens
Gardens

(☎08-8222 9311; www.botanicgardens.sa.gov.au; cnr North Tce & East Tce, Adelaide; ☺7.15am-sunset Mon-Fri, from 9am Sat & Sun)

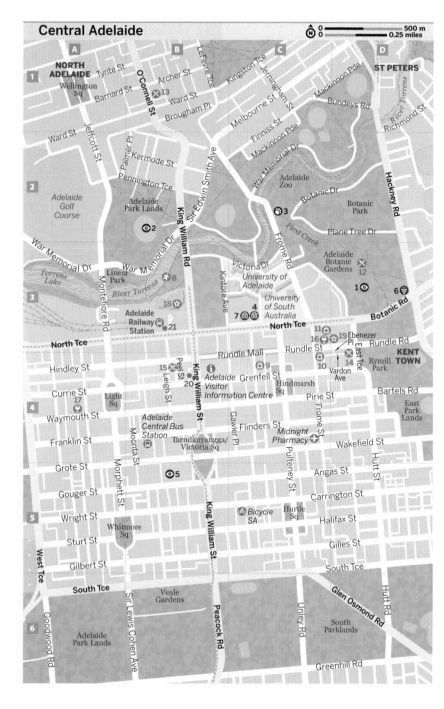

Central Adelaide

N 0 ⊙ | 500 m
0 | 0.25 miles

A

NORTH ADELAIDE

Tynte St
Wellington Sq
Barnard St
Archer St
O'Connell St
Ward St
Brougham Pl

1

Ward St
Jeffcott St
Palmer Pl
Kermode St
Pennington Tce

2

Adelaide Golf Course
Adelaide Park Lands
⊙2

War Memorial Dr
Montefiore Rd
Linear Park
War Memorial Dr
Torrens Lake
River Torrens

3

18✪
Adelaide Railway Station
21

North Tce
Hindley St
Peel St
15 ✕
Leigh St
20
Light Sq
17

4

Currie St
Waymouth St
Franklin St
Adelaide Central Bus Station
Moonta St
Morphett St

5

Grote St
Gouger St
Wright St
Whitmore Sq
Sturt St
West Tce
Gilbert St
South Tce

6

Goodwood Rd
Adelaide Park Lands
Sir Lewis Cohen Ave

B

LeFevre Tce
13✕
King William Rd
Sir Edwin Smith Ave

8✕

North Tce
Rundle Mall
King William St
9
Adelaide Visitor Information Centre
Grenfell St

Pirie St
Adelaide Central Bus Station
Tarndanyangga/ Victoria Sq
Gawler Pl
Flinders St
⊙5

King William St
Bicycle SA
Veale Gardens

Peacock Rd

C

Kingston Tce
Jerningham St
Melbourne St
Finniss St
Mackinnon Pde
Mackinnon Dr
War Memorial Dr

Adelaide Zoo
Botanic Dr
⊙3
First Creek
Victoria Dr
University of Adelaide
Kintore Ave
4
University of South Australia
7
North Tce

Rundle St
10
Hindmarsh Sq
Frome St
Midnight Pharmacy ✛
Pulteney St
Angas St
Hurtle Sq
Halifax St
Gilles St
South Tce
Unley Rd
Glen Osmond Rd
South Parklands
Greenhill Rd

D

ST PETERS
Mackinnon Pde
Bundeys Rd
River Torrens
Richmond St

Adelaide Botanic Gardens
Botanic Park
Hackney Rd
Plane Tree Dr
Adelaide Botanic Gardens
12✕
1⊙
6

Botanic Rd

11
16 19 Ebenezer Pl
Rundle Rd
East Tce
KENT TOWN
14✕
Rymill Park
Vardon Ave
Bartels Rd
East Park Lands
Wakefield St
Hutt St
Carrington St

Hutt St

Central Adelaide

FREE Meander, jog or chew through your trashy airport novel in these lush city-fringe gardens. Highlights include a restored 1877 palm house, the water-lily pavilion (housing the gigantic *Victoria amazonica*), the First Creek wetlands, the engrossing **Museum of Economic Botany** and the fabulous steel-and-glass arc of the **Bicentennial Conservatory** (10am to 4pm), which re-creates a tropical rainforest. Free 1½-hour guided walks depart the Schomburgk Pavilion at 10.30am daily. The classy **Botanic Gardens Restaurant** (☑08-8223 3526; www.botanicgardensrestaurant.com.au; Adelaide Botanic Gardens, off Plane Tree Dr; 3/4 courses $70/90; ☻noon-2.30pm Tue-Sun, 6.30-9pm Fri & Sat) is here too.

😊 ACTIVITIES

Adventure Kayaking SA   Kayaking
(☑08-8295 8812; www.adventurekayak.com.au; tours adult/child from $50/25, kayak hire per 3hr 1-/2-/3-seater $40/60/80) ✐ Family-friendly guided kayak tours around the Port River estuary (dolphins, mangroves, shipwrecks). Also offers kayak and stand-up paddleboard hire, plus self-guided tours.

😊 TOURS

Adelaide City Explorer   Walking
(www.adelaidecityexplorer.com.au) **FREE** Excellent downloadable walking tours around the city, co-sponsored by the Adelaide City Council and the National Trust (there's a definite architectural bias here, which we like!). There are 27 themed trails in all – art deco, pubs, North Tce, outdoor art, trees etc – get 'em on your phone and get walking.

Escapegoat   Mountain Biking
(☑0422 916 289; www.escapegoat.com.au) ✐ Careen down the koala-studded slopes of 727m Mt Lofty into Adelaide below ($129; Monday, Thursday and Saturday), or take a day trip through McLaren Vale by bike ($159; Wednesday, Friday and Sunday).

RoofClimb Adelaide Oval   Climbing
(☑08-8331 5222; www.roofclimb.com.au; Adelaide Oval, King William Rd, North Adelaide; adult day/twilight/night $104/114/119, child day/twilight $70/80) As per the Sydney Harbour Bridge and Brisbane's Story Bridge, you can scale the lofty, scalloped rooftops of the Adelaide Oval (p216). And the views are astonishing! Kids can climb too (day and at twilight), but all climbers must be

⛵ Glenelg – 'The Bay'

Glenelg, or 'the Bay' – the site of SA's colonial landing – is Adelaide at its most LA. Glenelg's beach faces towards the west, and as the sun sinks into the sea, the pubs and bars burgeon with surfies, backpackers and sun-damaged sexagenarians. The tram rumbles in from the city, past the Jetty Rd shopping strip to the al fresco cafes around Moseley Sq.

The **Glenelg Visitor Information Centre** (📞08-8294 5833; www.glenelgsa. com.au; Glenelg Town Hall, Moseley Sq; ⏰10am-4pm) has the local lowdown, including information on diving and sailing opportunities and Aboriginal heritage.

From the city, take the tram or bus 167, 168 or 190 to get here.

Glenelg jetty
KEITMA/SHUTTERSTOCK ©

at least 120cm tall, and at most 136kg. Ask about climbing experiences when the cricket or football is happening down below ($235).

Adelaide's Top Food & Wine Tours
Food & Drink

(📞08-8386 0888; www.topfoodandwinetours. com.au) Get out of bed early and uncover Adeaide's gastronomic soul with a dawn ($75 including breakfast) or morning ($55) tour of the buzzing Central Market (p216), where stallholders introduce their produce. Adelaide Hills, McLaren Vale, Barossa and Clare Valley wine tours are also available.

🛍 SHOPPING

Streetlight
Books, Music

(📞08-8227 0667; www.facebook.com/street lightadelaide; 2/15 Vaughan Pl, Adelaide; ⏰10am-6pm Mon-Thu & Sat, to 9pm Fri, noon-5pm Sun) Lefty, arty and subversive in the best possible way, Streetlight is the place to find that elusive Miles Davis disc, Del Amitri rock biography or Bukowski poetry compilation.

Adelaide Arcade
Shopping Centre

(📞08-8223 5522; www.adelaidearcade.com. au; 112-118 Grenfell St, Adelaide; ⏰9am-7pm Mon-Thu, to 9pm Fri, 9am-5pm Sat, 11am-5pm Sun) Running between Rundle Mall and Grenfell St, the 1885 Adelaide Arcade is a high-Victorian commercial masterpiece, lined with high-end watchmakers, jewellers, coffee shops, coin dealers and tailors. You mightn't want to buy anything here, but it's worth a look for its lavish architectural stylings. There's a little free **museum** on the upper level, with some amazing photos of old-time Adelaide.

Miss Gladys Sym Choon
Fashion & Accessories

(📞08-8223 1500; www.missgladyssymchoon. com.au; 235a Rundle St, Adelaide; ⏰9.30am-6pm Mon-Thu, to 9pm Fri, 10am-5.30pm Sat, 11am-5pm Sun) Named after a famed Rundle St trader from the 1920s (the first woman in SA to incorporate a business) this hip shop is the place for fab frocks, rockin' boots, street-beating sneakers, jewellery, watches and hats. Guys and gals.

🍴 EATING

Argo on the Parade
Cafe $

(📞08-8431 1387; www.argo.love; 212 The Parade, Norwood; mains $10-24; ⏰6am-5pm Mon-Fri, 6.30am-5pm Sat, 7am-5pm Sun) The best cafe in affluent, eastern-suburbs Norwood is arguably the best cafe in Adelaide, too. It is in Norwood, so by default it's a bit thin on soul. But the food, coffee, service and quirky design all take the cake. As does the breakfast burrito. And the marinated tuna bowl. And the coffee. And the sweet potato fries...

Central Market
Market $

(📞08-8203 7494; www.adelaidecentralmarket.
com.au; Gouger St, Adelaide; ⏰7am-5.30pm Tue
& Thu, 9am-5.30pm Wed, 7am-9pm Fri, 7am-3pm
Sat) This place is an exercise in sensory
bombardment: a barrage of smells, colours
and cacophonous stallholders selling
fresh vegetables, breads, cheeses, seafood
and gourmet produce. Cafes, hectic food
courts, a supermarket and Adelaide's Chinatown are here too. Just brilliant – don't
miss it!

Gin Long Canteen
Asian $$

(📞08-7120 2897; www.ginlongcanteen.com.
au; 42 O'Connell St, North Adelaide; small plates
$8-16, mains $18-45; ⏰noon-2.30pm Tue-Fri,
5.30pm-late Tue-Sat) This energetic food
room is a winner. Chipper staff allocate you
a space at the communal tables (bookings
only for six or more) and take your order
pronto. The food arrives just as fast: fab
curries, slow-braised Thai beef and pork,
netted spring rolls, Malay curry puffs...
It's a pan-Asian vibe, bolstered by jumbo
bottles of Vietnamese beer and smiles all
round.

Peel
Street
Modern Australian, Asian $$

(📞08-8231 8887; www.peelst.com.au; 9 Peel St,
Adelaide; mains $20-35; ⏰7.30am-10.30pm Mon
& Wed-Fri, 7.30am-4.30pm Tues, 6-10.30pm Sat)
Peel St itself – a long-neglected service lane
in Adelaide's West End – is now Adelaide's
after-dark epicentre, lined with hip bars and
eateries, the best of which is this one. It's
a super cool cafe/bistro/wine bar that just
keeps packing 'em in: glam urbanites sit at
window seats nibbling parmesan-crumbed
parsnips and turkey meatballs with preserved lemon. Killer wine list.

Orana
Modern Australian $$$

(📞08-8232 3444; www.restaurantorana.com;
Level 1, 285 Rundle St, Adelaide; tasting menus
lunch/dinner $120/240, wine extra $90/170;
⏰noon-2pm Fri, 6-9pm Tue-Sat) Racking up
recent 'Australia's Best Restaurant' awards,
Orana is a secretive beast, with minimal
signage and access via a black staircase at
the back of Bistro Blackwood restaurant
on Rundle St. Upstairs rockstar chef Jock
Zonfrillo's tasting menu awaits: at least
seven courses for lunch, and 18 for dinner

Central Market

National Wine Centre of Australia (p217)

(18!). Add wine to the experience to fully immerse yourself in SA's top offerings.

⊙ DRINKING & NIGHTLIFE

Grace Emily Hotel   Pub
(☎08-8231 5500; www.graceemilyhotel.com.au; 232 Waymouth St, Adelaide; ⊙4pm-late) One of the top pubs in Adelaide, the Grace has live music most nights (alt-rock, country, acoustic, open-mic nights), kooky '50s-meets-voodoo decor, open fires and great beers. Regular cult cinema; no pokies. Are the Bastard Sons of Ruination playing tonight?

Exeter Hotel   Pub
(☎08-8223 2623; www.theexeter.com.au; 246 Rundle St, Adelaide; ⊙11am-late) Adelaide's best pub, this legendary boozer attracts an eclectic brew of postwork, punk and uni drinkers, shaking the day off their backs. Pull up a bar stool or nab a table in the grungy beer garden and settle in for the evening. Original music nightly (indie, electronica, acoustic); no pokies. Book

for curry nights in the upstairs restaurant (Wednesdays).

Maybe Mae   Bar
(☎0421 405 039; www.maybemae.com; 15 Peel St, Adelaide; ⊙5pm-late Mon-Sat, 6pm-late Sun) Down some stairs down an alleyway off a laneway, Maybe Mae doesn't proclaim its virtues loudly to the world. In fact, if you can't find the door, you won't be the first thirsty punter to wander back upstairs looking confused. But once you're inside, let the good times roll: classic rock, cool staff, booth seats and brilliant beers. Love it!

Nola   Bar
(www.nolaadelaide.com; 28 Vardon Ave, Adelaide; ⊙4pm-midnight Tue-Thu, noon-2am Fri & Sat, noon-midnight Sun) This hidden back-lane space was once the stables for the adjacent Stag Hotel. Out with the horse poo, in with 16 craft beers on tap, American and Australian whiskies (no Scotch!), Cajun cooking (gumbo, oysters, jambalaya, fried chicken) and regular live jazz. A saucy bit of Deep South in the East End.

⭐ ENTERTAINMENT

Adelaide
Festival Centre
Performing Arts

(☑08-8216 8600; www.adelaidefestivalcentre.com.au; King William Rd, Adelaide; ⊘box office 9am-6pm Mon-Fri) The hub of performing arts in SA, this crystalline white Festival Centre opened in June 1973, four proud months before the Sydney Opera House! The **State Theatre Company** (www.statetheatrecompany.com.au) is based here. Festival Plaza, linking the Centre and city, was undergoing a major upgrade when we visited – a project that may elevate the Centre's (deserving) iconic status.

Governor Hindmarsh Hotel
Live Music

(☑08-8340 0744; www.thegov.com.au; 59 Port Rd, Hindmarsh; ⊘11am-late) Ground zero for live music in Adelaide, 'The Gov' hosts some legendary local and international acts. The odd Irish band fiddles around in the bar, while the main venue features rock, folk, jazz, blues, salsa, reggae and dance. A huge place with an inexplicably personal vibe, far enough from the city to sidestep any noise complaints from the neighbours. Good food too.

Palace Nova Eastend
Cinema

(☑08-8125 9312; www.palacenova.com.au; 3 Cinema Pl, Adelaide; adult/child $20/16; ⊘10am-late) Just off Rundle St, handily poised down the alley next to the Exeter Hotel, this plush city complex screens new-release art-house, foreign-language and independent films, as well as some mainstream flicks. Fully licensed.

ℹ️ INFORMATION

Adelaide Visitor Information Centre (☑1300 588 140; www.adelaidecitycouncil.com; 9 James Pl, off Rundle Mall, Adelaide; ⊘9am-5pm Mon-Fri, 10am-4pm Sat & Sun) Adelaide-specific information, plus abundant info on SA, including fab regional booklets.

Midnight Pharmacy (☑08-8232 4445; www.healthdirect.gov.au; 192-198 Wakefield St, Adelaide; ⊘9am-midnight) Late-night presciptions.

Royal Adelaide Hospital (☑08-7074 0000; www.rah.sa.gov.au; Port Rd, Adelaide; ⊘24hr) Emergency department (not for blisters!) and STD clinic in this impressive hospital, opened in 2018 – the most expensive public building in Australian history.

ℹ️ GETTING THERE & AWAY

AIR

International, interstate and regional flights via a number of airlines service **Adelaide Airport** (ADL; ☑08-8308 9211; www.adelaideairport.com.au; 1 James Schofield Dr,), 7km west of the city centre. Domestic services include with **Jetstar** (www.jetstar.com.au), **Qantas** (www.qantas.com.au), **Tigerair Australia** (www.tigerair.com.au) and **Virgin Australia** (www.virginaustralia.com).

BUS

Adelaide Central Bus Station (☑08-8203 7532; www.cityofadelaide.com.au; 85 Franklin St, Adelaide; ⊘6am-9.30pm) is the hub for all major interstate and statewide bus services. Note: there is no Adelaide–Perth bus service.

Firefly Express (☑1300 730 740; www.fireflyexpress.com.au) Runs between Sydney and Adelaide via Melbourne.

Greyhound Australia (☑1300 473 946; www.greyhound.com.au) Australia's main long-distance player, with services from Adelaide to Melbourne and Alice Springs, with onward connections.

V/Line (☑1800 800 007; www.vline.com.au) Bus and bus/train services between Adelaide and Melbourne.

TRAIN

Interstate trains run by **Great Southern Rail** (☑08-8213 4401; www.greatsouthernrail.com.au) grind into the **Adelaide Parklands Terminal** (☑13 21 47; www.greatsouthernrail.com.au; Railway Tce, Keswick; ⊘6am-3pm Mon & Tue, 9am-3pm Wed, 9am-9.30pm Thu, 6am-3pm Fri, noon-12.30pm Sat, 8.30am-12.30pm Sun), 1km southwest of the city centre.

The following trains depart Adelaide regularly; fares include all meals, booze and off-train excursions en route:

○ *The Ghan* to Alice Springs (from $1059, 26 hours)

○ *The Ghan* to Darwin (from $1959, 54 hours)

○ *The Indian Pacific* to Perth (from $1599, 42 hours)

○ *The Indian Pacific* to Sydney (from $779, 25 hours)

○ *The Great Southern* to Brisbane (from $1649, 55 hours)

🛈 GETTING AROUND

TO/FROM THE AIRPORT

Prebooked private Adelaide Airport Flyer (📞08-8385 9967; www.adelaideairportflyer.com) minibuses run door to door between the airport and anywhere around Adelaide; get a quote and book online (into the city from the airport for one to three people costs $45).

Public Adelaide Metro **JetExpress and JetBus** (📞1300 311 108; www.adelaidemetro. com.au/timetables/special-services; $3.60-5.50; ⊙4.30am-11.30pm) bus services connect the airport with Glenelg and the CBD; standard Metro fares apply.

Taxis charge around $30 into the city from the airport (15 minutes.

BICYCLE

Adelaide is pizza-flat: great for cycling! With a valid passport or driver's licence you can borrow an **Adelaide Free Bike** from **Bicycle SA** (📞08-8168 9999; www.bikesa.asn.au; 53 Carrington St, Adelaide; ⊙9am-4.30pm); helmet and lock provided. There are a couple of dozen locations around town: you can collect a bike at any of them, provided you return it to the same place. Multiday hires also available.

Down at the beach, hire a bike from **Glenelg Bicycle Hire** (📞08-8376 1934; www.glenelg bicyclehire.com.au; Norfolk Motel, 71 Broadway, Glenelg South; bikes per half/full day $15/25; ⊙8.30am-7pm).

PUBLIC TRANSPORT

Adelaide Metro (📞1300 311 108; www.adelaide metro.com.au; cnr King William & Currie Sts, Adelaide; ⊙9am-5pm Mon-Fri, 9am-4pm Sat) runs Adelaide's decent and integrated bus, train and tram network.

Tickets can be purchased on board, at staffed train stations and in delis and newsagents across the city. Ticket types include day trip ($10.40), two-hour peak ($5.50) and two-hour off-peak ($3.60) tickets. Peak travel time is before 9am and after 3pm. Kids under five ride free. There's also a three-day, unlimited-travel visitor pass ($25). If you're here for longer, save at least $1 per trip with a rechargable multi-trip Metrocard.

BUS

Adelaide's buses start around 6am and run until midnight.

Every 30 minutes daily, Adelaide Metro's free **City Connector** (📞1300 311 108; www. adelaidemetro.com.au/timetables/special-services; ⊙9am-7.15pm Sat-Thu, to 9.15pm Fri) buses – routes 98A and 98C – run clockwise and anticlockwise around the CBD fringe, passing North Tce, Victoria Sq, Hutt St and Central Market, and winding through North Adelaide en route. The 99A and 99C buses ply the same route (minus North Adelaide) Monday to Friday – the net effect is a free bus every 15 minutes Monday to Friday.

TRAIN

Adelaide's hokey old diesel trains are slowly being electrified. Trains depart from **Adelaide Station** (www.railmaps.com.au/adelaide.htm; North Tce, Adelaide), plying five suburban routes (Belair, Gawler, Grange, Seaford and Outer Harbour). Trains generally run between 6am and midnight (some services start at 4.30am).

TRAM

Adelaide's state-of-the-art trams rumble to/from Moseley Sq in Glenelg, through Victoria Sq in the city and along North Tce to the Adelaide Entertainment Centre. A 2018 line extension runs east along North Tce to the Adelaide Botanic Gardens. Trams run approximately every 10 minutes on weekdays (every 15 minutes on weekends) from 6am to midnight daily. Standard Metro ticket prices apply, but the sections between South Tce and the Adelaide Entertainment Centre, and along Glenelg's Jetty Rd, are free. Further route extensions are being discussed (the city once had an extensive tram network, but the rails were ripped up in the 1950s. Go figure.)

TAXI

Adelaide Independent Taxis (☑13 22 11; www. aitaxis.com.au) Regular and wheelchair-access cabs.

Adelaide Transport (☑08-8212 1861; www. adelaidetransport.com.au) Minibus taxis for four or more people, plus airport-to-city transfers.

Suburban Taxis (☑13 10 08; www.suburban taxis.com.au) Taxis, all suburbs.

Yellow Cabs (☑13 22 27; www.yellowcabgroup. com.au) Regular cabs (most of which are white).

Barossa Valley

The Barossa is one of the world's great wine regions – an absolute must for wine fans. It's a compact valley – just 25km long – but the Barossa produces 21% of

Australia's wine, and it makes a no-fuss day trip from Adelaide, 65km away.

The local towns – Tanunda, Angaston and Nuriootpa are the big three – have a distinctly German heritage, dating back to 1842. Fleeing religious persecution in Prussia and Silesia, settlers (bringing their vine cuttings with them) created a Lutheran heartland where German traditions endure today (a passion for oompah bands, wurst, pretzels and sauerkraut).

And of course, before the shiraz, this was – and is – Peramangk country, bordering on Ngadjuri lands further north.

◎ SIGHTS

Mengler's Hill Lookout   Viewpoint

(Menglers Hill Rd, Tanunda; ⊘24hr) `FREE`
From Tanunda, take the scenic route to Angaston via Bethany for hazy valley views (just ignore the naff sculptures in the foreground). The road tracks through beautiful rural country, studded with huge eucalypts.

View from Mengler's Hill Lookout

Keg Factory   Factory
(☑08-8563 3012; www.thekegfactory.
com.au; 25 St Hallett Rd, Tanunda; ◷8am-
4pm Mon-Fri, 11am-4pm Sat) **FREE** Watch
honest-to-goodness coopers make and
repair wine barrels, 4km south of town.
Amazing! If you want to roll one home,
kegs start at $325.

🅖 TOURS

**Barossa Wine
Lovers Tours**   Wine
(☑08-8270 5500; www.wineloverstours.com.
au; full day from $99) Small-group tours to
wineries, lookouts, shops and heritage
buildings around the valley...a good blend.
Prices are based on numbers (more than
$90 per person if fewer than six travellers).
Lunch not included: bring a sandwich or eat
on the run.

 **Barossa
Festivals**

Time your visit with one of the valley's
big parties – great fun!
Barossa Gourmet Weekend (www.
barossagourmet.com; ◷Sep) Fab food
matched with winning wines at select
wineries; usually happens in September.
The number-one event in the valley
(book your beds *waaay* in advance).
Barossa Vintage Festival (www.barossa
vintagefestival.com.au; ◷Apr) A week long
festival with music, maypole dancing,
tug-of-war contests etc; around Easter
(harvest time – very atmospheric) in
odd-numbered years.

Barossa Vintage Festival grape treading
ART DIRECTORS & TRIP/ALAMY ©

**Barossa Taste
Sensations**   Food & Drink
(☑0457 101 487; www.barossatours.com.au;
half-/full day from $160/250) Flavour-packed
small-group tours in a comfy VW, focusing
on food as much as wine. The half-day
'fast-track' tour (ex-Barossa only) is a zippy
oversight of the whole valley.

🅐 SHOPPING

Barossa Farmers Market   Market
(☑0402 026 882; www.barossafarmersmarket.
com; cnr Stockwell & Nuriootpa Rds, Angaston;
◷7.30-11.30am Sat) Happens every Saturday
in the big farm shed behind Vintners Bar &
Grill, a few kilometres west of central Angaston. Expect hearty Germanic offerings,
coffee, flowers, lots of local produce and
questionable buskers.

🅧 EATING

Barista Sista   Cafe $
(☑08-8562 2882; www.facebook.com/barista
sistabeanery; 29d Murray St, Nuriootpa; mains
$6-16; ◷8.30am-4.30pm Mon-Fri, 8am-noon
Sat; 🖋) Mad-keen on beans, this little
main-street cafe zeroes in on organic
single-origin coffee to go along with its
crowd-pulling vegan and cafe fare. Grab
a slice of potato-and-leek quiche, some
scrambled tofu or a lemon tart and sip
your ristretto in the secret garden out the
back. Does non-vegan food too (ace egg-
and-bacon rolls).

Red Door Espresso   Cafe $$
(☑08-8563 1181; www.reddoorespresso.com;
79 Murray St, Tanunda; mains $8-29; ◷7.30am-
5pm Wed-Sat, 9.30am-4pm Sun; 🛜👪) A
decent cafe shouldn't be hard to create,
but it's rare in the Barossa for good food,
coffee, staff, music and atmosphere to
come together this well. The avocado and
basil-infused eggs Benedict is a winner,
best consumed with an eye-opening coffee
in the pot-planted courtyard. Live music
over weekend brunch; wine, cheese and
antipasto in the afternoons.

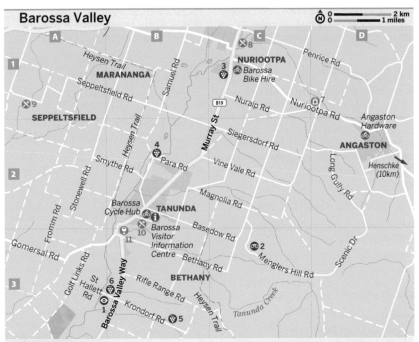

Barossa Valley

Fino
Seppeltsfield   Modern Australian $$$
(☏08-8562 8528; www.fino.net.au; 730 Seppeltsfield Rd, Seppeltsfield; 3/4/5 plates $48/65/75, incl wine $83/115/135; ⊙noon-3pm daily, 6-8.30pm Fri & Sat) From humble beginnings in a little stone cottage on the Fleurieu Peninsula, Fino has evolved into one of Australia's best restaurants, now ensconced in the gorgeous 1851 Seppeltsfield estate west of Tanunda. Food from the understated, deceptively simple menu highlights local ingredients, and is designed to be shared. Try the dry-aged sirloin with anchovies, chard and butter.

🍷 DRINKING & NIGHTLIFE
Barossa Valley Brewing   Craft Beer
(☏08-8563 0696; www.bvbeer.com.au; 2a Murray St, Tanunda; ⊙noon-4pm Mon-Wed, noon-9pm Thu-Sun) Beer! Real beer, here among all the wine! On Tanunda's southern fringe, BVB has a paved terrace beneath some astoundingly big eucalypts, just made for an afternoon with a few easy-drinking IPAs.

You can also peer at the stout steel tanks in the brewery, or grab a pizza, burger or some ribs from the **brasserie** (mains $17 to $33).

ℹ INFORMATION

Barossa Visitor Information Centre (☏1300 852 982, 08-8563 0600; www.barossa.com; 66-68 Murray St, Tanunda; ☺9am-5pm Mon-Fri, 9am-4pm Sat, 10am-4pm Sun; ☎) The low-down on the whole valley, plus bike hire and accommodation and tour bookings. Stocks the *A Town Walk of Tanunda* brochure.

ℹ GETTING THERE & AWAY

The best way to explore the Barossa is with your own vehicle or on a guided tour.

Alternatively, **Adelaide Metro** (www.adelaide metro.com.au) runs regular daily trains from Adelaide to Gawler ($5.50, one hour), from where **LinkSA** (www.linksa.com.au) buses run

---

🚲 Cycling the Barossa

From Tanunda, a 14km rail trail continues through Nuriootpa to Angaston, passing plenty of wineries. Pick up the Barossa by Bike brochure at the Barossa Visitor Information Centre, or download one from its website.

Based in Nuriootpa, **Barossa Bike Hire** (☏0400 537 770; www.barossabike hire.com; 5 South Tce, Nuriootpa; ☺9am-5pm) rents out quality cycles/tandems from $40/70 per day (pick-up price; bikes can be delivered for $10/20 extra). In Tanunda, the **Barossa Cycle Hub** (☏1300 852 982; www.barossa.com/ visit/see-do/cycling/barossa-cycle-hub; 70 Murray St, Tanunda; ☺9am-5pm Mon-Fri, 9am-4pm Sat, 10am-4pm Sun) has bikes per half-/full day for $30/44. **Angaston Hardware** (☏08-8564 2055; www.angas tonhardware.com.au; 5 Sturt St, Angaston; ☺8.30am-5.30pm Mon-Fri, 9am-4pm Sat, 10am-4pm Sun) also rents out bikes for $25/35 per half-/full day.

---

to Lyndoch ($5.90, 30 minutes), Tanunda ($10.70, 45 minutes), Nuriootpa ($13.50, one hour) and Angaston ($16.40, 1¼ hours).

ℹ GETTING AROUND

Tanunda, Angaston and Nuriootpa are all a 10-minute drive from each other.

Barossa Taxis (☏0411 150 850; www.barossa taxis.com.au; ☺24hr) Taxis for up to nine people.

McLaren Vale

On the Fleurieu Peninsula, flanked by the wheat-coloured Willunga Scarp and striated with vines, McLaren Vale is just 40 minutes south of Adelaide. Servicing the wine industry, it's an energetic, utilitarian town with some great eateries and easy access to some truly excellent winery cellar doors.

⊘ ACTIVITIES

Shiraz Trail   Cycling
(www.walkingsa.org.au; ☺24hr) FREE Get the McLaren Vale vibe on this 8km walking/cycling track, along an old railway line between McLaren Vale and Willunga. If you're up for it, the trail continues another 30km to Marino Rocks as the **Coast to Vines Rail Trail**. Hire a bike from **Oxygen Cycles** (☏08-8323 7345; www.oxygencycles.com; 143 Main Rd, McLaren Vale; bike hire per 3hr single/tandem $20/40; ☺10am-6pm Tue-Fri, 9am-5pm Sat) or **McLaren Vintage Bike Hire** (☏0410 067 199; www.mclarenvintagebikehire. com; 189 Main Rd, McLaren Vale; per day $45; ☺9am-5pm); ask the visitor centre for a map or download one from www.walking-sa.org.au.

✕ EATING

Blessed Cheese   Cafe, Deli $
(☏08-8323 7958; www.facebook.com/blessed cheese; 150 Main Rd, McLaren Vale; mains $11-18; ☺8am-4pm Mon-Fri, to 5pm Sat, 9am-4pm Sun) The staff at this blessed cafe crank out great coffee, croissants, wraps, salads,

Fino Seppeltsfield (p227)

tarts, burgers, cheese platters, massive cakes and funky sausage rolls. The menu changes every couple of days, always with an emphasis on local produce. Sniff the aromas emanating from the cheese counter – deliciously stinky! Love the lime citrus tarts and Spanish baked eggs.

Pizzateca   Pizza $$

(📞0431 700 183; www.pizza-teca.com; 319 Chalk Hill Rd; pizzas $20-28, set menu $38-55; ⊘noon-4pm Mon, noon-9pm Fri & Sat, noon-5pm Sun; 👪) Crazy-busy-popular Pizzateca occupies a little back-blocks cottage, with a broad deck beneath a couple of huge old redgum trees. Generously sized pizzas wheel out from the woodfired oven, as kids careen across the lawns – it's an effervescent scene. Try the devilishly hot 'Diablo' (sugo, dried chilli, *fontina* cheese, salami and house-made chilli honey). More prosecco, anyone?

d'Arenberg Cube   Fusion $$$

(📞08-8329 4888; www.darenberg.com.au/darenberg-cube-restaurant; d'Arenberg, 58 Osborn Rd; degustation menu from $190, wine pairings from $95, museum $10; ⊘noon-3pm Thu-Sun, museum 10am-5pm) The product of d'Arenberg winemaker Chester Osborne's vision, the d'Arenberg Cube is an eccentric, surprising place – a towering, multi-tiered, black-and-white Rubik's cube, educating with a museum ($10), stimulating with wine tastings, and satisfying with a fabulous regional degustation restaurant. There are lounge areas, viewing platforms, artful installations and McLaren Vale's only elevator. Failing to enjoy yourself here just isn't an option.

ℹ️ INFORMATION

McLaren Vale & Fleurieu Visitor Information Centre

(📞08-8323 9944; www.mclarenvale.info; 796 Main Rd; ⊘9am-5pm Mon-Fri, 10am-4pm Sat & Sun) At the northern end of McLaren Vale's main strip. Winery info, plus the *McLaren Vale Heritage Trail* brochure for an historic walk around town.

ⓘ GETTING THERE & AWAY

It is possible to get here via public transport via train then bus, but hey, life's too short. Drive or take a tour instead.

Adelaide Metro (p224) suburban trains run between Adelaide and Seaford (one hour). From here, bus 751 runs to McLaren Vale (45 minutes). Regular Adelaide Metro ticket prices apply (from $3.60).

Adelaide Hills

When the Adelaide plains are desert-hot in the summer months, the Adelaide Hills (technically the Mt Lofty Ranges) are always a few degrees cooler, with crisp air, woodland shade and labyrinthine valleys. Early colonists built stately summer houses around Stirling and Aldgate, and German settlers escaping religious persecution also arrived, infusing towns like Hahndorf with European values and architecture.

◉ SIGHTS

Mt Lofty Summit   Viewpoint
(www.parks.sa.gov.au; Mt Lofty Summit Rd, Crafers; ⊘24hr) **FREE** From Cleland Wildlife Park you can bushwalk (2km) or drive up to Mt Lofty Summit (a surprising 727m), which has show-stopping views across the Adelaide plains to the shimmering Gulf St Vincent. **Mt Lofty Summit Visitor Information Centre** (☑08-8370 1054; www.parks.sa.gov.au; Mt Lofty Summit Rd, Crafers; ⊘9am-5pm) has info on local attractions and walking tracks, including the steep Waterfall Gully Track (8km return, 2½ hours) and Mt Lofty Botanic Gardens Loop Trail (7km loop, two hours). There's a decent **cafe** (☑08-8839 2600; www.mountloftysummit.com; mains $9-25; ⊘9am-5pm Mon-Fri, 8.30am-5pm Sat & Sun) here too. Parking is an irritating $2.

**Cleland
Wildlife Park**   Wildlife Reserve
(☑08-8339 2444; www.clelandwildlifepark.sa.gov.au; 365 Mt Lofty Summit Rd, Crafers; adult/child/family $25.50/12/61; ⊘9.30am-

Haus on Hahndorf main street

5pm, last entry 4.30pm) Within the steep **Cleland Conservation Park** (www.parks. sa.gov.au; Mt Lofty Summit Rd, Crafers; ⊗24hr) **FREE**, this place lets you interact with all kinds of Australian beasts. There are keeper talks and feeding sessions throughout the day, plus occasional Night Walks (adult/child $51/40.50) and you can have your mugshot taken with a koala ($30.50; 2pm to 3pm daily, plus 11am to noon Sundays). There's a **cafe** (☑08-8339 2444; www.envi ronment.sa.gov.au/clelandwildlife; mains $5-15; ⊗9.30am-5pm) here too. From the city, take bus 864 or 864F from Grenfell St to Crafers for connecting bus 823 to the park.

🄯 TOURS

Tour Adelaide Hills   Tours
(☑08-8563 1000; www.touradelaidehills.com; full day incl lunch per person $250) Full-day tours through the Hills with pick-up locally, or from Adelaide or the Barossa Valley. Views, vines and fine food (chocolate, strawberries and cheese – not all at once).

🄯 SHOPPING

Stirling Markets   Market
(☑0488 770 166; www.stirlingmarket.com. au; Druid Ave, Stirling; ⊗10am-4pm 4th Sun of the month, 3rd Sun in Dec) 'Bustling' is such a corny, overused adjective...but in this case it applies! Market stalls fill oak-lined Druid Ave: much plant-life, busking, pies, cakes, affluent locals with dogs, and Hills knick-knackery.

🄯 EATING

Fred Eatery   Cafe $$
(☑08-8339 1899; www.fredeatery.com.au; 220 Mt Barker Rd, Aldgate; mains $12-26; ⊗7.30am-4pm Tue-Fri, 7.30am-3.15pm Sat & Sun, plus 6-9pm Fri; ❸) Build it, and they will come... For decades Aldgate eked out a cafe lifestyle with no quality cafe offerings. Then along came Fred, a rather urbane fellow, decked out in green, black and white,

with a savvy cityside menu, killer coffee and great staff. The house bircher muesli makes a solid start to the day, while the bodacious Reuben sandwich is calorific heaven.

Haus   Bistro $$
(☑08-8388 7555; www.haushahndorf.com.au; 38 Main St, Hahndorf; breakfast $7-23, lunch & dinner mains $20-42; ⊗7.30am-11pm) Haus brings some urban hip to the Hills. Rustic-style pizzas are laden with local smallgoods, and the wine list is gargantuan (lots of Hills drops). Also on offer are baguettes, pasta, burgers, steaks, salads and quiches. Prop yourself on the street-side terrace if it's warm. Good coffee and interesting craft beers, too. Nice one, Haus.

🄯 DRINKING & NIGHTLIFE

Prancing Pony   Craft Beer
(☑08-8398 3881; www.prancingponybrewery. com.au; 42 Mt Barker Rd, Totness; ⊗10am-6pm Mon, 4-10pm Wed & Thu, 10.30am-10pm Fri-Sun) Trophy-winning craft beers, burgers, platters, bar snacks and live troubadours all make an appearance at this funky beer shed, on the road out of Mt Barker heading for Hahndorf. Kick back with an Indie Kid Pilsener or three and revel in the fact that you're not in a winery or a pub.

🄯 INFORMATION

Adelaide Hills Visitor Information Centre
(☑08-8393 7600; www.adelaidehills.org.au; 68 Main St, Hahndorf; ⊗9am-5pm Mon-Fri, 10am-5pm Sat & Sun) The usual barrage of brochures, plus accommodation bookings; the **Hahndorf Academy** (☑08-8388 7250; www.hahndorf academy.org.au; 68 Main St, Hahndorf; ⊗10am-5pm) **FREE** art gallery and museum is here too.

🄯 GETTING THERE & AWAY

To best explore the Hills, BYO wheels. Alternatively, Adelaide Metro (p224) runs buses between the city and most Hills towns.

ULURU &
THE OUTBACK

Uluru & the Outback at a Glance...

Nothing can prepare you for the immensity, grandeur, changing colours and stillness of Uluru – a sight that will sear itself into your memory. This World Heritage–listed icon has attained pilgrimage status for many Australians. Equally impressive Kata Tjuta and the surrounding desert are of deep cultural significance to the traditional owners, the Anangu people.

Alice Springs is the biggest town in the Australian outback, and an urban oasis, while Yulara is Uluru's busy service town, 20km from 'the Rock'.

Uluru & the Outback in Two Days

Fly directly to Yulara to maximise your time in **Uluru-Kata Tjuta National Park** (p237). Head straight to the **Uluru-Kata Tjuta Cultural Centre** (p236) and book yourself onto a ranger-led tour of Uluru. Head to the **sunset viewing area** at dusk to see the desert colours shift. On day two, take a tour or a drive to explore Kata Tjuta.

Uluru & the Outback in Four Days

With four days to play with, you might want to do some bike riding around Uluru, sign up for a **scenic flight** (p239), or at least tackle a couple of independent walks. **Alice Springs** (p243) is also worth a visit – a unique, isolated desert town with a brilliant **wildlife park** (p245) and excellent Aboriginal art galleries.

Previous page: Visitors at Sounds of Silence (p239)

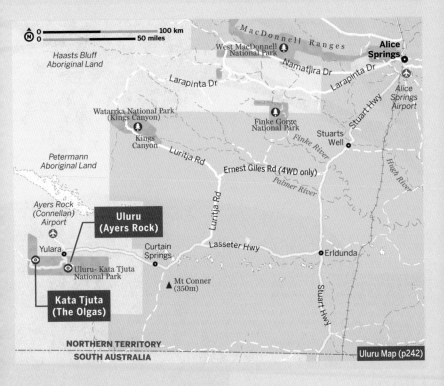

Arriving in Uluru & the Outback

Yulara is the gateway to the park and has an **airport** (p242) with flights from major Australian cities. There are also buses and tours from Alice Springs. If you're driving, the sealed route from Alice Springs (447km) is via the Stuart and then Lasseter Hwys.

Sleeping

Alice Springs has plenty of hotels, motels and resorts if you're spending any time there. Out at Uluru, the only accommodation is at Yulara, 20km away from Uluru. There are 5000 beds here – campgrounds, a hostel, apartments and resort-style hotels – but you still need to book ahead through a central reservations system. Expect premium prices, reflecting the remote locale.

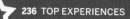

Uluru

The first sighting of Uluru (Ayers Rock) on the horizon will astound even the most jaded traveller. Solitary and prodigious, it's 3.6km long and towers 348m above the surrounding scrub.

Great For...

☑ **Don't Miss**

Wonderful rock art in shelters along the Mala Walk and Kuniya Walk to Mutitjulu Waterhole.

The Big Rock

Uluru is undeniably huge, but it's believed that two-thirds of the rock lies beneath the sand. Close inspection reveals a wondrously contoured surface concealing numerous sacred sites of particular significance to the Anangu.

If your first look at Uluru is in the afternoon, it appears to be ochre-brown, scored and pitted by dark shadows. As the sun sets, it illuminates the rock in burnished orange, then a series of deeper reds before it fades into charcoal. A performance in reverse, with marginally fewer spectators, is given at dawn.

Exploring Uluru

Uluru-Kata Tjuta Cultural Centre

(☎08-8956 1128; www.parksaustralia.gov.au/uluru; ☺7am-6pm) is 1km before Uluru on

TOURISM NT/SEAN SCOTT ©

ⓘ Need to Know

https://parksaustralia.gov.au/uluru; adult/
child/family 3-day passes $25/12.50/65;
☉sunrise-sunset

✕ Take a Break

The **Tali Wiru** (☏02-8296 8010; www.
ayersrockresort.com.au/tali-wiru; per person
$360; ☉Apr–mid-Oct) outdoor dining ex-
perience (atop a dune!) can be magical.

★ Top Tip

The sunset viewing area is the best
place for those classic, saffron-red Rock
shots.

the road from Yulara and should be your
first stop. Displays and exhibits focus
on *tjukurpa* (Aboriginal law, religion and
custom) and the history and management
of the national park. The information desk
in the Nintiringkupai building is staffed by
park rangers who supply the information,
leaflets and walking notes.

Walks

There are several established walking
tracks around Uluru. Ranger-led walks explain the area's plants, wildlife, geology and
cultural significance. The excellent *Visitor
Guide & Maps* brochure from the Cultural
Centre details a few self-guided walks.

Base Walk This track (10.6km, three to four
hours) circumnavigates the rock, passing caves,
paintings, sandstone folds and geological abra-
sions along the way.

Liru Walk Links the Cultural Centre with the
start of the Mala walk and climb, and winds
through strands of mulga before opening up near
Uluru (4km return, 1½ hours).

Mala Walk From the base of the climbing point
(2km return, one hour), interpretive signs explain
the *tjukurpa* of the Mala (hare-wallaby people),
which is significant to the Anangu, as well as fine
examples of rock art. A ranger-guided walk (free)
along this route departs at 10am (8am from
October to April) from the car park.

Kuniya Walk A short walk (1km return, 45
minutes) from the car park on the southern
side leads to the most permanent waterhole,
Mutitjulu, home of the ancestral watersnake.
Great birdwatching and some excellent rock art
are highlights of this walk.

Sunset & Sunrise Views

About halfway between Yulara and Uluru,
the **sunset viewing area** has plenty of car
and coach parking for that familiar post-
card view. The **Talinguru Nyakunytjaku**

sunrise viewing area is perched on a sand dune and captures both Uluru and Kata Tjuta in all their glory. It also has two great interpretive walks (1.5km) about women's and men's business. There's a shaded viewing area, toilets and a place to picnic.

Closed for Climbing

Many visitors consider climbing Uluru to be a highlight of a trip to the Centre, and even a rite of passage. But for the traditional owners, the Anangu, Uluru is a sacred place. The path up the side of Uluru is part of the route taken by the Mala ancestors on their arrival at Uluru and has great spiritual significance – and is not to be trampled by human feet. Since 2017 there has been a sign at Uluru from the Anangu saying 'We don't climb', and requesting that you don't climb either. From 26 October 2019 you won't be allowed to.

The Anangu are the custodians of Uluru and take responsibility for the safety of visitors. Any injuries or deaths that occur are a source of distress and sadness to them. For similar reasons of public safety, Parks Australia preferred that people didn't climb, even while the walk remained open. It's a very steep ascent, not to be taken lightly, and each year there are several air rescues, mostly for people suffering heart attacks.

Consider visiting the Cultural Centre (p236) and taking an Anangu guided tour instead.

Seit Outback Australia sunset tour at Uluru

Tours of Uluru

Sounds of Silence
Australian $$$

(☑08-8957 7448; www.ayersrockresort.com.
au/sounds-of-silence; adult/child $210/105)
Waiters serve Champagne and canapés on
a desert dune with stunning sunset views
of Uluru and Kata Tjuta. Then it's a buffet
dinner (with emu, croc and roo) beneath
the southern sky, which, after dinner, is
dissected and explained with the help of
a telescope. If you're more of a morning
person, try the similarly styled **Desert
Awakenings 4WD Tour** (☑1300 134 044;
www.ayersrockresort.com.au; adult/child from

> ### 🚲 On Your Bike
> A wonderful new way of experiencing
> the rock is by bike, available for hire at
> the Cultural Centre (p236).

$179/139). Neither tour is suitable for chil-
dren under 10 years.

Uluru
Aboriginal Tours
Cultural Tour

(www.facebook.com/Uluru-Aboriginal-Tours-248
457278623328/; guided tours from $99) Owned
and operated by Anangu from the Mutitjulu
community, this company offers a range of
trips to give you an insight into the signifi-
cance of the Rock through the eyes of the
traditional owners. Tours depart from the
Cultural Centre (p236), Yulara Ayers Rock
Resort and from Alice Springs.

Ayers Rock
Helicopters
Scenic Flights

(☑08-8956 2077; www.flyuluru.com.au; 15/30
/36min scenic flights per person $150/ 285/310)
One of the most memorable ways to see
the Rock; you'll need the 40-minute flight
to also take in Kata Tjuta.

Seit Outback Australia
Bus

(☑08-8956 3156; www.seitoutbackaustralia.
com.au) This small-group tour operator
has dozens of Uluru and Kata Tjuta tours,
including sunset tours around Uluru and
sunrise tours at Kata Tjuta.

Wira
Walking

(☑08-8956 1128; Uluru-Kata Tjuta Cultural Cen-
tre; ⏱4.30-6pm Mon, Wed & Fri) **FREE** This free
tour is a lovely way to spend an afternoon,
walking through the bush surrounding the
cultural centre with a local Anangu guide
who'll teach you all about bush plants.
You'll never look at the desert in the same
way again.

> ### 🚌 Tours from
> ### Alice Springs
>
> Several bus/tour companies can take
> you from Alice to Uluru and back in a
> day. Try **Emu Run Experience** (☑1800
> 687 220, 08-8953 7057; www.emurun.com.
> au; 72 Todd St, Alice Springs) or **Gray Line**
> (☑1300 858 687; www.grayline.com; Capri-
> cornia Centre 9, Gregory Tce , Alice Springs).

Kata Tjuta

No journey to Uluru is complete without a visit to Kata Tjuta (also known as the Olgas), a striking group of domed rocks huddled together about 35km west of the Rock.

Great For...

☑ **Don't Miss**

Kata Tjuta at sunset, when the boulders are at their glorious, blood-red best.

Big Boulders

There are 36 boulders shoulder to shoulder here, forming deep valleys and steep-sided gorges. The tallest rock, namesake **Kata Tjuta** (aka Mt Olga; 546m, 1066m above sea level) is approximately 200m higher than Uluru, and indeed, many visitors find them even more captivating than their prominent neighbour...but why choose?

Trails weave in among the red rocks, leading to pockets of silent beauty and spiritual gravitas. Kata Tjuta is of great *tjukurpa* significance (relating to Aboriginal law, religion and custom), particularly for Indigenous men, so stick to the tracks.

As a curious aside (astound friends around the campfire), the English name for Kata Tjuta – the Olgas – was bestowed in 1872 by Ernest Giles, in honour of Russian Queen Olga of Württemberg, the daughter of Tsar Nicholas I.

TOURISM NT/SEAN SCOTT ©

Yulara

Kata Tjuta
Uluru-Kata Tjuta
National Park
Kata Tjuta Rd

Uluru Rd

❶ Need to Know

https://parksaustralia.gov.au/uluru; adult/
child/family 3-day passes $25/12.50/65;
☼sunrise-sunset

✕ Take a Break

There's a picnic and sunset-viewing
area with toilet facilities just off the
access road.

★ Top Tip

The Valley of the Winds walk sidesteps
the crowds and rewards hikers with
sensational views.

Indigenous Significance

The name 'Kata Tjuta' in the Pitjantjatjara
language means 'many heads'. Sacred to
the Anangu people, the 500-million-year-
old rocks are said to be the home of the
snake king Wanambi, who only comes
down from his fastness atop Mt Olga in
the dry season. This is, however, by no
means the only legend told about the site.
The majority of myths about Kata Tjuta,
and the ceremonies still practised by its
traditional owners, are off limits to women
and outsiders.

Walks

The 7.4km **Valley of the Winds** loop (two
to four hours) is one of the most challenging and rewarding bushwalks in the park. It
winds through the gorges giving excellent
views of the surreal domes and traversing

varied terrain. It's not particularly arduous,
but wear sturdy shoes and take plenty of
water. Starting this walk at first light often
rewards you with solitude, enabling you to
appreciate the sounds of the wind and bird
calls carried up the valley. When the weather gets too hot, trail access is often closed
by late morning.

The short signposted track beneath
towering rock walls into pretty **Walpa
Gorge** (2.6km return, 45 minutes) is
especially beautiful in the afternoon, when
sunlight floods the gorge. Watch for rock
wallabies in the early morning or late
afternoon.

Tours

Unless you're on a tour, you'll need your own
wheels to reach Kata Tjuta. Many companies
offering tours of Uluru can also take you to
Kata Tjuta, including Seit Outback Australia
(p239), Sounds of Silence (p239) and Ayers
Rock Helicopters (p239).

Yulara

Yulara is the service village and necessary base for exploring Uluru-Kata Tjuta National Park, and has effectively turned one of the world's least hospitable regions into a comfortable place to stay with a full range of amenities. It lies just outside the national park, 20km from Uluru and 53km from Kata Tjuta.

🍴 EATING

Kulata Academy Cafe   Cafe $

(Town Sq; breakfast $4.80-8, sandwiches, pies & light meals $10.50; ⏲7.30am-5pm) Run by trainees of Uluru's Indigenous training academy, Kulata is a good place to pick up a coffee in the morning and a light lunch (including pies) later in the day.

Geckos Cafe   Mediterranean $$

(Town Sq; mains $19-29; ⏲noon-2.30pm & 6.30-9pm) For great value, a warm atmosphere

and tasty food, head to this buzzing licensed cafe. The wood-fired pizzas and kangaroo burgers go well with a carafe of sangria, and the courtyard tables are a great place to enjoy the desert night air. There are several veggie and gluten-free options, plus meals can be made to take away.

Outback Pioneer Barbecue   Barbecue $$

(Outback Pioneer Hotel & Lodge; burgers/meat/salad bar $20/35/20; ⏲6-9pm) For a fun, casual night out, this lively tavern is the popular choice for everyone from backpackers to grey nomads. Choose between kangaroo skewers, prawns, veggie burgers, steaks and emu sausages, and grill them yourself at the communal BBQs. The deal includes a salad bar.

Arngulli Grill & Restaurant   Australian $$$

(☎08-8957 7888; Desert Gardens Hotel; mains $30-56; ⏲6-9pm) Celebrated by many as

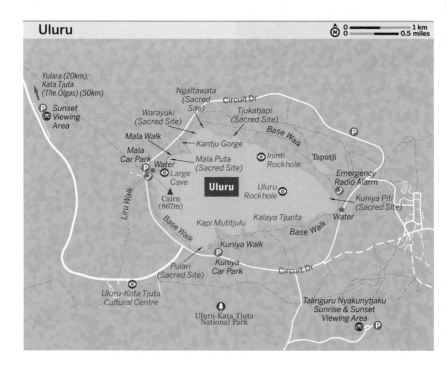

Uluru

Yulara's best restaurant, Arngulli serves up fabulous, locally sourced steaks, as well as kangaroo fillet and wild mushroom risotto. It's an elegant place where you might want to dress nicely.

ℹ️ INFORMATION

The useful *Manta* flyer is available at hotel desks. Most of the village's facilities are scattered around Yulara Town Sq.

Most tour operators and car-hire firms have desks at the **Tour & Information Centre** (☑08-8957 7324; Resort Shopping Centre; ⊙8am-7pm)

ℹ️ GETTING THERE & AWAY

AIR

Ayers Rock Airport (Connellan Airport; ☑08-8956 2266; Coote Rd) About 4km north of Yulara.

Jetstar (☑13 15 38; www.jetstar.com) Yulara to/from Melbourne and Sydney.

Qantas (☑13 13 13; www.qantas.com.au) Connects Yulara with Cairns, Sydney and Melbourne.

Virgin Australia (☑13 67 89; www.virginaustralia.com) Flies Yulara–Sydney with onward connections.

BUS

There is no public bus transport to/from Yulara. Emu Run Experience (p239) operates services between Alice Springs and Yulara (one way adult/child from $145/110), as does Gray Line ($105).

CAR & MOTORCYCLE

The main route from Alice to Yulara is sealed all the way, with regular food and petrol stops. It's 200km from Alice to Erldunda on the Stuart Hwy, where you turn west for the 245km journey along the Lasseter Hwy. The journey takes four to five hours.

ℹ️ GETTING AROUND

A free shuttle bus meets all flights (pick-up is 90 minutes before your flight when leaving) and drops off at all accommodation points around

🔭 Desert Star-Gazing

See the stars of central Australia in the desert outside Alice with terrific nightly astronomy tours with **Earth Sanctuary** (☑08-8953 6161; www.earth-sanctuary.com.au; astronomy tours adult/child $36/25). Tours last for an hour and the informative guides have high-powered telescopes to get you feeling up close and personal with the stars. You'll need to ring ahead – they'll know by 4pm if clear skies are forecast.

the resort. Another free shuttle bus loops through the resort – stopping at all accommodation points and the shopping centre – every 20 minutes from 10.30am to 6pm and from 6.30pm to 12.30am daily.

Uluru Hop-On Hop-Off (☑08-8956 2019; www.uluruexpress.com.au; adult 1-/2-day passes $120/160, child $40/60, Uluru return adult/child $49/15, Kata Tjuta $95/40) falls somewhere between a shuttle-bus service and an organised tour. It provides return transport from the resort to Uluru and Kata Tjuta with one- to three-day passes also available. Check the website for timetables.

Alice Springs

Alice Springs wouldn't win a beauty contest, but there's more going on here than first meets the eye, from the inspirational (excellent museums, a fine wildlife park and outstanding galleries of Indigenous art) to the practical (a wide range of accommodation, good dining options and travel connections). It's the gateway to some of central Australia's most stirring landscapes: Uluru-Kata Tjuta National Park is a four- to five-hour drive away.

Alice is a key touchstone for understanding Aboriginal Australia in all its complexity and its present-day challenges. The Aboriginal name for Alice Springs is Mparntwe, and the region's traditional owners are the Arrernte, although many different Aboriginal communities now call Alice Springs home.

⊙ SIGHTS

Araluen Arts Centre
Gallery

(🕿08-8951 1122; www.araluenartscentre.nt.gov.au; cnr Larapinta Dr & Memorial Ave; ⊙10am-4pm) For a small town, Alice Springs has a thriving arts scene and the Araluen Arts Centre is at its heart. There is a 500-seat **theatre** and four galleries with a focus on art from the Central Desert region. The Albert Namatjira Gallery features works by the artist, who began painting watercolours in the 1930s at Hermannsburg mission, 127 km from Alice. The exhibition draws comparisons between Namatjira and his initial mentor, Rex Battarbee, and other Hermannsburg School artists.

Anzac Hill
Landmark

For a tremendous view, particularly at sunrise and sunset, take a hike (use Lions Walk from Wills Tce) or a drive up to the top of Anzac Hill, known as Untyeyetweleye in Arrernte. From the war memorial there is a 360-degree view over the town down to Heavitree Gap and the MacDonnell Ranges.

Royal Flying Doctor Service Base
Museum

(RFDS; 🕿08-8958 8411; www.rfdsalicesprings.com.au; Stuart Tce; adult/child/family $17/10/52; ⊙9am-5pm Mon-Sat, 1-5pm Sun) This excellent museum, filled with interactive information portals, is the home of the Royal Flying Doctor Service, whose dedicated health workers provide 24-hour emergency retrievals across an area of around 1.25 million sq km. State-of-the-art facilities includes a hologram of John Flynn (the RFDS founder) and a look at the operational control room, as well as some ancient medical gear and a flight simulator. Guided tours leave every half-hour, with the last at 4pm.

Olive Pink Botanic Garden
Nature Reserve

(🕿08-8952 2154; www.opbg.com.au; Tuncks Rd; ⊙8am-6pm) FREE A network of meandering trails leads through this lovely arid zone

RT Tours chef and Arrernte guide Bob Taylor

botanic garden, which was founded by the prominent anthropologist Olive Pink. The garden has more than 500 central Australian plant species and grows bush foods and medicinal plants such as native lemon grass, quandong and bush passion fruit.

⚙ TOURS

RT Tours — Tours
(☑08-8952 0327; www.rttoursaustralia.com; tours per person from $150) Chef and Arrernte guide Bob Taylor runs a popular lunch and dinner tour at Simpsons Gap or the Telegraph Station Historical Reserve, where he whips up a bush-inspired meal. Other tours available, too.

Dreamtime Tours — Cultural
(☑08-8955 5095; 72 Hillside Gardens; adult/child $85/42, self-drive $66/33; ☺8.30-11.30am) Runs the three-hour Dreamtime & Bush-tucker Tour, where you meet Warlpiri Aboriginal people and learn a little about their traditions. As it caters for large bus groups it can be impersonal, but you can tag along with your own vehicle.

Alice Springs
Walking Tours — Walking
(☑0432 511 492; www.facebook.com/aspwalkingtours; cnr Parsons St & Todd Mall; per person $28) These 90-minute walking tours around Alice are a terrific way to get to know the town. Local guide James Acklin is a mine of information. Tours leave from outside the visitor information centre.

🔒 SHOPPING

Papunya Tula Artists — Art
(☑08-8952 4731; www.papunyatula.com.au; Todd Mall; ☺9am-5pm Mon-Fri, 10am-1pm Sat) This stunning gallery showcases artworks from the Western Desert communities of Papunya, Kintore and Kiwirrkurra – even if you're not buying, it's worth stopping by to see the magnificent collection.

Tjanpi Desert Weavers — Art
(☑08-8958 2336; www.tjanpi.com.au; 3 Wilkinson St; ☺10am-4pm Mon-Fri, closed Jan)

🐦 Alice Springs Desert Park

Head to this **park** (☑08-8951 8788; www.alicespringsdesertpark.com.au; Larapinta Dr; adult/child $32/16, nocturnal tours adult/child $45.50/28.50; ☺7.30am-6pm, last entry 4.30pm, nocturnal tour 7.30pm Mon-Fri), where the creatures of central Australia are all on display in one place, including many that are extremely difficult to find out on the trail. The predominantly open-air exhibits faithfully re-create the animals' natural environments in a series of habitats: inland river, sand country and woodland. It's an easy 2.5km cycle to the park. Pick up a free audio guide (available in various languages) or join one of the free ranger-led talks throughout the day.

Try to time your visit to coincide with the terrific birds of prey show, featuring free-flying Australian kestrels, kites and awesome wedge-tailed eagles. To catch some of the park's rare and elusive animals, such as the bilby, visit the excellent nocturnal house. If you like what you see, come back at night and spotlight endangered species on the guided nocturnal tour (bookings essential).

Desert Park Transfers (☑08-8952 1731; www.tailormadetours.com.au; adult/child $40/22) offers transfers from town to the park, five times daily during park hours. The cost includes park entry and pick-up and drop-off at your accommodation. Alice Wanderer (p247) offers a similar service.

Eagle in Alice Springs Desert Park
MMARTIN/SHUTTERSTOCK ©

This small enterprise by the Ngaanyatjarra Pitjantjatjara Yankunytjatjara (NPY) Women's Council employs and supports more than 400 Central Desert female weavers from 26 remote communities. The shop is well worth a visit to see the superb woven baskets and quirky sculptures created from grasses collected locally – *tjanpi* means 'wild harvested grass'.

Red Kangaroo Books Books
(☏08-8953 2137; www.redkangaroobooks.com; 79 Todd Mall; ◷9am-5.30pm Mon-Fri, to 3pm Sat, to 1pm Sun market days) Excellent bookshop specialising in central Australian titles: history, art, travel, novels, guidebooks and more. It also has small but well-chosen wildlife section.

✖ EATING

Kungkas Cafe Cafe $
(☏08-8952 3102; shop 17, Diarama Village, Larapinta Dr; snacks & light meals from $10; ◷7.30am-3pm Mon-Fri) Now here's something a little different. The coffee at this Indigenous catering place is good, but we love it for its snacks that put wild-harvested bush foods (eg bush tomatoes, lemon myrtle) front and centre. Take-home treats include saltbush or wattleseed dukkah, bush tomato chutney and quandong relish.

Page 27 Cafe Cafe $
(☏0429 003 874, 08-8952 0191; www.facebook.com/Page27Cafe; Fan Lane; mains breakfast $8-22, lunch $14-20; ◷7am-2.30pm Tue-Fri, 7.30am-2pm Sat & Sun; ☏) Alice's locals duck down this arcade for great coffee or fresh juice. There are wholesome home-style breakfasts (eggs any style, pancakes), pita wraps and fancy salads such as chicken fattoush with herbed quinoa, rocket and baba ganoush. Excellent vegetarian menu.

Montes Australian $$
(☏08-8952 4336; www.montes.net.au; cnr Stott Tce & Todd St; mains $13-28; ◷2pm-2am Wed-Sun) Travelling circus meets outback homestead. Montes is family friendly with a play area for kids, and the food ranges from gourmet burgers, pizzas and tapas to curries and seafood. Sit in the leafy beer garden (with a range of beers) or intimate booth seating. Patio heaters keep patrons warm on cool desert nights.

Epilogue Lounge Tapas $$
(☏08-8953 4206; www.facebook.com/epiloguelounge; 58 Todd Mall; mains $18-22; ◷7.30am-11.30pm Wed-Sat, 8am-3pm Sun & Mon) This urban, retro delight is definitely the coolest place to hang in town. With a decent wine list, food served all day and service with a smile, it is a real Alice Springs stand-out. Expect dishes such as halloumi burgers and steak sandwiches. They also have live music at 8pm Saturdays and open-mike comedy from 7.30pm on Thursdays.

ⓘ INFORMATION

Alice Springs Visitor Information Centre
(☏08-8952 5800, 1800 645 199; www.discovercentralaustralia.com; cnr Todd Mall & Parsons St; ◷8am-6pm Mon-Fri, 9.30am-4pm Sat & Sun; ☏) This helpful centre can load you up with stacks of brochures and the free visitors' guide. Weather forecasts and road conditions are posted on the wall. National parks information is also available. Ask about the unlimited kilometre deals if you are thinking of renting a car.

Alice Springs Hospital (☏08-8951 7777; https://nt.gov.au/wellbeing; Gap Rd)

Alice Springs Pharmacy (☏08-8952 1554; shop 19, Yeperenye Shopping Centre, 36 Hartley St; ◷8.30am-9pm Mon-Fri, 8.30am-7pm Sat, 9am-4.30pm Sun)

ⓘ GETTING THERE & AWAY

AIR

Alice Springs is well connected, with **Qantas** (☏13 13 13, 08-8950 5211; www.qantas.com.au) and **Virgin Australia** (☏13 67 89; www.virginaustralia.com) operating regular flights to/from capital cities. Airline representatives are based at **Alice Springs airport** (☏08-8951 1211; www.alicespringsairport.com.au; Santa Teresa Rd).

Anzac Hill (p244) memorial

BUS

Greyhound (1300 473 946; www.greyhound.
com.au; Shop 3, 113 Todd St) has regular services
to points north and south (check the website for
timetables and discounted fares). Buses arrive at,
and depart from, the Greyhound office in Todd St.

Emu Run Experience (p239) runs daily connections between Alice Springs and Yulara (one way
adult/child from $145/110). Gray Line (p239) also
runs between Alice Springs and Yulara (one way
from $100).

CAR & MOTORCYCLE

Alice Springs is a long way from everywhere.
It's 1180km to Mt Isa in Queensland, 1490km
to Darwin, 1531km to Adelaide and 441km (4½
hours) to Yulara (for Uluru).

All the major car-hire companies have offices
in Alice Springs and many have counters at the
airport. A conventional (2WD) vehicle will get you
out to Uluru via sealed roads.

TRAIN

The train station is at the end of George Cres, off
Larapinta Dr.

A classic way to enter or leave the NT is by
the **Ghan** (13 21 47; www.greatsouthernrail.
com.au), which can be booked through Great
Southern Rail. Discounted fares are sometimes
offered, especially in the low season (February to
June). Bookings are essential.

ⓘ GETTING AROUND

TO/FROM THE AIRPORT

Alice Springs airport is 15km south of the town;
it's about $50 by taxi. A bus from **Alice Wander-
er** (08-8952 2111, 1800 722 111; www.alice
wanderer.com.au) meets all flights and drops off
passengers at city accommodation. Book a day
in advance for pick-up from accommodation.

BUS

The public bus service, **AS Bus** (08-8944
2444), departs from outside the **Yeperenye
Shopping Centre** in Hartley St.

TAXI

Taxis congregate near the visitor information
centre. To book one, telephone 13 10 08 or
08-8952 1877.

KAKADU
NATIONAL PARK

Kakadu National Park

Kakadu is more than a national park: it's a vibrant, living acknowledgement of the elemental link between the Aboriginal people and the country they've nurtured for millennia. At almost 20,000 sq km, it's a truly spectacular ecosystem, overrun with wildlife and dotted with waterfalls and mind-blowing ancient rock art.

It's accessed from Darwin, Australia's only tropical capital. Closer to Bali than Bondi, Darwin can certainly feel removed from the rest of the country – just the way the locals like it! More than 50 nationalities live here, clearly represented in the city's wonderful markets.

Kakadu in Two Days

Just two days in this glorious national park seems like an error in judgement. But if time is tight, do the essentials: wildlife spotting with **Yellow Water Cruises** (p261), a hike to see the rock art at spectacular **Nourlangie** (p253), and an Indigenous-led guided tour at **Ubirr** (p253), with views from Nardab Lookout.

Kakadu in Four Days

Spend three days in Kakadu, ticking off the big-ticket sights then exploring some of the more remote locations such as **Jim Jim Falls** and **Twin Falls** (p256). Recover in **Darwin** (p257) with a visit to the **Museum & Art Gallery of the Northern Territory** (p257) and drinks and nocturnal shenanigans along Mitchell St.

Previous page: Kakadu National Park
TOURISM NT/JOHAN LOLOS ©

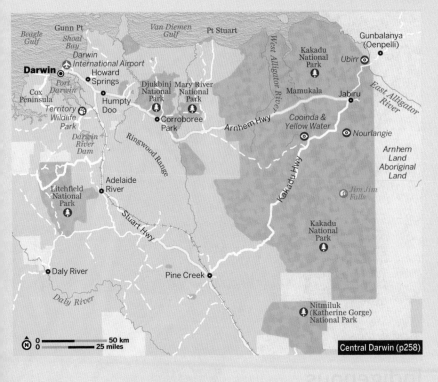

Central Darwin (p258)

Arriving in Kakadu

Many people access Kakadu on a tour from Darwin (253km to Jabiru), seeing the major sights with the minimum of hassles, but it's just as easy with your own wheels. Note that some sights (eg Jim Jim Falls and Twin Falls) are 4WD-access only.

Greyhound Australia (p264) runs buses from Darwin to Jabiru ($75, 3½ hours).

Darwin international airport (p264) has connections to all capital cities.

Sleeping

If you want to stay within Kakadu (as opposed to just day-tripping in from Darwin – not recommended!), Jabiru has the best choice of accommodation within the park, including a couple of good resorts. The resort at Cooinda and wilderness lodge near Ubirr are also worthwhile. Booking ahead is essential, especially from June to September.

Indigenous Rock Art

Kakadu is one of Australia's richest, most accessible repositories of Aboriginal rock art. There are more than 5000 sites here, which date from 20,000 years to 10 years ago.

Significance & Preservation

For local Aboriginal people, Kakadu's ancient rock-art sites are a major source of traditional archival knowledge. Some older paintings are believed by many Aboriginal people to have been painted by mimi spirits, connecting people with creation legends and the development of Aboriginal lore.

As the paintings are all rendered with natural, water-soluble ochres, they are very susceptible to water damage. Drip lines of clear silicon rubber have been laid on the rocks above the paintings to divert rain. As the most accessible sites receive up to 4000 visitors a week, boardwalks have been erected to keep the dust down and to keep people at a suitable distance from the paintings.

Great For...

☑ Don't Miss

Touring Ubirr with an Indigenous guide and hearing Dreaming stories.

TOURISM NT/PETER EVE ©

Ubirr

It'll take a lot more than the busloads of visitors here to disturb Ubirr's inherent majesty and grace. Layers of **rock-art paintings**, in various styles and from various centuries, command a mesmerising stillness. Part of the main gallery reads a menu, with images of kangaroos, tortoises and fish painted in X-ray, the dominant style about 8000 years ago. Look for the yam-head figures, which date back around 15,000 years.

The magnificent **Nardab Lookout** is a 250m scramble from the main gallery. Surveying the billiard-table-green floodplain and watching the sun set and the moon rise, like they're on an invisible set of scales, is glorious, to say the least. **Ubirr** (⊗8.30am-sunset Apr-Nov, 2pm-sunset Dec-Mar) is 39km north of the Arnhem Hwy via a sealed road.

Nourlangie

The sight of this looming outlier of the Arnhem Land escarpment makes it easy to understand its ancient importance to Aboriginal people. Its long red-sandstone bulk, striped in places with orange, white and black, slopes up from surrounding woodland to fall away at one end in stepped cliffs. Below is Kakadu's best-known collection of **rock art**.

The 2km looped walking track (open 8am to sunset) takes you first to the **Anbangbang Shelter**, used for 20,000 years as a refuge and canvas. Next is the **Anbangbang Gallery**, featuring Dreaming characters repainted in the 1960s. Look for the virile Nabulwinjbulwinj, a dangerous spirit who likes to eat females after banging them on the head with a yam. From here it's a short walk to **Gunwarddehwarde Lookout**, with views of the Arnhem Land escarpment.

Native Wildlife

Kakadu is home to 60 mammal species, 280-plus bird species, 120 species of reptile, 25 frog species, 55 freshwater fish species and at least 10,000 different kinds of insect.

Great For...

☑ Don't Miss

The weird alien 'cities' formed by the cathedral termite mounds found right through Kakadu.

Birds

Abundant waterbirds are a Kakadu highlight. This is one of the chief refuges in Australia for several species, including the magpie goose, green pygmy goose and Burdekin duck. Other waterbirds include pelicans, brolgas and the jabiru – technically the black-necked stork, Australia's only stork – with its distinctive red legs and long beak. Herons, egrets, cormorants, wedge-tailed eagles, whistling kites and black kites are common. Open woodlands harbour rainbow bee-eaters, kingfishers and the endangered bustard. Majestic white-breasted sea eagles are seen near inland waterways.

At night, you might hear barking owls calling – they sound just like dogs – or the plaintive wail of the bush stone curlew. The

Plumed whistling ducks, Kakadu

TOURISM NT/JEWELS LYNCH ©

raucous call of the spectacular red-tailed black cockatoo is often considered the signature sound of Kakadu.

Mammals

Several types of kangaroo and wallaby inhabit the park; the shy black wallaroo is unique to Kakadu and Arnhem Land – look for them at Nourlangie Rock. At Ubirr, short-eared rock wallabies can be spotted in the early morning. You may see a sugar glider or a shy dingo in wooded areas in the daytime. Kakadu has 26 bat species, four of them endangered.

Reptiles

Twin Falls and Jim Jim Falls have resident freshwater crocodiles, which have narrow snouts and rarely exceed 3m, while the dangerous saltwater variety is found throughout the park.

Kakadu's other reptiles include the frilled lizard, 11 species of goanna, and five freshwater turtle species, of which the most common is the northern snake-necked turtle. Kakadu has many snakes, though most are nocturnal and rarely encountered. The striking Oenpelli python was first recorded by non-Aboriginal people in 1976. The odd-looking file snake lives in billabongs and is much sought after as bush tucker. They have square heads, tiny eyes and saggy skin covered in tiny rough scales (hence 'file'). They move very slowly, eating only once a month and breeding once every decade.

Fish

You can't miss the silver barramundi, which creates a distinctive swirl near the water's surface. Renowned sportfish, 'barra' can grow to more than 1m long.

Jabiru

It may seem surprising to find a town of Jabiru's size and structure in the midst of a wilderness national park, but it exists solely because of the nearby Ranger uranium mine. With the closure of the mine slated for 2021, the town's future appears uncertain and will be dependent upon the extent to which it can build on its other role as the national park's major service centre. In this capacity, it has just about everything you'd need, with a bank, newsagent, medical centre, supermarket, bakery and service station, as well as some good accommodation and an improving culinary scene.

Jim Jim Falls & Twin Falls

Remote and spectacular, these two falls epitomise the rugged Top End. **Jim Jim Falls**, a sheer 215m drop, is awesome after rain (when it can only be seen from the air), but its waters shrink to a trickle by about June. **Twin Falls** flows year-round (no swimming), but half the fun is getting here,

involving a little **boat trip** (adult/child $15/ free; h7.30am-5pm, last boat 4pm) and an over-the-water boardwalk.

These two iconic waterfalls are reached via a 4WD-only track that turns south off the Kakadu Hwy between the Nourlangie and Cooinda turn-offs. Jim Jim Falls is about 56km from the turn-off (the last 1km on foot) and it's a further five corrugated kilometres to Twin Falls. The track is open in the Dry only and can still be closed into late May; it's off limits to most rental vehicles (check the fine print). A couple of tour companies make trips here in the Dry.

Cooinda & Yellow Water

Cooinda is one of the main tourism hubs in Kakadu. An all-purpose resort has grown up around the wetlands, which are known as Yellow Water, or to give its rather challenging Indigenous name, Ngurrungurrundjba. The cruises (p261), preferably taken around sunrise or sunset, are undoubted highlights of any visit to Kakadu.

Jim Jim Falls

About 1km from the resort (an easy 15 minutes' walk), the **Warradjan Aboriginal Cultural Centre** (www.kakadutourism.com; Yellow Water Area; ⊙9am-5pm) **FREE** depicts Creation stories and has an excellent permanent exhibition. You'll be introduced to the moiety system (the law of interpersonal relationships), languages and skin names, and there's a minitheatre with a huge selection of films from which to choose. A mesmeric soundtrack of chants and didgeridoos plays in the background.

The turn-off to the Cooinda accommodation complex and Yellow Water wetlands is 47km down the Kakadu Hwy from the Arnhem Hwy intersection.

Darwin

Australia's only tropical capital city and gateway to the Top End, Darwin, on the traditional lands of the Larrakia, gazes out across the Timor Sea. It feels quite removed from the rest of the country, which is just how the locals like it.

Tables spill out of street-side restaurants and bars, innovative museums celebrate the city's past, and galleries showcase the region's rich Indigenous art. Nature is well and truly part of Darwin's backyard: the national parks of Kakadu and Litchfield are only a few hours' drive distant.

◎ SIGHTS

Crocosaurus Cove   Zoo
(☑08-8981 7522; www.crocosauruscove.com; 58 Mitchell St; adult/child/family $35/23/110; ⊙9am-6pm, last admission 5pm) If the tourists won't go out to see the crocs, then bring the crocs to the tourists. Right in the middle of Mitchell St, Crocosaurus Cove is as close as you'll ever want to get to these amazing creatures. Six of the largest crocs in captivity can be seen in state-of-the-art aquariums and pools, while you can be lowered right into a pool with the crocs in the transparent Cage of Death (one/two people $170/260).

 ### Kakadu National Park Admission

Admission to the **park** (☑08-8938 1120; www.parksaustralia.gov.au/kakadu; adult/child/family Apr-Oct $40/20/100, Nov-Mar $25/12.50/65) is via a seven-day Park Pass. Passes can be bought online or at various places around the park, including **Bowali Visitor Information Centre** (☑08-8938 1120; www.parksaustralia.gov.au/kakadu; Kakadu Hwy, Jabiru; ⊙8am-5pm), where you can also pick up the excellent *Visitor Guide* booklet. Carry your pass with you at all times as rangers conduct spot checks – penalties apply for nonpayment.

Other places to purchase the pass include the following:

Cooinda Lodge & Campground (☑1800 500 401; www.kakadutourism.com; powered/unpowered sites $50/38, budget/lodge r from $175/200; 🅿❄❈)

Katherine Visitor Information Centre (☑1800 653 142; www.visitkatherine.com.au; cnr Lindsay St & Stuart Hwy; ⊙8.30am-5pm daily mid-Apr–Sep, 8.30am-5pm Mon-Fri, 10am-2pm Sat & Sun Oct–mid-Apr)

Tourism Top End (p264)

Bowali Visitor Information Centre
PARKS AUSTRALIA ©

Museum & Art Gallery of the Northern Territory   Museum
(MAGNT; ☑08-8999 8264; www.magnt.net.au; 19 Conacher St, Fannie Bay; ⊙10am-5pm) **FREE** This superb museum and art gallery boasts beautifully presented galleries of Top End–centric exhibits. The **Aboriginal**

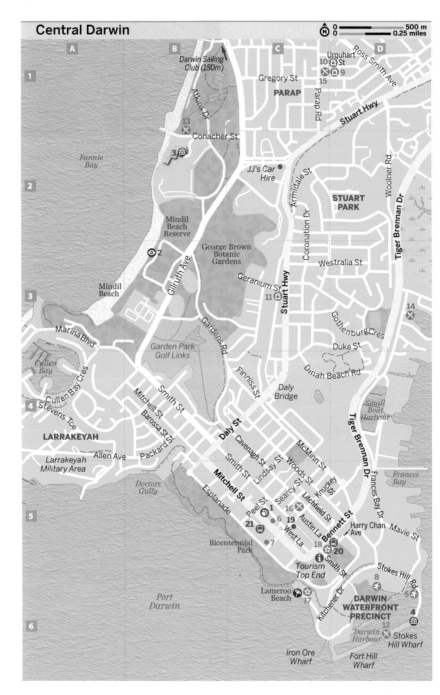

Central Darwin

N 0 _____ 500 m
   0 _____ 0.25 miles

A B C D

1

Darwin Sailing
Club (150m)

Gregory St

PARAP

Urquhart
St
10
15
9

Ross Smith Ave

13
Conacher St

Atkins Dr

Stuart Hwy

3

*Fannie
Bay*

2

JJ's Car
Hire

Armidale St

**STUART
PARK**

Woolner Rd

Coronation Dr

Tiger Brennan Dr

Mindil
Beach
Reserve

George Brown
Botanic
Gardens

Westralia St

Geranium St

Stuart Hwy

2

Gilruth Ave

*Mindil
Beach*

11

3

Gardens Rd

Gothenburg Cres

Duke St

14

*Cullen
Bay*

Marina Blvd

*Garden Park
Golf Links*

Finniss St

Dinah Beach Rd

Daly
Bridge

Cullen Bay Cres

Stevens Tce

Mitchell St

Smith St

Barossa St

Daly St

Cavenagh St

McMinn St

Tiger Brennan Dr

*Small
Boat
Harbour*

LARRAKEYAH

*Larrakeyah
Military Area*

Allen Ave

Packard St

Smith St

Lindsay St

Woods St

Searcy St

Knuckey St

Litchfield St

*Frances
Bay*

*Doctors
Gully*

Mitchell St

Esplanade

Peel St

1
6
19
West La
18

16

Austin La

Bennett St

Harry Chan
Ave

Mavie St

5

21

7

*Bicentennial
Park*

20

Tourism
Top End

Smith St

8

Stokes Hill Rd

*Port
Darwin*

Lameroo
Beach

17

Kitchener Dr

**DARWIN
WATERFRONT
PRECINCT**

12
*Darwin
Harbour*

Stokes
Hill Wharf

5

4

6

*Iron Ore
Wharf*

Fort Hill
Wharf

Central Darwin

art collection is a highlight, with carvings from the Tiwi Islands, bark paintings from Arnhem Land and dot paintings from the desert. An entire room is devoted to **Cyclone Tracy**, in a display that graphically illustrates life before and after the disaster. You can listen to the whirring sound of Tracy at full throttle – a sound you won't forget in a hurry.

Royal Flying Doctor Service
Museum

(☏08-8983 5700; http://rfdsdarwin.com.au/; Stokes Hill Wharf; adult/child/family $28/16/70; ◷9.30am-6pm, last entry 5pm Jun-Sep, 9.30am-5pm, last entry 4pm Oct-May) This outstanding museum on Stokes Hill Wharf is the way all museums should be. There's a 55-seat hologram cinema, virtual-reality glasses that enable you to relive in vivid detail the 1942 Japanese bombing raid on Darwin Harbour, a decommissioned Pilatus PC-12 aircraft from the Royal Flying Doctor Service (RFDS), a live map showing the current location of RFDS planes, and a series of touch screens that take you through the story of the RFDS and Darwin during WWII.

Territory Wildlife Park
Zoo

(☏08-8988 7200; www.territorywildlifepark.com.au; 960 Cox Peninsula Rd; adult/child/family $32/16/54.50; ◷9am-5pm) This excellent park showcases the best of Top End Aussie wildlife. Pride of place must go to the aquarium, where a clear walk-through tunnel puts you among giant barramundi, stingrays, sawfish and saratogas, while a separate tank holds a 3.8m saltwater crocodile. The turn-off is 48km down the Stuart Hwy from Darwin; from here it's 12km further down Cox Peninsula Rd to the park.

⊕ ACTIVITIES
Wave & Recreation Lagoons
Water Park

(☏08-8985 6588; www.waterfront.nt.gov.au; Wave Lagoon adult/child $7/5; ◷Wave Lagoon 10am-6pm) The hugely popular **Wave Lagoon** is a hit with locals and travellers alike. There are 10 different wave patterns produced, along with lifeguards, a kiosk and a strip of lawn to bask on. Adjacent is the **Recreation Lagoon** with a sandy beach, lifeguards and stinger-filtered seawater (although the nets and filters are not guaranteed to be 100% effective).

🎯 TOURS

Darwin Harbour Cruises   Cruise

(📞08-8942 3131; www.darwinharbourcruises.
com.au; Stokes Hill Rd; ⏰6pm mid-Feb–mid-Dec)
Variety of cruises from Stokes Hill Wharf,
including evening cruise options aboard the
Charles Darwin, a tri-level catamaran. Possibilities include a 2½-hour sunset cruise
(adult/child $58/35), or the same deal but
with a buffet dinner ($102/68).

Darwin Walking Tours   Walking

(📞08-8981 0227; 50 Mitchell St; adult/child
$50/free) 🚶 Two-hour guided heritage walks
around the city, enlivened by local anec-
dotes from good local guides.

Ethical Adventures   Tours

(📞0488 442 269; www.ethicaladventures.com) A
cut above most of those offering day tours
to Litchfield National Park from Darwin,
Ethical Adventures runs sunrise-to-sunset
tours that take in all of the main attractions, and provide excellent food (including
barbecued crocodile and buffalo) and good
guides. Its focus on small groups, cultural
engagement and ethical practices is a
highlight. Tours cover Kakadu, Litchfield
and attractions around Darwin.

🎯 Kakadu Tours from Darwin

Northern Territory
Indigenous Tours   Cultural Tour

(📞1300 921 188; www.ntitours.com.au; cnr
Esplanade & Knuckey St, Lyons Cottage; day
tours adult/child from $249/124) Upmarket
Indigenous-led tours to Litchfield National
Park and Kakadu.

Sacred Earth Safaris   Adventure

(📞08-8536 2234; www.sacredearthsafaris.com.
au; ⏰May-Oct) Multiday, small-group 4WD
camping tours around Kakadu, Katherine
and the Kimberley. The three-day Kakadu
tour starts at $1800, while the five-day Top
End National Parks Safari is $3100.

Kakadu Dreams   Tours

(📞1800 813 269; www.kakadudreams.com.au)
Backpacker day tours to Litchfield (adult/
child $149/129), and boisterous two-/
three-day trips to Kakadu ($445/665).

See p261 for more Kakadu tours.

Juvenile saltwater crocodile, Crocosaurus Cove (p257)

🔒 SHOPPING

Outstation Gallery   Art

(📞08-8981 4822; www.outstation.com.au;
8 Parap Pl, Parap; ⏰10am-1pm Tue, to 5pm Wed-
Fri, to 2pm Sat) One of Darwin's best galleries
of Indigenous art, Outstation presents the
works of nine different Aboriginal art centres from across the NT, from Arnhem Land
to the Western Desert.

Provenance Arts   Art

(📞08-6117 5515; www.provenancearts.com.au;
Stuart Hwy, Stuart Park; ⏰10am-5pm Tue-Fri,
to 3pm Sat & Sun) A fabulous initiative from
Injalak Arts (📞08-8979 0190; www.injalak.
com; ⏰8am-5pm Mon-Fri, 9am-2pm Sat) FREE,
an outstanding Indigenous art centre
in Arnhem Land, Provenance Arts is a
gallery with works from over 30 Aboriginal art centres from across the NT, WA
and Queensland, but their ambitions run
further – visitors can sometimes interact
with the artists themselves and there are
plans for an Indigenous cultural tourism
information centre.

Parap
Village Market   Market

(📞0438 882 373; www.parapvillage.com.au;
Parap Shopping Village, 3/3 Vickers St, Parap;
⏰8am-2pm Sat) This compact, crowded
food-focused market is a local favourite.
There's the full gamut of Southeast Asian
cuisine, as well as plenty of ingredients to
cook up your own tropical storm. It's open
year-round.

✖ EATING

Frying Nemo   Fish & Chips $

(📞08-8981 2281; www.fryingnemo.com.au; shop
10, 90 Frances Bay Dr, Stuart Park; mains from
$12; ⏰5pm-late Mon-Fri, 11.30am-9pm Sat &
Sun) They've won various awards here and
are consistently ranked among Australia's
best fish and chips. Lightly battered, wild-
caught NT fish are the mainstays, but the
burgers (barra, croc, buffalo) are all worth
considering too.

Kakadu Tours

Yellow Water Cruises (📞1800 500 401;
www.kakadutourism.com; per person $72-99)
Cruise the South Alligator River and
Yellow Water Billabong spotting wildlife.
Purchase tickets from Gagudju Lodge,
Cooinda; a shuttle bus will take you
from here to the tour's departure point.
The best ones are at sunrise and sunset,
when the wildlife's at its most active.

Kakadu Cultural Tours (KCT; 📞1800
525 238; www.kakaduculturaltours.com.au)
Aboriginal-owned and -operated, the
excellent Kakadu Cultural Tours covers
northern Kakadu and Arnhem Land. The
**Arnhemlander Cultural & Heritage
Tour** (adult/child $273/218; ⏰May-Nov) is
the best way to see western Arnhem
Land and covers rock art, billabongs
and the fabulous Injalak Arts. The
Guluyambi Cultural Cruise (adult/child
$79/52; ⏰9am, 11am, 1pm & 3pm May-Nov)
along the East Alligator River is similarly
outstanding, with Indigenous stories
and plenty of crocs.

Kakadu Animal Tracks (📞0429 676 194;
www.animaltracks.com.au; adult/child $220/55;
⏰1pm May-Sep) Based at Cooinda, this
outfit runs seven-hour tours with an Indigenous guide combining a wildlife safari
and Aboriginal cultural tour. You'll see
thousands of birds and get to hunt, gather,
prepare and consume bush tucker.

Kakadu Air (📞1800 089 113, 08-8941 9611;
www.kakaduair.com.au; 30min flights adult/
child $150/120, 60min flights $250/200,
20/30min helicopter flights adult $245/345)
Offers both fixed-wing and helicopter
scenic flights – both are a wonderful way
to get a sense of the sheer scale and
beauty of Kakadu and Arnhem Land.

Ayal Aboriginal Tours (📞0429 470
384; www.ayalkakadu.com.au; adult/child
$220/99) Full-day Indigenous-run tours
around Kakadu with former ranger and
local Victor Cooper, shining a light on
art, culture and wildlife.

Litchfield National Park

It's not as famous as Kakadu, but **Litchfield** (☑08-8976 0282; www.nt.gov.au/leisure/parks-reserves) is one of the best places in the NT for walking, camping and swimming. Just 115km south of Darwin, it makes a brilliant day trip or tour: try Ethical Adventures (p260).

The 1500-sq-km national park encloses much of the Tabletop Range, a wide sandstone plateau with waterfalls pouring off the edge, feeding crystal-clear, croc-free plunge pools.

Entering the park from Batchelor, the tombstones you see after 17km are, in fact, magnetic termite mounds.

Another 6km in is the turn-off to **Buley Rockhole** (2km), with a series of rock pools. This turn-off also takes you to **Florence Falls** (5km), accessed by a 15-minute, 135-step descent to a deep pool surrounded by forest. About 18km beyond the turn-off is another turn-off to spectacular **Tolmer Falls**. A 1.6km loop track affords beaut views.

It's a further 7km along the main road to the turn-off for Litchfield's big-ticket **Wangi Falls** ('wong-guy'; 1.6km). The falls flow year-round, filling an enormous swimming hole bordered by rainforest. Bring your goggles!

TOURISM NT/SHAANA MCNAUGHT ©

Parap Fine Foods
Market $

(☑08-8981 8597; www.parapfinefoods.com; 40 Parap Rd, Parap; ⊙8am-6.30pm Mon-Fri, 8am-6pm Sat, 9am-1pm Sun) A gourmet food hall in Parap shopping centre, stocking organic and health foods, deli items and fine wine – perfect for a picnic.

PM Eat & Drink
Australian, International $$

(☑08-8941 3925; www.pmeatdrink.com; cnr Knuckey St & Austin Lane; lunch mains from $16, dinner mains $16-24; ⊙noon-late Tue-Sat) This place buzzes with atmosphere, not to mention great food and excellent service – this is the pick for a casual city-centre meal if your time in town is limited. The tempura fish burger is outstanding, but the beef brisket soft tacos and Angus sirloin with cauliflower puree also have their fans.

Saffron Restaurant
Indian $$

(☑08-8981 2383; https://saffrron.com; 14/34 Parap Rd; mains lunch $20-41, dinner $17-28; ⊙5.30-9pm Tue, Wed, Sat & Sun, 11am-2pm & 5.30-9pm Thu & Fri) ✿ At the forefront of Parap's burgeoning culinary scene and one of Darwin's best Indian restaurants, multi-award-winning Saffrron puts sustainability and local ingredients front and centre. The cooking is assured and the service attentive and knowledgeable. You could take your pick of the menu and leave happy, but the Barramundi masala and Kerala mussel curry are highly recommended.

Darwin Ski Club
Australian $$

(☑08-8981 6630; www.darwinskiclub.com.au; Conacher St, Fannie Bay; mains $22-32; ⊙noon-10pm) This place just keeps getting better. Already Darwin's finest location for a sunset beer, it now does seriously good tucker too. The dishes are well prepared, and the menu is thoughtful and enticing. The red curry is particularly tasty. Highly recommended by locals.

Pee Wee's at the Point
Australian $$$

(☑08-8981 6868; www.peewees.com.au; Alec Fong Lim Dr, East Point Reserve; mains $41-55; ⊙from 6.30pm) Arguably Darwin's premier kitchen, this is indeed a place for a treat. Enjoy your double-roasted duckling or the wild-caught barramundi with macadamia, herb and lemon myrtle among tropical palms at **East Point Reserve** (🕙mangrove boardwalk 8am-6pm), right on the waterfront.

Crustaceans   Seafood $$$

(📞08-8981 8658; www.crustaceans.net.au; Stokes Hill Wharf; mains $19-45; 🕙5.30-11pm, last order 8.30pm) This casual, licensed restaurant features fresh fish, Moreton Bay bugs, lobster, oysters and even crocodile, as well as succulent steaks. It's all about the location, perched right at the end of Stokes Hill Wharf with sunset views over Frances Bay. The cold beer and a first-rate wine list seal the deal.

🍺 DRINKING & NIGHTLIFE

Darwin Ski Club   Pub

(📞08-8981 6630; www.darwinskiclub.com.au; Conacher St, Fannie Bay; 🕙noon-late) Leave Mitchell St behind and head for a sublime sunset at this laid-back waterski club on **Vesteys Beach**. The view through the palm trees from the beer garden is a winner, and there are often live bands. Hands down the best venue for a sunset beer in Darwin.

Darwin Sailing Club   Sports Bar

(📞08-8941 0580; www.dwnsail.com.au; Atkins Dr, Fannie Bay; 🕙noon-late Mon-Fri, 10.30am-late Sat & Sun) More upmarket than the ski club, the sailing club is always filled with yachties enjoying a sunset beer overlooking the Timor Sea. Tunes on the sound system are surprisingly un-yacht club-like (no Christopher Cross or Rod Stewart). Sign in as a visitor at the door (bring some ID).

One Mile Brewing Company   Brewery

(📞0429 782 870; www.onemilebrewery.com.au; 8/111 Coonawarra Rd, Winnellie; 🕙5-8pm Thu & Fri, noon-7.30pm Sat) A good place to start your Darwin night out, this brewery's tasting bar showcases some of the Top End's tastiest beers. We like the 4:21, a beer cheekily named after the time Darwin's civil servants famously finish work, but the Pink Lady Cider, too, has its devotees. Ask about a brewery tour if you're a beer aficionado.

🍴 Mindil Beach Market

Food is the main attraction at this **market** (www.mindil.com.au; off Gilruth Ave; 🕙4-9pm Thu & Sun May-Oct; 🚌4, 6)— from Thai, Sri Lankan, Indian, Chinese and Malaysian to Brazilian, Greek, Portuguese and more. Don't miss a flaming satay stick from Bobby's brazier. Top it off with fresh fruit salad, decadent cakes or luscious crepes.

But that's only half the fun! Arts and crafts stalls bulge with handmade jewellery, fabulous rainbow tie-dyed clothes, Aboriginal artefacts, and wares from Indonesia and Thailand.

Mindil Beach is about 2km from Darwin's city centre; an easy walk or hop on buses 4 or 6 that go past the market area.

⭐ ENTERTAINMENT

Deckchair Cinema   Cinema

(📞08-8981 0700; www.deckchaircinema. com; Jervois Rd, Waterfront Precinct; adult/ child $16/8; 🕙box office from 6.30pm Apr-Nov) During the Dry, the Darwin Film Society runs this fabulous outdoor cinema below the southern end of the Esplanade. Watch a movie under the stars while reclining in a deckchair. There's a licensed bar serving food or you can bring a picnic (no BYO alcohol). There are usually double features on Friday and Saturday nights (adult/child $26/13).

Where to Stay

You can stay in Kakadu itself – there are resorts, safari-tent lodges and lots of fab camping sites. If you're booked on a tour, your accommodation will probably be included at one of these operators.

Back in Darwin, most accommodation is right in the city centre, close to all the restaurants and nightlife, or in quieter Larrakeyah just to the north of the CBD. Cullen Bay is another option, with lots of apartments and some good waterside eateries, though it's not really walking distance to any of the action.

Darwin
MARCO TALIANI DE MARCHIO/SHUTTERSTOCK ©

Happy Yess Live Music
(www.happyyess.tumblr.com; Brown's Mart, 12 Smith St; ⊘6pm-midnight Thu-Sat) This venue is Darwin's leading place for live music. A not-for-profit venue for musicians run by musicians, you won't hear cover bands in here. Original, sometimes weird and always fun.

ℹ INFORMATION

Royal Darwin Hospital (✐08-8920 6011; www. health.nt.gov.au; 105 Rocklands Dr, Tiwi; ⊘24hr)

Tourism Top End (✐08-8980 6000, 1300 138 886; www.tourismtopend.com.au; cnr Smith & Bennett Sts; ⊘8.30am-5pm Mon-Fri, 9am-3pm Sat & Sun) Helpful office with hundreds of brochures; books tours and accommodation for Darwin and beyond.

ℹ GETTING THERE & AWAY

AIR

Darwin International Airport (✐08-8920 1811; www.darwinairport.com.au; Henry Wrigley Dr, Marrara) is 12km north of the city centre, and handles both international and domestic flights. The following airlines operate from the airport and fly to all other capital cities: **Jetstar** (www. jetstar.com; Darwin Airport), **Qantas** (www.qan tas.com.au; Darwin Airport) and **Virgin Australia** (www.virginaustralia.com; Darwin Airport).

BUS

Greyhound (✐1300 473 946; www.greyhound. com.au) runs at least one service per day up and down the Stuart Hwy, the only road in and out of Darwin. Buses depart from the rear of the **Transit Centre** (www.enjoy-darwin.com; 69 Mitchell St).

For Kakadu, there's a daily return service from Darwin to Jabiru ($79, 3¾ hours).

CAR & CAMPERVAN

Most car-rental companies offer only 100km free, which won't get you far (you pay per kilometre beyond 100km). Rates start at around $40 per day for a small car with 100km per day. All the usual car-hire suspects operate here, or **JJ's Car Hire** (✐0427 214 229; www.jjscarhire. com.au; 7-9 Goyder Rd, Parap) is a good local operator.

There are also plenty of 4WD vehicles available in Darwin, but you have to book ahead and fees/deposits are higher than for 2WD vehicles.

TRAIN

The legendary **Ghan** (✐08-8213 4401; www. greatsouthernrail.com.au; Berrimah Rd, East Arm, Darwin Train Station) train, operated by Great Southern Rail, runs weekly (twice weekly May to July) between Adelaide and Darwin via Alice Springs. The Darwin terminus is on Berrimah Rd, 15km/20 minutes from the city centre. A taxi fare into the centre is about $40, though there is a shuttle service to/from the Transit Centre.

Wave Lagoon (p259)

ℹ️ GETTING AROUND

TO/FROM THE AIRPORT

Darwin City Airport Shuttle Service (📞08-8947 3979; www.darwincityairportshuttleservice.com.au; per person $18) is one of a number of private airport shuttle companies that will pick up or drop off almost anywhere in the centre. When leaving Darwin book a day before departure. A taxi fare into the centre is $40 to $45.

PUBLIC TRANSPORT

Darwinbus (📞08-8944 2444; www.nt.gov.au/driving/public-transport-cycling) runs a comprehensive bus network that departs from the **Darwin Bus Terminus** (Harry Chan Ave), opposite Brown's Mart. For timetables,

check out the website at the **Department of Transport** (📞08-8924 7666; https://nt.gov.au/driving/public-transport-cycling/public-bus-timetables-maps-darwin).

A $3 adult ticket gives unlimited travel on the bus network for three hours (validate your ticket when you first get on). Daily ($7) and weekly ($20) travel cards are also available from bus interchanges, newsagents and the visitor centre.

TAXI

Taxis wait along Knuckey St, diagonally opposite the north end of Smith St Mall, and are usually easy to flag down. Call **Darwin Radio Taxis** (📞13 10 08; www.131008.com).

PERTH &
MARGARET RIVER

Perth & Margaret River at a Glance...

In Wadjuk country, way out west in the Indian Ocean breeze, Perth regularly attracts that most easy-going of adjectives – 'liveable'. Under a near-permanent canopy of blue sky, life here unfolds at a pleasing pace. Throw in superb beaches, global eats and booming small-bar and street-art scenes, and Perth seems downright hip.

Not far away to the south is the Margaret River wine region, with vineyard restaurants, artisan food producers, and some of Australia's most spectacular surf beaches and rugged coastline. It's a fabulous place to spend a few days.

Perth in Two Days

A day in Perth, a day in Fremantle: nice! Have breakfast in Mt Lawley or the CBD, then check out the **Art Gallery of Western Australia** (p274). Grab lunch in hip Leederville, explore view-friendly **Kings Park** (p271) then go drinking in Northbridge. Next day in Freo, visit **Fremantle Markets** (p274) then go Gothic at **Fremantle Prison** (p275). A beer and dinner at waterside **Little Creatures** (p278) is the ideal Freo sign-off.

Perth & Margaret River in Four Days

Make for Margaret River and spend a couple of days sampling the region's wines, craft beers and artisanal produce. Take tour that combines all three with **Wine for Dudes** (p272), learn cooking techniques at **Wildwood Valley Cooking School** (p272), then lose any added kilos by learning to surf at **Yallingup Surf School** (p273) or stretching your legs with **Cape to Cape Tours** (p273).

Previous page: Cottesloe Beach (p274), Perth

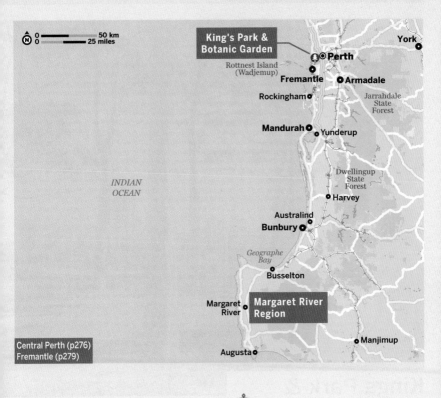

Central Perth (p276)
Fremantle (p279)

Arriving in Perth

Perth Airport (p280) is about 10km east of the city, with flights winging in from overseas and other Australian capitals. A cab will cost around $45 into the centre. Connect runs shuttles to/from city accommodation. Fremantle is 30 minutes from Perth by train or bus, or an easy drive.

Sleeping

Perth CBD (hotels, apartments) and Northbridge (backpackers, boutique hotels) are close to public transport. If you're a beach fan, consider staying at Cottesloe or Scarborough. Alternatively, head to Fremantle for a good mix of sleeping options: pubs, boutique hotels, B&Bs and hostels. In Margaret River, rural B&Bs and excellent boutique accommodation are the standouts.

Kings Park & Botanic Garden

Rising above the Swan River on Perth's western flanks, the 400-hectare, bush-filled Kings Park is the city's pride and joy.

Great For...

☑ **Don't Miss**

The epic glass-and-steel bridge on the Lotterywest Federation Walkway.

Parklife

Kings Park is a top spot for a picnic or to let the kids off the leash. Its numerous tracks are popular with walkers and joggers, with an ascent of the steep stairs from the river rewarded with fab city views.

At the park's heart is the 17-hectare **Botanic Garden**, containing over 2000 plant species indigenous to WA. In spring there's an impressive display of WA's famed wildflowers.

Another highlight is the Federation Walkway, a 620m path including a 222m-long glass-and-steel bridge that passes through the canopy of a stand of eucalypts.

Leading into the park, Fraser Ave is lined with towering lemon-scented gums that are dramatically lit at night. At its culmination are the State War Memorial, a

❶ Need to Know

☑08-9480 3600; www.bgpa.wa.gov.au;
🕒free guided walks 10am, noon & 2pm; `FREE`

✕ Take a Break

Fraser's (p271) plates up mod-
American food in a beaut location
at the top of Kings Park.

★ Top Tip

The hop-on, hop-off **City Sightseeing
Perth Tour** (☑08-9370 1000; www.
perthexplorer.com.au; 24hr ticket adult/
child/family $40/12/95) bus rolls
through the park, too...so hop off!

cafe, a gift shop, **Fraser's** (☑08-9481 7100;
www.frasersrestaurant.com.au; Fraser Ave, Kings
Park; mains $32-45; 🕒noon-late Mon-Fri, from
11.30am Sat & Sun) restaurant and the Kings
Park Visitor Centre. Free guided walks
leave from here.

Indigenous Heritage

The Noongar people knew the Kings Park
area as Kaarta Gar-up and used it for thousands of years for hunting, food gathering,
ceremonies, teaching and tool-making. A
freshwater spring at the base of the escarpment, now known as Kennedy Fountain but
before that as Goonininup, was a home of
the Wargal, mystical snake-like creatures
that created the Swan River and other
waterways.

For today's Aboriginal perspective on
Kings Park, sign up for an Indigenous Heritage Tour – a 90-minute Indigenous-themed
stroll around the park. Bookings essential.

Kings Park Festival

Held annually throughout September to
coincide with the park's rampant wildflower
blooms, the super-popular **Kings Park Festival** (www.kingsparkfestival.com.au) involves
floral displays, workshops, exhibitions,
artworks and installations, guided walks,
family distractions and live music every
Sunday. Running since 1964, the festival
these days is a polished act.

Getting Here

Take bus 935 from St Georges Tce to near
the visitor centre. You can also walk up
(steep) Mount St from the city or climb
Jacob's Ladder from Mounts Bay Rd.

Margaret River Region

The Margaret River region combines many of modern Australia's most enduring attractions, from quality food and wine, to surfing and enjoying a beautiful coast.

Great For...

☑ **Don't Miss**

A winery tour of the Margaret River vineyards.

Wine for Dudes   Wine

(☑0427 774 994; www.winefordudes.com; per person $105) Includes a brewery, a chocolate factory, four wineries, a wine-blending experience and lunch.

Wildwood Valley Cooking School   Cooking

(☑08-9755 2120; www.wildwoodvalley.com. au; 1481 Wildwood Rd; classes per person $140; ⊙Dec-Mar) Set amid the shaded grounds of the **Wildwood Valley Cottages** (cottages from $250; 🛈), the cooking school offers hands-on classes in Thai or Italian cuisine. Sioban's CV includes cooking at Longrain and living in Tuscany. Cooking classes include Wood Fired cooking and Taste of Tuscany and are wildly popular with Perth visitors, so check the schedule online and book early. Most classes occur on a Wednesday, Friday or Saturday, but this does vary.

Cape to Cape coastal walk

PAUL KINGSLEY/ALAMY ©

route or just parts of the stunning Cape to Cape coastal walk (p283) on self-guided and guided itineraries. Trips include camping or lodge accommodation and excellent meals, and options from three to eight days are available. Various day tours exploring the Margaret River region are also offered.

Margaret River Distilling Company — Distillery

(📞08-9757 9351; www.distillery.com.au; Maxwell St, off Carters Rd; ⏰10am-6pm, to 7pm Fri & Sat; 🚻) Limeburners single malt whisky, Tiger Snake sour mash, Great Southern gin and White Shark vodka can all be sampled at this edge-of-the-forest tasting room. There are also local beers to go with pizzas and shared platters.

Yallingup Surf School — Surfing

(📞08-9755 2755; www.yallingupsurfschool.com) Grab a 1½-hour group lesson for beginners or private coaching sessions. Also offers six-day surf and yoga safaris for women at www.escapesafaris.com.au.

Naturaliste Charters — Whale Watching

(📞08-9750 5500; www.whales-australia.com.au; from $90; ⏰mid-May–Aug) ✔ This operator runs two-hour whale-watching cruises departing Augusta from mid-May to August. During May, the emphasis switches to an Eco Wilderness Tour showcasing beaches and wildlife, including dolphins, seals and lots of seabirds.

Cape Mentelle — Winery

(www.capementelle.com.au; 331 Walcliffe Rd; tours from $30; ⏰10am-5pm; 🚻) A cellar door, wine tours and tastings (with optional and food pairings), pétanque, and an outdoor cinema in summer. This Margaret River winery is one of the originals from 1970.

Cowaramup Brewing Company — Brewery

(📞08-9755 5822; www.cowaramupbrewing.com.au; North Treeton Rd, Cowaramup; ⏰11am-6pm) Microbrewery with an award-winning Pilsner and a moreish English-style Special Pale Ale. Four other beers and occasional seasonal brews also feature. It's 15 minutes back up Busselton Hwy past Cowaramup.

Cape to Cape Tours — Walking

(📞0459 452 038; www.capetocapetours.com.au; per couple from $1300) Negotiate the entire

Perth & Fremantle

◎ SIGHTS

Art Gallery of
Western Australia   Gallery

(☎08-9492 6622; www.artgallery.wa.gov.au; Perth Cultural Centre; ⊙10am-5pm Wed-Mon) **FREE**
Founded in 1895, this excellent gallery houses the state's pre-eminent art collection as well as regular international exhibitions that, increasingly, have a modern, approachable bent. The permanent collection is arranged into wings, from contemporary to modern, historic to local and Indigenous. Big-name Australian artists such as Arthur Boyd, Russell Drysdale and Sidney Nolan are there, as are diverse media including canvasses, bark paintings and sculpture. Check the website for info on free tours running most days at 11am and 1pm.

Cottesloe Beach   Beach

(Marine Pde; 🚹) The safest swimming beach, Cottesloe has cafes, pubs, pine trees and fantastic sunsets. From Cottesloe train station (on the Fremantle line) it's 1km to the beach; there's a free shuttle that runs between the stop and the sand during the annual Sculpture by the Sea exhibition, each March. Bus 102 ($4.80) from Elizabeth Quay Busport goes straight to the beach.

Aquarium of
Western Australia   Aquarium

(AQWA; ☎08-9447 7500; www.aqwa.com.au; Hillarys Boat Harbour, 91 Southside Dr; adult/child $30/18; ⊙10am-5pm) Dividing WA's vast coastline into five distinct zones (Far North, Coral Coast, Shipwreck Coast, Perth and Great Southern), AQWA features a 98m underwater tunnel showcasing stingrays, turtles, fish and sharks. (The daring can snorkel or dive with the sharks with the aquarium's in-house divemaster.) By public transport, take the Joondalup train to Warwick Station and then transfer to bus 423. By car, take the Mitchell Fwy north and exit at Hepburn Ave.

Fremantle Markets   Market

(www.fremantlemarkets.com.au; cnr South Tce & Henderson St; ⊙8am-8pm Fri, to 6pm Sat &

Fremantle Markets

BEEBOYS/SHUTTERSTOCK ©

Sun) **FREE** Originally opened in 1897, these colourful markets were rebooted in 1975 and today draw slow-moving crowds combing over souvenirs. A few younger designers and artists have introduced a more vibrant edge. The fresh-produce section is a good place to stock up on supplies and there's an excellent food court featuring lots of global street eats.

Fremantle Prison Historic Building
(☑08-9336 9200; www.fremantleprison.com.au; 1 The Terrace; day tour adult/child $22/12, combined day tour $32/22, Torchlight Tour $28/18, Tunnels Tour $65/45; ⊘9am-5pm) With its forebidding 5m-high walls, the old convict-era prison dominates Fremantle. Various daytime tours explore the jail's maximum security past, give insights into criminal minds and allow you into solitary-confinement cells. Book ahead for the Torchlight Tour through the prison, with a few scares and surprises, and the 2½-hour Tunnels Tour (minimum age 12 years), venturing into subterranean tunnels and doing an underground boat ride.

🟢 ACTIVITIES

Spinway WA Cycling
(☑0413 343 305; www.spinwaywa.bike; per 1/4/24hr from $11/22/33) Spinway WA has 14 self-serve bicycle-hire kiosks in handy spots around central Perth, Kings Park, South Perth, Scarborough and Fremantle. Swipe your credit card and follow the prompts. Helmets and locks are included, available from partner businesses (often hotel reception desks) where bikes are parked outside.

🟢 TOURS

Djurandi Dreaming Cultural
(☑0458 692 455; www.djurandi.com.au; tours adult/child $45/35) 🏃 Indigenous walking tours around the booming Elizabeth Quay precinct in central Perth: 45 minutes of Nyungar cultural immersion, focusing on stories of the Dreaming, art, native flora

🏝️ Rottnest Island

'Rotto' has long been the family-holiday playground of choice for Perth locals. Although it's only about 19km offshore from Fremantle, this car-free, off-the-grid slice of paradise, ringed by secluded beaches and bays, feels a million miles away. A day trip spent cycling around the 11km-long, 4.5km-wide island is a real pleasure: you're bound to spot quokkas, the island's famed native mammals.

Rottnest Express (☑1300 467 688; www.rottnestexpress.com.au; return ex-Fremantle adult/child from $64/30, ex-Perth from $103/49) runs ferries from Perth's Barrack Street Jetty (p281), which take 1¾ hours (once daily) and **Fremantle** (☑1300 467 688; www.rottnestexpress.com.au), which take 30 minutes (five times daily).

Bikes can be booked through **Rottnest Island Bike Hire** (☑08-9292 5105; www.rottnestisland.com/see-and-do; cnr Bedford Way & Welch Rd; bikes per half-/full day from $16/30; ⊘8am-6pm). The ferry companies and island visitor centre also hire bikes.

Cyclists on Rottnest Island
SAPHOTOGS/SHUTTERSTOCK ©

and fauna, traditional diet, seasons and family structures.

Oh Hey WA Walking
(☑0408 995 965; www.ohheywa.com.au; 45 St Georges Tce; tours from $35) Highly rated central Perth walking tours, zeroing in on the city's booming street-art scene,

Central Perth

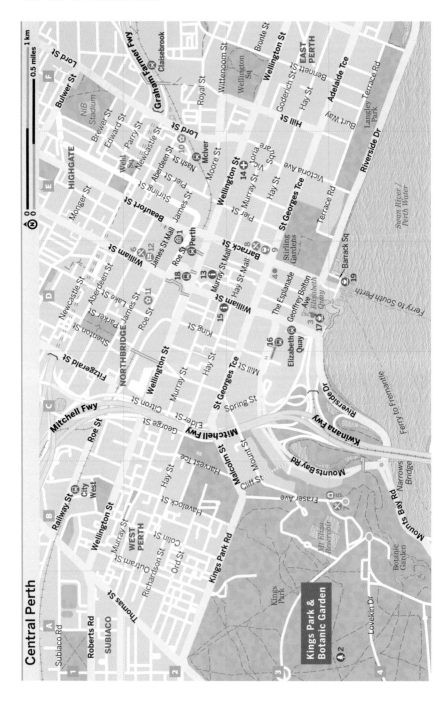

Kings Park & Botanic Garden

Central Perth

hip small bars, throbbing nightlife zones and architectural heritage. Self-guided audio tours and two-hour bike tours also available.

Little Ferry Co   Boating
(☑0488 777 088; www.littleferryco.com.au; Elizabeth Quay; 1/2/3 stops adult $12/18/22, child $10/16/20, day pass adult/child $32/28; ⊙10am-5.30pm) ⚑ This heritage-style electric ferry travels between the Elizabeth Quay terminal and the cafes and restaurants of Claisebrook Cove – an excellent Swan River snapshot. Either take a return trip, or bus it back to the city on the free CAT bus. Also connects to **Optus Stadium** (Perth Stadium; www.optusstadium.com.au; Victoria Park Dr, Burswood) on big-game days.

🔒 SHOPPING

Aboriginal Art & Craft Gallery   Art
(☑08-9481 7082; www.aboriginalgallery.com.au; Fraser Ave, Kings Park; ⊙10.30am-4.30pm Mon-Fri, 11am-4pm Sat & Sun) Work from around WA; more populist than high end or collectible. The gallery is slightly hidden below the Kaarta Gar-up lookout.

Common Ground Collective   Design
(☑0418 158 778; www.facebook.com/cmmngrnd; 82 High St, Fremantle; ⊙10am-5pm Mon-Sat, from 11am Sun) An eclectic showcase of jewellery, apparel and design, much of it limited-edition and mainly from local Fremantle artisans and designers. The coffee at the in-house cafe is pretty damn good too.

✖ EATING

Pinchos   Tapas $
(☑08-9228 3008; www.pinchos.me; 112-124 Oxford St, Leederville; small plates $11-18, larger plates $25-27; ⊙8am-10pm Sun-Tue, to 10.30pm Wed-Thu, to 11pm Fri & Sat) Iberian-inspired good times constantly rock this corner location amid Leederville's many cafes, casual restaurants and bars. The must-have tapas are the pork-belly chicharrons and the Pedro Ximénez and blue-cheese mushrooms – they've never left the menu. Those and the beef cheeks are perfect drinking fodder with the attractively priced Spanish beer, wine, sherry and on-tap sangria.

Bread in Common   Bistro, Bakery $$
(☑08-9336 1032; www.breadincommon.com.au; 43 Pakenham St, Fremantle; shared platters $15-19, mains $23-33; ⊙11.30am-10pm Mon-Fri,

8am-late Sat & Sun; ❄) ✦ Be lured by the comforting aroma of the in-house bakery before staying on for cheese and charcuterie platters, or larger dishes such as lamb ribs, octopus or pork belly. The focus is equally on comfort food and culinary flair, while big shared tables and a chic warehouse ambience encourage conversation over WA wines and Aussie craft beers and ciders.

Manuka Woodfire Kitchen
Barbecue, Pizza $$

(✆08-9335 3527; www.manukawoodfire.com.au; 134 High St, Fremantle; shared plates $7-38, pizzas $19-22; ⊙5-9pm Tue-Fri, noon-3pm & 5-9pm Sat & Sun) ✦ Relying almost exclusively on a wood-fired oven, the kitchen at Manuka is tiny, but it's still big enough to turn out some of the tastiest food in town. The passionate chef has become an expert at taming the flame; his seasonal menu could include whole roasted fish, coal-grilled eggplant or peppers and basil pesto. The pizzas are also excellent.

Wildflower
Modern Australian $$$

(✆08-6168 7855; www.wildflowerperth.com. au; State Bldgs, 1 Cathedral Ave; mains $42-49, 5-course tasting menu without/with wine $145/240; ⊙noon-2.30pm & 6pm-late Tue-Fri, 6pm-late Sat) Filling a glass pavilion atop the restored State Buildings, Wildflower offers fine-dining menus inspired by the six seasons of the Indigenous Noongar people of WA. There's a passionate focus on Western Australian produce: dishes often include Shark Bay scallops or kangaroo smoked over jarrah embers, as well as indigenous herbs and bush plants like lemon myrtle and wattle seed.

🍷 DRINKING & NIGHTLIFE

Little Creatures
Brewery

(✆08-6215 1000; www.littlecreatures.com.au; Fishing Boat Harbour, 40 Mews Rd, Fremantle; ⊙10am-late Mon-Fri, from 9am Sat, to 11pm Sun; 🍴) Try everything on tap – particularly the Pale Ale and Rogers. The floor's chaotic and fun, and the wood-fired pizzas ($20

to $24) are worth the wait. Shared plates ($8 to $27) include kangaroo with tomato chutney and marinated octopus. There's a sandpit out the back for kids and free bikes for all, plus regular brewery tours ($20). No bookings.

Petition Beer Corner
Craft Beer

(✆08-6168 7773; www.petitionperth.com/beer; State Bldgs, cnr St Georges Tce & Barrack St; ⊙11.30am-late Mon-Sat, from noon Sun; 🛜) Distressed walls provide the backdrop for craft brews at this spacious bar. There's a rotating selection of 18 independent beers on tap – check out Now Tapped on the website – and it's a great place to explore the more experimental side of the Australian craft-beer scene. Servings begin at just 150mL, so the curious beer fan will be in heaven.

Mechanics Institute
Bar

(✆08-9228 4189; www.mechanicsinstitute bar.com.au; 222 William St , Northbridge; ⊙noon-midnight Mon-Sat, to 10pm Sun) Negotiate the laneway entrance via the James St cul-de-sac – behind **Alex Hotel** (✆08-6430 4000; www.alexhotel.com.au; 50 James St; d from $209; ❄🛜) – to discover one of Perth's most easy-going rooftop bars. Share one of the big, pine tables on the deck or nab a bar stool. Brilliant cocktails are readily shaken, craft beers are on tap, and you can even order in a gourmet burger from sister venue, **Flipside** (✆08-9228 8822; www.flipsideburgerbar.com.au; 222 William St; burgers $8-15; ⊙11.30am-9.30pm Mon-Wed, to late Thu-Sat, noon-9pm Sun), downstairs.

Norfolk Hotel
Pub

(✆08-9335 5405; www.norfolkhotel.com.au; 47 South Tce , Fremantle; share plates $9-24, mains $19-40; ⊙11am-midnight Mon-Sat, to 10pm Sun) Slow down to Freo pace at this 1887 pub. Interesting guest beers wreak havoc for the indecisive drinker, and the food and pizzas are very good. The heritage limestone courtyard is a treat, especially when sunlight dapples through elms and eucalypts. Downstairs, the **Odd Fellow** channels a bohemian small-bar vibe and has live music Wednesday to Saturday from 7pm.

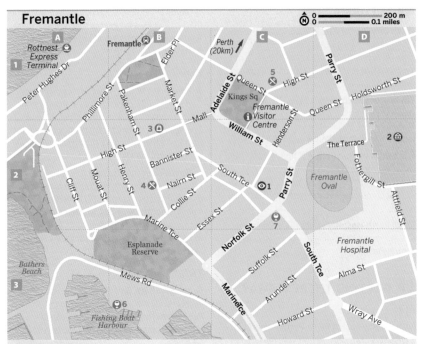

Fremantle

⊙ Sights
1 Fremantle Markets.....................................C2
2 Fremantle Prison.......................................D2

🛍 Shopping
3 Common Ground Collective.....................B2

🍽 Eating
4 Bread in Common B2
5 Manuka Woodfire Kitchen.........................C1

🍸 Drinking & Nightlife
6 Little Creatures..B3
7 Norfolk Hotel...C2

⭐ ENTERTAINMENT

Badlands Bar
Live Music

(📞0498 239 273; www.badlands.bar; 3 Aberdeen St; ⏱6pm-2am Fri & Sat) Located on the fringes of Northbridge, Badlands has shrugged off its previous incarnation as a retro 1950s-inspired nightclub to be reborn as an edgy rock venue. The best WA bands are regulars, and if an up-and-coming international band is touring, Badlands is the place to see them before they become really famous. Check online for listings.

Rooftop Movies
Cinema

(📞08-9227 6288; www.rooftopmovies.com.au; 68 Roe St , Northbridge; online/door $16/17; ⏱Tue-Sun late Oct-late Mar) Art-house, classic movies and new releases screen under the stars on the 6th floor of a Northbridge car park. Beanbags, wood-fired pizza and craft beer all combine for a great night out. Booking ahead online is recommended and don't be surprised if you're distracted from the on-screen action by the city views. Score $14 tickets on cheap Tuesdays.

ⓘ INFORMATION

Perth City Visitor Kiosk (www.visitperth.com.
au; Forrest Pl, Murray St Mall; ⊘9.30am-4.30pm
Mon-Thu & Sat, to 8pm Fri, 11am-3.30pm Sun)
Volunteers here answer questions and run
walking tours.

WA Visitor Centre (⊘08-9483 1111; www.
wavisitorcentre.com.au; 55 William St; ⊘9am-
5pm Mon-Fri, 9.30am-4pm Sat & Sun) Excellent
resource for information across WA.

Fremantle Visitor Centre (⊘08-9431 7878;
www.visitfremantle.com.au; Town Hall, Kings
Sq; ⊘9am-5pm Mon-Fri, to 4pm Sat, from 10am
Sun) Accommodation and tour bookings; bike
rental.

Royal Perth Hospital (⊘08-9224 2244; www.
rph.wa.gov.au; 197 Wellington St; ⊘24hr) In
central Perth.

ⓘ GETTING THERE & AWAY

AIR

Around 10km east of Perth, **Perth Airport** (⊘08-
9478 8888; www.perthairport.com.au; Airport Dr)
is served by numerous airlines, including **Qantas**
(QF; ⊘13 13 13; www.qantas.com.au), with daily
flights to and from international and Australian
destinations.

BUS

Transwa (⊘13 62 13; www.transwa.wa.gov.au;
East Perth Station, West Pde, East Perth; ⊘office
8.30am-5pm Mon-Fri, to 4.30pm Sat, 10am-4pm
Sun) operates services from the bus terminal at
East Perth train station to/from many destina-
tions around the state.

   South West Coach Lines (⊘08-9753 7700;
www.southwestcoachlines.com.au) focuses on
the southwestern corner of WA, running services
from **Elizabeth Quay Bus Station** (⊘13 62 13;
www.transperth.wa.gov.au; Mounts Bay Rd) to
most towns in the region. Destinations include
Margaret River ($77, 4½ hours).

TRAIN

Great Southern Rail (⊘1800 703 357; www.
greatsouthernrail.com.au) runs the *Indian
Pacific* train between Perth and Sydney – a
four-day, three-night, 4352km cross-continen-
tal epic.

Cape Naturaliste

ℹ GETTING AROUND

TO/FROM THE AIRPORT

Taxi fares to the city from the airport are around $45 from all terminals.

Just Transfers (📞0400 366 893; www.just-transfers.com.au) runs prebooked shuttle-buses between Perth Airport and the city/Fremantle (one way per person $25/60, cheaper for multiple travellers).

PUBLIC TRANSPORT

Transperth (📞13 62 13; www.transperth.wa.gov.au) operates Perth's excellent network of public buses, trains and ferries.

BUS

Perth's central **Free Transit Zone** (FTZ) is served by regular buses and is well covered during the day by the four free **Central Area Transit** (CAT) services.

The broader metropolitan area is serviced by a wide network of Transperth buses.

FERRY

A ferry runs every 20 to 30 minutes between **Elizabeth Quay Jetty** (📞13 62 13; www.transperth.wa.gov.au; off William St) and Mends St Jetty in South Perth – a great way to get to get a from-the-river glimpse of the Perth skyline.

The highly professional Rottnest Express (p275) runs ferries to Rottnest Island from both **Elizabeth Quay** (pier 2, Barrack St Jetty) and Fremantle, which stops at **Victoria Quay** (B Shed; ⊗6.45am-5.15pm) and **Rous Head** (1 Emma Pl, Northport; ⊗7.30am-5pm).

TRAIN

Transperth operates five train lines from around 5.20am to midnight weekdays and to about 2am Saturday and Sunday.

TAXI

The two main companies are **Swan Taxis** (📞13 13 30; www.swantaxis.com.au) and **Black & White Cabs** (📞08-9230 0440; www.blackandwhitecabs.com.au); both have wheelchair-accessible cabs. **Uber** also operates throughout Perth.

Margaret River

◎ SIGHTS

The main towns in the Margaret River region are Margaret River, Yallingup, Augusta and Dunsborough.

Leeuwin-Naturaliste National Park   National Park

(Caves Rd) Despite the vast areas of aridity it contains, Western Australia also boasts a startling variety of endemic wildflowers. The Leeuwin-Naturaliste National Park explodes with colour in the spring months. The leached, sandy soils of WA produce a surprising variety of vividly coloured wildflowers.

Cape Leeuwin Lighthouse   Lighthouse

(📞08-9780 5911; www.margaretriver.com; tour adult/child $20/14; ⊗8.45am-4.30pm) Wild and windy Cape Leeuwin, where the Indian and Southern Oceans meet, is the most southwesterly point in Australia. It takes its name from a Dutch ship that passed here in 1622. The lighthouse (1896), Western Australia's tallest, offers magnificent views of the coastline. Whale watching opportunities abound in the migration season. There is a good cafe on-site too.

Jewel Cave   Cave

(📞08-9780 5911; www.margaretriver.com; Caves Rd; adult/child $22.50/12; ⊗9.30am-3.30pm) The most spectacular of the region's caves, Jewel Cave has an impressive 5.9m straw stalactite, so far the longest seen in a tourist cave. Fossil remains of a Tasmanian tiger (thylacine), believed to be 3500 years old, were discovered here. It's near the south end of Caves Rd, 8km northwest of Augusta. Access to the cave is by guided tours, which run hourly.

Cape Naturaliste Lighthouse   Lighthouse

(📞08-9780 5911; www.margaretriver.com/members/cape-naturaliste-lighthouse; adult/child $14/7; ⊗9.30am-4pm; 🅿♿) Built in 1903, this lighthouse can only be visited as

Margaret River Region

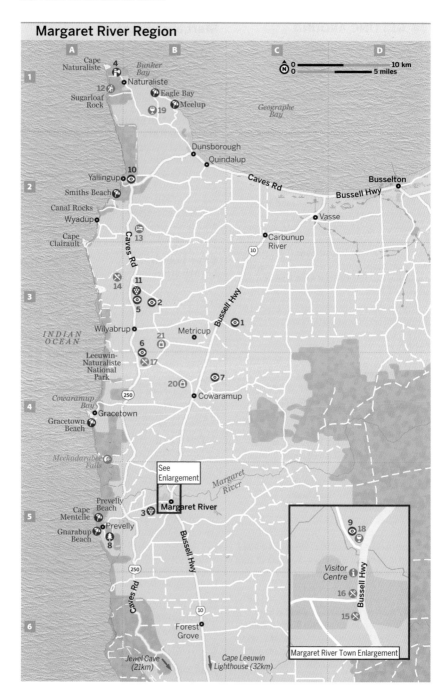

Cape
Naturaliste
4

*Bunker
Bay*

12

Naturaliste

19

Eagle Bay

Meelup

*Geographe
Bay*

Sugarloaf
Rock

Dunsborough

Quindalup

10

Yallingup

Smiths Beach

Canal Rocks

Wyadup

Cape
Clairault

Caves Rd

Caves Rd

Busselton

Bussell Hwy

Vasse

Carbunup
River

13

14

11

5

2

*INDIAN
OCEAN*

Wilyabrup

Metricup

6

21

17

20

7

Cowaramup

*Cowaramup
Bay*

Gracetown

Gracetown
Beach

*Meekadarabee
Falls*

250

See
Enlargement

*Margaret
River*

Prevelly
Beach

Cape
Mentelle

Prevelly

3

Margaret River

Gnarabup
Beach

8

250

Bussell Hwy

Caves Rd

10

Forest
Grove

*Jewel Cave
(21km)*

*Cape Leeuwin
Lighthouse (32km)*

10 km

5 miles

9

18

*Visitor
Centre*

Bussell Hwy

16

15

Margaret River Town Enlargement

Margaret River Region

part of a guided tour, which run half-hourly and help fund the upkeep of the site. The view of two oceans meeting is spectacular. A museum and cafe are also on-site.

Stormflower Vineyard
Winery

(www.stormflower.com.au; 3503 Caves Rd, Wilyabrup; ⊙11am-5pm) Rustic and relaxed, with beautiful Australian natives in the garden, this is the antidote to some of Margaret River's more grandiose tasting rooms and formal wine estates. The compact organic vineyard is just 9 hectares, and Stormflower's cabernet shiraz is highly regarded.

⊕ ACTIVITIES
Cape to Cape Track
Walking

(www.capetocapetrack.com.au) Stretching from Cape Naturaliste to Cape Leeuwin, the 135km Cape to Cape Track passes through the heath, forest and sand dunes of the Leeuwin-Naturaliste National Park (p281), with Indian Ocean views. Most walkers take about seven days to complete the track (staying in a combination of national park campgrounds and commercial accommodation). You can walk it in five days, or break up the route into a series of day trips.

⊕ TOURS
Koomal Dreaming
Tours

(☎0413 843 426; www.koomaldreaming.com.au; adult/child from $78/44) Charismatic Yallingup local and Wardandi man Josh Whiteland runs a range of tours showcasing Indigenous food, culture and music, including walks and exploration of the **Ngilgi Cave** (☎08-9755 2152; www.margaretriver.com; Yallingup Caves Rd; adult/child $22.50/12; ⊙9am-5pm; ℗🚻). Don't leave the region without learning about its Aboriginal cultural story.

Augusta River Tours
Cruise

(www.augustarivertours.com.au; Eliis St Jetty; from $35; ⊙Sep-Jun; 🚻) Spot waterbirds such as black swans, cormorants and pelicans on a 1½-hour cruise up the Blackwood River with the knowledgeable skipper Graeme Challis.

⊙ SHOPPING
Providore
Deli

(☎08-9755 6355; www.providore.com.au; 448 Tom Cullity Dr, Wilyabrup; ⊙9am-5pm) Has been voted one of Australia's Top 100 Gourmet Experiences by *Australian Traveller* magazine – and given its amazing range of artisanal produce, including organic olive oil, tapenades and preserved fruits, we can only agree. Look forward to loads of free samples.

Craft Beer Breweries

Margaret River is not just about wines – craft beers are everywhere, especially in the Caves Road area.

Caves Road Collective (☑08-9755 6500; https://cavesroadcollective.com.au; 3517 Caves Rd, Wilyabrup; tasting paddles from $20; ⊙11am-5pm; P♠) This tastings temple, in a spectacular location on a private lake, has an excellent restaurant. Dune Distilling boasts local botanicals, and on-site Ground to Cloud winery has a small but confident list.

Cheeky Monkey (☑08-9755 5555; www.cheekymonkeybrewery.com.au; 4259 Caves Rd, Wilyabrup; ⊙10am-6pm) Set around a pretty lake, Cheeky Monkey has an expansive restaurant. Try the Hatseller Pilsner with bold New Zealand hops or the Belgian-style Hagenbeck Pale Ale.

Bootleg Brewery (☑08-9755 6300; www.bootlegbrewery.com.au; Puzey Rd, off Yelverton Rd, Wilyabrup; ⊙11am-5pm) More rustic than some of the area's flashier breweries, but lots of fun with a pint in the sun, especially with live bands on Saturday. Try the award-winning WA-classic Raging Bull Porter.

Beer Farm (☑08-9755 7177; www.beerfarm.com.au; 8 Gale Rd, Metricup; ⊙11am-6pm, to 10.30pm Fri, to 7pm Sat; ♠) In a former milking shed down a sleepy side road, this is the area's most rustic brewery. Loyal locals crowd in with their kids and dogs, supping on Beer Farm brews.

Bootleg Brewery
SAPHOTOG/SHUTTERSTOCK ©

Margaret River Regional Wine Centre
Winery

(☑08-9755 5501; www.mrwines.com; 9 Bussell Hwy, Cowaramup; ⊙10am-7pm, noon-6pm Sun) A one-stop shop for buying up a selection of 600 Margaret River wines and craft beers in nearby Cowaramup.

🍴 EATING

Margaret River Farmers Market
Market $

(☑0438 905 985; www.margaretriverfarmersmarket.com.au; Lot 272 Bussell Hwy, Margaret River Education Campus; ⊙8am-noon Sat; ♠) ✿ The region's organic and sustainable artisanal producers come to town every Saturday. It's a top spot for breakfast. Check the website for your own foodie hit list.

Blue Ocean Fish & Chips
Fish & Chips $

(73 Blackwood Ave, Augusta; ⊙11.30am-2pm & 5-8pm; P♠) Oft-rated best fish and chips ever eaten (no overstatements here obviously), this very basic blue-plastic-chairs and simple-wall-menu fast-food joint boasts excellent locally caught fish, perfectly crisp batter and optional chicken salt on your chips. At night there are not many other choices in sleepy Augusta.

Amiria
Winery $$

(☑08-9755 2528; https://arimia.com.au; 242 Quininup Rd, Yallingup; 2-course menu $55) Down an unsealed road you'll find this organic and biodynamic winery and restaurant creating excellent seasonal meals with ingredients almost entirely sourced from the property.

Vasse Felix
Bistro $$$

(☑08-9756 5050; www.vassefelix.com.au; cnr Caves Rd & Tom Cullity Dr, Cowaramup; mains $37-39; ⊙10am-3pm, cellar door to 5pm; P❋) Vasse Felix winery is considered by many to have the best fine-dining restaurant in the region, the big wooden dining room reminiscent of an extremely flash barn. The grounds are peppered with sculptures,

Providore (p283)

while the gallery displaying a revolving exhibition from the Holmes à Court collection is worth a visit. Vegans catered for with 24 hours' notice.

🍷 DRINKING & NIGHTLIFE

Eagle Bay Brewing Co   Brewery
(☑08-9755 3554; www.eaglebaybrewing.com.au; Eagle Bay Rd, Dunsborough; ⊙11am-5pm) A lovely rural outlook; interesting beers and wines served in modern, spacious surroundings; and excellent food, including crisp wood-fired pizzas. Keep an eye out for Eagle Bay's Single Batch Specials.

Brewhouse   Microbrewery
(☑08-9757 2614; www.brewhousemargaretriver.com.au; 35 Bussell Hwy, Margaret River; ⊙11am-7pm, to 9pm Fri-Sun; 👫) A craft-beer place you can walk to! Brewhouse is nestled amid karri forest with a rustic bar and restaurant serving three guest beers and six of its own brews. Try the Inji Pale Ale with the chilli salt

squid, and check out live music on Friday nights and Sunday afternoons.

ℹ️ INFORMATION

Visitor Centre (☑08-9780 5911; www.margaretriver.com; 100 Bussell Hwy, Margaret River; ⊙9am-5pm) Bookings and information plus displays on local wineries.

ℹ️ GETTING THERE & AWAY

Margaret River is easily reached by bus from Perth. To drive from Perth to Margaret River township takes around three hours.

South West Coach Lines (p280) Runs services between Busselton and Augusta, stopping at Cowaramup and Margaret River, and linking with Perth on the weekends.

Transwa (p280) The SW1 service (12 weekly) from Perth to Augusta stops at Yallingup and Margaret River.

Surfer at Bondi Beach (p44)

In Focus

Australian Parliament House (p86)

Australia Today

Australia is at a crossroads and much work remains to be done to reconcile with and recover Aboriginal civilisation. Today Australia projects images of itself that are often in opposition: strong economic growth, but notably laid-back people. Identity politics plays out in the national conversation while Australians attempt to answer a long-standing question: what is Australian culture?

First Peoples

The First Peoples of Australia are still fighting for recognition more than 200 years since the declaration of terra nullius – the legal fiction that stated Australia was devoid of human settlement – which underpinned the justification of the British Empire's colonisation at the time. The 20th century saw colonialist practices continue, such as forcibly removing children from their Aboriginal mothers; eugenics to 'breed out the black', and slavery-like conditions that saw the routine theft of wages and land continue.

The ongoing impact of these policies are still being felt today, with key indicators showing Indigenous peoples have poorer health outcomes, lower life expectancy and some of the highest incarceration rates in the world.

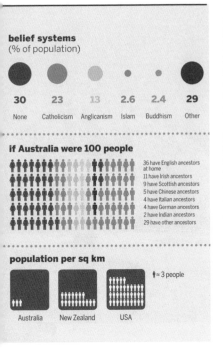

belief systems
(% of population)

30	23	13	2.6	2.4	29
None	Catholicism	Anglicanism	Islam	Buddhism	Other

if Australia were 100 people

36 have English ancestors at home
11 have Irish ancestors
9 have Scottish ancestors
5 have Chinese ancestors
4 have Italian ancestors
4 have German ancestors
2 have Indian ancestors
29 have other ancestors

population per sq km

⋔ ≈ 3 people

Australia   New Zealand   USA

Treaty negotiations are currently under way in many states, with Victoria leading the way. More recently a document, titled the Uluru Statement from the Heart, called for a Voice to be enshrined in the country's Constitution so that Indigenous people would have more say over policies that affect their lives. It also stated that the nation needs to go through a truth-telling process.

With debates growing stronger each year over Australia's 'national day', the legitimacy of the Australian flag and national anthem, and statues celebrating controversial colonial figures, Australia is at a crucial moment where it must confront questions about its past and its future identity.

The Rise of Populism?

There are growing signs that disaffection with mainstream politics is growing globally and Australia is no exception. Independent politicians are an increasingly powerful force in Australian parliaments. One Nation leader Pauline Hanson returned to the fore with proposals like capping immigration from 'Muslim countries' and compulsory DNA tests for Indigenous people to 'prove their ancestry'. Other signs populism has infected the political discourse in Australia include the parliamentary declaration that 'It's okay to be white', and the copy-and-paste populist slogans plastered on billboards around the country calling for the people to 'Make Australia Great Again'.

Revolving-Door Politics

After decades of seemingly stable governments and democratic transitions of power, the two major parties – the centre-left Australian Labor Party (ALP) and the centre-right Coalition of the Liberal and National Parties – have destabilised with a politics of the revolving door (perhaps not helped by the 24-hour news cycle scrutinising politicians' every move). Since 2010, the prime minster of Australia has changed seven times, though the revolving door syndrome has slowed with the win of the LNP coaltion in May 2019, meaning Prime Minister Scott Morrison remains in office.

Climate of Confusion

Australia's economy weathered the Global Financial Crisis of 2009 with barely a blip, and the country continues to enjoy low unemployment, low inflation and generally high wages – though the cost of living has soared to levels that threaten to leave behind a generation of would-be home-owners.

Economists have, however, warned that storm clouds could be gathering unless governments undertake meaningful economic reform, while environmentalists are alarmed that the federal government continues to keep the environment a low priority. Recent decisions, such as the approval of a new coal mine in Queensland, arguably pose serious threats to Australia's environment, including the Great Barrier Reef.

History

The story of Australia is an epic where 'the New World meets the Old' in a clash of two very different versions of history. It's only in recent years that the story of Indigenous Australians – here for more than 50,000 years before British colonisation – has come to occupy its rightful place at centre stage. It is a further sign, perhaps, that this dynamic, sometimes progressive and often laid-back country is really starting to grow up.

80 million years ago
Continental Australia breaks free from the Antarctic landmass and drifts north.

50,000 years ago
The first Australians arrive by sea to northern Australia.

1606
Dutch Navigator Willem Janszoon makes the first authenticated European landing on Australian soil.

Uluru (p236)

ALDO MANGANARO/SHUTTERSTOCK ©

First Australians

Human contact with Australia is thought by many to have begun around 60,000 years ago, when Aboriginal people journeyed across the straits from what is now Indonesia and Papua New Guinea. Aboriginal people, however, believe they have always inhabited the land. Undoubtedly, Indigenous life in Australia marked the beginning of the world's longest continuous cultural history.

Across the continent, Aboriginal peoples traded goods, items of spiritual significance, songs and dances across central Australia and beyond, using routes that followed the paths of ancestors from the Dreaming, the complex system of country, culture and beliefs that defines Indigenous spirituality.

An intimate understanding of plant ecology and animal behaviour ensured that food shortages were rare. Even central Australia's hostile deserts were occupied year-round, thanks to scattered permanent wells. Fire-stick farming was practised in forested areas,

1770
First Lieutenant James Cook claims the entire east coast of Australia for England.

1788
Captain Arthur Phillip and the First Fleet – 11 ships and about 1350 people – arrive at Botany Bay.

1835
John Batman negotiates a land deal with the Kulin nation; Melbourne is settled that same year.

involving the burning of undergrowth and dead grass to encourage new growth, to attract game and reduce the threat of bushfires.

For more information on Aboriginal Australia, see p298.

Strangers Arrive

In April 1770, Aboriginal people standing on a beach in southeastern Australia saw an astonishing spectacle out at sea. It was an English ship, the *Endeavour*, under the command of then-Lieutenant James Cook. His gentleman passengers were English scientists visiting the Pacific to make astronomical observations and to investigate 'new worlds'. As they sailed north along the edge of this new-found land, Cook began drawing the first British chart of Australia's east coast. This map heralded the beginning of conflicts between European settlers and Indigenous peoples.

A few days after that first sighting, Cook led a party of men ashore at a place known to the Aboriginal people as Kurnell. Though the Kurnell Aboriginal people were far from welcoming, the botanists on the *Endeavour* were delighted to discover that the woods were teeming with unfamiliar plants. To celebrate this profusion, Cook renamed the place Botany Bay.

When the *Endeavour* reached the northern tip of Cape York, Cook and his men could smell the sea-route home. And on a small, hilly island (Possession Island), Cook raised the Union Jack. Amid volleys of gunfire, he claimed the eastern half of the continent for King George III.

Cook's intention was not to steal land from the Aboriginal peoples. In fact he rather idealised them. 'They are far more happier than we Europeans', he wrote. 'They think themselves provided with all the necessaries of Life and that they have no superfluities.'

Convict Beginnings

Eighteen years after Cook's arrival, in 1788, the English were back to stay. They arrived in a fleet of 11 ships, packed with supplies including weapons, tools, building materials and livestock. The ships also contained 751 convicts and more than 250 soldiers, officials and their wives. This motley 'First Fleet' was under the command of a humane and diligent naval captain, Arthur Phillip. As his orders dictated, Phillip dropped anchor at Botany Bay. But the paradise that had so delighted Joseph Banks filled Phillip with dismay. So he left his floating prison and embarked in a small boat to search for a better location. Just a short way up the coast his heart leapt as he sailed into the finest harbour in the world. There, in a small cove, in the idyllic lands of the Eora people, he established a British penal settlement. He renamed the place after the British Home Secretary, Lord Sydney.

Phillip's official instructions urged him to colonise the land without doing violence to the local inhabitants. Among the Indigenous people he used as intermediaries was an Eora man named Bennelong, who adopted many of the white people's customs and manners. But Bennelong's people were shattered by the loss of their lands. Hundreds died of smallpox, and many of the survivors, including Bennelong himself, succumbed to alcoholism and despair.

1851	1880	1901
A gold rush in central Victoria brings settlers from across the world. Democracy is introduced in the eastern colonies.	Bushranger Ned Kelly is hanged as a criminal – and remembered as a folk hero.	The Australian colonies form a federation of states. The federal parliament sits in Melbourne.

In 1803, English officers established a second convict settlement in Van Diemen's Land (now Tasmania). Soon, reoffenders filled the grim prison at Port Arthur on the beautiful and wild coast near Hobart.

From Shackles to Freedom

At first, Sydney and the smaller colonies depended on supplies brought in by ship. Anxious to develop productive farms, the government granted land to soldiers, officers and settlers. After 30 years of trial and error, the farms began to flourish. The most irascible and ruthless of these new landholders was John Macarthur.

Macarthur was a leading member of the Rum Corps, a clique of powerful officers who bullied successive governors (including William Bligh of *Bounty* fame) and grew rich by controlling much of Sydney's trade, notably rum. But the Corps' racketeering was ended in 1810 by a tough new governor named Lachlan Macquarie. Macquarie laid out the major roads of modern-day Sydney, built some fine public buildings (many of which were designed by talented convict-architect Francis Greenway) and helped to lay the foundations for a more civil society. Macquarie also championed the rights of freed convicts, granting them land and appointing several to public office.

Southern Settlements

In the cooler grasslands of Van Diemen's Land, sheep farmers were thriving. In the 1820s they waged a bloody war against the island's Indigenous population, driving them to the brink of extinction. Now these settlers were hungry for more land.

In 1835 an ambitious young man named John Batman sailed to Port Phillip Bay on mainland Australia. On the banks of the Yarra River, he chose the location for Melbourne, famously announcing 'This is the place for a village'. Batman persuaded local Aboriginal peoples to 'sell' him their traditional lands (a whopping 250,000 hectares) for a crate of blankets, knives and knick-knacks. Back in Sydney, Governor Bourke declared the contract void, not because it was unfair, but because the land officially belonged to the British Crown.

At the same time, a private British company settled Adelaide in South Australia. Proud to have no links with convicts, these God-fearing folk instituted a scheme under which their company sold land to well-heeled settlers, and used the revenue to assist poor British labourers to emigrate. When these worthies earned enough to buy land from the company, that revenue would in turn pay the fare of another shipload of labourers.

Gold & Rebellion

Transportation of convicts to eastern Australia ceased in the 1840s. This was just as well: in 1851, prospectors discovered gold in New South Wales and central Victoria, including at Ballarat. The news hit the colonies with the force of a cyclone. Young men and some women from every social class headed for the diggings. Soon they were caught up in a great rush of prospectors, publicans and prostitutes. In Victoria the British governor was

1915
The Anzacs join a British invasion of Turkey: this military disaster spawns a nationalist legend.

1939
Prime Minister Robert Menzies announces that Britain is at war; 'as a result, Australia is also at war'.

1942
The Japanese bomb Darwin, the first of numerous air strikes on the northern capital.

Port Arthur Historic Site, Tasmania

SARAWUT KONGANANTDECH/SHUTTERSTOCK ©

★ Convict History

Port Arthur Historic Site (Tasmania)
Parramatta (Sydney, NSW)
Rottnest Island (Perth, WA)
Hyde Park Barracks (Sydney, NSW)

alarmed – both by the way the Victorian class system had been thrown into disarray, and by the need to finance the imposition of law and order on the goldfields. His solution was to compel all miners to buy an expensive monthly licence.

But the lure of gold was too great, and in the reckless excitement of the goldfields, the miners initially endured the thuggish troopers who enforced the government licence. After three years, though, the easy gold at Ballarat was gone, and miners were toiling in deep, water-sodden shafts. They were now infuriated by a corrupt and brutal system of law that held them in contempt. Under the leadership of a charismatic Irishman named Peter Lalor, they raised their own flag, the Southern Cross, and swore to defend their rights and liberties. They armed themselves and gathered inside a rough stockade at Eureka, where they waited for the government to make its move.

In the predawn of Sunday 3 December 1854, a force of troopers attacked the stockade. It was all over in 15 terrifying minutes. The brutal and one-sided battle claimed the lives of 30 miners and five soldiers. But democracy was in the air and public opinion sided with the miners. The eastern colonies were already in the process of establishing democratic parliaments, with the full support of the British authorities.

Meanwhile, in the West...

Western Australia lagged behind the eastern colonies by about 50 years. Though Perth was settled by genteel colonists back in 1829, its material progress was handicapped by isolation, Aboriginal resistance and the arid climate. It was not until the 1880s that the discovery of remote goldfields promised to gild the fortunes of the isolated colony. At the time, the west was just entering its own period of self-government, and its first premier was a forceful, weather-beaten explorer named John Forrest. He saw that the mining industry would fail if the government did not provide a first-class harbour, efficient railways and reliable water supplies. Ignoring the threats of private contractors, he appointed the brilliant engineer CY O'Connor to design and build each of these as government projects.

1945
Australia's motto: 'Populate or perish!' Over the next 30 years more than two million immigrants arrive.

1965
Menzies commits Australian troops to the American war in Vietnam, and divides the nation.

1967
In a national referendum, white Australians vote overwhelmingly to give citizenship to Indigenous people.

Nationhood

On 1 January 1901, Australia became a federation. When the members of the new national parliament met in Melbourne, their first aim was to protect the identity and values of a European Australia from an influx of Asians and Pacific Islanders. The solution was a law that became known as the White Australia Policy. It became a racial tenet of faith in Australia for the next 70 years.

For whites who lived inside the charmed circle of citizenship, this was to be a model society, nestled in the skirts of the British Empire. Just one year later, white women won the right to vote in federal elections. In a series of radical innovations, the government introduced a broad social welfare scheme and it protected Australian wage levels with import tariffs.

Entering the World Stage

Living on the edge of a dry and forbidding land, isolated from the rest of the world, most Australians took comfort in the knowledge that they were a dominion of the British Empire. When war broke out in Europe in 1914, thousands of Australian men rallied to the Empire's call. They had their first taste of death on 25 April 1915, when the Australian and New Zealand Army Corps (the Anzacs) joined thousands of other British and French troops in an assault on the Gallipoli Peninsula in Turkey. It was eight months before the British commanders acknowledged that the tactic had failed. By then 8141 young Australians were dead. Before long the Australian Imperial Force was fighting in the killing fields of Europe. By the time the war ended, 60,000 Australians had died.

In the 1920s Australia embarked on a decade of chaotic change. The country careered wildly through the 1920s until it collapsed into the abyss of the Great Depression in 1929. World prices for wheat and wool plunged. Unemployment brought its shame and misery to one in three households.

War with Japan

After 1933, the economy began to recover. Daily life was hardly dampened when Hitler hurled Europe into a new war in 1939. Though Australians had long feared Japan,

The Long Walk to Ballarat

Robe set up shop as a fishing port in 1846 – one of SA's earliest settlements. During the 1850s gold rush in Victoria, Robe came into its own when the Victorian government whacked a $10-per-head tax on Chinese gold miners arriving to work the goldfields. Thousands of Chinese miners dodged the tax by landing at Robe in SA, then walking the 400-odd kilometres to Bendigo and Ballarat in Victoria; 16,500 arrived between 1856 and 1858, with 10,000 in 1857 alone! But the flood stalled as quickly as it started when the SA government instituted its own tax on the Chinese. The 'Chinamen's wells' along their route (including one in the Coorong) can still be seen today, as can a memorial to the Chinese arrivals on the Robe foreshore.

1975
Against a background of reform and scandal, Governor General Sir John Kerr sacks the Whitlam government.

1992
The High Court of Australia recognises the principle of native title in the Mabo decision.

2000
The Sydney Olympic Games is a triumph of spectacle and good will.

Australian War Memorial (p85), Canberra

they took it for granted that the British navy would keep them safe. In December 1941, Japan bombed the US Fleet at Pearl Harbor. Weeks later, the 'impregnable' British naval base in Singapore crumbled.

As the Japanese swept through Southeast Asia and into Papua New Guinea, the British announced that they could not spare any resources to defend Australia. But US commander General Douglas MacArthur saw that Australia was the perfect base for American operations in the Pacific. In fierce sea and land battles, Allied forces turned back the Japanese advance. Importantly, it was the USA, not the British Empire, who saved Australia. The days of alliance with Britain alone were numbered.

Visionary Peace

When WWII ended, a new slogan rang out: 'Populate or perish!' The Australian government embarked on a scheme to attract thousands of immigrants. People flocked from Britain and non-English-speaking countries. They included Greeks, Italians, Serbs, Croatians and Dutch, followed by Turks and many others.

In addition to growing world demand for Australia's primary products (wool, meat and wheat), there were jobs in manufacturing and on major public works, notably the mighty Snowy Mountains Hydro-Electric Scheme in the mountains near Canberra.

This era of growth and prosperity was dominated by Robert Menzies, the founder of the Liberal Party of Australia, and Australia's longest-serving prime minister. Menzies was steeped in British tradition, and was also a vigilant opponent of communism. As Asia succumbed to the chill of the Cold War, Australia and New Zealand entered a formal military alliance with the USA – the 1951 Anzus security pact. When the USA jumped into a civil war in Vietnam, Menzies committed Australian forces to battle. The following year Menzies retired, leaving his successors a bitter legacy.

In an atmosphere of youthful rebellion and new-found nationalism, the Labor Party was elected to power in 1972 under an idealistic lawyer named Gough Whitlam. In four short years his government transformed the country, ending conscription and abolishing

2007
Kevin Rudd is elected prime minister and delivers the National Apology to the Australia's Indigenous peoples.

2010
Kevin Rudd is ousted as prime minister by Julia Gillard, the first woman to hold the office.

2013
Rudd in turn ousts Gillard (touché!), then Rudd is again ousted, this time by right-wing nemesis Tony Abbott.

university fees. He introduced a free universal health scheme, no-fault divorce, and the principles of Indigenous land rights and equal pay for women.

By 1975, the Whitlam government was rocked by inflation and scandal. At the end of 1975 his government was infamously dismissed from office by the governor general.

Modern Challenges

Today Australia faces new challenges. In the 1970s the country began dismantling its protectionist scaffolding. New efficiency brought new prosperity. At the same time, wages and working conditions, which were once protected by an independent tribunal, became more vulnerable as egalitarian-

Sticky Wicket

The year 1932 saw accusations of treachery on the cricket field. The English team, under captain Douglas Jardine, employed a violent new bowling tactic known as 'bodyline'. The aim was to unnerve Australia's star batsman, the devastatingly efficient Donald Bradman. The bitterness of the tour provoked a diplomatic crisis with Britain and became part of Australian legend. Bradman batted on. When he retired in 1948 he had a still-unsurpassed career average of 99.94 runs.

ism gave way to competition. And after two centuries of development, the strains on the environment were starting to show – on water supplies, forests, soils, air quality and the oceans.

Under John Howard, Australia's second-longest-serving prime minister (1996–2007), the country grew closer than ever to the USA, joining the Americans in their war in Iraq. Some Australians were dismayed by the conservative Howard government's harsh treatment of asylum seekers, its refusal to acknowledge the reality of climate change, its anti-union reforms and the prime minister's lack of empathy with Aboriginal Australians. But Howard presided over a period of economic growth that emphasised the values of self-reliance and won him continuing support.

In 2007 Howard was defeated by the Labor Party's Kevin Rudd, an ex-diplomat who issued a formal apology to Indigenous Australians for the injustices they had suffered over the past two centuries. Though it promised sweeping reforms in environment and education, the Rudd government found itself faced with a crisis when the world economy crashed in 2008. In 2010 Rudd lost his position in a leadership spill.

Incoming Prime Minister Julia Gillard, along with other world leaders, now faced three related challenges: climate change, a diminishing fuel supply and a shrinking economy. Since 2013 the prime minister's chair has changed hands several times with a run of leaders after Gillard: Rudd (again); then three Liberal Party leaders in quick succession, Tony Abbott, Malcolm Turnbull and Scott Morrison. A May 2019 election saw the Morrison-led Liberal Party retain control.

Governing the nation, almost 120 years after it was created, has proven to be quite a challenge in the 21st century.

2015	**2016**	**2019**
Tony Abbott is replaced by Malcolm Turnbull in a Liberal Party leadership spill. Five prime ministers in five years!	Prime Minister Turnbull narrowly wins a federal election and returns to power with a wafer-thin majority in parliament.	Detained asylum-seeker Behrouz Boochani wins Australia's richest literary prize for his novel *No Friend but the Mountains*.

An Aboriginal artist dot painting at Maruka Arts gallery in Uluru-Kata Tjuta National Park (p236)

Aboriginal Australia

Aboriginal culture has evolved over thousands of years with strong links between the spiritual, economic and social lives of its people, kept alive by generations passing on knowledge and skills through oral history, rituals, art, cultural material and language. From the cities to the bush, there are opportunities to get up close and learn from a way of life that has existed for over 50,000 years.

Cathy Craigie

History of Aboriginal Australia

First Australians

Many academics believe Indigenous Australians came here from somewhere else, with scientific evidence placing them on the continent at least 40,000 to 60,000 years ago. Aboriginal people, however, believe they have always inhabited the land.

At the time of European contact the Aboriginal population was grouped into 300 or more different nations, with distinct languages and land boundaries. From the desert to the sea Aboriginal peoples shaped their lives according to their environments and developed different skills and a wide body of knowledge on their territories.

Colonised

The effects of colonisation started immediately after the Europeans arrived. It began with the appropriation of land and water resources and an epidemic of diseases – smallpox killed around half of the Indigenous people who were native to Sydney Harbour. A period of resistance occurred as Aboriginal people fought back to retain their land and way of life; as violence and massacres swept the country, many were pushed away from their traditional lands. Over the course of a century, the Aboriginal population was reduced by 90%.

By the late 1800s most of the fertile land had been taken and most Indigenous Australians were living in poverty on the fringes of settlements or on land unsuitable for settlement. Aboriginal people had to adapt to the new culture, but had few to no rights. Employment opportunities were scarce and most worked as labourers or domestic staff.

Rights & Reconciliation

The relationship between Indigenous Australians and other Australians hasn't always been an easy one. The history of forced resettlement, removal of children, and the loss of land and culture can never be erased, even with governments addressing some of the issues. Current policies focus on 'closing the gap' and better delivery of essential services to improve lives, but there is still great disparity between Indigenous Australians and the rest of the population, including lower standards of education, employment, health and living conditions; high incarceration and suicide rates; and a lower life expectancy.

Throughout all of this, Aboriginal peoples have managed to maintain their identity and link to country and culture. Many gains for Aboriginal peoples have been hard-won and initiated by Aboriginal communities themselves.

For more Australian history see p290.

Aboriginal Culture

Indigenous Australians originally had an oral tradition, and language has played an important role in preserving Aboriginal cultures. Today there is a national movement to revive Aboriginal languages and there's a strong Aboriginal art sector; traditional knowledge is being used in science, natural resource management and government programs. Aboriginal cultures have never been static, and continues to evolve with the changing times and environment.

The Land

Aboriginal cultures view humans as part of the ecology, not separate from it. Everything is connected – a whole environment that sustains the spiritual, economic and cultural lives of the people. In turn, Aboriginal people have sustained the land over thousands of years, through knowledge passed on in ceremonies,

The Stolen Generations

When Australia became a federation in 1901, a government policy known as the 'White Australia policy' was put in place. It was implemented mainly to restrict nonwhite immigration to Australia, but the policy also had a huge impact on Indigenous Australians. Assimilation into the broader society was encouraged by all sectors of government, with the intent to eventually 'fade out' the Aboriginal race. A policy of forcibly removing Aboriginal and Torres Strait Islander children from their families operated from 1909 to 1969. It is estimated that around 100,000 Indigenous children – or one in three – were taken from their families: they became known as the Stolen Generations.

On 13 February 2008 Kevin Rudd, then prime minister of Australia, offered a national apology to the Stolen Generations.

Aboriginal rock art in Ubirr (p253), Kakadu

★ Indigenous Art Encounters

rituals, songs and stories. Land is intrinsically connected to identity and spirituality; all land in Australia is reflected in Aboriginal lore, but particular places may be significant for religious and cultural beliefs.

Sacred sites can be parts of rocks, hills, trees or water and are associated with an ancestral being or an event that occurred. Often these sites are part of a Dreaming story and link people across areas.

Cultural tours to Aboriginal sites can provide opportunities to learn about plants and animals, hunting and fishing, bush food or dance.

The Arts

Rock Art

Rock art is the oldest form of human art and Aboriginal rock art stretches back tens of thousands of years. Rock art is found in every state of Australia and many sites are thousands of years old. There are a number of different styles of rock art across Australia. These include engravings in sandstone and stencils, prints and drawings in rock shelters.

Some of the oldest examples of engravings can be found in the Pilbara in Western Australia and in Olary in South Australia where there is an engraving of a crocodile. All national parks surrounding Sydney have rock engravings and can be easily accessed and viewed. At Gariwerd (the Grampians) in Victoria there are hand prints and hand stencils.

In the Northern Territory many of the rock-art sites have patterns and symbols that appear in paintings, carvings and other cultural material. Kakadu National Park has more than 5000 recorded sites, but many more are thought to exist.

The Importance of Storytelling

Aboriginal peoples traditionally had an oral culture so storytelling was an important way to learn. Stories gave meaning to life and were used to teach the messages of the spirit ancestors. Although beliefs and cultural practices vary according to region and language groups, there is a common world view that these ancestors created the land, the sea and all living things. This is often referred to as the Dreaming. Through stories, the knowledge and beliefs are passed on from one generation to another and set out the social mores. They also recall events from the past. Today artists have continued this tradition but are using new media such as film and writing. The first Aboriginal writer to be published was David Unaipon, a Ngarrindjeri man from South Australia who was a writer, scientist and advocate for his people. Born in 1872, he published *Aboriginal Legends* (1927) and *Native Legends* (1929).

Contemporary Art

The contemporary Indigenous art industry started in a tiny community called Papunya (NT) in central Australia. In 1971 an art teacher at Papunya school encouraged painting and some senior men took an interest. This started the process of transferring sand and body drawings onto modern mediums and the 'dot and circle' style of contemporary painting began. The emergence of dot paintings is one of the most important movements in 20th-century Australian art, and the Papunya Tula artists became a model for other Aboriginal communities.

> ### Torres Strait Islanders
>
> Aboriginal society is a diverse group of several hundred sovereign nations. Torres Strait Islanders are a Melanesian people with a separate culture from that of Aboriginal Australians, though they have a shared history. Together, these two groups form Australia's Indigenous peoples.

The National Gallery of Australia (p84) in Canberra has a fantastic collection, but contemporary Aboriginal art can also be viewed at any public art gallery or in one of the many independent galleries dealing in Aboriginal work.

Music

Music has always been a vital part of Aboriginal culture. The most well-known instrument is the *yidaki* (didgeridoo), which was traditionally played in northern Australia, and only by men. Other instruments included clapsticks, rattles and boomerangs; in southern Australia, animal skins were stretched across the lap to make a drumming sound.

Contemporary Aboriginal artists such as Dan Sultan, Thelma Plum and Jessica Mauboy have crossed over successfully into the mainstream, winning major music awards and appearing on popular programs and at major music festivals.

Performing Arts

Dance and theatre are a vital part of social and ceremonial life and important elements in Aboriginal cultures. Historically, dances often told stories to pass on knowledge. Like other art forms, dance has adapted to the modern world, and contemporary dance companies and groups have merged traditional forms into a modern interpretation. The best-known dance company is the internationally acclaimed Bangarra Dance Theatre (p69).

Theatre also draws on the storytelling tradition. Currently there are two major Aboriginal theatre companies: Ilbijerri (www.ilbijerri.com) in Melbourne and Yirra Yakin (www.yirrayaakin.com.au) in Perth. Traditionally drama and dance came together in ceremonies or corroborees and this still occurs in many contemporary productions.

TV, Radio & Film

Aboriginal people have developed an extensive media network of radio, print and television services. There are over 120 Aboriginal radio stations and programs operating across Australia – in cities, rural areas and remote communities. Program formats differ from location to location. Some broadcast only in Aboriginal languages or cater to specific music tastes.

From its base in Brisbane, the National Indigenous Radio Service (NIRS; www.nirs.org. au) broadcasts four radio channels of Aboriginal content via satellite and over the internet.

There is a thriving Aboriginal film industry and in recent years feature films such as *The Sapphires*, *Bran Nue Day*, *Samson and Delilah* and *Putuparri and the Rainmakers* have had mainstream success. Since the first Aboriginal TV channel, NITV, was launched in 2007, there has been a growth in the number of film-makers wanting to tell their stories.

Koala

Environment

Australia has been isolated from the other continents for a very long time: around 80 million years. Unlike those on other habitable continents linked by land bridges, Australia's birds, mammals, reptiles and plants have taken their own separate and very different evolutionary journeys. The result today is the world's most distinct natural realm.

Dr Tim Flannery

A Unique Environment

The first naturalists to investigate Australia were astonished by what they found. Here the swans were black – to Europeans this was a metaphor for the impossible – and mammals such as the platypus and echidna were discovered to lay eggs. It really was an upside-down world, where many of the larger animals hopped and where each year the trees shed their bark rather than their leaves.

If you are visiting Australia for a short time, you might need to go out of your way to experience some of the richness of the environment. That's because Australia is a subtle place, and some of the natural environment – especially around the cities – has been damaged or replaced by trees and creatures from Europe. Places like Sydney, however, have preserved extraordinary fragments of their original environment that are relatively easy to access. Before you enjoy them though, it's worthwhile understanding the basics about how nature operates in Australia. This is important because there's nowhere like Australia, and once you have an insight into its origins and natural rhythms, you will appreciate the place so much more.

Fuel-Efficient Fauna

Australia is, of course, famous as the home of the kangaroo (aka just plain 'roo') and other marsupials. Have you ever wondered why kangaroos hop? It turns out that hopping is the most efficient way of getting about at medium speeds. This is because the energy of the bounce is stored in the tendons of the legs – much like in a pogo stick – while the intestines bounce up and down like a piston, emptying and filling the lungs without needing to activate the chest muscles.

Marsupials are so energy efficient that they need to eat one-fifth less food than equivalent-sized placental mammals (everything from bats to rats, whales and ourselves). But some have taken energy efficiency much further: if you visit a wildlife park or zoo, you might notice that faraway look in a koala's eyes. Several years ago biologists announced that koalas are the only living creatures that have brains that don't fit their skulls. Instead they have a shrivelled walnut of a brain that rattles around in a fluid-filled cranium. We now believe that the koala has sacrificed its brain to energy efficiency – brains cost a lot to run. Koalas eat gum leaves, which are so toxic that they use 20% of their energy just detoxifying this food. This leaves little energy for the brain, but fortunately living in the treetops – where there are so few predators – means that they can get by with few wits at all.

The peculiar constraints of the Australian environment have not made everything dumb. The koala's nearest relative, the wombat (of which there are three species), has a large brain for a marsupial. These creatures live in complex burrows and can weigh up to 35kg, making them the largest herbivorous burrowers on earth.

Two unique monotremes (egg-laying mammals) live in Australia: the bumbling echidna, something akin to a hedgehog but bigger and spikier; and the platypus, a bit like an otter, with webbed feet and a duck-like bill. Echidnas are common along bushland trails, but platypuses are elusive, seen at dawn and dusk in quiet rivers and streams.

Current Environmental Issues

Headlining the environmental issues facing Australia's fragile landscape at present are climate change, water scarcity, nuclear energy and uranium mining. All are interconnected. For Australia, the warmer temperatures resulting from climate change spell disaster to an already fragile landscape. A 2°C climb in average temperatures on the globe's driest continent will result in an even drier southern half of the country and greater water scarcity. Scientists also agree that hotter and drier conditions will exacerbate bushfire conditions and increase cyclone intensity.

Pellegrini's Espresso Bar (p161)

MICHAEL HOLLOWAY/ALAMY ©

Food & Wine

Towards the end of last century Australians proudly still survived on a diet of 'meat and three veg'. Fine fare was a Sunday roast, and lasagne or croissants were considered exotic. Not any more. Today Australian gastronomy is keen to break rules, backed up by award-winning wines, world-class coffee, an organic revolution in the importance of fresh produce and a booming craft-beer scene.

Mod Oz?

The phrase Modern Australian (Mod Oz) has been coined to classify contemporary Australian cuisine: a melange of East and West; a swirl of Atlantic and Pacific Rim; a flourish of authentic French and Italian.

Immigration has been the key to this culinary concoction. An influx of immigrants since WWII, from Europe, Asia, the Middle East and Africa, introduced new ingredients and new ways to use staples. Vietnamese, Japanese, Fijian – no matter where it's from, there are expat communities and interested locals keen to cook and eat it. You'll find Jamaicans using Scotch bonnet peppers and Tunisians making tajine.

As the Australian appetite for diversity and invention grows, so does the food culture surrounding it. Cookbooks and foodie magazines are bestsellers and Australian celebrity

chefs – highly sought overseas – reflect Australia's multiculturalism in their backgrounds and dishes. Cooking TV shows, both competitions and foodie travel documentaries, have become mandatory nightly viewing.

If all this sounds overwhelming, never fear. The range of food in Australia is a true asset. You'll find that dishes are characterised by bold and interesting flavours and fresh ingredients. All palates are catered for: the chilli-meter spans gentle to extreme, seafood is plentiful, meats are full-flavoured, and vegetarian needs are considered (especially in the cities).

Vegemite

Vegemite: you'll either love it or hate it. Barack Obama undiplomatically called it 'horrible'. It's certainly an acquired taste, but Australians consume more than 22 million jars of the stuff every year. And they're particularly pleased that ownership of this national icon recently returned to Australian hands for the first time since 1928.

Cafes & Coffee

Cafes in Australia generally serve good-value food: they're usually more casual than restaurants and you can get a decent meal for around $20, although many only open for breakfast and lunch. Kids are usually more than welcome.

Coffee has become a nationwide addiction: there are Italian-style espresso machines in virtually every cafe, boutique roasters are all the rage and, in urban areas, the qualified barista (coffee-maker) is the norm. Sydney, Melbourne and even subtropical Brisbane have borne generations of coffee snobs, but Melbourne takes top billing as Australia's caffeine capital. The cafe scene here rivals the most vibrant in the world: the best way to dunk yourself in it is by wandering the city centre's cafe-lined lanes.

Fire up the Barbie

The iconic Australian barbecue (BBQ or 'barbie') is a near-mandatory cultural experience. In summer locals invite their friends around at dinner time and fire up the barbie, grilling burgers, sausages ('snags'), steaks, seafood, and veggie, meat or seafood skewers. If you're invited to a BBQ, bring some meat and cold beer. Year-round the BBQ is wheeled out at weekends for quick-fire lunches. There are plenty of free electric or gas BBQs in parks around the country, too – a terrific traveller-friendly option.

Cheers!

No matter what your poison, you're in the right country if you're after a drink.

Wine

Long recognised as some of the finest in the world, wine is now one of Australia's top exports. In fact, if you're in the country's cooler southern climes (particularly in South Australia, and even in southeast Queensland), you're probably not far from a wine region. Some regions have been producing wines from the early days of settlement more than 220 years ago. Most wineries have small cellar door sales where you can taste for a nominal fee (or often free). Although plenty of good wine comes from big producers with economies of scale on their side, the most interesting wines are usually made by smaller, family-run wineries.

National Wine Centre of Australia (p217)

★ Wine Tasting

National Wine Centre of Australia (p217), Adelaide, SA

McLaren Vale (p212), SA

Margaret River (p272), WA

Yarra Valley (p160), Vic

Beer

As the public develops a more sophisticated palate, local craft beers are rising to the occasion. There's a growing wealth of microbrewed flavours and varieties on offer, challenging the nation's entrenched predilection for mass-produced lager. Have a look at www.find abrewery.com.au for brewery listings. Most beers have an alcohol content between 3.5% and 5.5% – less than many European beers but more than most in North America.

The terminology used to order beer varies state by state. In NSW you ask for a schooner (425mL) if you're thirsty and a middy (285mL) if you're not quite so dry. In Victoria the 285mL measure is called a pot; in Tasmania it's called a 10-ounce. Pints can either be 425mL or 568mL, depending on where you are. Mostly you can just ask for a beer and see what turns up.

Spirits

In recent years, Tasmania – with its chilly Scotland-like highlands and clean water – has become a whisky-producing hotspot. There are about a dozen distillers around the state now, bottling superb single malt for a growing international market. Keep an eye out for excellent drops from Sullivans Cove Whisky (which won the prize for the world's best single malt for its French Oak Cask variety in 2014), Nant Distillery and Hellyers Road Distillery. Gins from Kangaroo Island Spirits in South Australia and Melbourne's Four Pillars are also impressive.

Etiquette

At the bar, 'shouting' is a revered custom, where people take turns to pay for a round of drinks. Leaving before it's your 'shout' won't win you many friends! Once the drinks are distributed, a toast of 'Cheers!' is standard practice: everyone should touch glasses and look each other in the eye as they clink – failure to do so purportedly results in seven years' bad sex.

Australian Rules football game, Melbourne

NEALE COUSLAND/SHUTTERSTOCK ©

Sport

Whether they're filling stadiums, glued to a pub's big screen or on the sofa in front of the TV, Australians invest heavily in sport. The federal government kicks in fairly substantial funding, enough to see Australia hold its own against formidable international sporting opponents. However, it's the passion for sport in almost every Aussie that truly defines the country's sporting life.

Australian Rules Football

Australia's very own sport, and one of the most watched, is Australian Rules football (aka 'footy' or 'Aussie rules'). Growing from the Victorian Football League, the Australian Football League (AFL; www.afl.com.au) gradually expanded its popularity into all states, though the majority of teams hail from Melbourne. The roar of up to 100,000 fans cheering inside 'The G' (Melbourne's MCG stadium) is something to experience once in a lifetime. The national women's league (AFLW) successfully debuted in 2017 with plans to expand to 14 teams by 2020. Footy season runs from March until late September; tickets can be purchased online or at various stadiums around the country on the day for all but the biggest games. The season culminates in the AFL Grand Final at the MCG, one of Australia's most-watched sporting events.

Rugby

The National Rugby League (NRL; www.nrl.com.au) is the most popular football code north of the Murray River, with the season highlight the annual State of Origin series between New South Wales and Queensland. To witness an NRL game is to fully appreciate Newton's laws of motion – bone-crunching! As with the AFL, a national women's team (NRLW) started in 2018 with four teams, including one from New Zealand.

Meanwhile, the national rugby union team, the Wallabies, won the Rugby World Cup in 1991 and 1999 and was runner-up in 2003 (to England) and 2015 (to eternal rivals New Zealand). In between World Cups, Bledisloe Cup games against New Zealand are hotly contested, though the All Blacks have dominated the Wallabies since the turn of the century.

Soccer

Australia's national soccer team, the Socceroos, has qualified for the last few FIFA World Cups after a long history of almost-but-not-quite getting there. The women's national team, the Matilda's, are ranked six in the world and made it to the round of 16 in the 2019 World Cup before being knocked out by Norway.

The national A-League (www.a-league.com.au) competition, with nine teams from around Australia and one from New Zealand, has enjoyed increased popularity in recent years.

Cricket

The Aussies dominated both international Test and One-Day International cricket for much of the 2000s, holding the number-one world ranking for most of the decade. But the retirement of once-in-a-lifetime players like Shane Warne, Adam Gilchrist, Ricky Ponting and the Waugh brothers sent the team into an extended rebuilding phase.

The pinnacle of Australian men's cricket is the biennial Test series played between Australia and England known as the Ashes. Shorter versions of the game – One-Day Internationals and Twenty20 matches are a more accessible spectator introduction than five-day Tests. Not to be outdone, the Australian women's cricket team, captained by Meg Lanning, is currently ranked number one in the world in all forms of the game.

Tennis

Every January, tennis shoes melt in the Melbourne heat at the Australian Open (www.aus open.com), one of the four Grand Slam tennis tournaments. In the men's comp, following the retirement of former world number-one Lleyton Hewitt, Australians don't quite know what to make of the talented-but-flawed enfants terrible, Nick Kyrgios and Bernard Tomic. Australia has enjoyed more success in the women's game: Australian Sam Stosur won the US Open in 2011 and Ash Barty the French Open in 2019.

Horse Racing

Australians have traditionally loved to bet on the 'nags'. On the first Tuesday in November the nation stops for a world-famous horse race, the Melbourne Cup (www.melbournecup. com). In Victoria it's a public holiday. Australia's most famous cup winner was Phar Lap, who won in 1930, and later died of a mystery illness in the USA. In recent years, sprint queens Black Caviar and Winx have taken the sport by storm, each registering long unbeaten runs. Increasing awareness of the injuries sustained by horses during the race, including broken legs and dying on track, has tempered celebrations in recent years.

Hiking in Blue Mountains National Park (p77)

MARINA J/SHUTTERSTOCK ©

Australia Outdoors

Australia serves up plenty of excuses to just kick back and stare at incredible landscapes, but these same landscapes lend themselves to boundless outdoor pursuits – whether it's getting active on the trails and mountains on dry land, or on the swells and reefs offshore.

Bushwalking

Bushwalking (aka hiking, trekking or tramping, depending on where you're from) is supremely popular in Australia, with national parks and vast tracts of untouched scrub and forest providing ample opportunities. June to August are the best walking months up north; down south, summer (December to February) is better.

Online, look at www.bushwalkingaustralia.org. The book *Sydney's Best Harbour & Coastal Walks* details the excellent 6km Bondi to Coogee Clifftop Walk and the 10km Manly Scenic Walkway, in addition to wilder walks.

Other good sources of bushwalking information and trail descriptions include outdoor stockists and the websites of the various state government national parks departments. Online, see www.lonelyplanet.com/australia/things-to-do/bushwalking-in-australia.

Surfing at Byron Bay (p98)

★ **The Best Surf Spots**

Byron Bay (p98) , NSW

Bells Beach (p178), Vic

Sydney's northern beaches (p56), NSW

Margaret River (p272), WA

Cycling

Cyclists in Australia have access to plenty of cycling routes and can tour the country for days, weekends or even on multi-week trips. Or you can just rent a bike for a few hours and cycle around a city.

Standout longer routes include the **Murray to the Mountains Rail Trail** (www.murrayto mountains.com.au) and the **East Gippsland Rail Trail** (www.eastgippslandrailtrail.com.au) in Victoria. In WA the **Munda Biddi Trail** (☑08-6336 9699; www.mundabiddi.org.au) offers 900km of mountain biking, or you can rampage along the same distance on the **Mawson Trail** in South Australia (SA). The 480km **Tasmanian Trail** (www.tasmaniantrail.com.au) is a north–south mountain-bike route across the length of the island state. Alice Springs (p243) in Central Australia also has a prospering mountain-biking scene.

Rental rates charged by most outfits for road or mountain bikes start at around $25/50 per hour/day. Deposits range from $50 to $250, depending on the rental period. Most states have bicycle organisations that can provide maps and advice.

Diving & Snorkelling

Professional Association of Diving Instructors (PADI) dive courses are offered throughout the country. Courses range from two to five days and cost anything between $350 and $850. Alternatively, hiring a mask, snorkel and fins is an affordable way to get underwater.

In Queensland, the Great Barrier Reef has more dazzling dive sites than you can poke a fin at. There are coral reefs off some mainland beaches and around many islands. Many day trips to the reef include snorkelling gear for free.

North of Sydney in New South Wales (NSW), try Broughton Island near Port Stephens; and, further north, Fish Rock Cave off South West Rocks is renowned for its excellent diving, with shells, schools of clownfish and humpback whales. On the NSW South Coast popular diving spots include Jervis Bay, Montague Island and Merimbula.

In Western Australia (WA), Ningaloo Reef is every bit as interesting as the east-coast coral reefs, without the tourist numbers. Rapid Bay jetty off the Gulf St Vincent coast in South Australia (SA) is renowned for its abundant marine life, while in Tasmania the Bay of Fires and Eaglehawk Neck are popular spots.

Check out www.diveoz.com.au online for nationwide info.

Skiing & Snowboarding

Australia has a small but enthusiastic skiing industry, with snowfields straddling the NSW–Victoria border. The season is relatively short, however, running from about mid-July to early September, and snowfalls can be unpredictable. See www.ski.com.au for ski-cams, forecasts and reports. The rest of the year these are hiking and mountain cycling hubs.

Some of Australia's best ski destinations include the following:

Falls Creek, Victoria (www.fallscreek.com.au)

Mt Buller, Victoria (www.mtbuller.com.au)

Mt Hotham, Victoria (www.mthotham.com.au)

Perisher Valley, NSW (www.perisher.com.au)

Thredbo, NSW (www.thredbo.com.au)

Surfing

World-class waves can be found all around Australia. If you've never surfed before, a lesson or two will get you started.

In NSW, Sydney is strewn with ocean beaches with decent breaks. Further north, Crescent Head is the longboard capital of Australia, and there are brilliant breaks at Lennox Head and Byron Bay. On the South Coast try Jervis Bay and Ulladulla.

There are magical breaks along Queensland's southeastern coast, notably at Coolangatta, Burleigh Heads, Surfers Paradise, North Stradbroke Island and Noosa.

Victoria's Southern Ocean coastline has impressive surf. Bells Beach hosts the annual Rip Curl Pro comp. For the less experienced, there are surf schools in Victoria at Anglesea, Lorne and Phillip Island.

Southern WA is a surfing mecca (head for Margaret River), while South Australia's Cactus Beach is remote but internationally lauded. Tasmania's cold-water surf spots include legendary Shipstern Bluff, Australia's heaviest wave.

See www.coastalwatch.com for forecasts and surf-cams.

Wildlife Watching

Wildlife is one of Australia's top selling points. Most national parks are home to native fauna. Australia is also a birdwatcher's haven.

In NSW, Border Ranges National Park is home to a quarter of all of Australia's bird species. Koalas are everywhere around Port Macquarie. In Victoria, Wilsons Promontory National Park teems with wildlife – wombats seem to have right of way! The Great Ocean Road is also excellent for koalas and kangaroos.

In Queensland, head to Magnetic Island for koalas; Fraser Island for dingoes, and the Daintree for cassowaries and other birdlife. In South Australia, Flinders Chase National Park on Kangaroo Island has platypuses, kangaroos and fur seals.

In Tasmania, Maria Island is another twitcher's paradise (Tasmanian devils, too!), while Mt William and Mt Field National Parks and Bruny Island teem with native fauna. In the Northern Territory, head to Kakadu National Park for birdlife and crocodiles.

Western Australia has whale sharks and manta rays at Ningaloo Marine Park, fur seals and sea lions at Rottnest Island, Esperance and Rockingham, and all manner of sea creatures at Monkey Mia. Canberra has the richest birdlife of any Australian capital city, plus grey kangaroos at Namadgi National Park.

Whale-watching hotspots include Victor Harbor and Head of Bight in South Australia, Warrnambool in Victoria, Hervey Bay in Queensland and out on the ocean beyond Sydney Harbour. If you're lucky enough to be out on the water with one of them, give them a wide berth – humanity owes them a little peace and quiet!

A Melbourne tram

Survival Guide

Directory A–Z

Accessible Travel

Australians are increasingly mindful of people with different access needs, and more operators are realising the social and economic benefits of accommodating them.

◦ Legislation requires that new accommodation meets accessibility standards for mobility-impaired travellers, and discrimination by tourism operators is illegal.

◦ Many of Australia's key attractions, including many national parks, provide access for those with limited mobility and a number of sites also address the needs of visitors with visual or aural impairments.

Book Your Stay Online

For more accommodation reviews by Lonely Planet authors, check out http://hotels.lonely planet.com/Australia. You'll find independent reviews, as well as recommendations on the best places to stay. Best of all, you can book online.

◦ Contact attractions you plan to visit in advance to confirm facilities available.

◦ Tour operators with vehicles catering to mobility impaired travellers operate from most capital cities.

◦ Facilities for wheelchairs are improving in accommodation, but there are still many older establishments where the upgrades haven't been implemented. Download Lonely Planet's free Accessible Travel guides from http://lptravel.to/AccessibleTravel.

Resources

Deaf Australia (www.deafaus tralia.org.au)
e-Bility (www.ebility.com)
Vision Australia (www.vision australia.org)

Air Travel

Qantas (🖉13 13 13; www.qantas.com.au) entitles a person with high-support needs and the carer travelling with them to a discount on full economy fares. Guide dogs travel free on Qantas, **Jetstar** (www.jetstar.com/au/en/home), **Virgin Australia** (www.virginaustralia.com) and their affiliated carriers. All of Australia's major airports have dedicated parking spaces, wheelchair access to terminals, accessible toilets, and skychairs to convey passengers onto planes via air bridges.

Public Transport

All of Australia's suburban rail networks are wheelchair accessible, and guide dogs and hearing dogs are permitted on all public transport.

Accommodation

Australia has accommodation for all budgets, but you still need to book ahead – especially through summer (December to February), over Easter and during school holidays, when prices are at their highest. Outside these times you'll find useful discounts and lower walk-in rates. Notable exceptions include central Australia, the Top End and Australia's ski resorts, where summer is the low season and prices drop substantially.

B&Bs

Australian bed-and-breakfast options include restored miners' cottages, converted barns, rambling old houses, upmarket country manors and beachside bungalows. Tariffs are typically in the midrange bracket, but can be higher. In areas that attract weekenders – historic towns, wine regions, forest regions such as the Blue Mountains in NSW and the Dandenongs in Victoria – B&Bs are often booked out for weekend stays.

Some places advertised as B&Bs are actually self-contained cottages with breakfast provisions supplied. In the cheaper B&Bs there may be shared bathroom facilities. Some hosts cook dinner for guests (though notice is required).

Online resources:

Airbnb (www.airbnb.com.au) Global homestay accommodation provider with variable options.

Beautiful Accommodation (www.beautifulaccommo dation.com) A select crop of luxury B&Bs and self-contained houses.

Hosted Accommodation Australia (www.australian bedandbreakfast.com.au) Local listings for B&Bs, farmstays, cottages and homesteads.

Holiday Apartments

Holiday apartments are particularly common in coastal areas, with reservations often handled by local real estate agents or online booking sites.

Costs For a two-bedroom flat, you're looking at anywhere between $150 and $250 per night, but you will pay much more in high season and for serviced apartments in major cities.

Facilities Self-contained holiday apartments range from simple, studio-like rooms with small kitchenettes, to two-bedroom apartments with full laundries and state-of-the-art entertainment systems: great value for multi-night stays. Sometimes they come in small, single-storey blocks, but in tourist hotspots such as the Gold Coast expect a sea of high-rises.

Hotels

Hotels in Australian cities or well-touristed places are generally of the business or luxury-chain variety (midrange to top end): comfortable, anonymous, mod-con-filled rooms in multistorey blocks. For these hotels we quote 'rack rates' (official advertised rates – usually upwards of $220 a night), though significant discounts can be offered when business is quiet.

Motels

Drive-up motels offer comfortable basic to midrange accommodation and are found all over Australia, often on the edges of urban centres. They rarely offer a cheaper rate for singles, so are better value for couples or groups of three. You'll mostly pay $120 to $180 for a simple room with a kettle, a fridge, a TV, air-con and a bathroom.

Pubs

Many Australian pubs (from the term 'public house') were built during boom times, so they're often among the largest, most extravagant buildings in town. Some have been restored, but generally rooms remain small and weathered, with

Climate

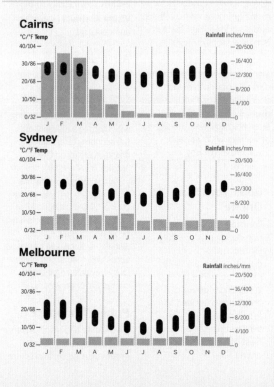

a long amble down the hall to the bathroom. They're usually central and cheap – singles/doubles with shared facilities cost from $60/100, more if you want a private bathroom. If you're a light sleeper, avoid booking a room above the bar and check whether a band is cranking out the rock downstairs that night.

Resorts

Australia does a nice line in resorts and other forms of accommodation that represent destinations in their own right. So good are they that you may not even need to move, other than to enjoy the activities and excursions offered in the surrounding area. Most work so well because their locations are prized patches of real estate, often on private concessions in remote areas that are for the exclusive enjoyment of guests. Rates are high – up to $3000 per night – and most have minimum stays, but prices usually include all meals and activities.

Customs Regulations

For detailed information on customs and quarantine regulations, contact the **Department of Home Affairs** (131 881, 02-6196 0196; www. homeaffairs.gov.au).

When entering Australia you can bring most articles in free of duty provided that customs is satisfied they are for personal use. Duty-free quotas per person (note the unusually low figure for cigarettes):

Alcohol 2.25L (over the age of 18)

Cigarettes 50 cigarettes (over the age of 18)

General goods Up to the value of $900 ($450 for people aged under 18)

Narcotics, of course, are illegal, and customs inspectors and their highly trained hounds are diligent in sniffing them out. Quarantine regulations are strict, so you must declare all goods of animal or vegetable origin – wooden spoons, straw hats, the lot. Fresh food (meat, cheese, fruit, vegetables etc) and flowers are prohibited. There are disposal bins located in airports where you can dump any questionable items if you don't want to bother with an inspection, a hefty on-the-spot fine or up to 10 years' imprisonment.

Discount Cards

The internationally recognised **International Student Identity Card** (www. isic.org) is available to full-time students globally. The card gives the bearer discounts on accommodation, transport and admission to various attractions. Home country student ID cards are sometimes accepted by proprietors.

Travellers over the age of 60 may be eligible for the same concession prices as locals with **Senior Citizen cards**, though not many 60-year-olds take kindly to being called 'senior'.

Electricity

Type I
230V/50Hz

Food

See the Food & Wine chapter (p304) for more information.

The following price ranges refer to a standard main course.

$ less than $20

$$ $20–40

$$$ more than $40

LGBTIQ+ Travellers

Australia is a popular destination for LGBTIQ+ travellers, with Sydney a big 'pink dollar' draw thanks largely to the city's annual, high-profile and spectacular Sydney Gay & Lesbian Mardi Gras. Australians are generally open-minded, but you may experience some suspicion or hostility in more conservative neighbourhoods or regions.

Throughout the country, but particularly on the east coast, there are tour operators, travel agents and accommodation places that cater specifically for the rainbow community.

The age of consent varies by state for homosexual relationships; same-sex marriages are now recognised in Australia after the question was finally put to a national vote in November 2017.

Major LGBTIQ+ Events

Midsumma Festival, Melbourne (www.midsumma. org.au)

Sydney Gay & Lesbian Mardi Gras (www.mardigras.org.au)

Feast Festival, Adelaide (www. feast.org.au)

PrideFest, Perth (www.pridewa. com.au)

Brisbane Pride Festival (www. brisbanepride.org.au)

Resources

Major cities have gay-community publications available from clubs, cafes, venues and newsagents. Lifestyle magazines include *Star Observer, Lesbians on the Loose (LOTL)* and *DNA*.

Gay & Lesbian Tourism Australia (Galta; www.galta. com.au) General information on gay-friendly businesses, places to stay and nightlife.

Gay Stay Australia (www. gaystayaustralia.com) A useful resource for accommodation.

Same Same (www.samesame. com.au) News, events and lifestyle features.

Health

Health-wise, Australia is a remarkably safe country in which to travel, considering that such a large portion of it lies in the tropics. Few travellers to Australia will experience anything worse than an upset stomach or a bad hangover and, if you do fall ill, the standard of hospitals and health care is high.

Availability & Cost of Health Care

Facilities Australia has an excellent health-care system with a mix of private clinics and hospitals complementing a public system funded by the Australian government.

Medicare Covers Australian residents for essential health care. Visitors from countries with which Australia has a reciprocal health-care agreement are able to access Medicare. However, private travel insurance is recommended. See www.humanservices. gov.au/customer/subjects/ medicare-services.

Medications Painkillers, antihistamines for allergies and skincare products are widely available at chemists throughout Australia. Some medications readily available over the counter in some countries are only available by prescription, such as the oral contraceptive pill and antibiotics.

Resources

There's a wealth of travel health advice on the internet, not all of it good for you.

The **World Health Organization** (WHO; www. who.int/ith) publishes *International Travel and Health*, revised annually and available free online.

The US-based **Centers for Disease Control and Prevention** (www.cdc.gov/ travel) provides complete travel-health recommendations for every country for different types of travel and traveller.

Other recommended sites:

Australia (www.smartraveller. gov.au)

Canada (www.hc-sc.gc.ca)

UK (www.nhs.uk/conditions/ travel-vaccinations)

Vaccinations

The **World Health Organization** (www.who. int) recommends that all travellers get immunised for diphtheria, tetanus, measles, mumps, rubella, chicken pox and polio, as well as hepatitis B, regardless of their destination.

Visit a physician eight weeks before departure to Australia to ensure you're up to date for all routine vaccinations. While Australia has high levels of childhood vaccination coverage, outbreaks of these diseases do occur.

Upon entering Australia you'll be required to fill out a travel history card detailing any recent visits to regions other than your home country.

If you're entering Australia after visiting a yellow-fever-infected country as listed by World Health Organization, you'll be asked for proof of yellow-fever vaccination or instructed on what to do immediately if you display any systems in the coming days.

Insurance

A travel-insurance policy to cover theft, loss and medical problems is a very good idea.

Level of cover Ensure your policy covers theft, loss and medical problems. Some policies specifically exclude designated 'dangerous activities' such as scuba diving, skiing and even bushwalking. Make sure the policy you choose fully covers

your planned (and perhaps unplanned) activities.

Health Check that the policy covers ambulances and emergency medical evacuations by air. Australia is a vast country so being airlifted to a hospital is a real possibility.

Where the Wild Things Are

Australia's profusion of dangerous creatures is legendary, but travellers needn't be alarmed – you're unlikely to see many of these creatures in the wild, much less be attacked by one.

Crocodiles Around the northern Australian coastline, saltwater crocodiles (salties) are a real danger. They also inhabit estuaries, creeks and rivers, sometimes a long way inland. Observe safety signs or ask locals before plunging in.

Jellyfish With venomous tentacles up to 3m long, box jellyfish (aka sea wasps or stingers) and their tiny, lethal relatives the irukandji, inhabit Australia's tropical waters. They're most common during the wet season (October to March). Stinger nets are in place at some beaches, but never swim unless you've checked. If you are stung, wash the skin with vinegar then get to a hospital.

Sharks Despite extensive media coverage, the risk of shark attack in Australia is no greater than in other countries with extensive coastlines. Check with surf life-saving groups about local risks.

Snakes Australia has some of the world's most venomous snakes. Most common are brown and tiger snakes, but few species are aggressive. If you are bitten, prevent the spread of venom by applying pressure to the wound and immobilising the area with a splint or sling. Stay put and get someone else to go for help.

Spiders The deadly funnel-web spider lives in NSW (including Sydney) – bites are treated as per snake bites (pressure and immobilisation before transferring to a hospital). Redback spiders live throughout Australia; bites cause pain, sweating and nausea. Apply ice or cold packs, then transfer to hospital. White-tailed spider bites may cause an ulcer that's slow and difficult to heal. Clean the wound and seek medical assistance. The disturbingly large huntsman spider is harmless.

Worldwide travel insurance is available at www.lonelyplanet.com/travel-insurance. You can buy, extend and claim online anytime – even if you're already on the road.

Internet Access

Wi-fi

Wi-fi is the norm in most (not all) Australian accommodation, but it is not always good.

Cafes, bars, malls, museums and town squares sometimes provide free wi-fi access, but again don't expect strong speeds.

There remains a surprising number of black spots without mobile phone or internet coverage in Australia. Most are in rural or outback areas. Let family and friends know when you are likely to be uncontactable, and then enjoy properly switching off from the web.

Access

There are fewer internet cafes around these days than there were five years ago (thanks to the advent of smart devices and wi-fi),

but you'll still find them in most sizeable towns. Most accommodation is phasing out internet terminals and kiosks in favour of wi-fi, although most hostels still have a public computer.

Most public libraries have internet access, but generally it's provided for research needs, not for travellers to check Facebook – so book ahead or find an internet cafe.

Legal Matters

Most travellers will have zero contact with Australia's police or legal system; if they do, it's most likely to be while driving.

Driving There's a significant police presence on Australian roads, and police have the power to stop your car, see your licence (you're required to carry it), check your vehicle for road-worthiness and insist that you take a breath test for

alcohol (and sometimes illicit drugs).

Drugs First-time offenders caught with small amounts of illegal drugs are likely to receive a fine rather than go to jail, but the recording of a conviction against you may affect your visa status.

Visas If you remain in Australia beyond the life of your visa, you'll officially be an 'overstayer' and could face mandatory detention and be prevented from returning to Australia.

Legal advice It's your right to telephone a friend, lawyer or relative before police questioning begins. Legal aid is available only in serious cases and is subject to means testing; for legal aid info see www.nationallegalaid.org. However, many solicitors do not charge for an initial consultation.

Money

Australia's currency is the Australian dollar, comprising 100 cents. There are 5c, 10c, 20c, 50c, $1 and $2 coins, and $5, $10, $20, $50 and $100 notes. Prices in shops are often marked in single cents then rounded to the nearest 5c when you come to pay.

ATMs & Eftpos

ATMs Australia's 'big four' banks – ANZ, Commonwealth, National Australia Bank and Westpac – and affiliated banks have branches all over Australia, plus a slew of 24-hour cashpoints (automated teller

---

Interstate Quarantine

When travelling within Australia, whether by land or air, you'll come across signs (mainly in airports and interstate train stations and at state borders) warning of the possible dangers of carrying fruit, vegetables and plants from one area to another. Certain pests and diseases (fruit fly, cucurbit thrips, grape phylloxera...) are prevalent in some areas, but not in others: authorities would like to limit their spread.

Quarantine control between states mostly relies on honesty, but some posts are staffed and officers are entitled to search your car for undeclared items. Generally they will confiscate all fresh fruit and vegetables, so it's best to leave shopping for these items until you're in the next state.

machines; ATMs). You'll even find them in some outback roadhouses.

Eftpos Most petrol stations, supermarkets, restaurants, cafes and shops have Electronic Funds Transfer at Point of Sale (Eftpos) facilities.

Banking fees Withdrawing cash through ATMs or Eftpos may attract significant fees – check associated costs with your home bank and enquire about fee-free options.

Credit Cards

Credit cards are widely accepted for everything from a hostel bed or a restaurant meal to an adventure tour, and are essential for hiring a car. They can also be used to get cash advances over the counter at banks and from many ATMs, depending on the card, though you'll incur immediate interest. Diners Club and American Express (Amex) are not as widely accepted in Australia.

Debit Cards

A debit card allows you to draw money directly from your home bank account. Any card connected to the international banking network – Cirrus, Maestro, Plus and Eurocard – should work with your PIN, but again expect substantial fees. Companies such as Travelex offer debit cards with set withdrawal fees and a balance you can top up from your personal bank account while on the road.

Exchanging Money

Changing foreign currency (or travellers cheques, if you're still using them!) is rarely a problem at banks and licensed money-changers such as Travelex in major cities and airports.

Taxes & Refunds

Goods & Services Tax The GST is a flat 10% tax on all goods and services included in the price. There are exceptions such as basic foods (milk, bread, fruit and vegetables etc).

Refund of GST If you purchase goods with a total minimum value of $300 from any one supplier no more than 30 days before you leave Australia, you are entitled under the Tourist Refund Scheme (TRS) to a refund of any GST paid. The scheme only applies to goods you take with you as hand luggage or wear onto the plane or ship. Check out www.abf.gov.au/entering-and-leaving-australia/tourist-refund-scheme for more details.

Income tax Nonresidents still pay tax on earnings made within Australia, and must lodge a tax return with the Australian Taxation Office. If too much tax was withheld from your pay, you will receive a refund.

Opening Hours

Most attractions close Christmas Day; many also close on New Year's Day and Good Friday.

Banks & post offices 9.30am–4pm Monday to Thursday; until 5pm Friday

Cafes 7am–5pm, some close later

Petrol stations & roadhouses 8am–8pm; some open 24 hours in cities

Restaurants Lunch noon–2.30pm and dinner from 6pm. Service ends early in country towns or on quiet nights.

Shops 9am–5pm Monday to Saturday; sometimes on Sunday; in larger cities, doors close at 9pm on Friday.

Supermarkets 7am–9pm; some open 24 hours

Post

Australia Post (www.auspost.com.au) runs a reliable national postal services; see the website for info on international delivery zones and rates. All post offices will hold mail for visitors: you need to provide some form of identification (such as a passport or a driving licence) to collect mail.

Public Holidays

Timing of public holidays can vary from state to state: check locally for precise dates. Some holidays are only observed locally within a state.

Practicalities

Newspapers Leaf through the daily Sydney Morning Herald (www.smh.com.au), Melbourne's Age (www.theage.com.au) or the national Australian broadsheet newspaper (www.theaustralian.com.au).

Radio ABC broadcasts national radio programs, many syndicated from the BBC, plus local regional stations. Check www.abc.net.au/radio for local frequencies.

Television The main free-to-air TV channels are the ABC, multicultural SBS, Seven, Nine and Ten, though locals are being seduced by pay TV options like Foxtel and Netflix.

Weights and measures Australia uses the metric system.

National

New Year's Day 1 January
Australia Day 26 January
Easter (Good Friday to Easter Monday inclusive) late March/early April
Anzac Day 25 April
Queen's Birthday Second Monday in June (last Monday in September in Western Australia)
Christmas Day 25 December
Boxing Day 26 December

In addition, each state has its own public holidays from Canberra Day to the Hobart Show Day.

School Holidays

○ The Christmas/summer school holidays run from mid-December to late January.

○ Three shorter school holiday periods occur during the year, varying by a week or two from state to state. They fall roughly from early to mid-April (usually including Easter), late June to mid-July, and late September to early October.

Safe Travel

Australia is a relatively safe and friendly place to travel, but natural disasters regularly wreak havoc. Bushfires, floods and cyclones can devastate local areas as weather events become more extreme and unpredictable.

○ Check weather warnings and don't venture into affected areas without an emergency plan.

○ Crime is low but don't let your guard *too* far down.

○ Beware of online lettings scams in Australia. Follow best practice when transferring money overseas.

○ Wild swimming can be dangerous here thanks to sharks, jellyfish and crocodiles – always seek reliable information.

○ Watch for wandering wildlife on roads, especially at night. Kangaroos are very unpredictable.

Telephone

Australia's main phone networks:
Optus (www.optus.com.au)
Telstra (www.telstra.com.au)
Virgin (www.virginmobile.com.au)
Vodafone (www.vodafone.com.au)

International Calls

From payphones Most payphones allow International Subscriber Dialling (ISD) calls, the cost and international dialling code of which will vary depending on which international phonecard provider you are using. International phone cards are readily available from internet cafes and convenience stores.

From landlines International calls from landlines in Australia are also relatively cheap and often subject to special deals; rates vary with providers.

Codes When calling overseas you will need to dial the international access code from Australia (0011 or 0018), the country code and then the area code (without the initial 0). So for a London telephone number you'll need to dial 0011-44-20, then the number. If dialling Australia from overseas, the country code is 61 and you need to drop the 0 in state/territory area codes.

Long-Distance Calls & Area Codes

Long-distance calls (over around 50km) are paid by time on the call, with peak and off-peak rates.

State/ Territory	Area code
ACT	📞02
NSW	📞02
NT	📞08
QLD	📞07
SA	📞08
TAS	📞03
VIC	📞03
WA	📞08

Area-code boundaries don't always coincide with state borders; for example some parts of NSW use the neighbouring states' codes.

Numbers with the prefix 04 belong to mobile phones.

Mobile (Cell) Phones

Either set up global roaming, or pick up a local SIM card with a prepaid recharge-able account on arrival in Australia. Shop around as deals vary depending on how much data or minutes you expect to use.

Toll-Free & Information Calls

○ Many businesses have either a toll-free 1800 number, dialled from anywhere within Australia for free, or a 13 or 1300 number, charged at a local call rate. None of these numbers can be di-alled from outside Australia (and often can't be dialled from mobile phones within Australia).

○ To make a reverse-charge (collect) call from any public or private phone, dial 📞12 550.

○ Numbers starting with 190 are usually recorded in-formation services, charged at anything from 35c to $5 or more per minute (even more from mobiles and payphones).

Time

Zones Australia is divided into three time zones: Western Standard Time (GMT/UTC plus eight hours), covering Western Australia; Central Standard Time (plus 9½ hours), covering South Australia and the Northern Territory; and Eastern Standard Time (plus 10 hours), covering Tasmania, Victoria, NSW, the Australian Capital Territory and Queensland.

Daylight saving Clocks are put forward an hour in some states during the warmer months (October to early April), but Queensland, WA and the NT stay on standard time.

Tourist Information

Tourist information is disseminated by various regional and local offices. Almost every major town in Australia has a tourist office of some type and staff can be super-helpful (often retiree volunteers) providing local information not readily available online. Some also sell books, souvenirs and snacks.

If booking accommoda-tion or tours through a local tourist offices, be aware that they usually only promote businesses that are paying members of the local tourist association.

Brisbane (📞07-3006 6290; www.visitbrisbane.com.au; The Regent, 167 Queen St; ⊙9am-5.30pm, to 7pm Fri, to 5pm Sat, 10am-5pm Sun; 🚉Central)

Hobart (📞03-6238 4222; www.hobarttravelcentre.com.au; 20 Davey St; ⊙8.30am-5pm Mon-Fri, from 9am Sat & Sun)

Melbourne (https://whatson.melbourne.vic.gov.au; Bourke St Mall; ⊙9am-5pm)

Perth (www.visitperth.com.au; Forrest Pl, Murray St Mall; ⊙9.30am-4.30pm Mon-Thu & Sat, to 8pm Fri, 11am-3.30pm Sun)

Sydney (www.cityofsydney.nsw.gov.au; Alfred St, Circular Quay; ⊙9am-8pm Mon-Sat, to 5pm Sun; 🚉Circular Quay)

Visas

All visitors to Australia need a visa, except New Zealanders. There are sev-eral different visas available from short-stay visitor visas to working-holiday visas.

If you want to stay in Australia for longer than your visa allows, you'll need to apply for a new visa via www.homeaffairs.gov.au. You can't apply for a new

Government Travel Advice

The following government websites offer travel advisories and information for travellers to Australia.

Australian Department of Foreign Affairs & Trade (www.smartraveller.gov.au)

Canadian Department of Foreign Affairs & International Trade (www.voyage.gc.ca)

French Ministère des Affaires Étrangères et Européennes (www.diplomatie.gouv.fr/fr/conseils-aux-voyageurs)

Italian Ministero degli Affari Esteri (www.viaggiaresicuri.mae.aci.it)

New Zealand Ministry of Foreign Affairs & Trade (www.safetravel.govt.nz)

UK Foreign & Commonwealth Office (www.gov.uk/foreign-travel-advice)

US Department of State (www.travel.state.gov)

visa in Australia if your current visa has expired so start the process well before your current visa expires.

If you require an Australian visa, eligibility depends on your nationality, your age, your skills and how long you are contemplating staying in Australia. For more information and to apply online visit www.home affairs.gov.au.

eVisitor (651)

○ Many European passport holders are eligible for a free eVisitor visa, allowing stays in Australia for up to three months within a 12-month period.

○ eVisitor visas must be applied for online (www.border.gov.au). They are electronically stored and linked to individual passport numbers, so no stamp in your passport is required.

○ It's advisable to apply at least 14 days prior to the proposed date of travel to Australia.

Electronic Travel Authority (ETA; 601)

○ Passport holders from eight countries that aren't part of the eVisitor scheme – Brunei, Canada, Hong Kong, Japan, Malaysia, Singapore, South Korea and the USA – can apply for either a visitor or business ETA.

○ ETAs are valid for 12 months, with stays of up to three months on each visit.

○ You can apply for an ETA online (www.border.gov.au), which attracts a nonrefundable service charge of $20.

Visitor (600)

○ Short-term Visitor visas have largely been replaced by the eVisitor and ETA.

However, if you're from a country not covered by either, or you want to stay longer than three months, you'll need to apply for a Visitor visa.

○ Standard Visitor visas allow one entry for a stay of up to three, six or 12 months, and are valid for use within 12 months of issue.

○ Apply online at www.homeaffairs.gov.au.

Volunteering

Lonely Planet's *Volunteer: A Traveller's Guide to Making a Difference Around the World* provides useful information about volunteering.

See also the following websites:

Conservation Volunteers Australia (www.conservation-volunteers.com.au) Nonprofit organisation involved in tree planting, walking-track construction and flora and fauna surveys.

Earthwatch Institute Australia (www.earthwatch.org) Volunteer expeditions focusing on conservation and wildlife.

GoVolunteer (www.govolunteer.com.au) Thousands of volunteering opportunities around the country.

Volunteering Australia (www.volunteeringaustralia.org) State-by-state listings of volunteering opportunities around Australia.

Willing Workers on Organic Farms (WWOOF: www.wwoof.com.au) WWOOFing sees travellers swap a day's work on a farm in return for bed and board. Most hosts are concerned to some extent with alternative lifestyles and have a minimum stay of two nights. Join online for a booklet listing participating enterprises.

Women Travellers

Australia is generally a safe place for women travellers, and the following sensible precautions all apply for men, as well as women.

Night-time Avoid walking alone late at night in any of the major cities and towns – keep enough money aside for a taxi back to your accommodation.

Pubs Be wary of basic pub accommodation unless it looks particularly well managed. Alcohol can affect people's behaviour and compromise safety.

Drink spiking Pubs in major cities sometimes post warnings about drugged or 'spiked' drinks. Be cautious if someone offers you a drink in a bar.

Sexual harassment Unfortunately still a fairly big problem in Australia from street harassment to 'nice guys' on dating apps.

Hitchhiking Hitching is never recommended for anyone, even when travelling in pairs. Exercise caution at all times.

Solo travel Most people won't bat an eyelid if you're female-identifying and travelling alone. Go forth and have the time of your life in Australia, without having to compromise just to have a buddy on the road.

Transport

Getting There & Away

Most travellers arrive on a long-haul flight. Pick your arrival city wisely. Sydney might be the obvious choice, but flights into smaller cities can make for a quicker trip through customs, and a happier transition to your accommodation. Flights, cars and tours can be booked online at lonely planet.com/bookings.

Entering the Country

Arrival in Australia is usually fairly quick and efficient. If you have a current passport and visa, and follow customs regulations, your entry should be straightforward.

Air

Airlines & Airports

Most major international airlines fly to/from Australia's larger cities. The national carrier is **Qantas** (☑13 13 13; www.qantas.com.au), which has an outstanding safety record, and code shares with British Airways.

Sydney and Melbourne are the busiest gateway cities, but Perth, Adelaide and Brisbane are all increasingly popular places to start your Australia adventure.

Adelaide Airport (ADL; ☑08-8308 9211; www.adelaideair port.com.au; 1 James Schofield Dr, Adelaide Airport)

Brisbane Airport (www.bne. com.au; Airport Dr)

Cairns Airport (☑07-4080 6703; www.cairnsairport.com; Airport Ave)

Darwin International Airport (☑08-8920 1811; www. darwinairport.com.au; Henry Wrigley Dr, Marrara)

Gold Coast Airport (www.gold coastairport.com.au; Eastern Ave, Bilinga)

Melbourne Airport (MEL; ☑03-9297 1600; www. melbourneairport.com.au; Departure Rd, Tullamarine)

Perth Airport (☑08-9478 8888; www.perthairport.com. au; Airport Dr)

Sydney Airport (Kingsford Smith Airport; Mascot Airport; ☑02-9667 6111; www.sydneyair port.com.au; Airport Dr, Mascot)

Getting Around

Air

Australia's main domestic airlines service the large centres with regular flights. The major players:

Jetstar (☑13 15 38; www.jetstar.com)

Qantas (☑13 13 13; www.qantas.com.au)

Tigerair (☑1300 174 266; www.tigerair.com.au)

Virgin Australia (⌕13 67 89; www.virginaustralia.com)

A number of regional airlines operate within smaller geographical parameters and fly into regional airports.

Air Passes

For the highly organised, **Qantas** (⌕13 13 13; www.qantas.com.au) has a **Qantas Explorer** (www.qantas.com/us/en/book-a-trip/flights/qantas-explorer.html) deal where you link up to 30 domestic Australian destinations for less than you'd pay if you booked flights individually, though you must book them together.

Bicycle

Cycling around Australia is possible but will take considerable fitness and excellent planning.

Transport If you're bringing your own bike, check with your airline for weight, costs and packing required. Within Australia, bus companies require you to dismantle your bike. Trains sometimes have separate bike-storage facilities on board.

Legalities Bike helmets are compulsory in all states and territories, as are white front lights and red rear lights for riding at night.

Maps You can get by with standard road maps, but to avoid low-grade unsealed roads, the government series is best. The 1:250,000 scale is suitable, though you'll need lots of maps if you're riding long distances.

Safety In summer carry plenty of water at all times. Distances between towns can be gruellingly far. Avoid cycling in the middle of the day in hot weather. Drivers will not be expecting to see cyclists on most country roads. Wear as much high-vis outerwear as possible.

Resources

The following websites offers information, news and links. Each Australian state also has its own cycling information networks.

Bicycles Network Australia (www.bicycles.net.au)

Bicycle Network (www.bicyclenetwork.com.au)

Cycling & Walking Australia & NZ (www.cwanz.com.au)

MTBA (www.mtba.asn.au)

Bus

Australia's extensive bus network is a reliable way to get around but distances are often vast. Most Australian buses are equipped with air-con, comfortable seats and decent toilets; all are smoke-free and some have wi-fi and USB chargers.

Greyhound Australia (⌕1300 473 946; www.greyhound.com.au; ⌕) Runs in every state except South Australia and Western Australia. Offers flexible hop-on hop-off fares. Discounts for seniors, students and children.

Firefly Express (⌕1300 730 740; www.fireflyexpress.com.au) Runs between Sydney, Canberra, Melbourne and Adelaide.

Integrity Coach Lines (⌕08-9274 7464; www.integritycoachlines.com.au; cnr Wellington St & Horseshoe Bridge) The main operator in WA.

Premier Motor Service (⌕13 34 10; www.premierms.com.au) Does the east coast from Eden to Cairns. Has flexible hop-on hop-off fares.

V/Line (⌕1800 800 007; www.vline.com.au; Southern Cross Station, Spencer St, Docklands) Covers all of Victoria with a mix of coaches and trains.

Guided Bus Travel

Another way to get around by bus is on a tour. Some offer the whole package including accommodation and meals; others are less formal options to get from A to B and see the sights on the way.

AAT Kings (⌕1300 556 100; www.aatkings.com) Big coach company (popular with the older set) with myriad tours around Australia.

Adventure Tours Australia (⌕1300 654 604; www.adventuretours.com.au) Affordable, young-at-heart tours in all states.

Autopia Tours (⌕03-9393 1333; www.autopiatours.com.au) One- to three-day trips from Melbourne, Adelaide and Sydney.

Groovy Grape Tours (⌕08-8440 1640; www.groovygrape.com.au) Small-group, SA-based operator running tours ex-Adelaide, Melbourne and Alice Springs.

Nullarbor Traveller (⌕08-8687 0455; https://nullarbortraveller.com.au) Small company running relaxed minibus trips across the Nullarbor Plain between SA and WA.

Oz Experience (⌕1300 300 028; www.ozexperience.com)

Packaged itineraries for younger travellers, partnering with Greyhound coaches.

Car & Motorcycle

Driving Licence

To drive in Australia you'll need to hold a current driving licence issued in English from your home country. If the licence isn't in English, you'll also need to carry an International Driving Permit, issued in your home country.

Choosing a Vehicle

2WD Depending on where you want to travel, a regulation 2WD vehicle might suffice. They're cheaper to hire, buy and run than 4WDs and are more readily available. Most are fuel efficient and easy to repair and sell. Downsides: no off-road capability and no room to sleep!

4WD Good for outback travel as they can access almost any track for which you get a hankering, and there might even be space to sleep in the back. Downsides: poor fuel economy, awkward to park and more expensive to hire or buy.

Campervan Creature comforts at your fingertips: sink, fridge, cupboards, beds, kitchen and space to relax. Downsides: slow and often not fuel-efficient, not great on dirt roads and too large for nipping around the city.

Motorcycle The Australian climate is great for riding, and bikes are handy in city traffic. Downsides: Australia isn't particularly bike-friendly in terms of driver awareness; there's limited luggage capacity, and exposure to the elements.

Climate Change & Travel

Every form of transport that relies on carbon-based fuel generates CO_2, the main cause of human-induced climate change. Modern travel is dependent on aeroplanes, which might use less fuel per kilometre per person than most cars but travel much greater distances. The altitude at which aircraft emit gases (including CO_2) and particles also contributes to their climate change impact. Many websites offer 'carbon calculators' that allow people to estimate the carbon emissions generated by their journey and, for those who wish to do so, to offset the impact of the greenhouse gases emitted with contributions to portfolios of climate-friendly initiatives throughout the world. Lonely Planet offsets the carbon footprint of all staff and author travel.

Renting a Vehicle

Larger car-hire companies have offices in major cities and airports. Most companies require drivers to be over the age of 21, though in some cases it's 18, and in others 25.

Suggestions to assist in the process:

● Read the contract cover to cover.

● Most companies will demand they put a 'hold' on a sum on your credit card to cover their insurance excess. This is released after the car is returned in one piece, but budget that into your finances.

● Ask if unlimited kilometres are included; it's almost essential in Australia as extra kilometres will add to your costs considerably.

● Find out what excess you'll have to pay if you have an accident, usually charged no matter who is at fault.

● Check if your personal travel insurance covers you for vehicle accidents and excess.

● Check whether you're covered on unavoidable unsealed roads (eg accessing campgrounds).

● Some companies also exclude parts of the car from cover, such as the underbelly, tyres and windscreen.

● At pick-up inspect the vehicle for any damage. Make a note of anything on the contract before you sign. Take photos, though they're usually not considered evidence if you get into a dispute.

● Make sure you know the breakdown and accident procedures.

● If you can, return the vehicle during business hours and insist on an inspection in your presence.

The following websites offer last-minute discounts and

the opportunity to compare rates between the big operators:

- www.carhire.com.au
- www.drivenow.com.au
- www.webjet.com.au

4WDs

Having a 4WD is essential for off-the-beaten-track driving into the outback. The major car-hire companies have 4WDs.

Renting a 4WD is affordable if a few people get together – something like a Nissan X-Trail (which can get you through most, but not all, tracks) costs $100 to $150 per day; for a Toyota Landcruiser you're looking at $150 to $200, which should include unlimited kilometres.

Check the insurance conditions, especially the excess (the amount you pay in the event of accident, which can be up to $5000), as they can be onerous. A refundable bond is also often required – this can be as much as $7500. The excess and policies might not cover damage caused when travelling off-road (which they don't always tell you when you pick up your vehicle). Some also name specific tracks as off limits and you may not be covered by the insurance if you ignore this.

Campervans

Companies for campervan hire – with rates from around $90 (two-berth) or $150 (four-berth) per day, usually with minimum five-day hire and unlimited kilometres – include the following:

Apollo (☏1800 777 779; www. apollocamper.com)

Britz (☏1300 738 087; www. britz.com.au)

Hippie Camper (☏1800 777 779; www.hippiecamper.com)

Jucy (☏1800 150 850; www. jucy.com.au)

Maui (☏1800 827 821; www. maui.com.au)

Mighty Campers (☏1800 821 824; www.mightycampers. com.au)

Spaceships (☏1300 132 469; www.spaceshipsrentals.com.au)

Travelwheels (☏0412 766 616; www.travelwheels.com.au)

Insurance

Third-party insurance With the exception of NSW and Queensland, third-party personal-injury insurance is included in the vehicle registration cost, ensuring that every registered vehicle carries at least the minimum insurance (if registering in NSW or Queensland you'll need to arrange this privately). It's recommended that you extend that minimum to at least third-party *property* insurance – minor collisions can be incredibly expensive.

Comprehensive cover Consider taking out comprehensive car insurance if you want your own vehicle insured, even when the accident is not your fault. An uninsured driver will be hard to extract money from, especially if you're not going to be in Australia for long.

Auto Clubs

Under the auspices of the **Australian Automobile Association** (AAA; ☏02-6247 7311; www.aaa.asn.au) there are automobile clubs in each state, which is handy

---

Going Greener

A few simple actions can help minimise the impact your journey has on the environment.

- Ensure your vehicle is well serviced and tuned.
- Travel lightly to reduce fuel consumption.
- Drive slowly – many vehicles use 25% more fuel at 110km/h than at 90km/h.
- Stay on designated roads and vehicle off-road tracks.
- Drive in the middle of tracks to minimise track widening and damage, don't drive on walking tracks and avoid driving on vegetation.
- Cross creeks at designated areas.
- Consider ride sharing where possible.
- Check out the electric-car options at major dealers. For more info, see www.greenvehicleguide.gov.au.

when it comes to insurance, regulations, maps and roadside assistance. Club membership (around $100 to $150) can save you a lot of trouble if things go wrong mechanically. The major Australian auto clubs generally offer reciprocal rights in other states and territories.

Automobile Association of the Northern Territory (AANT; ☑08-8925 5901; www.aant.com. au; 2/14 Knuckey St; ☺9am-5pm Mon-Fri, to 12.30pm Sat)

National Roads & Motorists Association (☑13 11 22; www. mynrma.com.au) New South Wales and the Australian Capital Territory

Royal Automobile Club of Queensland (☑13 19 05; www. racq.com.au)

Royal Automobile Club of Tasmania (RACT; ☑03-6232 6300, roadside assistance 13 11 11; www.ract.com.au; cnr Murray & Patrick Sts, Hobart; ☺8.45am-5pm Mon-Fri)

Royal Automobile Club of Victoria (☑13 72 28; www.racv. com.au)

Royal Automobile Club of Western Australia (RAC; ☑13 17 03; www.rac.com.au)

Road Rules

Australians drive on the left-hand side of the road and all cars are right-hand drive.

Give way An important road rule is 'give way to the right' – if an intersection is unmarked (unusual), and at roundabouts, you must give way to vehicles entering the intersection from your right.

Speed limits The general speed limit in built-up and residential areas is 50km/h. Near schools, the limit is usually 25km/h (sometimes 40km/h) in the morning and afternoon. On the highway it's usually 100km/h or 110km/h; in the NT it's either 110km/h or 130km/h. Police have speed radar guns and cameras and are fond of using them in strategic locations.

Seat belts and car seats It's the law to wear seat belts in the front and back seats; you're likely to get a fine if you don't. Small children must be belted into an approved safety seat.

Drinking and driving Random breath tests are common. If you're caught with a blood-alcohol level of more than 0.05%, expect a fine and the loss of your licence. Police can randomly pull any driver over for a breathalyser or drug test. It's best just to drive sober and make it alive.

Mobile phones Using a mobile phone while driving is illegal in Australia (excluding hands-free technology).

Hazards & Precautions

Behind the Wheel

Fatigue Be wary of driver fatigue; driving long distances (particularly in hot weather) can be utterly exhausting. Falling asleep at the wheel is a serious risk. Stop and rest regularly – do some exercise, change drivers or have a coffee.

Road trains Be careful overtaking road trains (trucks with two or three trailers stretching for as long as 50m); you'll need distance and plenty of speed. On single-lane tracks get right off the road when one approaches. Stones or debris can clip your car as it passes.

Unsealed roads Unsealed road conditions vary wildly and cars perform differently when braking and turning on dirt. Don't exceed 70km/h on dirt roads; if you go faster, you won't have time to respond to a sharp turn, stock on the road or an unexpected pothole.

Animal Hazards

Roadkill is a huge problem in Australia, particularly in the NT, Queensland, NSW, SA and Tasmania. Many Australians in rural areas avoid travelling once the sun drops because of the risks posed by nocturnal animals on the roads.

Kangaroos are common on country roads, as are cows and sheep in the unfenced outback. Kangaroos are most active around dawn and dusk and often travel in groups: if you see one hopping across the road, slow right down, as its friends may be just behind it.

If you injure an animal while driving, call the relevant wildlife rescue line:

Department of Environment & Heritage Protection (☑1300 264 625; www.ehp.qld.gov.au) Queensland

Department of Parks & Wildlife (☑Wildcare Helpline 08-9474 9055; www.parks.dpaw. wa.gov.au) WA

Fauna Rescue of South Australia (☑08-8289 0896; www. faunarescue.org.au)

NSW Wildlife Information, Rescue & Education Service (WIRES; ☑1300 094 737; www. wires.org.au)

Parks & Wildlife Service
(☑1300 827 727; www.parks.
tas.gov.au) Tasmania

Wildcare Inc NT (☑0408 885
341; www.wildcarent.org.au)

Wildlife Victoria (☑1300 094
535; www.wildlifevictoria.org.au)

Fuel

Fuel types Unleaded and diesel
fuel is available from petrol
stations sporting well-known
international brand names. LPG
(liquefied petroleum gas) has
waned in popularity with fewer
places stocking refills – it's
best to have dual-fuel capacity.
Electric recharging spots are
popping up all over Australia,
making hybrid and electric road
trips a viable alternative.

Costs Prices vary between the
city and country, days of the
week, and political situation.
At the time of writing petrol
hovered around $1.50 a litre,
but under certain conditions it
can be as high as $2 per litre.

Availability In cities and towns,
petrol stations are plentiful,
but distances between fill-ups
can be huge in the countryside
so pay attention to your fuel
gauge. On main roads there'll

be a small town or roadhouse
roughly every 200km.

Local Transport

All of Australia's major towns
have reliable, affordable public bus networks, and there
are suburban train lines in
Sydney, Melbourne, Bris-
bane, Adelaide and Perth.

Melbourne also has trams
(Adelaide has one!), Sydney
and Brisbane have ferries,
and Sydney has a light-rail
line.

Taxis operate in all major
cities and towns, which is
especially handy if you're
having a few drinks out.
However, not every city has
a pool of mobile app-booked
taxi drivers – yet.

Train

Long-distance rail travel
in Australia is something
you do because you really
want to – not because it's
cheap, convenient or fast.
That said, trains are more
comfortable than buses,
and there's a certain long-
distance 'romance of the
rails' that's alive and kicking.

Shorter-distance rail
services within most states
are run by state rail bodies,
either government or
private.

The most notable
long-distance rail journeys
in Australia are run by the
following:

Great Southern Rail (☑08-
8213 4401, 1800 703 357; www.
greatsouthernrail.com.au) Operates the *Indian Pacific* between
Sydney and Perth, the *Overland*
between Melbourne and
Adelaide, the *Great Southern*
between Brisbane and Adelaide,
and the *Ghan* between Adelaide
and Darwin via Alice Springs.

Queensland Rail (☑1300 131
722; www.queenslandrailtravel.
com.au) Runs the high-speed
Spirit of Queensland service
between Brisbane and Cairns.

NSW TrainLink (☑13 22 32;
www.nswtrainlink.info) Trains
from Sydney to Brisbane,
Melbourne and Canberra.

V/Line (☑1800 800 007; www.
vline.com.au; Southern Cross
Station, Spencer St, Docklands)
Trains within Victoria, linking up
with buses for connections into
NSW, SA and the ACT.

Behind the Scenes

Acknowledgements

Climate map data adapted from Peel MC, Finlayson BL & McMahon TA (2007) 'Updated World Map of the Köppen-Geiger Climate Classification', *Hydrology and Earth System Sciences*, 11, 1633–44.

Cover artwork: Forecourt Mosaic Pavement, Parliament House Canberra (created 1986–87), original design by Michael Nelson Jagamara (born 1945) of the Luritja/Warlpiri peoples, fabricated by William McIntosh, Aldo Rossi and Franco Colussi; Parliament House Art Collection, Department of Parliamentary Services, Canberra. Michael Nelson Jagamara/Aboriginal Artists Agency Ltd ©

Cover photo: Bosiljka Zutich/Alamy Stock Photo ©

Illustration pp 42-3 by Javier Zarracina.

This Book

This 3rd edition of Lonely Planet's *Best of Australia* guidebook was curated by Anthony Ham and researched and written by Anthony, Andrew Bain, Fleur Bainger, Samantha Forge, Paul Harding, Trent Holden, Sofia Levin, Hugh McNaughtan, Kate Morgan, Charles Rawlings-Way, Andy Symington and Tasmin Waby. The previous edition was written by Brett Atkinson, Cristian Bonetto, Peter Dragicevich, Anthony Ham, Paul Harding, Trent Holden, Kate Morgan, Charles Rawlings-Way, Tamara Sheward, Tom Spurling, Andy Symington and Donna Wheeler. We would also like to thank the following people for their contributions to this guide: Dr Michael Cathcart, Cathy Craigie,

Rachel Hocking and Dr Tim Flannery. This guidebook was produced by the following:

Destination Editor Tasmin Waby

Senior Product Editor Anne Mason

Regional Senior Cartographer Julie Sheridan

Product Editor Kate Kiely

Book Designer Clara Monitto

Assisting Editors James Bainbridge, Sarah Bailey, Judith Bamber, Imogen Bannister, Andrea Dobbin, Peter Cruttenden, Emma Gibbs, Carly Hall, Paul Harding, Kellie Langdon, Joel Cotterell, Lou McGregor, Kristin Odjik, Fionnuala Twomey

Cartographer Julie Dodkins

Cover Researcher Brendan Dempsey-Spencer

Thanks to Geoff Brew, Jennifer Carey, Laura Crawford, Sasha Drew, David Hodges, Claire Naylor, Anna Tyler, Brana Vladisavljevic

Send Us Your Feedback

We love to hear from travellers – your comments keep us on our toes and help make our books better. Our well-travelled team reads every word on what you loved or loathed about this book. Although we cannot reply individually to postal submissions, we always guarantee that your feedback goes straight to the appropriate authors, in time for the next edition. Each person who sends us information is thanked in the next edition, the most useful submissions are rewarded with a selection of digital PDF chapters.

Visit lonelyplanet.com/contact to submit your updates and suggestions or to ask for help. Our award-winning website also features inspirational travel stories, news and discussions.

Note: We may edit, reproduce and incorporate your comments in Lonely Planet products such as guidebooks, websites and digital products, so let us know if you don't want your comments reproduced or your name acknowledged. For a copy of our privacy policy visit lonelyplanet.com/privacy.

Index

Symbols & Map Key

Look for these symbols to quickly identify listings:

◎ Sights
❸ Activities
❸ Courses
❸ Tours
❸ Festivals & Events

❽ Eating
❺ Drinking
❸ Entertainment
❸ Shopping
❶ Information & Transport

These symbols and abbreviations give vital information for each listing:

🌿 Sustainable or green recommendation

FREE No payment required

📞 Telephone number
🕙 Opening hours
ℙ Parking
🚭 Nonsmoking
❄ Air-conditioning
@ Internet access
🛜 Wi-fi access
🏊 Swimming pool

🚌 Bus
⛴ Ferry
🚊 Tram
🚆 Train
📖 English-language menu
🥗 Vegetarian selection
👪 Family-friendly

Find your best experiences with these Great For... icons.

🖼 Art & Culture
🏖 Beaches
💳 Budget
☕ Cafe/Coffee
🚲 Cycling
↪ Detour
🍷 Drinking
🎫 Entertainment
🎆 Events
👨‍👩‍👧 Family Travel
🍽 Food & Drink

📔 History
💬 Local Life
🐦 Nature & Wildlife
📷 Photo Op
🔭 Scenery
🛍 Shopping
🎒 Short Trip
🏸 Sport
🚶 Walking
❄ Winter Travel

Sights

👼 Beach
🐦 Bird Sanctuary
☸ Buddhist
🏯 Castle/Palace
✝ Christian
卍 Confucian
🕉 Hindu
☪ Islamic
卍 Jain
✡ Jewish
❶ Monument
🏛 Museum/Gallery/ Historic Building
❸ Ruin
⛩ Shinto
🪯 Sikh
☯ Taoist
🍇 Winery/Vineyard
🐾 Zoo/Wildlife Sanctuary
◎ Other Sight

Points of Interest

Ⓒ Bodysurfing
🏕 Camping
☕ Cafe
🛶 Canoeing/Kayaking
● Course/Tour
🤿 Diving
🍸 Drinking & Nightlife
❽ Eating
❸ Entertainment
🛀 Sento Hot Baths/ Onsen
🛍 Shopping
⛷ Skiing
🛏 Sleeping
🤿 Snorkelling
🏄 Surfing
🏊 Swimming/Pool
🚶 Walking
🏄 Windsurfing
❸ Other Activity

Information

💲 Bank
❸ Embassy/Consulate
✚ Hospital/Medical
@ Internet
🚓 Police
📮 Post Office
📞 Telephone
🚻 Toilet
❶ Tourist Information
● Other Information

Geographic

🏖 Beach
⊶ Gate
🏠 Hut/Shelter
🗼 Lighthouse
🔭 Lookout
▲ Mountain/Volcano
🌴 Oasis
🌳 Park
)(Pass
🧺 Picnic Area
💧 Waterfall

Transport

✈ Airport
Ⓑ BART station
❌ Border crossing
Ⓣ Boston T station
🚌 Bus
🚡 Cable car/Funicular
🚲 Cycling
⛴ Ferry
Ⓜ Metro/MRT station
🚝 Monorail
ℙ Parking
⛽ Petrol station
Ⓢ Subway/S-Bahn/ Skytrain station
🚕 Taxi
🚉 Train station/Railway
🚊 Tram
Ⓤ Underground/ U-Bahn station
● Other Transport

Paul Harding

As a writer and photographer, Paul has been travelling the globe for the best part of two decades, with an interest in remote and offbeat places, islands and cultures. He's an author and contributor to more than 50 Lonely Planet guides to countries and regions as diverse as India, Belize, Vanuatu, Iran, Indonesia, New Zealand, Iceland, Finland, Philippines and – his home patch – Australia.

Trent Holden

A Geelong-based writer, located just outside Melbourne, Trent has worked for Lonely Planet since 2005. He's covered 30-plus guidebooks across Asia, Africa and Australia. With a penchant for megacities, Trent's in his element when assigned to cover a nation's capital – the more chaotic the better – to unearth cool bars, art, street food and underground subculture. On the flipside he also writes books to idyllic tropical islands across Asia, in between going on safari to national parks in Africa and the subcontinent. When not travelling, Trent works as a freelance editor and reviewer, spending all his money catching live gigs. You can catch him on Twitter @hombreholden.

Sofia Levin

Seasoned traveller and food journalist Sofia believes that eating in a country other than one's own is the best way to understand a culture. It's why she feels so lucky to call Melbourne home, where the city's diversity allows her to eat all over the world without catching a flight. With Insta-famous toy poodle, @lifeofjinkee, on her lap, she writes for newspapers and travel magazines, acts as Lonely Planet's Melbourne Local and co-authors international guidebooks – often rewarding herself with regional Vietnamese noodle soups for dinner. Follow her culinary adventures or ask her where to eat via Instagram at @sofiaklevin.

Hugh McNaughtan

A former lecturer and restaurant critic, Hugh is a native Melbournite with deep family roots in New South Wales and Queensland. Jumping behind the wheel (and up the gangplank) to explore New England and the Queensland coast, islands and hinterland from Fraser Island to the Whitsunday was a dream assignment, made all the more memorable by the many kindnesses he encountered.

Kate Morgan

Having worked for Lonely Planet for over a decade now, Kate has been fortunate enough to cover plenty of ground working as a travel writer on destinations such as Shanghai, Japan, India, Russia, Zimbabwe, the Philippines and Phuket. She has done stints living in London, Paris and Osaka but these days is based in one of her favourite regions in the world – Victoria, Australia. In between travelling the world and writing about it, Kate enjoys spending time at home working as a freelance editor.

Charles Rawlings-Way

Charles is a veteran travel, food and music writer who has penned 40-something titles for Lonely Planet – including guides to Singapore, Toronto, Sydney, Tonga, New Zealand, the South Pacific and every state in Australia, including his native terrain of Tasmania and current homeland of South Australia – plus too many articles to recall. After dabbling in the dark arts of architecture, cartography, project management and busking for some years, Charles hit the road for Lonely Planet in 2005 and hasn't stopped travelling since. Charles is also the author of a best-selling rock biography, *These are Such Perfect Days,* on Glasgow band Del Amitri. Follow Charles on the socials @crawlingsway and www.facebook.com/chasrwmusic.

Andy Symington

Andy has written or worked on over a hundred books and other updates for Lonely Planet (especially in Europe and Latin America) and other publishing companies, and has published articles on numerous subjects for a variety of newspapers, magazines, and websites. He part-owns and operates a rock bar, has written a novel and is currently working on several fiction and non-fiction writing projects. Andy, from Australia, moved to Northern Spain many years ago. When he's not off with a backpack in some far-flung corner of the world, he can probably be found watching the tragically poor local football side or tasting local wines after a long walk in the nearby mountains.

Tasmin Waby

A London-born writer with Kiwi *whānau* (extended family) who grew up in Australia, Tasmin loves cartography, starry night skies, and getting off the beaten track. When not on the road for Lonely Planet she lives in a narrowboat and is planning her next adventure with her two school-aged kids.

Our Story

A beat-up old car, a few dollars in the pocket and a sense of adventure. In 1972 that's all Tony and Maureen Wheeler needed for the trip of a lifetime – across Europe and Asia overland to Australia. It took several months, and at the end – broke but inspired – they sat at their kitchen table writing and stapling together their first travel guide, *Across Asia on the Cheap*. Within a week they'd sold 1500 copies. Lonely Planet was born.

Today, Lonely Planet has offices in Franklin, London, Melbourne, Oakland, Dublin, Beijing, and Delhi, with more than 600 staff and writers. We share Tony's belief that 'a great guidebook should do three things: inform, educate and amuse'.

Our Writers

Anthony Ham

Anthony is a freelance writer and photographer who specialises in Spain, East and Southern Africa, the Arctic and the Middle East. When he's not writing for Lonely Planet, Anthony writes about and photographs Spain, Africa and the Middle East for newspapers and magazines in Australia, the UK and US.

Andrew Bain

Andrew is an Australia-based writer, specialising in outdoors and adventure. He's cycled and trekked across every continent bar the icy one, and is the author of *Headwinds*, the story of his 20,000km bike ride around Australia, and of Lonely Planet titles such as *A Year of Adventures*, *Walking in Australia* and *Cycling Australia*. Find him on Instagram at @bainonbike.

Fleur Bainger

Having worn her first backpack to Europe when she was just 10 years old, Perth-based journalist Fleur gets a heck of a buzz from being a freelance travel and food writer. As Western Australia's weekly food reviewer for the *Sunday Times Magazine*, she's constantly on the hunt for Perth's best new eateries, while her weekly 'what's on' slot on 6PR talkback radio means she's always got the lowdown on events and openings around town. She's a Lonely Planet Local, a destination expert for the *Telegraph* (UK) and regular contributor to *Australian Traveller*, *Escape*, ABC radio and and more.

Samantha Forge

Samantha became hooked on travel at the age of 17, when she arrived in London with an overstuffed backpack and a copy of LP's *Europe on a Shoestring*. After a stint in Paris, she moved back to Australia to work as an editor in LP's Melbourne office. Eventually her wanderlust got the better of her, and she now works as a freelance writer and editor.

◄— More Writers —◄

STAY IN TOUCH LONELYPLANET.COM/CONTACT

AUSTRALIA The Malt Store, Level 3, 551 Swanston St, Carlton, Victoria 3053
☎03 8379 8000, fax 03 8379 8111

IRELAND Digital Depot, Roe Lane (off Thomas St), Digital Hub, Dublin 8, D08 TCV4, Ireland

USA 124 Linden Street, Oakland, CA 94607
☎510 250 6400, toll free 800 275 8555, fax 510 893 8572

UK 240 Blackfriars Road, London SE1 8NW
☎020 3771 5100, fax 020 3771 5101

 twitter.com/lonelyplanet

facebook.com/lonelyplanet

instagram.com/lonelyplanet

 youtube.com/lonelyplanet

lonelyplanet.com/newsletter